INDUSTRIAL ARCHAEOLOGY IN BRITAIN

New Edition

R. A. Buchanan

Allen Lane

ALLEN LANE
Penguin Books Ltd
536 Kings Road
London SW10

First published in Pelican Books 1972
Published by Allen Lane 1974
Second edition 1980

ISBN 0 7139 0956 0 *for 1st ed.*

Set in Monotype Ehrhardt
Printed in Great Britain by Billing and Sons Ltd,
London, Guildford and Worcester

For Andrew and Thomas

Contents

List of Plates 9
List of Line Drawings and Maps 13
Preface 15

Part 1: Introduction

1. Definitions and Techniques 21
2. The Historical Framework 35

Part 2: The Industrial Categories

3. The Coal-Mining Industry 55
4. The Metal Industries 73
5. The Engineering Industries 93
6. The Textile Industries 116
7. The Chemical Industries 139
8. Building, Agriculture, and Rural Crafts 163
9. Consumer Industries and Urban Crafts 192

Part 3: Power, Transport, and Public Services

10. Power I – Animal, Wind, and Water 219
11. Power II – Steam, Internal Combustion, and Electricity 244

12. Transport I – Ports, Roads, and Waterways   267
13. Transport II – Tramways, Railways, and Other Systems   300
14. Community and Public Services   327

Part 4: The Progress of Industrial Archaeology

15. The Organization of the Subject   355
16. The Study of Industrial Archaeology   372

Part 5: Regional Survey

Region 1. Scotland   397
2. North England   404
3. Wales   411
4. The English Midlands   416
5. South-East England   423
6. South-West England   430

Notes and Bibliographical References   437

Index   453

List of Plates

1. Cornish engine house, Tregurtha Down, Cornwall (R. A. Buchanan)
2. Engine house, Beamish Colliery, Co. Durham (North of England Open-Air Museum)
3. Horizontal steam winding engine (G. Watkins)
4. The Levant Mine, Cornwall (R. A. Buchanan)
5. Parys Mountain, Anglesey (R. A. Buchanan)
6. Mine winding engine, by Agricola, 1555
7. Water-pressure pumping engine (R. A. Buchanan)
8. Annealing oven, Kelston Brassworks, Bath (R. A. Buchanan)
9. Condenser flues at Charterhouse on Mendip, Somerset (John Cornwell)
10. Coalbrookdale furnace (R. A. Buchanan)
11. Bonawe furnace (John Hume)
12. The Iron Bridge, Telford, Shropshire (Eric de Maré)
13. 'Missionary' cooking-pot (R. A. Buchanan)
14. Triphammer and anvil (Sheffield City Museum)
15. Hamsterley cementation furnace (North of England Open-Air Museum)
16. Forge hammer (John Cornwell)
17. Crucible furnaces (John Cornwell)
18. Pottery kilns (J. Kenneth Major)

19. 'An English Glass Works'
20. Glass cone, Catcliffe (R. A. Buchanan)
21. Paper mill (John Cornwell)
22. Hand-made paper
23. Brewery (R. A. Buchanan)
24. Chemical factory (John Cornwell)
25. China clay (R. A. Buchanan)
26. Cheddleton flint mill (Cheddleton Flint Mill Industrial Heritage Trust)
27. Albert Mill, Keynsham, Avon (Roy Day Associates)
28. Edge-runners, Albert Mill (Roy Day Associates)
29. New Lanark
30. Marshall's flax mill, Leeds (R. A. Buchanan)
31. Salt's Mill, Saltaire (R. A. Buchanan)
32. Dunkirk Mill (R. A. Buchanan)
33. Masson Mill, Cromford (R. A. Buchanan)
34. Bage's Mill, Shrewsbury (R. A. Buchanan)
35. Stanley Mill, Stroud (John Cornwell)
36. Machine tools (S. Jacobi)
37. Workers' housing, Cromford (R. A. Buchanan)
38. Artisan dwellings, Sheffield (R. A. Buchanan)
39. Bath Stone (R. A. Buchanan)
40. Brick kilns (John Cornwell)
41. Portland Stone (R. A. Buchanan)
42. Marble quarry (R. A. Buchanan)
43. Industrial monument (R. A. Buchanan)
44. Applied Science (R. A. Buchanan)
45. Royal Albert Bridge (John Cornwell)
46. Smock Mill (J. Kenneth Major)

47. Post mill (J. Kenneth Major)
48. Tower mill (J. Kenneth Major)
49. High-breast water wheel (R. A. Buchanan)
50. Over-shot water wheel (North of England Open-Air Museum)
51. Over-shot water wheel (Sheffield City Museum)
52. Under-shot water wheel (R. A. Buchanan)
53. Cheddleton flint mill (Cheddleton Flint Mill Industrial Heritage Trust)
54. Laxey, Isle of Man (R. A. Buchanan)
55. Horse gin (John Cornwell)
56. Elsecar engine (R. A. Buchanan)
57. Crofton Pumping Station (R. A. Buchanan)
58. Lound Pumping Engine (G. Watkins)
59. Dee Mill, Shaw (G. Watkins)
60. Stoke Bruerne (R. A. Buchanan)
61. Sapperton Canal Tunnel (John Cornwell)
62. Pont Cysyllte Aqueduct (British Waterways Board)
63. James Brindley Walk, Birmingham (R. A. Buchanan)
64. Causey Arch, Tanfield, Co. Durham (North of England Open-Air Museum)
65. Coal chaldron, Co. Durham (North of England Open-Air Museum)
66 and 67. Old Temple Meads Station, Bristol (R. A. Buchanan)
68. Railway signal box (John Cornwell)
69. Graveyard of steam locomotives (John Cornwell)
70. Narrow-gauge revival (R. A. Buchanan)
71. Toll house (R. A. Buchanan)
72. A plateway
73. Albert Dock, Liverpool (Merseyside County Council)
74. Cast-iron bollard (G. Farr)

75. Seaham Harbour, Co. Durham (North of England Open-Air Museum)
76. The S.S. *Great Britain* in Bristol (Port of Bristol Authority)
77. Brunel dredger (Exeter Maritime Museum)
78. S.S. *Great Britain* (John Cornwell)
79. Nottingham Waterworks (R. A. Buchanan)
80. Hull Waterworks (R. A. Buchanan)
81. Papplewick pumping engine (R. A. Buchanan)
82. Fakenham Gas Works, Norfolk (R. A. Buchanan)
83. Horizontal gas retorts (R. A. Buchanan)
84. Electricity generating (John Cornwell)
85. Clevedon Pier (John Cornwell)
86. Airship at Cardington in 1930 (John Cornwell)

List of Line Drawings and Maps

1. The coalfields of Britain 58
2. Types of coal-mining activities 64
3. Miners' lamps 66
4. Killhope lead-crushing mill, Co. Durham 79
5. The lead shot tower, Bristol 81
6. Diagram of a typical blast furnace 86
7. Mechanical hammers used in the iron and steel industry 90
8. The lathe with and without the slide-rest 96
9. Nasmyth's steam hammer 99
10. Mortising machine 102
11. Fulling stocks 122
12. Handloom weaver's cottage 128
13. Cotton factory 135
14. Staffordshire pottery kilns 148
15. Simplified cross-section of an English glass cone 150
16. Paper-making machine 153
17. Types of wooden-frame buildings 165
18. Chief building stones and quarries 167
19. Some basic types of brick bonds 174
20. Farm wagons 188
21. Redditch needle mill 190
22. Brindley's corn mill at Leek 194
23. Mill stones 195
24. Arrangement of processes in a typical malt whisky distillery 204
25. The Horsemill, Woolley Park, Berkshire 225
26. The post mill: three variations 228

27. The tower mill: three variations   229
28. Windmills: three less common types   231
29. Water wheel types   238
30. Diagram of steam engine of *c*. 1800   251
31. Eight types of steam engine   258-9
32. The Port of London   271
33. Smeaton's Eddystone Lighthouse   275
34. Turnpike trusts: roadside relics   284
35. Types of canal lock   289-91
36. Some typical tram-plate sections; some early types of edge
      rail   304
37. The railway bridge over the Menai Straits   314
38. London main-line railway termini   316-17
39. *North Star*   321
40. Chimney Types   332
41. Two unusual pillar boxes   350

REGIONAL SURVEY MAPS:

Key Map   394-6
Scotland   402-3
North England   408-9
Wales   414
The English Midlands   420-21
South-East England   428-9
South-West England   434-5

Preface to the Second Edition

As I observed in the Preface to the first edition of this book, a work such as this must inevitably draw heavily upon the experience of others. No one person can hope to be an expert on all the specialized subjects touched upon in these pages. However, the interdisciplinary character of industrial archaeology is one of its delights, so that it is necessary to make excursions into subjects of which I have no mastery, and although my lack of expertise will be apparent to the experts in each of these subjects, I hope that I have avoided major errors and succeeded in giving an exposition which is both reasonably fair and clear.

I have attempted, in the Notes and Bibliographical References, to show my main debts as far as documentary sources of information and interpretation are concerned, but these are only the more formal aspects of my obligations and I would like to acknowledge fully that I have relied, probably even more than I realize, upon the comments, judgements, and incidental phrases of my many friends in the study of industrial archaeology. I have been greatly touched by the generosity of these friends when I have called upon them for help, and their response encourages me to believe that a real fellowship has developed in the field of our common concerns.

This fellowship has grown rapidly during the 1960s and 1970s and has manifested itself in a wealth of local studies and publications, in preservation protests and conservation attempts, as well as in a striving to achieve a national organization. The cynical or the envious may be tempted to describe the popularity of industrial archaeology in this period as a 'band-wagon', but such a description does less than justice to the sheer enjoyment which has made the majority of industrial archaeologists enthusiastic about their subject. This is not to deny that industrial archaeology has its handful of prickly people who are difficult to please, but the dominant impression in a gathering of industrial archaeological practitioners is one of exhilaration at the discovery of a new way of looking at the landscape, of seeing things to which one was blind before, of understanding processes and machines which previously had an unfamiliar and even an alien quality. In being privileged to share this experience I have made many friends and it is to them that I would like to express my gratitude for their contributions, direct and indirect, to the formulation of this book.

Sadly, some of those to whom I have most cause to be grateful are no longer able to receive my thanks. Sir Arthur Elton died in 1973 and L. T. C. Rolt in 1974. Both were pioneers of the study of industrial archaeology in Britain, and both gave me the enormous benefit of their encouragement and advice. They also set standards of perceptive judgement and professional excellence which have provided models for the rest of us.

I would like also to thank the following friends for special services: Mr George Watkins, my research colleague in the Centre for the Study of the History of Technology at the University of Bath, with whom I count it exceptional good fortune to have been so closely associated over the past twelve years, and who has made many valuable suggestions on my text; Mr Neil Cossons; Mr Keith Gale; Mr Rex Wailes; Mr Michael Rix; and all my colleagues on the staff and Advisory Council of the Centre for the Study of the History of Technology. For special help with photographs and illustrations I would like to thank

Dr Cyril Boucher; Mr J. Kenneth Major; Mr Frank Atkinson and the North of England Open-Air Museum; Mr Frank Wightman; the Ironbridge Gorge Museum Trust Limited; the Tramway Museum, Crich; the Ryhope Pumping Engines Preservation Fund; British Waterways; and the Science Museum.

Various members of the Bristol Industrial Archaeological Society have also helped me with their advice and support over the years, particularly Mr Brian Attwood; Mr John Mosse; Mr Martin Watts; Mr Don Browning; Mr Douglas Jeffery; Mr Roy Day; Mrs Joan Day; Mr Alan Tonkin; and Mr Paul Elkin, Curator in Technology to Bristol City Museum. I am grateful to Mrs Annette Bond and Miss Joanna Valentine for help in preparing the typescripts of the two editions of the book. The second edition, moreover, has benefited from the close working relationship which I have enjoyed with Mr Keith A. Falconer, and also with my brother, Sandy Buchanan. My wife, Brenda, and my sons, Andrew and Thomas, greeted my acknowledgement to them in the first edition with some derision, pointing out that, far from allowing me to direct our family holidays towards industrial archaeological investigation, they had in fact taken the initiative and had, in more cases than I care to be reminded, insisted on us visiting sites when I would have been prepared to pass them by with a distant view and a photograph. Nevertheless, they do deserve my thanks for the constant refreshment and stimulation provided by an increasingly historically orientated household.

Finally, I must make it clear in the customary manner that none of these many friends and helpers can be held responsible for any errors of commission or omission in this book. The design and execution of the work is entirely my own responsibility, and some of my friends might wish to disown me or the book or both in consequence. All the same, it remains true to say that without their help and advice the book could not have been written, and I am profoundly grateful to them all.

R. A. BUCHANAN
University of Bath

Part 1   Introduction

1. Definitions and Techniques

Industrial archaeology has become a popular subject in Britain during the last twenty years because it offers something for everybody. It is concerned with that common heritage of the population, their shared past, and in particular with the outstanding national achievement of the last two centuries. The gist of this achievement may be summed up as success in maintaining a rising standard of living for an ever-increasing population: it is the achievement of higher productivity which has resulted in the comparative affluence of Western societies in the twentieth century. This has been made possible by industrialization, the dynamic but complex process whereby the nations of Western civilization have developed their resources of raw materials, skills, and enterprise, transforming them into usable wealth in some form or other. Industrial archaeology is concerned with an examination of this process of industrialization through a systematic study of its surviving monuments and artefacts. It is a study to which everybody can bring some expertise, whether it be the skill of the architect or engineer, the experience of the manual worker or housewife, or the craft of the teacher or historian, and expect to find a useful and rewarding field of investigation. In the best sense of the term, industrial archaeology is thus an interdisciplinary study.

Whether or not the subject can maintain this attractive non-specialist character as more and more people become interested in it and it acquires, possibly, the status of an academic discipline in its own right, remains to be seen. It will depend largely on the resolution with which the practitioners of industrial archaeology attempt to preserve the open-ended nature of their subject, and their ability to define and to develop it in ways which maintain its interdisciplinary character. This book is conceived in the belief that this can be done and that it is worth doing. On the one hand, the need to formulate the subject matter of industrial archaeology into a systematic and organic study is recognized. On the other hand, however, the breadth of treatment over a wide range of industrial categories and chapters devoted to power, transport systems, and public services indicates the scope for specialist studies in depth in a way in which no one student of the subject, and certainly not the present author, could hope to give adequate attention. Hitherto the study of industrial archaeology has tended to be regional, and even parochial, in its emphasis. This book attempts to suggest a framework within which such local studies can be integrated as parts of a general pattern of development. The element of development is important, because it is only in a historical perspective of economic growth and social transformation that the real significance of industrial monuments can be seen. Hence the decision to include a chapter on the historical framework as part of the introduction to the subject.

Before tackling this historical outline, however, there are some preliminary points of definition and technique which will be dealt with in this chapter. The inchoate quality of the subject is reflected in the lack of any generally agreed definition of industrial archaeology. The most satisfactory definition which I have managed to devise is that industrial archaeology is a field of study concerned with investigating, surveying, recording and, in some cases, with preserving industrial monuments. It aims, moreover, at assessing the significance of these monuments in the context of social and technological history. For the purposes of this definition, an 'industrial monument' is any relic of an obsolete phase of an industry or transport system, ranging from a Neolithic flint mine to a newly obsolete aircraft or electronic computer. In practice, however, it is useful to confine attention to monuments of the last two hundred years or so, both because earlier periods are dealt with by more conventional archaeological or historical techniques, and because of the sheer mass of material dating from the beginning of the Industrial Revolution. The study is 'archaeological' in so far as it deals with physical objects and requires field-work, even if the excavatory techniques of the classical archaeologist are not often applicable. Professor Hoskins, borrowing a phrase from R. H. Tawney, has said that the primary article of equipment of the local historian is a strong pair of walking shoes, and Michael Rix has capped this with the observation that the industrial archaeologist requires gum boots. Such remarks justly emphasize the practical aspects of industrial archaeology, rooted as it is in an examination of the tangible relics of industrialization, and it is by the success and validity of its practical techniques that the claim of industrial archaeology to academic attention must, in the last resort, be judged.

The functions of investigating, surveying, recording and preserving industrial monuments are all part of the subject. 'Investigating' implies a systematic search and appraisal, either following clues in search of new evidence, or re-examining material already known: it is surprising how frequently an industrial monument can be found almost literally at the bottom of the garden, in the form of an abandoned railway, a spoil heap, or a piece of machinery, once a search is undertaken. 'Surveying' involves using whatever techniques are available to measure, photograph, and date a monument. 'Recording' is the process of ensuring that there is a permanent notification of the monument in an appropriate national and local repository. 'Preserving' only arises in certain cases, where a monument is judged to be of outstanding value. Few of us would wish to live in a museum, but it is of great importance that a representative selection of industrial monuments should be preserved for posterity, and the criteria by which such monuments are selected are a matter to which we must return. At this point it is only necessary to indicate that a discriminating regard for preservation is one of the essential functions included within our definition of industrial archaeology.

However important these practical functions of industrial archaeology, they can only achieve scholarly significance as part of a general interpretation of industrialization. Hence the second part of our definition, which recognizes the need to assess the significance of industrial monuments in the context of social and technological history. At this level the skills required of the industrial archaeologist are those of the historian and the social scientist, and particularly the techniques of documentary research and analysis. An enormous amount of useful information about industrial monuments can be culled from business archives, the files of local newspapers, and regional topographical studies, to mention only a few of the more obvious documentary sources. Even more important, however, in a subject which is always in danger of lapsing into the quaint antiquarianism of so much parish-pump literature and the 'I-spy' approach to locomotive or canal spotting, is the need to relate industrial archaeological evidence to existing interpretations of economic growth and social transformation and, indeed, to use such evidence to modify the interpretations.

The need to formulate a working definition of industrial archaeology indicates the novelty of the subject, although it is not an entirely brand-new field of study. Enthusiasts for engineering history have long been taking a constructive interest in industrial monuments through such organizations as the Newcomen Society, and economic historians have done much to elucidate the development of machines and processes. But there is also an important element of novelty in the subject, in so far as the great interest aroused by it in the last two decades has been caused by a sense of urgency. All over Britain – and elsewhere – traces of past phases of industrialization are being rapidly wiped out by the pressing forces of industrial modernization, urban renewal, and motorway construction. It should be said that industrial archaeologists are rarely opposed to such processes themselves, but only in so far as they may lead to the loss of significant artefacts without even an opportunity to record them adequately for posterity. It may almost be said that industrial archaeology was born out of the battle to preserve the Doric Portico at Euston Station, which was finally pulled down by British Railways in 1962 despite strong protests from amenity bodies and other organizations. The last fifteen years have seen many similar confrontations and some successes, such as the preservation of Telford's suspension bridge at Conway. The mounting efficiency with which the case for preservation of significant industrial monuments has been presented in these years reflects the vigorous development of local industrial archaeological societies throughout the country.

Apart from the response to such urgent practical problems as those posed by the high wastage rate of industrial monuments, and apart also from the fact, not to be disregarded or minimized, that many people get great pleasure from it as a recreational activity, there have been two complementary incentives to the study of industrial archaeology. On the one hand, there is the cultural incentive to preserve that which is valuable from the past, and there is now a widening recognition that obsolete industrial artefacts deserve consideration in this respect. Old churches and old castles have long been given such attention, and it is a well-justified if belated acknowledgement of the importance of the British industrial heritage which is bringing the same sort of attention to industrial monuments. On the other hand, there is the historical incentive, which is motivated by the need to preserve as much information as possible about the physical remains of the industrial past. To the historian, all information is good information. Every generation of historians makes its selection from the surviving body of information about the past, and the larger the base of such factual material the better the analysis and interpretation derived from it. Historians are now realizing that there is an abundance of potentially valuable information to be gleaned from industrial artefacts, so that the surveying and recording of such material has assumed a new significance.

We will have more to say about the cultural incentive and the policy for preservation which it implies in a later chapter, but it will be convenient to pursue a little further here the nature of the historical incentive. There are four distinct ways in which industrial archaeological information can provide useful evidence for the social, economic, and technological historian. In the first place, it is capable of giving a practical dimension to historical studies which so easily become second-hand and devoid of imaginative depth. How many authors of the standard text-books, one wonders, know how a set of fulling stocks works? Or a spinning jenny, or Watt's separate condenser? Even when the authors have mastered such elementary technical detail, they rarely manage to convey it to their students. Economic historians often seem to lack a geographical consciousness, using such terms as 'Flanders', for example, with bewildering diversity of meaning. Even the Cambridge Economic History of Europe, for all its monumental and urbane scholarship, could be improved with some more maps. To add to this weakness a lack of technical consciousness is to remove the subject one stage further from reality and to make it so much the less significant and understandable. This is not to say, of course, that all economic historians suffer from such blind-spots, but only to maintain that the identification of such blind-spots is an admission of the importance of the practical dimension to the subject. At this level, therefore, industrial archaeology is capable of opening the imaginative eye of the student of history to new perspectives, in much the same way as a knowledge of architecture enables a person to see and appreciate more about the landscape of a town than he could hope to see without it.

Secondly, there is the potential value of possessing a comprehensive archive of industrial monuments such as has not hitherto been available. The utility of this to economic historians, human geographers, and even to city planners, should be clear enough. It promises to put at their disposal information about the siting, distribution, and size of industries to supplement and correct the picture available from other sources. The lack of such evidence can occasionally have a serious practical result, as when the desirable properties erected by suburban developers in ancient coal-mining areas like that of Kingswood to the east of Bristol subside into old mine workings. Or on a more sombre note, the mining disaster at Lofthouse Colliery, Yorkshire, in 1973, spotlighted the need for information about long-abandoned coal workings. Of more consequence to the economic historian, perhaps, the example of the lead industry on the Mendips may be mentioned. This was the subject of an excellent study in 1930 by the late Dr J. W. Gough, then Lecturer in History at Bristol University. The work was compiled largely from the papers of the Waldegrave family, however, and gave little attention to the technical details or to the precise location of particular workings. The important point about this case is that subsequent fieldwork by industrial archaeologists is bringing to light much new evidence about the location of the industry and about the techniques employed in it. This is the sort of evidence which will eventually find its way into local and national archives, providing future historians with richer sources of material than those which have previously been at their disposal.

A third source of value of industrial archaeological evidence is an extension of this point regarding archival records. It is the provision of technical information on specific aspects of now obsolete processes which would be virtually unobtainable from other sources. The diligence with which some industrial archaeologists have taped the reminiscences of elderly workers who were once engaged in industries which have since disappeared has proved worth-while. In some cases, the details of processes have been recovered and recorded, while in others problems of specialized terminology, inexplicable by any other method, have been resolved. Although the distorting qualities of old men's recollections must be taken into account, there is a useful source of information available here. A similar service is provided by old films, although the task of assembling collections of industrial film has hardly been begun and the wastage of old film is disturbingly high. Another source of technical information which has been exploited by industrial archaeologists is that of photographs. An example of this medium being skilfully used is the collection of Mr George Watkins's photographs of stationary steam engines. His book *The Stationary Steam Engine* covers all the main types of reciprocating steam engine used in industry and illustrates them with a wealth of technical detail. As most of the engines illustrated have now been scrapped, the photographs are the best remaining source of information about them. A final source that should be mentioned here is that of written material in the form of ephemeral semi-technical literature which does not normally find its way into library collections. Such are the voluminous trade catalogues put out by firms, which are often valuable sources of information about equipment and about commodities on the market, but which can often only be used to advantage by somebody already familiar with the type of physical material they describe.

The fourth contribution of industrial archaeology to historical evidence is that it can supply a useful measuring-rod of economic growth and social change. Classical archaeology has long made use of pottery shards for fixing dates, and there is an interesting extension of this technique into modern times in the utilization of fragments of clay tobacco pipes for dating sites, particularly in North America, where there is often a dearth of documentary evidence about early settlements. Admittedly, there is little opportunity to exercise this technique in Europe, but in other ways industrial archaeological material may reflect the successive stages of industrial development. The evolution of a port, for example, can frequently be interpreted from the physical remains of docks, wharves, cranes, locks, bridges, warehouses, and workshops. Similarly, the changes which have overtaken the metallurgical industries in Britain can be unravelled by a careful study of the mass of industrial monuments which they have left, and an investigation of the transport relics of a region can show how one means of transport has been superseded by another. Such remains contribute to the 'palimpsest' quality of the British landscape, whereby successive generations have modified the environment without completely destroying the artefacts of their predecessors, so that a discerning eye can read the current face of a city and reconstruct the significant phases of its development. While economic growth can be assessed by the nature and distribution of the industries of a region over a period of time, social change can be judged from the ancillary features of the industrial landscape – the homes of the workers, their public houses, parks, and chapels, all of which deserve and receive the passing attention of industrial archaeologists. It is fashionable now to look for psychological changes in response to the early stages of rapid industrialization in Britain, but it may also be relevant to look for physiological changes, and the surviving evidence of workers' houses in a model community like Robert Owen's New Lanark, where all the doorways seem less than the modern standard in height, does suggest a marked change in this respect.

There is, then, a definite subject matter to industrial archaeology: a field of study to be explored, a work of selective preservation to be undertaken, and a scholarly task of relating physical remains of obsolete industries to a general interpretation of the processes of industrialization to be performed. The techniques which help the industrial archaeologist in performing these functions are many and varied. It has already been observed that specialist skills from other fields of study can find a ready application in industrial archaeology. Thus, the professional skills of the architect and surveyor in measuring up buildings are of tremendous value when complex industrial buildings require careful recording, and those of the engineer are similarly indispensable when it is necessary to make a drawing of a complicated piece of machinery. Again, the techniques of the classical archaeologist assume great importance when industrial sites require excavation, and the expert knowledge of the metallurgist has proved invaluable in the interpretation of many metal-working sites. All these are skills which are not lightly acquired, and however great their service to industrial archaeology it is a mistake to regard the possession of any one of them as an essential part of the equipment of every industrial archaeologist. It is here that the interdisciplinary nature of the subject is such an asset, and it is not necessary to appropriate the special skills of other professions as techniques of industrial archaeology.

Nonetheless, certain basic techniques may be defined as part of the stock-in-trade of any practising industrial archaeologist. To begin with, he must have a receptive eye. This is not as elementary and trivial as it sounds. It is abundantly clear that it is possible to live virtually surrounded by industrial monuments without seeing in them anything of interest, significance, or value: it is not being too unfair to say that most people in Britain today seem to manage to do just this. The fundamental technique of the industrial archaeologist is thus a posture of imaginative sympathy towards the subject, whereby he acquires a receptive eye – that is, a facility for noticing and appreciating industrial artefacts of all sorts. Without such a keen awareness for his environment, no industrial archaeologist can hope to derive much from the subject, and will certainly not be able to put anything into it.

Once this happy state of mind has been achieved, a number of other basic techniques may be usefully acquired. An efficient and systematic method of note-taking for field-work is prominent amongst these. Although some industrial archaeologists manage with the backs of envelopes, the better-organized members of the fraternity keep proper note-books for their field-work, in which they can enter measurements, observations, grid references, and any other appropriate details while they are actually on the job of surveying a site or artefact. The important thing, however, is to work out a personal technique for collecting the information which will later be transcribed into a written report, either for a record card or for an alternative account. The record cards issued by the Council for British Archaeology for the National Record of Industrial Monuments indicate the sort of headings under which field notes can usefully be summarized. These include a description of the nature of the site or artefact, its dimensions and present condition, its machinery and fittings if any, a note on any danger of demolition or other damage and on any printed, manuscript, or photographic records, and the reporter's name. The cards also provide space for locating the site carefully in a county and parish, and for a grid reference. If there is one elementary technique which all field-workers in industrial archaeology could most usefully acquire, it is that of facility in map-reading, which would enable them to give precise six-figure grid references with the two-letter prefix of the National Grid.

Another basic technique is photography. Not every industrial archaeologist will have the ability or the inclination to become even competent as a photographer, but the camera is by far the most convenient tool of the field-worker, allowing him to make a rapid pictorial record which can in many cases make further detailed surveying unnecessary, so that it is a technique which is worth acquiring. Whether he takes black-and-white photographs or colour slides will depend upon the sort of use to which he puts the pictures: black-and-white are the best way of making a permanent record, but for purposes of teaching and lecturing colour slides are preferable. Like so many other aspects of industrial archaeology, good photography will reflect the expertise of the photographer, and the help of professionals using high-quality cameras and the best techniques is of enormous value. But the ground that can be covered by such experts is obviously severely limited so that for most purposes the fieldworker must depend upon his own resources, and by learning to become a reasonably competent photographer he can add greatly to the value of his reports.

There is really little more that needs to be said about the basic techniques of industrial archaeology. Equipped with a receptive eye and a sympathetic imagination, and suitably clad in gum boots or whatever other weather-resistant gear is appropriate, the industrial archaeologist can begin to tackle his fieldwork armed only with a note-book and a pencil, a camera, and a tape-measure or measuring-rod. He will soon learn when he requires the skills of his colleagues to make a detailed survey, to conduct an excavation, or to do a metallurgical analysis, and he will probably not have to look far to find the help he needs. In the normal run of events, it would be unwise or even harmful for him to attempt such specialized tasks which are beyond his competence: many fine sites in the fields of both classical and industrial archaeology have been ruined for posterity by over-enthusiastic and unskilled excavation, and similar damage can be done by other well-intentioned but ill-informed attempts to survey, move, or preserve industrial monuments. It is thus an important part of the technique of the industrial archaeologist to recognize one's limitations and, in a subject involving a lot of interdisciplinary team-work, to be prepared to call in colleagues to help with their special skills.

One skill which is fairly easily acquired and involves no damage to the industrial monuments concerned is the historian's technique of documentary research. Any industrial archaeologist with spare time and patience can find material to enlighten him on the industrial remains of his own neighbourhood in local library archives and record offices. At the most superficial level, it is often useful to consult the files of local newspapers to read contemporary accounts of the opening of a bridge or the launching of a ship, and such work can frequently illuminate the study of physical remains. The facility with which such local documentary material can be made available, however, should not mislead the student into thinking that this is all there is to historical research. It is particularly important that industrial archaeologists should be aware of the range of historical interpretations which have evolved around the processes of industrialization, because it is only within such a general understanding of the pattern of historical development that the physical remains of past industrial systems assume their fullest significance. It is for this reason that the next chapter is devoted to a consideration of the historical framework of industrialization.

In this chapter we have introduced the subject of industrial archaeology by formulating a definition, by presenting a case for regarding it seriously as a branch of historical studies, and by suggesting the basic techniques which are desirable for the effective practice of the subject. In the next chapter we will continue this introduction by treating the historical content of industrial archaeology. Most of the remainder of the book is then devoted to a study of the main areas of industry in which industrial remains can help in the interpretation of industrial history. For convenience this is divided into a series of the major industrial categories (coal, metals, textiles, etc.) in Part Two, and into power, transport systems, and public services in Part Three. Part Four then attempts to draw some conclusions about the development of industrial archaeology. In the final section there is an outline regional survey, showing the geographical distribution of industrial monuments in Britain. The book is designed to be read either straight through, by the reader requiring a general over-view of the subject matter of industrial archaeology, or as a series of independent chapters, for the benefit of the industrial archaeological field-worker wanting information on a particular industry or process. In the interests of simplicity notes have been kept to the minimum, but they include bibliographical references which are designed to assist readers who desire to follow the subject in greater depth in one or other of the particular fields surveyed.

2. The Historical Framework

We have established, as part of our attempt to define industrial archaeology, that the subject is most usefully confined to the artefacts and processes of the last two hundred years or so. This temporal limitation implies that industrial archaeology is intimately related to that phenomenon of economic and social history known as the 'Industrial Revolution'. The concept of Industrial Revolution, however, is a difficult one, about which it is desirable to have a clear understanding as a crucial element in the historical framework of our subject.

The idea of an Industrial Revolution became current in the second half of the nineteenth century, although there are anticipations of it earlier in the writings of such astute observers of socio-economic change as Friedrich Engels, who pointed out in the opening sentences of his book *The Condition of the Working Class in England in 1844* that:

These inventions [the steam engine and cotton machines] gave rise, as is well known, to an industrial revolution, a revolution which altered the whole civil society; one, the historical importance of which is only now beginning to be recognized.[1]

Credit for using the term in academic circles is usually attributed to Arnold Toynbee (uncle of the distinguished historian of the same name), whose course at Oxford was published under the title *Lectures on the Industrial Revolution in England* in 1884.

Thereafter it became widely used in works of economic and social history, being generally applied to the events in Britain between the mid-eighteenth and the mid-nineteenth centuries whereby the industry and economic prosperity of the country expanded with what was, on any estimation, unprecedented speed. This usage of the term has been perpetuated, so that even such a distinguished text-book as that by the late Professor T. S. Ashton took the title, quite specifically, of *The Industrial Revolution, 1760–1830*.

This usage is, however, misleading, and it is necessary for the student of industrial archaeology to recognize the problematical qualities of the term. To begin with, there is a semantic difficulty. The Industrial Revolution is not a revolution at all in the mechanical sense of the term, meaning that something is moving in a circle. It is only appropriate in so far as it is derived from the Marxist conception of violent political upheaval marking the transition from one politico-social system to another. By analogy, the term Industrial Revolution marks the application of such thinking about sudden and violent change to the spheres of social and economic development. It may be legitimately doubted whether any event in the course of such social and economic development can justify this connotation of violent change, but the expression Industrial Revolution has become so widely used and remains so useful as a piece of historical shorthand that it would be unreasonable to reject it on grounds of linguistic imprecision alone.

A more substantial objection to the term is that it implies a sudden beginning and a sudden end to a process which, in the nature of socio-economic development, cannot be sudden. The determination of the Industrial Revolution by such dates as 1760–1830 emphasizes this difficulty. If the concept is used rigidly, a picture emerges of a short period of violent industrial activity preceded by an epoch of rural stagnation, and followed by a period of comparative calm once the effects of rapid industrialization had been assimilated. The vision of a predominantly agricultural Golden Age, with a few small-scale craft industries amid a scene of idyllic bliss in which Englishmen ate roast beef and quaffed English ale while their wives and children danced round English maypoles, was projected backwards by warm-hearted Radicals in the nineteenth century who rejected the 'dark Satanic mills' and the evils of urban, industrial, life.

Such a view, however, is a manifest distortion. It is, indeed, so obvious that the changes which occurred after 1760 had been prepared for over a long period of time that historians have introduced prior 'industrial revolutions' to explain the build-up to the classic Industrial Revolution of the eighteenth century. Most notably, Professor Nef spoke of an industrial revolution in coal production in the sixteenth and seventeenth centuries, and Professor Carus-Wilson has written of an industrial revolution in the thirteenth century, caused by the invention of mechanical fulling mills in the woollen cloth industry.[2] The 'stepped' interpretation of history which emerges from these successive qualifications is an improvement on the short sharp change model of the classic Industrial Revolution, but it still does less than justice to the facts of socio-economic growth because it involves selecting particular aspects of economic life as being of outstanding significance at the time in question, and the selection will depend in part on the historian and on the area of his specialization.

It is more helpful to see the process as a continuum, a current of mounting economic activity which has fluctuated but has suffered no catastrophic reverse over the past thousand years, and of which the area of operation has expanded from Western Europe to encompass most of the modern world. This is the process by which Western civilization (so called – despite the geographical anomalies of using the title in the present century – because of its origin in Western Europe) emerged from the period of comparative chaos and socio-economic collapse which has been habitually described as the 'Dark Ages', and developed into the position of world dominance which it holds today. The process of growth was slow at first, the first five hundred years from around A.D. 1000 to 1500 being spent almost entirely in isolation from the rest of the world, except for the crusading expeditions against Islam and the first tentative voyages of exploration. Nevertheless, it was during this period that the foundations for much of the subsequent economic expansion were laid: strong political units were established, trading relationships were made and flourished, vigorous town life spread all over Western Europe, agricultural organization and techniques were improved and made more productive, and the population grew steadily.

The causes of this expansion of economic activity do not concern us here, but the fact that it took place is important because it provides the roots of many subsequent developments, and not only in the socio-economic field. It is, after all, no accident that the origin of such important contemporary institutions as Parliament, the Common Law, and the Universities must be sought in the context of these five hundred years of steady growth. By 1500, the new nation states which had emerged in Western Europe were prepared to begin the process of expansion which has carried Western civilization all over the world. Beginning with the great voyages of discovery, made possible by the improved sailing ship and navigational techniques, and going on to the establishment of vast colonial empires, achieved by the superior weapon technology of the European powers, this process culminated in the emergence of powerful new states, politically independent of Europe, but adopting the pattern of socio-economic development which had been pioneered in Western Europe.

This final phase of the expansion of Western Europe began in 1776 when the British colonies in North America declared their independence of the mother-country, and subsequently achieved this objective by the establishment of the United States of America. Their example has been followed, with varying degrees of violence, all over the world, so that the powers of the European nations which initiated the expansive movement have now been greatly curtailed. This has not involved, however, any curtailment of industrial and economic development, but rather the contrary. The American Declaration of Independence coincided almost exactly with the publication of Adam Smith's enormously influential treatise on *The Wealth of Nations*, which gave both a stimulus and a theoretical justification to individualism in trade and industry; and both events stand close to the beginning of the classic Industrial Revolution. However significant the preceding centuries in preparing for the socio-economic transformation of the last two hundred years, they appear in retrospect to be only the precursors of the dramatic events which have acquired for themselves the description 'Industrial Revolution' and which provide the main subject matter for the industrial archaeologist.

Of course, it is not suggested that industrial archaeology is or should be exclusively concerned with the events of the last two hundred years. Many industries and processes made significant innovations long before the middle of the eighteenth century, and when, as in the case of the iron industry, these left substantial artefacts, they require the attention of the industrial archaeologist. Indeed, as exponents of the practical aspect of the history of technology, industrial archaeologists are entitled to take an even longer view of their subject, for a study of the origins of technological innovation involves going back to the beginning of the human species and surveying the development of fire, pottery, the wheel, early tools, and building techniques on the way. Again, there is no reason why industrial archaeologists should limit their attention to Western civilization, as there is certainly plenty of evidence of obsolete industrial techniques to be collected from other civilizations, in India, China, the Middle East, and Central America. In the course of such inquiries, useful analogies can be found between practices still operating in these parts of the world and those which have long since disappeared from Western Europe. For example, iron is still worked in parts of central India in bloomeries which resemble those which were widespread in Europe until the blast furnace superseded them in the sixteenth century.

The industrial archaeologist is thus entitled, in pursuit of physical remains and explanatory detail, to extend the range of his subject in both space and time beyond the limits of Western civilization in the last two hundred years. But for most practical purposes his study will be concentrated within these limits, because the acceleration of the processes of industrialization in this period has caused both a vast quantitative increase in the amount of material requiring his attention and the threat to obsolete buildings and equipment which has given a particular poignancy to the study of industrial archaeology in the last two decades. It is this intensification of interest in modern Western civilization which makes it especially appropriate that the industrial archaeologist should be equipped with some understanding of the process of the Industrial Revolution.

What, then, was the Industrial Revolution? So far we have been concerned to correct misleading impressions conveyed by the traditional uses of the term, but we have accepted its convenience and intend to continue using it, so we must be clear about the way in which we are using it. Despite all qualifications, something dramatic began to happen in Britain in the middle of the eighteenth century. The apocryphal schoolgirl essay began: 'In the Industrial Revolution there was a flood of inventions . . .' and she obviously had a point. One of the most spectacular features of the period, both to contemporaries and in retrospect, was the success with which new inventions were introduced into industry. The cotton textile industry was the outstanding example, for between 1760 and 1830 – the classic dates of the Industrial Revolution – the British cotton industry was almost completely mechanized by a series of innovations which transformed the organization of the industry and brought about a staggering increase in productivity. Elsewhere, however, in the iron and steel industry, in the chemical processes, in the incipient engineering industry, and in the manufacture of steam engines, the same successful application of new ideas could be seen, and was marked by the rapid increase in the number of patents taken out. Obviously, there had been many inventions before the eighteenth century, some of which had been the cause of important technological developments, but never before had there been such a spate of successful inventions. So extraordinary was this feature of the Industrial Revolution that it requires some explanation.

For an invention to become a commercial success, three conditions are necessary, and these are all factors, in part or in whole, of the social environment. The first of these conditions is the existence within society of key groups who are prepared to consider innovation seriously and sympathetically. Recent research has stressed the profound importance of such a socially influential group – in this case the new industrial middle class – being willing to cultivate new ideas and inventors, the breeders of such ideas, in Britain in the second half of the eighteenth century. So pronounced was this encouragement that many inventors from other countries found in Britain a better market for their ideas than in their native countries. Inventors in Britain were able to work, not in the isolation of ridicule or contempt, but in a society which recognized the value of their labours and rewarded them with honour and respect, even if not always with material wealth. Whatever the psychological basis of inventive genius, therefore, there can be no doubt that the existence of a socially important group prepared to receive new ideas is a crucial factor in the development of technological change, and that Britain possessed such a group in the eighteenth century.[3]

However important this first factor, it can only operate effectively when technological innovation is being encouraged to match social needs. Such needs must be explicit – that is, they must be *felt* to be needs. It would be unrealistic to say that an Indian peasant labouring in his paddy field has a need for a television set, or even for a tractor; his needs are in fact much more fundamental and intractable. On the other hand, a sense of social need can be generated artificially, and this is the function of salesmanship and advertising in modern societies. What is important is that the need should be felt, so that people are prepared to devote resources to its fulfilment. It may be that the pressure of increasing population is creating social need in the form of an enlarged market, or, paradoxically, that shortage of labour in specific areas of the economy is creating a need for labour-saving machines. Or it may be that some obdurate technical problem sets up a pressure for new solutions, like the shortage of timber and the problem of using coal fuels in blast furnaces, or the flooding of mines and the ineffectiveness of existing pumps. All these factors and many more existed in eighteenth-century Britain, and they bore precisely on that social group – the new industrial middle class – which was temperamentally most receptive to new ideas. While the basic human needs of the French peasantry were no less and were probably greater than those of their British counterparts, France lacked a social group of sufficient size and power to articulate these needs and to resolve them through increasing productivity by technological innovations.

The third factor – social resources – is similarly indispensable. Many inventions have foundered because the social resources vital for their realization – capital, materials, and skilled personnel – were not available. The note-books of Leonardo da Vinci, for instance, are full of most ingenious ideas for helicopters, submarines, and aeroplanes (amongst many others), but few of these reached even the model stage because of deficient resources of one sort or the other. The resource of capital involves the existence of surplus productivity and the organization of a 'capital market' capable of directing the available wealth into channels where the inventor can use it. It presupposes, in other words, an adequate economic system. The resource of materials involves the availability of appropriate metallurgical, ceramic, and plastic substances, which in turn presupposes an adequate industrial system. The resource of skilled personnel implies the presence of expertise and technical 'know-how' capable of constructing artefacts and devising processes, and this presupposes an adequate educational system. A society, in short, has to be well primed in order to undertake an Industrial Revolution, and in eighteenth-century Europe only Britain possessed these social resources in a form which made them available when they were required. Elsewhere, they were deficient in one or more respects. It may well be argued, for example, that France at this time possessed a system of technical education which was superior to that of Britain, and that it had an elaborate and highly skilled range of industries capable of producing most of the new materials required for technological innovation. But its economic system was not as capable of the expansion and flexibility necessary to take advantage of new ideas: in a word, it was short of capital. Consequently Britain, with its rough and ready but practicable system of industrial apprenticeship, its broad industrial base, and its elaborate and expanding capital market, was in an advantageous position denied to France and other countries in the eighteenth century.

This review of the social preconditions necessary for successful invention provides a conceptual framework for a theory of invention by which the development and application of any invention can be explained. It cannot claim to predict invention, because there is a human and imponderable element in every

invention, and as yet we have, fortunately, found no way of cir-
cumventing this element. But it can be useful in negative predictions, in so far as it can be stated pretty clearly where particular
inventions will not be successful because of the lack of one or
other of the social factors described: the example of the Indian
peasant and the television set has already been mentioned. To
this extent, a theory of invention is valuable in determining
industrialization programmes for developing countries. In the
present context, however, we are concerned with it as an aid to
explaining the rapid rise in the number of successful inventions
in Britain in the second half of the eighteenth century, and the
conclusion to be drawn from this analysis is that Britain had
achieved a social environment which was receptive to new
ideas, which needed new ideas, and which had the essential
resources available for the development of new ideas, at least a
generation before its neighbours and rivals. For these social
reasons, therefore, the processes of industrialization began to
accelerate in Britain around the middle of the eighteenth century.

The acceleration was a hen-and-egg process in which it is
impossible to disentangle cause and effect with any precision,
but one of the stimuli to further expansion in what was already
a dynamic and expanding economy was the awareness of certain
technological constraints on production which posed problems
of social need and which, in their solution, led to substantial
increases in production. The major constraints of this nature in
the first half of the eighteenth century were the shortage of timber for building and for fuel, the flooding of mines because of
the inefficiency of existing pumping apparatus, and the series of
bottlenecks in production which frustrated enterprising manufacturers in the cotton industry. The timber shortage must not
be over-stated, for Britain has remained a well-wooded country,
but at a time when large quantities of top-quality timber were
required for national defence in the shape of the traditional
man-o'-war, and when the demands for small timber for domes-

tic and industrial fuel were increasing, there was good cause for anxiety about the depletion of the national stock of wood. It seems certain that the British iron industry would have been seriously embarrassed by shortage of fuel if it had continued to rely completely on charcoal for all its major processes in the eighteenth century. As it was, the timely invention by Abraham Darby in 1709 of means of using coke in iron-smelting began the shift from dependence upon timber to dependence upon coal fuels, and by the end of the century the whole iron and steel industry was expanding in response to the opportunities presented by the use of coal.

The coal industry, however, had its own problems, and the availability of more and more coal for the expanding industries of the eighteenth and nineteenth centuries was dependent upon the satisfactory solution of these problems, of which by far the most restrictive was the inadequacy of the conventional pumps to cope with the water which collected in the mines as the shafts were sunk deeper and deeper. The steam engine provided the solution to this problem, at first only partially but with steadily increasing efficiency, so that by the end of the eighteenth century deep coal-mines in all the main coalfields were equipped with reliable steam pumps. Moreover, the improved steam engines of James Watt and the engineers who followed him provided pumps for the metalliferous mines of Cornwall and Devon as well as for coal-mines, so that the non-ferrous metal industries also benefited from increasing production of their raw materials. Again, the conversion of the steam engine to rotary action opened up the possibility of its utilization in a wide range of industrial processes and aroused a sense of urgent social need in industries which had hitherto managed with less reliable prime movers.

Amongst the first industries to benefit from steam power was the cotton textile industry. Until the middle of the eighteenth century, this industry consisted of a series of traditional domestic

processes which made uneven demands on the available labour
and frustrated the industrialists who were anxious to increase
production. These industrialists were thus eager to experiment
with mechanical devices which would remove bottlenecks in
production, beginning with the spinning process and going on
to weaving, carding, and printing, and installing steam power to
drive the new machines whenever water power was inadequate
to deal with the ever-increasing load. Not all the bottlenecks in
cotton production could be removed by mechanical innovations.
One of the most serious delays occurred in the bleaching process,
and the incentive to produce an efficient chemical bleaching
agent stimulated the emergence of a new major industry in the
shape of the chemical industry which was able to meet the needs
of many other developing industries for new materials. The
soap, pottery, and glass industries, for example, were all able to
obtain essential materials from the new chemical plant and thus
to expand their own production.

This increasing industrial activity created new social needs
in the fields of transport and communications. Industries
required better facilities to collect their raw materials and to
distribute their manufactured goods, so that there was a constant pressure to improve transport which led to the remarkable
developments in road, canal, and railway construction during
the eighteenth and nineteenth centuries. Likewise, the demand
for better communications led to improvements in the postal
service and eventually to the electric telegraph, the telephone,
and the modern mass media. These improvements in transport
and communications fed back into industrial expansion by
making possible the development of hitherto inaccessible
districts.

The picture which emerges from this review of the 'growth-
points' of the British economy in the eighteenth and nineteenth
centuries is one of generally quickening activity and increasing
production. Some of the well-established traditional industries

such as woollen textiles were comparatively slow in responding to this new tempo of industrial activity, but even these came to adopt the new machines and processes or, in some cases of old craft industries such as the coopers, virtually faded away. To complete the outline, however, one further group of factors must be mentioned. The population of Britain had been increasing gradually for several centuries before the Industrial Revolution. There are no exact statistics available on this growth until the nineteenth century, so that assessments are necessarily somewhat speculative, but contemporaries did not need precise statistics to convince them of the fact that the population was growing. The towns were becoming larger and more crowded, and problems of law and order and poor relief were becoming more pressing. T. R. Malthus published his famous *Essay on Population* in 1799, two years before the first National Census in 1801, but this did not prevent him from making confident (even if gloomy) predictions about what we in the twentieth century have come to know as the 'population explosion'.

We now know that his predictions were unnecessarily gloomy; the experience of Western civilization has shown that an ever-increasing population can be accommodated, not just without starvation but even with a rising standard of life, provided that the processes of industrialization can be developed in order to raise productivity. Nonetheless, contemporary experience should warn us not to be too confident that this remedy can be applied universally and indefinitely, for the continued growth of population in South-East Asia, Latin America, and elsewhere appears to be outstripping the capacity of governments to develop their programmes of industrialization, so that the Malthusian nightmare of mass starvation has reappeared to haunt us. Although this is a sombre prospect for the future, the achievement of Western nations in the last two centuries in not only preventing this sort of catastrophe, but actually turning the population boom to advantage, has been outstanding. The demographic transition from a comparatively thinly populated and predominantly rural country to a heavily populated urban and industrial country has been, after all, the outstanding physical fact of the last two centuries, and this alone makes it a fact of importance to industrial archaeologists. As the growth of population has stimulated markets, encouraged agricultural reforms in order to increase the production of food and drink, and promoted the development of many sorts of consumer industries, it has also been instrumental in the creation of a large number of industrial remains which engage the attention of industrial archaeologists.[4]

Just as historians have tried to qualify the sharp discontinuity with previous developments at the beginning of the Industrial Revolution, so they have attempted to modify its point of termination, and the same sort of criticisms can be made of this as of the former exercise. The traditional Industrial Revolution terminated about 1830, at which point the British cotton textile industry was judged to have become completely mechanized. The spectacular conversion of this industry, within a single lifetime, from a scattered series of domestic processes into a highly concentrated, mechanized, factory- and urban-based industry was impressive both to contemporaries and to historians looking back at it subsequently. But however impressive, the transformation of the cotton industry did not in itself constitute the Industrial Revolution, even in the traditional interpretation of the term, and there are strong reasons for not ending the process in 1830. This was, after all, the year in which the Liverpool and Manchester Railway, the first fully scheduled passenger and goods railway service in the world, opened, and it is absurd to wind up the Industrial Revolution just as the Railway Age was beginning. The 1830s, moreover, marked important theoretical and experimental developments in electrical engineering and in organic chemistry, both of which grew into massive industries in the following hundred years, so on these grounds also it is hardly reasonable to close the period of Industrial Revolution in 1830. When it is remembered that the electric telegraph and modern communications did not appear until the late 1830s, and that the production of cheap steel, which has been of such profound importance in the modern world, did not begin until Bessemer's experiments in 1856, it appears nonsensical to regard the Industrial Revolution as having ended in 1830 to be followed by a period of comparative stagnation.

Some historians have attempted to avoid the absurdity of this conclusion by suggesting a series of subsequent 'revolutions', and in recent years we have heard of 'the second Industrial Revolution'. The latter appears to be a journalistic invention to describe the developments which have occurred during and since the Second World War – jet engines, rocketry, radar, electronics, computers, antibiotics, insecticides, atomic power, and so on. However astonishing this list of modern scientific and technological achievements, the attempt to cast it as another Industrial Revolution is open to exactly the same kind of objections as we have brought against the text-book interpretation of the first such Revolution, and particularly the criticism that it involves a conception of discontinuity which does not agree with the realities of socio-economic development. A more serious methodological approach to our understanding of industrialization has been made by economic historians such as Professor Rostow who have tried to analyse the phases of the Industrial Revolution and to suggest a model of the process which can be transferred to other countries.[5] This has been a fruitful approach, but from our point of view it is open to the objection that it conceives the process of industrialization entirely in terms of economic growth, and does less than justice to the matrix of social and political transformation into which changes of productivity need to be fitted in order to make sense. This criticism applies both to our understanding of the Industrial Revolution in Britain, which is inseparable from the social and political changes culminating in modern democratic institutions, and to that of the subtle process whereby the Midas-touch of rapidly increasing productivity can be acquired by developing countries. We are still looking, therefore, for a satisfactory view of the Industrial Revolution.

The idea that Industrial Revolution can be transferred from one country to another is worth considering, because it is necessary to avoid the insular view that the process was peculiar to Britain. There is little disagreement about the assertion that it *began* in Britain, although it is probably true to say that insufficient credit has been given by British historians of the Industrial Revolution to the contributions of Italian silk-throwing machines in the establishment of Lombe's factory at Derby, to French scientific expertise in fields such as chemistry, where Berthollet provided the pioneer work on chlorine bleaches and Lavoisier laid the basis of modern chemical theory, and to American scientists and engineers such as Franklin, Oliver Evans, and Robert Fulton. Still, Britain in the eighteenth century provided the essential social environment within which the rapid acceleration in the processes of industrialization could commence and be sustained. The reasons for this are complex and bound up in the social and political history of the preceding centuries, and particularly in the establishment of a strong government responsive to the interests of an influential land-owning, commercial and industrial class, and in the crucial role of the nonconformist religious groups in Britain who, denied political representation, devoted themselves to industrial and commercial activity. For our purposes, it is sufficient to recognize this British primacy and to observe, as has already been said, that it gave Britain a lead of a generation over its national rivals.

Where Britain led the way, however, other nations were bound to follow. But whereas the British Industrial Revolution was largely spontaneous, in the sense that it received no direct guidance from central government, in most other countries it was promoted by governments who were actively trying to model their development on British experience, often mediated through British businessmen and workmen and using British machines. The process of this diffusion of British experience is fascinating, but it need not concern us here, except in so far as it is useful to recognize that because British experience was paralleled and reproduced all over the world the industrial archaeological evidence of British industries may be found in unlikely places, such as coal-fuel blast furnaces in Pennsylvania, Cornish mining equipment in Central America and South Africa, Newcomen engines in Central Europe, and Telford canals in Sweden. By the middle of the nineteenth century British leadership in industrialization was being challenged by Prussia, America and France, with Belgium, Switzerland, and other countries developing strongly in particular industries, and by the end of the century both Germany and the USA had overtaken Britain in key sectors of economic life. In the present century, other countries such as Japan and Russia have undergone rapid industrialization, and the trend has been set towards the goal of general world industrialization. Whether or not this will solve all the world's problems is doubtful, but it is an aspiration which cannot be denied the less-developed countries as they try to increase their productivity and to improve their standards of living along lines pioneered first of all by the Industrial Revolution in Britain.

To return, finally, to the question which we have been pursuing throughout this chapter: what do we understand by the term 'Industrial Revolution'? Despite all its difficulties and anomalies, we are committed to retaining it because it is such a widely used and expressive term. Only we must be clear about what it expresses. It should *not* be taken to mean a particular period – whether this be the period 1760 to 1830 or any other terminal dates in British history, or later periods in the history of other nations – because we have tried to show the inadequacy of any such precise temporal limitation. Rather, the Industrial Revolution should be understood as a broad movement of socio-economic transformation, springing out of a social environment which is responsive to change and innovation, gathering momentum, and becoming an accelerating process of industrialization with corresponding adjustments in social and political institutions. Whether or not this curve of accelerating industrialization will slow down and flatten out remains to be seen: the spectacular developments of the past few decades should be enough to convince anybody that the pace of transformation is still very high, and there are as yet few signs of any serious slackening in it while so many parts of the world remain underdeveloped. It is thus as a continuing process of rapid social and economic transformation that the term Industrial Revolution can be most usefully employed. In this sense, it is not an event which happened once for all some time, somewhere, in history. It is a dynamic process in which Britain led the way some two hundred years ago, but which has now caught up the whole of Western civilization, and, indeed, the world. An understanding of the internal operation and social ramifications of this process should be part of the education of any citizen of the modern world, and in studying the physical remains of the process industrial archaeology is making a potentially valuable contribution to our comprehension of it.

Part 2   The Industrial Categories

3. The Coal-Mining Industry

Probably the greatest natural asset of Britain in the early stages of the Industrial Revolution was the possession of large coal deposits. Over extensive areas of the Midlands and northern counties, coal is available at or near the surface. Although the exploitation of these resources called for capital, labour, new techniques, and new methods of organization, the basic geological fact is that the British Isles are well endowed with coal, and when the need to find a substitute for wood as the fuel for fires and furnaces became pressing, means were developed to obtain the coal. Thus the story of the British coal industry, at least until the beginning of the present century, is a record of ever-increasing productivity as the obstacles to removing the coal were progressively overcome and the output of the mines responded to the enormous world hunger for the material which had become an essential ingredient in virtually all industries and transport systems. Nef estimated that coal production in Britain rose from about 200,000 tons per annum in the mid-sixteenth century to nearly 3 million tons per annum in the early eighteenth century, and this indicates the importance of coal fuel even before the traditional 'Industrial Revolution'.[1] Production continued to rise steeply, passing 10 million tons per annum around 1800 and reaching over 270 million tons in 1913. This year marked a turning-point, for the unsettled world situation culminating in the outbreak of the First World War, together with the rapid

growth in the popularity and accessibility of the internal combustion engine, brought a change in the world demand for coal.
The British coal industry passed through a period of intense
disturbance and depression between the wars, and even though
coal production has stabilized around the 200 million tons per
annum mark in the years since the Second World War, it has
never again reached the high point of 1913. In recent years the
National Coal Board, which inherited a complex mass of colliery
interests in 1946, has taken drastic steps to rationalize and to
modernize the industry, so that while production has been
generally maintained through the installation of machinery and
more intensive working of mines, these improvements have been
accompanied by a reduction in the number of operative mines
and in the size of the mining community. In traditional coal-
mining districts such as South Wales and County Durham this
process of contraction is clearly and sometimes painfully apparent. The overall effect of the modernization programme will,
it is hoped, be beneficial, but in the meantime it is causing large-
scale and rapid obsolescence of mines and machinery, which
poses a big problem for students of industrial archaeology.

The Geology of Coal

The geological conditions which give rise to coal measures are
worth considering in outline because they help to explain the
geographical location of the coal-mining industry, and hence the
location of many coal-consuming industries. It should be observed, to begin with, that coal is a rock, and that it is subject to
the same processes of distortion, faulting, and erosion as any
other rock, and that like any other stone it can be quarried or
mined. Coal is, in fact, a sedimentary rock formed by the
accumulation of vegetable matter which has been subjected to
pressure, causing shrinkage and progressive devolatilization.
There can be no coal amongst the most ancient rocks, because

these were formed long before the appearance of vegetation on the surface of the earth, but most of the coalfields of Britain date from the period of the first great rain forests, appropriately called the 'Carboniferous' period in geological terminology. The only exception in Britain, and this is not a very significant one, is the existence of some coal seams in the Jurassic strata of north-east Yorkshire and at Brora in Sutherland. These cause the outcrop of 'Whitby jet', used for decorative purposes, in Yorkshire, and a coal-mine at Brora. The latter has a curiosity interest as a piece of industrial archaeology, for as well as being the most northerly coal-mine in Britain it is a co-operative venture, being too small to fall within the scope of the National Coal Board. These pockets of Jurassic coal are unusual, but there is no physical reason why coal should not exist amongst rocks younger than Carboniferous measures. As a general rule, however, climatic conditions or some other factors do not seem to have favoured coal formation on a massive scale since the end of the Carboniferous period, although peat has been formed in Tertiary and even later deposits, to provide the raw material for a fuel industry in parts of the world where it can be used as a substitute for coal. The outstanding example in Britain of peat working is in the Highlands of Scotland, but smaller workings, almost as a by-product of agriculture, occur in the Sedgemoor Plain of Somerset, parts of Wales, and elsewhere. Another unusual coal is 'cannel coal', mined near Wigan and in parts of Scotland. This occurs in irregular lens-shaped masses and appears to consist largely of fine plant detritus. Its name derives from the word 'candle' because it burns with a bright luminous flame. It was highly valued by the gas industry for this quality when gas lighting was widely used and before the introduction of the incandescent mantle.

Most British coals, then, are the bituminous coals of the Carboniferous series, but even within these considerable variations of chemical composition occur, depending upon the

1. The coalfields of Britain. Coalfields are shaded; concealed coalfields are indicated by dots.

proportion of carbon, oxygen, and other elements. The volatility of the coal (i.e. the ease with which it burns) varies inversely with the proportion of carbon, so that anthracite, the least volatile, has the highest carbon content of any coal fuel, and the geological 'ranks' of coal are graded downward from anthracite through steam coal, coking coal, gas coal, to lignite ('brown coal') and peat, which have the lowest carbon content and the highest volatility. As the older deposits are usually the least volatile, the normal order of their occurrence in the ground is the reverse of their rank – i.e. the anthracites are normally the deeper rocks because these are older. Long-term land movements and faulting, however, have frequently combined to interrupt this natural sequence, and it was often impossible for the early mining engineers to predict with any certainty what type of seams they were likely to encounter. The work of William Smith, the 'Father of English Geology', and other pioneers established the value of fossils as a clue to the relative ages of seams, and hence to their probable places in a sequence of rock strata. It is significant that Smith was himself in business as a coal and canal engineer. The strictly utilitarian aspect of this science is nicely illustrated by Trueman's story of the mining engineer who declared: 'I don't care if you call it *Carbonicola communis* or *Anthraconaia modiolaris*; if I get one of the fat little b—s I know that I am in the Brass Vein'.[2] The difficulty of identifying coal seams is accentuated by the unevenness with which the coal was originally deposited. Coal formation seems to have taken place in a cyclical sequence over a prolonged period in Carboniferous times, so that many distinct seams appear throughout the depth of the coal measures. These may vary in thickness from a fraction of an inch to several feet, so that out of a total sequence of coal measures some hundreds of feet in depth, only a few tens of feet may represent coal, and an even smaller proportion will be workable coal. Most of the coal seams which have been worked in Britain range between $2\frac{1}{2}$ feet and 6 feet in thickness, although seams as

narrow as 1 foot have been worked in some of the poorer fields
such as that of North Somerset. But even in the richest coalfields, such as that of Yorkshire, the seams rarely exceed a thickness of 6 feet. Another result of the cyclical formation of coal is
that the adjacent strata also repeat themselves, with fireclay immediately below the coal (associated with the remains of the
plant roots) and below that there is frequently a band of sandstone or mudstone (associated with the swamp in which the
Carboniferous vegetation grew).

Not only are seams distributed unevenly within the coal
measures, but the coal measures themselves also occur irregu-
larly across the country. All the exposed coalfields of England
and Wales occur in a broad belt to the west of a north–south line
connecting Middlesbrough and Southampton, and to the east
of the ancient rocks of Cornwall and Devon, central Wales, the
Lake District and Scotland. This band is divided in the north of
England by the fold of the Pennines, which brings to the surface
older Carboniferous series of sandstones and limestones which
are not coal-bearing, so that the coal measures are confined to
the flanks of these hills. The band is terminated in the south by a
similar exposure of Carboniferous limestone in the Mendip
Hills. The coalfields of Scotland occur in a band of similar
geological age and composition running across the central Lowlands, sandwiched between the older and non-coal-bearing rocks
to north and south. Within these broad bands of potentially coal-
bearing rocks the actual disposition of the coalfields is the result
of almost random factors of local configuration and erosion. At
the southern end of the main band in England and Wales are the
coalfields of Bristol, North Somerset, the Forest of Dean, and
South Wales. In the Midlands, there is a scatter of small coalfields between Leicester and Wolverhampton, and to the north
of these the more extensive fields on either side of the Pennines
of South Lancashire to the west and of Yorkshire–Derbyshire–
Nottinghamshire to the east. The latter is the largest and least

disturbed coalfield in Britain. Further north again, there are fields in north Cumberland around Whitehaven to the west of the Pennines, and in Northumberland and Durham to the east. The fact that this latter is a large coalfield with easy access to the sea along the Tyne and, to a lesser extent, the Wear and the Tees, meant that the North-East coalfield had distinct advantages over the other fields of the country, because sea transport made its product more readily available in London than coal from any other area. Thus the North-East field had a long lead over all other areas in the development of its coal-mining industry. In the Lowlands of central Scotland, the largest coalfield is in the west, in Lanarkshire and Ayrshire, but there are very productive smaller fields around Stirling and Fife, and in Midlothian. There are also extensive shale-oil deposits at Bathgate in West Lothian which have been worked since the late nineteenth century and which have left waste heaps similar to those of collieries in the area.

So far only the exposed coalfields have been mentioned, although most of these have a penumbra around them in which coal seams are accessible below overlying deposits. In parts of North Somerset, for instance, coal was discovered in the late eighteenth century by sinking shafts at Radstock through several hundred feet of post-Carboniferous rock strata. In some coalfields, the hidden coal strata have assumed paramount importance as the exposed coal seams have become exhausted. In the large fields of Durham and Yorkshire, the search for deep coal has carried the main area of operations eastward from the original mines into the agricultural landscape of the Permo-Triassic rocks. The first large colliery to venture into this area was sunk near Worksop in 1859, when it began to work the Top Hard Coal seam at a depth of 1,530 feet. This is the Barnsley seam, which has been found to maintain an excellent quality over an unusually large area, so that it has become the main objective of the deep mines of the concealed coalfield. In County

Durham, also, there has been a marked shift of emphasis from the traditional inland coalfield to the seams concealed below the younger Permian strata on the coast. At Vane Colliery outside Seaham Harbour, for example, modern equipment is being used to carry the workings out below the sea. One other concealed coalfield should be mentioned, because it is completely covered by younger rocks and its discovery was the result of geological research. This is the Kent coalfield, in the south-east corner of the county north of Dover, where the typical coal-industry landscape has been re-created on a small scale in a way which is as unexpected and anomalous as that of the small field at Brora, at the opposite extremity of Britain.

The Development of the Industry

In his classic study, *The Rise of the British Coal Industry*, J. U. Nef observes that coal has been used extensively only in modern Western civilization:

Its use on a large scale as a combustible is clearly a peculiar feature of our own time. There is, perhaps, no other natural product which is so essential a part of our life, and which yet has been of so little importance in the lives of ancient people.[3]

Nef considers that coal working did not begin in Europe until the end of the twelfth century and that it expanded only very gradually until the sixteenth century. In the early centuries of the industry the British coalfields were handicapped by their distance from any substantial urban markets, whereas at Liège in Flanders coal was actually mined within the town and its extraction had already become a highly organized business by the sixteenth century. The development of the sea trade from the Tyne to London during this century made possible the growth of the Tyneside coalfield, which took full advantage of its favourable position in relation to the other coalfields of the country in the subsequent three hundred years. Capital was invested in the sinking of larger and deeper shafts, much of it coming from the landed proprietors of the north-eastern counties, who saw it as a method of improving their estates. Even more important, a complex organization of overseers, engineers, shippers and middlemen arose to supervise the mining operations and to handle the traffic in coal, which increased steadily in volume from the middle of the sixteenth century. Tyneside provided a fund of technical expertise and managerial competence which later served the development of coal-mining elsewhere in much the same way as Cornish experience served the world-wide spread of metalliferous mining.

Even in this period of acknowledged Tyneside superiority, however, the exposed coalfields in other parts of the country were beginning to develop in order to serve strictly local markets, and as soon as the severe operational problems could be solved they were ready to expand to meet the rapidly growing domestic and industrial demand for coal. The chief of these problems was transport from the colliery to the market, and this was overcome by the acquisition of a national transport system in the Industrial Revolution. But there were other problems of a more internal nature which restricted the development of Tyneside as well as that of the inland coalfields. These were, first, the problem of water accumulating in coal workings; second, the problem of explosive gases (methane, known as 'firedamp' to the miners); third, the problem of suffocating gases (carbon dioxide – 'chokedamp' to the miners); and fourth, the problem of moving coal from the coal face to the pit-head.

The first and seemingly most intractable problem was that of excess water. The earliest coal workings had been surface quarries or shallow bellpits, in which no serious accumulation of water had occurred. But as soon as the shafts began to go deeply through the coal measures they pierced the water table and acted like wells, gathering water at their bases. Attempts to counter this by excavating 'adits' to drain the mine through an adjoining hillside, or even by driving a nearly horizontal 'drift' mine into the coal-bearing strata, were only of limited value, because most of the available coal lay at too deep a level for this remedy. Deep mining consequently came to rely completely upon effective pumping machinery, and herein lay the first and greatest contribution of the steam engine to the coal industry. It was not in any

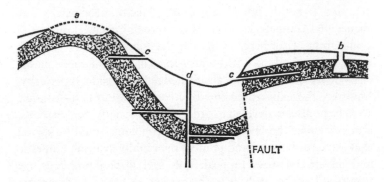

2. Types of coal-mining activities. Coal measures are shaded. a = Open-cast excavation; b = bell pit; c = drift mines; d = deep mines with shaft and galleries.

sense of frivolity that Thomas Savery called his first steam engine 'The Miner's Friend'. It was intended to replace the unreliable and ineffective horse-gins, treadmills and water-powered pumps which had previously served as the only available means of keeping mines clear of water. In the event, the Savery engine was not distinguished for its reliability, but the Newcomen engine which succeeded it was an efficient machine, even though wasteful of energy by later standards, so that it was soon adopted in the coalfields. This was particularly the case in the Tyneside coalfield, where mines were already being sunk deeper than elsewhere, and it has been calculated that at least a hundred Newcomen-type atmospheric 'fire engines' were at work in this district by 1765.[4] Successive improvements in the steam engine then kept pace with the extension of deep mining techniques in the nineteenth century, so that the problem of flooding in coal-mines was effectively solved.

The problems of explosive and suffocating gases were further difficulties which increased as coal workings became more extensive. The gases collected in pockets, depending on the configuration of the workings and the nature of the strata encountered. They were a problem not only directly for their danger to life and limb, but also indirectly because they hampered seriously the introduction of an effective form of lighting, all means of which until the nineteenth century involved a naked flame of some sort. Miners had traditionally worked in some areas by the phosphorescent light of decaying fish, and in other areas the 'steel mill' had been introduced to provide short-lived illumination from a shower of sparks produced by grinding a metal wheel against a flint. In places where firedamp was known to have collected, it was sometimes exploded deliberately by sending in a well-shrouded miner pushing before him a long pole with a lighted candle on the end. As for the suffocating chokedamp, the traditional remedy was to take a caged canary into the mine, because these birds responded more quickly than human beings to the toxic effects of the gases.

All these customary solutions to the gas menace were inadequate, but were better than nothing in what was after all the most hazardous form of mass employment ever devised by human societies. An effective answer came at last with the installation of efficient ventilating apparatus and the perfection of the safety lamp. Early attempts at ventilation involved creating a convection current through the workings by placing a brazier in one of the shafts or, if there was only one shaft, in a part of the shaft screened by canvas from the down-draught section. Here again, the development of **reliable steam engines** made a valuable contribution to coal-mining, because they could be used to drive surface fans which would draw a stream of air through the underground workings and thus remove the more dangerous

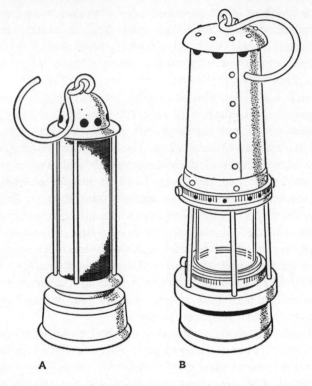

A   B

3. Miners' lamps. (A) Early Davy lamp; (B) developed Davy lamp – late nineteenth century (10 ins. high, without the hook).

concentrations of gas. Forms of safety lamp were developed simultaneously in 1813 by Sir Humphry Davy and George Stephenson, the principle of both being the separation of the naked flame from its immediate environment by a piece of gauze or a perforated cylinder which prevented the flame from causing an explosion in the gas outside the lamp. Changes in the colour of the flame could also be used by the expert miner to detect the presence of dangerous gases. Equipped with this greatly improved method of illumination, miners were sent into seams which had previously been deemed too dangerous to work, with the ironical result that the introduction of the safety lamp actually contributed to an increase in the accident rate in coal-mines.[5]

The last of the problems facing the coal industry as it strove to increase its production in order to meet the rapidly expanding demands of the eighteenth and nineteenth centuries was that of moving coal from the coal face to the pit-head. No matter how much coal the hewer could cut, if it could not be cleared smoothly and efficiently to the surface his efficiency would be impaired, as it almost invariably was when underground workings became extensive. Traditionally, the removal of coal from the coal face to the shaft, and then up the shaft, had been performed by women and children. The notorious drawings which accompanied the Report of the Select Committee on the Employment of Women and Children in Mines in 1840–42 show vividly the fearsome nature of this work, as the coal was dragged along burrow-like underground tunnels in trucks or sledges, and then hefted up the shafts in baskets carried across the women's shoulders. The public outcry which followed the publication of this Report led to the prohibition of female labour underground and of that of children under ten years of age in all coal-mines in the Mines Act of 1842, and provided an incentive to the introduction of animal and mechanical aids in the process. Pit ponies became widely used in coal-mines along the larger corridors, and although the labour remained arduous it became considerably less severe and more efficient than it had been previously. Also, the development of reliable steam winding engines performed yet another great service to the coal industry by mechanizing the process of raising the coal up the shaft, particularly with the introduction of steel cable in the middle of the nineteenth century.

By the progressive solution of these problems and the development of the surface transport network, the British coal industry was able to maintain a steady increase in production throughout the nineteenth century as all the coalfields of the country were enabled to operate more and more efficiently. In the process, there was a great deal of standardization between different coalfields as management practices and new techniques were transmitted throughout the country. Some differences remained, however. The North-East coalfield, in particular, being by far the oldest area of large-scale operation, retained a number of organizational peculiarities. Tyneside miners, for example, adopted the safety lamp of the local worthy George Stephenson rather than the Davy model which became standard elsewhere. They also retained the 'pillar and stall' method of working, with each hewer cutting into his own section of the coal face separated from his neighbours by pillars of rock left to support the roof, in preference to the 'longwall' system, whereby the miners worked as a team cutting the coal from the face and piling up the waste in the space behind them, which was almost universally adopted elsewhere. And in steam winding engines they showed a preference in the North-East for a vertical type of engine which gave rise to a distinctive high and narrow engine house. Unlike the safety lamp and the method of working underground, the vertical engine house was a feature of the industrial landscape and thus properly an item of industrial archaeology. Although very few still survive, one at a disused pit at Beamish in County Durham has been preserved and re-erected at the adjacent site of the North of England Open-Air Museum.

The Coal-Mining Landscape

Geographical conditions give a certain distinctiveness to some mining areas. The crowded valleys of the South Wales coalfield, for example, with their steep uncultivated sides and over-shadowing spoil heaps, contrast starkly with the mines set amongst the open farmlands and Sherwood Forest of Notting-hamshire. The urban setting of the Tyneside coalfield again contrasts with the rural countryside in which the North Somerset coal industry flourished. Despite these differences, however, there is a broad similarity about the conditions of the coal industry which have promoted standardization, especially since the National Coal Board has put into action its determined process of modernization. Viewed as features in the landscape, coal-mines, with their complex of pit-head buildings – winding gear, engine houses, sorting and washing sheds, bath houses and amenities, railways and sidings – are much the same wherever they occur, as are the attendant spoil heaps. Few industries ravage the landscape as badly as coal-mining, as the scars on the surface of County Durham, the 'green valleys' of South Wales, or the parts of Derbyshire between Staveley and Barlborough which have been opened up to view by the construction of the M1, all demonstrate. On the other hand, it is remarkable how quickly the landscape can revert to normal once a mine has closed, the pit-head buildings have been demolished, the railway track has been removed, and the waste heaps have been seeded with grass or planted with trees. It is difficult now to believe that some of the valleys of North Somerset were until quite recently part of a thriving coal-mining district, so complete has been the reversion to a rural landscape. Even the miners' villages, which as elsewhere tended to consist of drab terraced houses, have been taken over and remodelled gradually as the homes of a dormitory commuter population which finds its way into Bristol and Bath for work. Still more surprisingly, even the extensive open-cast workings which mutilated the fields and hedgerows of Yorkshire and elsewhere in the decades after the Second World War have caused little permanent disfiguration of the landscape, with the loss of forest trees being the only serious defect in the reconstruction which followed the removal of the coal. Thankfully, there is nothing in Britain to parallel the ghastly landscape of excavated territory in the Pittsburgh coalfield of Western Pennsylvania, USA.

For all this transitoriness of the coal industry, and the general unattractiveness of its outward and visible signs, there is much of interest to the industrial archaeologist as the British coal industry contracts the areas of its operations and concentrates more efficiently on a few sites and with more regard to amenity and other public considerations than it showed in its nineteenth-century heyday. As large areas of the traditional British coalfields become increasingly obsolete, it is important that evidence of the physical features of the mines should be recorded. The tramways, railways, and harbours which served the coalfields are also well worth attention. At one time, for instance, the mines of South Wales were served by a complicated strand of railways, canals, and roads in the valley bottoms, leading down to special coal-loading facilities at Newport, Cardiff, and Barry Dock for shipment all over the world. County Durham had a rather similar although less concentrated network leading to Seaham Harbour, and West Yorkshire had another converging on Goole. These all deserve careful recording and judicious attention to the preservation of particular items. Seaham Harbour, for example, is now virtually obsolete, but it boasted until recently some splendid coal staithes (wharves) with several coal drops (swing lifts for conveying the load from the quay to the waiting ships), several steam paddle tugs, and some wooden coal chaldrons. One of the coal drops has been removed and preserved for restoration in the Regional Open-Air Museum at Beamish already mentioned. One of the paddle tugs has been preserved in the National

Maritime Museum and another has made its own way to the Golden Gate Collection at San Francisco. Of the wooden coal chaldrons, once a very distinctive feature of the North-East coalfield, very few now remain intact, but several have been procured for the Beamish collection. Nobody has yet made out a serious case for preserving a colliery spoil heap, although even this would be a useful reminder to posterity of the nature of the industry, and some of the surface features of coal-mines are certainly worth preserving. Until quite recently, the National Coal Board possessed a considerable number of steam winding engines, some of which had run efficiently and with minimum maintenance for the greater part of a hundred years. Many of these have now gone with colliery closures and with the plan to modernize the remaining mines by introducing electric winding gear. A few have been preserved as museum pieces, and some are still operational. In the Scottish coalfields in particular a number survive, including a large engine at Lady Victoria colliery, Midlothian, installed in 1903 when it was already ten years old and run continuously ever since.

There is thus much that is worth recording systematically about the physical remains of the coal industry, and it is strange how little of this has yet been tackled. There is also much that is worth noting about the human community of miners. The typical pattern of coal-mining settlement has been the colliery village, often set down in regular terraces within easy reach of the mine. The reason for this nucleated settlement in the first place was the need to bring labourers from a distance to work in the mines once the mining operations became large-scale regular affairs. In the early days of the industry, men and women had mined coal as a supplement to work on the farms, and in some of the smaller coalfields this close relationship with agriculture was never lost. But in the large coalfields the mines were usually sited away from the centres of population, so that it became essential to provide accommodation for the miners, and basic community needs (shops, chapels, public houses) followed to compose the typical mining village of County Durham, South Wales, Yorkshire, or wherever the industry flourished. A natural clannishness amongst the workers in this most dangerous of industries reinforced the isolation of the villages, and tended also to emphasize a persistent masculinity in the social relationships of mining communities: the role of the women remained a subordinate one, maintaining the home and the family. The early novels and short stories of D. H. Lawrence are set against a background of such a community in South Derbyshire and Nottinghamshire and describe movingly the anxieties and tensions within it (see especially *Sons and Lovers*). The location, planning, and furnishing of the miners' cottages is a legitimate and important interest of industrial archaeologists. The new museums in County Durham and Telford New Town are hoping to reconstruct such cottages, which is an indication of the growing importance of this kind of industrial monument.

4. The Metal Industries

It would be difficult to exaggerate the importance of metals in the evolution of human societies. Developments in metallurgical techniques, indeed, are used to differentiate the main stages in the emergence of early civilizations, from the Copper Age through the Bronze Age to the Iron Age. The discovery of metallic minerals and of methods of extracting them from the ores in which they normally occur and of working them into useful implements represents one of the outstanding achievements of man, liberating him from the restrictions of a technology based on wood, stone, and fire, and bringing about the transformation of the advanced agricultural societies of the New Stone Age in parts of the Middle East into urban civilizations carrying on extensive industries and commercial activity. This achievement has been essentially cumulative, with new skills being slowly acquired and transmitted from generation to generation of craftsmen. As in other respects, however, the Industrial Revolution of the last two hundred years has caused a great acceleration in the advance of metallurgical knowledge, so that many old processes have become obsolete and ripe for the attention of the industrial archaeologist.

Non-ferrous Metals

The modern technical definition of a metal includes the great majority of the materials in the periodic table of elements and is virtually meaningless to the layman. The classification of the ancient world with its seven metals (gold, silver, copper, tin, lead, mercury, and iron) came closer to the common understanding of metals, and for the highly practical purposes of this chapter we may define a metal as a material which can be made ductile by heating and then moulded, cast, or hammered into useful shapes. The first of such metals to be widely used in antiquity was copper, largely because of the comparatively low temperature at which it can be reduced from the ores in which it occurs (in combination with oxygen and other elements) and becomes malleable. Even primitive furnaces, therefore, could make available a supply of copper for tools and ornaments once a supply of suitable ore had been located. Unfortunately, the high ductility of copper meant that it was too soft for many uses. It could not, for example, take a sharp edge on a blade, so that its military use was very limited. Early metallurgists tackled the problem of hardening copper sufficiently to increase its utility and eventually discovered the process of mixing (or 'alloying') copper with other metals. In particular, they alloyed copper with tin in proportions of nine parts of copper to one of tin to produce bronze. Tin itself is a soft white metal which is rarely used on its own but which has acquired a wide range of important subsidiary uses either for giving a protective coating to other more perishable metals or in the form of alloys. The only way in which tin is used as the predominant material is in the manufacture of pewter, when it is usually alloyed with one part of lead to nine parts of tin. The copper-tin alloy bronze became the most important metal of early civilizations in the second millennium before the Christian era, after which it gradually lost ground to the new metal, iron.

One important consequence of the use of tin was that it provided an incentive for the extension of trade. Because of its relative rarity in the Eastern Mediterranean, the civilized communities of that region were compelled to seek it far afield, and hence the trading exploits of the Phoenicians, which possibly brought them to Cornwall by 500 B.C. There is no doubt that the Cornish tin resources were well known by Roman times, but the Romans were more interested in prospecting for gold and silver in Britain than in exploiting Cornish tin. This search resulted in the development of mining settlements on the carboniferous limestone of the Mendips and elsewhere, the by-product of which was the extraction of lead. This came to exceed in value that of silver obtained from these sources.

The nature of early techniques for extracting metal ores is largely a matter of speculation, but they seem unlikely to have been very elaborate. There was probably plenty of tin fairly easily available in the alluvial deposits of Cornish rivers and streams, so that proper mining methods did not become common until the Middle Ages. On the Mendips the remains of Roman silver and lead workings have been almost entirely obliterated by later operations so that it is impossible to say with any precision what methods were used. Similarly, evidence of Roman furnaces has been lost, but lead, like copper, tin, and the precious metals (used largely for coins and ornamentation), is a relatively soft metal so that the techniques for working it require less sophistication than, say, iron.

By Roman times, iron had replaced copper and tin as the most important metal in the manufacture of tools and weapons, but it will be convenient to complete our treatment of the non-ferrous metals before considering the development of iron and steel. During the Middle Ages, the Cornish tin and copper industries grew in importance and organization. The mining communities, known as 'stannaries' (from the Latin *stannum*, meaning tin, although the word was also used for an alloy of silver and lead), possessed extensive privileges and rights of self-government. Similar privileges were enjoyed by the lead-miners of Mendip, and the Peak District, although it should be observed that these 'liberties' were largely the result of the isolation of the areas which were being mined, and that the way of life of the miner was often both brutish and brutal. As with the remains of Roman metal workings, the labours of these medieval miners have often been removed from view by later mining. It is possible, however, to find evidence of medieval mining in 'rakes' – lines of shallow workings following veins of metal – over fields and open moorland, and in the 'gruffy' or disturbed ground which on Mendip and elsewhere has successfully resisted the encroachment of subsequent cultivation.

Modern deep-mining techniques in Britain date effectively from the sixteenth century, when the government of Elizabeth I stimulated the metallurgical industries for military and nationalistic purposes by the creation of two monopolistic companies – the Mines Royal and the Mineral and Battery Company. German miners, practising the advanced techniques which were so brilliantly illustrated by G. Agricola in his sixteenth-century masterpiece *De Re Metallica*, were brought over to prospect for new sources of metal in Wales and the Lake District, while the Mineral and Battery Company was encouraged to develop new methods of metal working. This government support and the increasing industrial demand for metals produced a slow but steady development of the non-ferrous-metal industries in the following centuries.

Mining for copper and tin in Cornwall and Devon reached its peak about the end of the nineteenth century. Since then the exploitation of alternative world resources, and particularly the excavation of alluvial tin in Malaya, has so brought down the price of these metals in the international market that Cornish mines have become uneconomic and most of them have closed down. The industry has not become quite extinct, however; several tin mines are still in business at Camborne and Pendeen, but the fluctuations in world metal prices make their future uncertain. Even though most of the mines in Cornwall became very deep and extensive, there seems little doubt that the county is still rich in metallic mineral resources. A certain amount of tin 'streaming' is still carried on in Cornwall, to recover metal from the waste and tailings of earlier workings. A successful enterprise of this nature operates on the Tolgus Stream, near Redruth, complete with water wheel, Cornish stamps, and gravity-sifting apparatus.

During the last quarter of the eighteenth century the mines of Cornwall had been one of the most important markets for the improved steam engines produced by Boulton and Watt. With their economic fuel consumption compared with that of the standard Newcomen-type 'atmospheric' engines, these machines provided the essential pumping, winding and ventilating functions in the tin and copper mines, enabling them to go deeper than had ever been possible before. For all its great service to the Cornish mining industry, the firm of Boulton and Watt was not popular with the mining companies of the duchy, so that when the native genius of Richard Trevithick (his birthplace can still be visited at Camborne) led the way in designing a yet more efficient engine it became so generally adopted in the county that it has been known ever since as the 'Cornish engine'. The distinctive houses of these engines, built in local granite with a chimney incorporated in one corner and usually with the upper third of the chimney stack built of brick, occur in many parts of the county. The most accessible group is probably that around Camborne and the peninsula of Land's End. Most of the engine houses are derelict and ruinous, but a few, including two at Camborne, have been preserved by the Cornish Engines Preservation Society. Those at Camborne are now administered by the National Trust and contain two different types of Cornish engine: the larger one was used for pumping and the smaller one as a 'whimsy' or winding engine. Cornish engines were installed in many other parts of the country, where the benefits of an economical and reliable engine for mine pumping and winding

were important. Indeed, they have been built in mining communities all over the world, often introduced by immigrant
Cornish miners. At one time in the nineteenth century it used
to be said that at the bottom of every hole there was a Cornish-
man, which shows the significance of the Cornish contribution
to mining development.[1]

Lead-mining in Britain has followed a pattern of rise and
decline similar to that of copper and tin. Though it began as a
by-product of the search for silver, the Romans came to appreciate the value of lead for lining their elaborate baths and for other
plumbing purposes. It is an interesting speculation that the
careless use of lead piping for water-supply purposes caused lead
poisoning and thus contributed to the decline of the Roman
Empire! During the later Middle Ages the metal was used
extensively as a roofing material for large buildings such as
cathedrals, and the mining communities on the Mendips and
elsewhere were well established at this time. Lead-mining
continued to flourish on the Mendips until the eighteenth
century, when the superior quality of Welsh, Peak District, and
Pennine lead caused a decline in demand for the Mendip product, with its comparatively high arsenic content. Mining for
lead died out on the Mendips, although the mining communities
were preserved into the nineteenth century by the development
of calamine working in the district, producing zinc for the
flourishing brass industry in the valley of the Bristol Avon. They
were then given a further lease of life in the second half of the
nineteenth century, by a revival of the lead industry based upon
the introduction of more efficient processes for recovering lead
(and, incidentally, silver) from the waste heaps left by earlier
operations.

The initiative for these new processes was Cornish, and consisted largely of applying techniques which had been used in the
copper and tin industries. These included 'buddles', new
furnaces, and 'condensers'. Buddling is a method of extracting

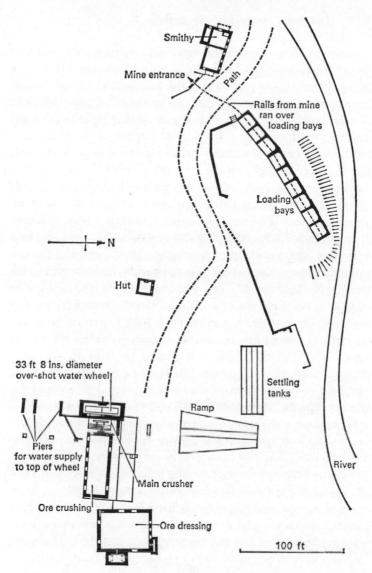

Smithy

Mine entrance

Path

Rails from mine
ran over
loading bays

Loading
bays

N

Hut

33 ft 8 ins. diameter
over-shot water wheel

Settling
tanks

Ramp

Piers
for water supply
to top of wheel

Main crusher

Ore crushing

Ore dressing

River

100 ft

4. Killhope lead-crushing mill, Co. Durham (based on a plan by D. Crockitt
in *Bulletin 6* of the North East Industrial Archaeology Society, July 1968).
See plate 50.

metal-rich deposits from the waste accompanying them in slag or ore which has been crushed and mixed with water to form a slime. When this is poured into the buddles the heavier metal-bearing material settles first and can be separated from the waste sludge. Buddling is still used in the metal-mining industries and a similar sedimentation process is used in some modern sewage-treatment works. The metal-bearing material was taken from the buddles and fed into the furnaces. One of the problems in working lead had been the low temperature at which it volatilized, or turned into a gaseous state in which it was quickly lost in the furnace smoke. The new furnaces found means of overcoming this problem, so that they were able to work at high temperatures and thus fully reduce the ore or slag. The solution to the low volatility temperature of lead was to provide condensers in which the gaseous lead could be recovered by allowing it to cool and be deposited on the walls of horizontal flues. These were usually constructed in stone and sometimes followed intricate maze-like patterns in order to make them as long as possible while saving space. They normally ended in a high chimney to provide a draught through the system, and they were made sufficiently large for the metallic materials to be recovered manually from the inside walls. An additional advantage of such condensers in lead working was that they provided a safeguard against the release of lead-charged gases to the atmosphere. Not only was this wasteful from the point of view of the owner of the lead workings, but it also poisoned the surrounding landscape and could involve the owner in expensive litigation with his neighbours.

Lead-mining and working has dwindled almost to vanishing point in Britain in the twentieth century; the remaining lead-working businesses now use imported lead. But the industry has left extensive relics in the areas already mentioned. Curiously few furnaces have survived, but crushing equipment for ore and slag, buddles, elaborate condenser flue systems, ponds for water supply, and piles of the shiny black furnace slag can still be found in remote parts of the limestone moorlands of Britain. The disturbed ground around such derelict plant is frequently all that remains visible of the mines from which the lead was originally

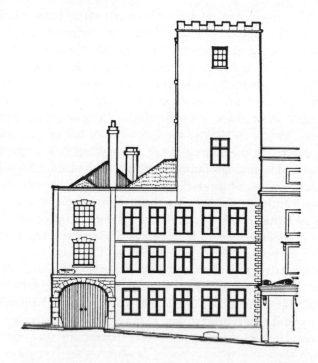

5. The lead shot tower, Bristol (John Mosse and Bristol City Museum). The tower was built on to a seventeenth-century house by William Watts, who patented the method of making lead shot by allowing molten lead to fall through the air in 1782. It was demolished in 1968.

extracted, although in parts of Derbyshire and the Northern Pennines the lines of workings can be traced in long 'rakes' across the moorland. Another monument to the lead industry is the occurrence of shot towers in towns where lead shot was made by pouring molten lead from a height. Few of these now remain, although a new one has recently been constructed in Bristol to replace the first-ever shot tower on Redcliff Hill, demolished in 1968.[2]

Brass is a modern metal, having been first manufactured satisfactorily in Europe at the end of the seventeenth century, when its golden colour and its property of being easily worked made it attractive for both decorative and functional purposes. It was developed commercially mainly in a sheet form, when as 'brass battery' it could be hammered into pots and pans for culinary and other domestic uses, but brass wire also became an important product. Brass is an alloy of copper and zinc, but metallic zinc was unknown to metallurgy before the eighteenth century, so that brass was first produced from the zinc oxide known as calamine. This was excavated on the Mendips and transported after very little preliminary treatment into Bristol, where the first large British brass works were established. Copper ore was usually brought to the site of the brass works and smelted on the spot before being alloyed to make brass. The waste from the copper furnaces was often cast into rectangular or triangular moulds, in which shape it set to form an excellent hard building material; the survival of such copper slag blocks in walls provides a useful clue to the location of brass works in the valley of the Bristol Avon. Several such sites remain in the region, although the last firm went out of production at Keynsham in 1927. A number of interesting buildings associated with this once important industry survive, including some spectacular annealing ovens at Kelston Mill, but most of them are in a neglected or actually ruinous condition. The Bristol region was superseded in this, as in other aspects of the non-ferrous metal industries, by the Swansea valley in the nineteenth century; this in turn has become obsolete and has presented the planning authorities of the region with a formidable problem in redeveloping a large area of industrial dereliction (the 'Swansea Valley Project'). In recent times, a part of the industry has returned to the south side of the Bristol Channel with the erection of a large new lead and zinc smelting enterprise at Avonmouth. Brass has long been used in a wide range of manufacturing industries in Birmingham and other parts of the Midlands, but it has left no distinctive features on the landscape in these areas.[3]

Other non-ferrous metals, including the precious metals, have been mined and worked sporadically in various parts of the British Isles. There were, for instance, gold-mines at Dolaucothi in Central Wales and in Merionethshire, and the remote valley of Kildonan in Sutherland even experienced a gold rush in 1869. The Ogofau Mine at Dolaucothi has been worked sporadically since Roman times, but at present the fascinating series of caves are abandoned and require great care in exploration.[4] Celestine, the ore of strontium, is still excavated in opencast workings near Yate in Gloucestershire for use in the manufacture of fireworks. Of much more importance amongst modern metal industries has been the establishment of large aluminium smelters in parts of the Highlands of Scotland such as Kinlochleven. Aluminium is the commonest of all metallic materials in the crust of the Earth, but it is only in the present century that means have been found of reducing the metal from its ores on a commercially viable scale. These means involve massive consumption of electricity, so that the Highlands became an attractive location for the industry because of the abundant cheap electricity available there in the form of hydro-electric power.

Iron and Steel

Despite the continuing importance of many non-ferrous metals in modern industry and the great developments in other materials such as plastics, our industrial civilization is still based predominantly on iron in its various forms. Iron began to replace bronze as the most useful metal in the first millennium B.C., and since then it has become the essential material for the technology of the 'Iron Age'. Although iron is one of the most abundant elements, its high melting point (1,535° C.) compared with that of copper (1,083° C.) made it an intractable material until techniques of furnace construction had advanced sufficiently to reach such temperatures. Iron always occurs in nature in combination with oxygen and other elements. There are many types of iron ore, three of which are important for industrial purposes (not including *magnetite*, which is the best ore of all, with 65 per cent of iron, but is not available in Britain). These are, first, *haematite*, in which form the iron frequently occurs in separate bluish nodules (giving the name 'kidney' iron) of high-grade (*c*. 50 per-cent) ore; secondly, *blackband* iron, of medium quality (*c*. 30 per-cent), occurring in discontinuous strata usually associated with coal measures; and thirdly, *jurassic* iron, found across Britain in a broad belt from the North Yorkshire Moors near Cleveland to the Cotswolds, being of a low grade (*c*. 20 per-cent) and a comparatively high phosphorus content. Evidence of iron extraction survives in many parts of the country. Amongst the most intensive areas of exploitation has been that in Cumbria around Millom and Furness, where extraction of high-grade haematite has only recently ceased and left a landscape littered with Cornish engine houses and other industrial monuments. Also, jurassic ores are still being excavated by open-cast methods over a wide area of Northamptonshire.

Early techniques of iron-making were hampered by the inadequacies of the furnaces available. To begin with, these were little more than partially enclosed fires, usually built on hill-tops or exposed positions to give the maximum blast of natural wind for the draught. Many of these sites survive as 'bole hills' in various parts of the country. They also became known as 'bloomeries' because the putty-like mass of red-hot iron would be taken from the furnace and hammered into a 'bloom'. The heating reduced the ore to metallic iron but inevitably left many impurities in the body of the metal, and the hammering helped to consolidate the iron and expelled some of the remaining slag. Repeated treatment in this way by a skilled smith, however, could produce a metal with the characteristics of wrought iron or even steel, although steel normally required much further processing and was limited to 'case hardening' – that is, carburizing the surface of wrought iron to give it a steel case. The output of a bloomery was very small – a few pounds of metal a day – so that there was little chance of a large-scale industrial development at this stage.

Furnace design began to improve significantly in the sixteenth century, with increases in size, the application of mechanical draught by water-powered bellows, and other refinements. Together, these improvements constituted the 'blast furnace' which has remained unchanged in its basic features to the present day. Essentially, the blast furnace is a fire in a hearth which is completely enclosed at the bottom except for the 'tuyéres' (pronounced 'tweers') or blast-holes through which the air is blown, while the fuel for the fire and the ore to be reduced to metal are fed in from the top together with fluxes to assist the chemical reaction in the furnace. At the high temperatures reached inside the furnace, the ore becomes completely molten and impurities combine with the carbon in the fuel to produce waste gases and slag, the latter forming as a scum on the molten iron which can be drawn off separately before the iron is 'tapped'. It normally takes about twelve hours to reach this stage, and a furnace can remain in blast for months at a time, producing two batches of iron every day.

The molten iron was traditionally allowed to run off into shapes moulded in sand which resembled a sow with her sucklings, giving the name 'pig-iron' to the product. It was soon realized that other shapes could be cast in this way, ranging from cannon and cylinders to complicated decorative articles, so that this form of iron is more usefully known as 'cast iron'. This is a crystalline metal which can be cast into almost any shape but cannot subsequently be worked into other shapes because of its brittle nature. Cast iron, indeed, still contains a proportion of about 4 per cent carbon, which has to be removed by further

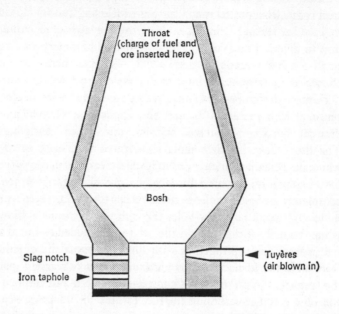

Throat
(charge of fuel and
ore inserted here)

Bosh

Slag notch ▶

Iron taphole ▶

Tuyères
(air blown in)

6. Diagram of a typical blast furnace. The slightly funnelled area above the bosh is known as the 'stack'. The circular pit below the bosh is the 'hearth', at the bottom of which a mass of clinker forms (the 'bear') which has to be periodically removed. The entire furnace is lined with firebrick, and traditionally encased in a box of brick, although modern blast furnaces have a metal shell.

processing to produce 'wrought iron' – that is, iron capable of being worked.

The only fuel used in the early blast furnaces was charcoal, and this fact, together with the reliance upon water power for

his forge at Fareham, Cort devised a method of using coal fuel in the manufacture of wrought iron. This consisted of melting cast iron in a 'reverberatory' furnace, where the heat was thrown down on to the metal from a low sloping roof rather than passing through it. The metal was stirred (or 'puddled') while molten and then taken from the furnace to be rolled into the required shapes. Some remains of Cort's forge survive today. The effect of his invention was to start the movement of the iron forges from the Weald and elsewhere to the coalfields in the wake of the blast furnaces.

The great attraction of wrought iron was its strength and adaptability: the fact that it was sometimes known as 'malleable' iron could refer to its utility as much as to its metallurgical characteristics. It could be rolled into bars, sheets and strip, and slit into rods for nail-making and other purposes. It could also be rolled in angle sections or reworked into complicated patterns. Wrought iron has now been almost entirely superseded by steel and little is now produced, but many forging processes have continued with few changes into steel-making. The arrangement of a modern automated high-speed continuous steel rolling mill, for instance, is an extension of the principles first applied to the working of wrought iron.

Steel-making was, until the mid-nineteenth century, a small and highly specialized part of the iron industry, because the processes involved were time-consuming, expensive, and produced only a small quantity of metal. Steel is an alloy of iron and carbon, containing less carbon than cast iron but more than wrought iron. The characteristics of steel can vary greatly according to the proportion of carbon, which can be as little as 0·25 per cent in the case of 'mild' steel, and never exceeds 1·4 per cent, and according also to the amount of other elements (tungsten, manganese, nickel, chromium, etc.) introduced into the alloy. The earliest method of making steel systematically was the 'cementation' process, whereby iron and charcoal (carbon)

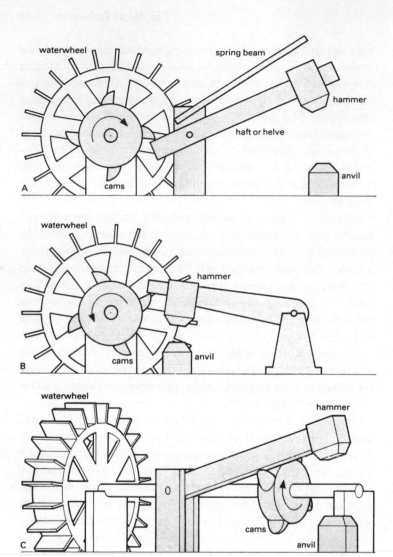

7. Mechanical hammers used in the iron and steel industry. (A) Tail helve or tilt hammer for delivering light rapid blows; (B) nose helve hammer. A heavy hammer used for shingling; (C) belly helve hammer used for heavy forgings.

were heated together for up to ten days in order to achieve 'carburization' – that is, the chemical combination of the iron with carbon. In the mid-eighteenth century, Benjamin Huntsman made an important step forward in steel-making techniques with his 'crucible' steel, in which the constituent elements were carefully measured and sealed in crucibles for treatment in a coal fired furnace; as a result of this, steel-making joined the movement to the coalfields, and a good steel of consistent quality could be produced, although still only in small quantities. The big breakthrough in quantity steel production came a century later, when Bessemer and Siemens invented methods of making bulk steel in 1856, with their 'converter' and 'open hearth' processes respectively. These and subsequent refinements such as the Gilchrist–Thomas process (1879) for using phosphoric iron in steel-making had the effect of making steel as abundant and cheap as wrought iron by the end of the nineteenth century, so that it gradually replaced wrought iron in virtually all of its many uses.

For some purposes, such as edge-tools requiring a sharp blade, steel had always been indispensable, and some of the most interesting surviving relics of the iron and steel industry are the forges where such implements were made. At Sticklepath in Devon and at Abbeydale and Wortley in South Yorkshire, examples of such forges have been carefully restored, with their water wheels, hammers, hearths for heating the metal, and grindstones for putting the edges on the blades. Abbeydale is a particularly interesting site, because the Huntsman crucible process continued to be practised here into the present century, and the various stages in the preparation of high-quality crucible steel are vividly displayed. The steel ingots cast from the crucibles were then used in the adjacent forge for the production of knives and other edge-tools. This was done by 'steeling', a process of welding a steel face on to a wrought-iron tool.

The modern iron and steel industry has become an extremely

large-scale and highly integrated organization, so that some plant contains the whole series of processes from taking in the iron ore to sending out steel plate, rails, joists, and so forth. The increase in the size of enterprises and the concentration of processes has meant that some smaller-scale sites have been abandoned (the Blorenge district of Monmouthshire is a good example), and these have become areas of immediate interest to industrial archaeologists. Such is the importance of the industry in the national economy, however, that these sites are often quickly redeveloped for other iron and steel processes. The factors which drew the industry to the coalfields in the eighteenth and nineteenth centuries are not now so strong as they were, with the widespread adoption of electrical power both for furnaces (but not blast furnaces) and for rolling mills, yet the traditions of craftsmanship and a certain industrial inertia have tended to keep the industry in the same general regions, South Wales, the 'Black Country' of the Midlands, South Yorkshire, and Teesside still being the most important. Access to convenient ores, however, has stimulated the development of the industry at such places as Scunthorpe and Corby, and also in areas like Monmouthshire and Tees-side with easy access to imported ores. Wherever it is established, the industry still marks the landscape and the atmosphere with its characteristic shapes, colours, and smells, and because of its slowly changing foci of concentration it has left parts of the countryside such as the Carron district near Falkirk in Scotland and the Coalbrookdale area in Shropshire ripe for redevelopment, and the object of urgent attention by industrial archaeologists if the main sites are to be plotted in time and adequate consideration given to the preservation of specimens of blast furnace, forge, or other processes. The iron and steel industry has provided one of the major themes of the British Industrial Revolution. The physical record of its history thus deserves sympathetic treatment at the hands of posterity.[5]

5. The Engineering Industries

Probably more than any other industry, that of engineering can be regarded as the creation of the Industrial Revolution. Its emergence as a distinct industry in its own right dates from the end of the eighteenth century and is marked by the convergence of several different lines of development, all associated with the process of industrialization. First, there was the development of the millwright from the tradition of the village blacksmith, wheelwright, and carpenter, who had worked with wrought iron or wood and with the skills transmitted by generations of previous craftsmen. Such men could shoe horses, make cart wheels, or turn pieces of wood on simple lathes and assemble the parts into furniture which could be graceful or utilitarian. They were the vital craftsmen of the early industrial community, but the new demands and resources of this community stimulated the emergence of the millwright as a sort of itinerant specialist in the construction of machines, industrial buildings, or improved roads and canals. The millwright was thus the representative of a significant transitional stage from the traditional crafts to the modern engineer.

Secondly, there was the tradition of precision-instrument making represented by the clock and watch makers, and by the manufacturers of telescopes, theodolites, and small arms. Eighteenth-century master craftsmen such as John Harrison, who devoted his life to the creation of an accurate marine chronometer and won a government prize for his success even though he only made five chronometers, and Jesse Ramsden, the instrument maker who made the first screw-cutting lathe, were outstanding representatives of this tradition, which was one of growing importance as the need for reliable navigational tools, better maps, locks, and small arms increased, together with the incentive for even better instruments provided by the scientific investigation of the universe and the more immediate environment. Like the millwrights, they were an essential element in the transition to an engineering industry.

There was a third tradition, different again from the other two, which contributed to the emergence of an engineering industry. The original 'engineers', after all, had been military personnel – the 'sappers' who constructed fortifications and devised ingenious methods of undermining those of the enemy - and there was a significant link between the army engineers and the rise of civil engineering in the eighteenth century represented, by such engineering work as the construction of military roads in Scotland under General Wade. By the second half of the century, a professionally conscious group of experts were beginning to style themselves 'civil engineers' to distinguish themselves from their military counterparts, and forming societies such as the Society of Civil Engineers, nicknamed 'the Smeatonians' after their most distinguished member, which was a precursor to the Institution of Civil Engineers founded in 1818. The role of civil engineering can be explored more appropriately in relation to the transport and other constructional achievements by which it has been distinguished, but it nevertheless played a vital part in the growth of the engineering industry because it set standards of professional competence and aspiration.

These various traditions were brought together in the second half of the eighteenth century by the growing pressure of demand for more large machines – water wheels, steam engines, spinning machines, power looms – all requiring an ever-increasing standard of precision. At first it was the millwright – part blacksmith, part carpenter, part odd-job man – who was called upon to do this work. It was to such a man that the Duke of Bridgewater turned to construct his first canals, and in James Brindley he found a millwright of genius, who, for all his many eccentricities, devised from scratch a method of canal construction. But as the degree of specialization and of precise skills increased, the role of the jobbing millwright diminished in significance. The new combination of old skills with those of the precision-instrument maker under the supervision of technical and professional management was already becoming apparent in the employment of Matthew Boulton's skilled workmen on the manufacture of Watt's steam engine, so that the Soho factory can be regarded as the first complete engineering workshop. The pattern was followed and made more explicit in the machine-tool workshops of Bramah and Maudslay, so that by the beginning of the nineteenth century the modern engineering industry had certainly been born.

The Machine Tools

The engineering industry underwent a process of rapid development in the first half of the nineteenth century, after which it began to proliferate into a variety of specialized industries, among which electrical engineering, marine engineering, and different sorts of vehicle construction were prominent. What all these industries had – and have – in common is a number of basic machine tools, and it is by the presence of these instruments that the existence of the engineering industry can be recognized. It is important, therefore, for the industrial archaeologist to be able to recognize them when he sees them.

A recent study of the subject defines a machine tool as 'a machine designed to cut or shape metal or other substance. The essence of a machine tool is that there is built into it some element of the skill which would be necessary to carry out a similar operation manually with the aid of a hand tool'.[1] In other words, a machine tool is an advance upon a hand tool, wholly or

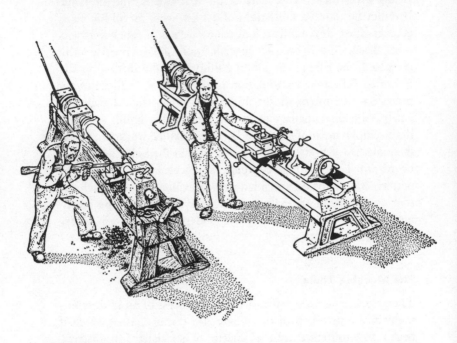

8. The lathe with and without the slide-rest, based on a sketch by James Nasmyth designed to show the advantage of the slide-rest over the traditional manually-operated cutting tool (*left*).

partially mechanized, used particularly but not exclusively for metal working. The oldest machine tool is the *lathe*, evidence of which survives from antiquity. The principle of the lathe is that the work-piece is rotated while the cutting edge is applied to it, producing a continuous smooth cut which is essential in any shaping and constructional work. The rotary action seems first to have been applied by wrapping a cord or thong around the work-piece and pulling it backwards and forwards: by fixing the cord to a bow it became a 'bow lathe', and the turner could operate it himself, while by fixing one end to a flexible pole and the other to a treadle he could operate it himself and keep both hands free to control the cutting tool, this being the form known as the 'pole lathe'. The mechanization of the lathe was extended by Henry Maudslay, who constructed all-metal machines driven off steam engines and with adjustable slide-rests so that the cutting or traversing tool could be held rigidly instead of depending upon the unaided hand and eye of the operator. Maudslay also built a screw-cutting lathe in 1800, applying on a large scale the principles which Ramsden had already established for precision-instrument construction. The lathe has undergone no major change in form since Maudslay's improvements, but its operation has been greatly refined and increased in versatility by the application of electric power and the introduction of the turret lathe, carrying a series of different cutting tools mounted on a turret so that they can be changed quickly and automatically.

If the lathe is regarded as a sort of mechanized chisel, the machine-tool form of the hammer is the *steam hammer*. This is the invention for which James Nasmyth, a pupil of Maudslay, is chiefly remembered, although he made many other distinguished contributions to engineering progress. The steam hammer was a tool of great importance in the growth of the heavy engineering industry, for it placed tremendous but controllable power at the disposal of the engineer. The hammer consists essentially of a piston which is raised by steam in a cylinder and then allowed to fall on the work-piece. Many specimens, of various shapes and sizes, survive, but not many remain in operation because with the general decline of steam plant it is not economic to maintain steam for a hammer.

Another group of machine tools is that concerned with

drilling and punching holes, particularly in metal plates. *Drilling machines* are usually recognizable by the cutting screw or drill, which is set rotating against the piece (i.e. as distinct from a lathe, in which the piece is rotated). A *boring machine* is also designed to cut holes, but in this case it is the inside surface of a cylinder which is involved. The problem of improving the bore of cannon had led the ironfounder John Wilkinson to invent a machine which carried a cutting tool on a rotating bar through the middle of the rough-cast work-piece. This was in 1774, and his patent coincided with the need of Boulton and Watt to improve the quality of the cylinders for their steam engine, so that they were able to take advantage of Wilkinson's invention, which set the pattern for subsequent boring machines. Holes can be punched and ends trimmed in a *punching and shearing machine* by the application of intense pressure to a localized area of the work-piece.

For producing flat, smooth surfaces another range of machine tools was developed: the grinding, milling, and planing machines. The *grinding machine* is essentially a development of the grindstone and dates from antiquity, being primarily used to put an edge on knives and other instruments, but it is also capable of being used for smoothing off a surface. The *milling machine* performs a similar function, but uses rapidly rotating cutters to do it. A *planing machine* is a development of the woodworker's plane, performing its cut by the lateral movement of the cutting edge. The refinement of the milling and planing machines into really efficient machine tools had to await the development of resistant cutting edges, and is associated with the outstanding success of Joseph Whitworth, another pupil of Maudslay, who set up in business in Manchester in 1833 and became the leading machine-tool manufacturer in the middle decades of the century. Many machines made by Whitworth's factory in the second half of the nineteenth century, including some robust lathes, planing machines, drilling and slotting machines, and so on, have survived, and some are still at work. It would be useful to know how many survive and where they can be found: the composition of a catalogue of such machines would be a worth-while task of industrial archaeology. They generally displayed the name

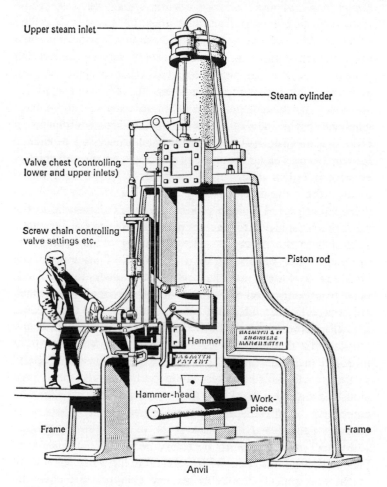

9. Nasmyth's steam hammer.

of their maker prominently, together with the date of construction.

Many other machine tools could be mentioned, such as *shaping, mortising,* and *slotting machines, gear-cutting machines, sawing machines* and various sorts of *copying machines,* whose function is clear enough from their titles; but the ones described so far are the most important in the sense that they have become the standard equipment of almost every sort of engineering workshop. It is worth stressing that all these machine tools are performing basically simple operations, for it is easy enough for an industrial archaeologist with no engineering skill to be overwhelmed by the sight of a workshop full of such equipment. In order to achieve complicated operations, it is necessary to arrange for work to pass along the series of machines, any one of which is engaged in only a small part of the process. Hence the development of the complex engineering establishment, with the workpiece being moved along a production line, culminating in the modern mass-production factory with a high degree of automatic control over the processes. The beginning of this pattern of production can be discerned in the series of machines made by Maudslay for the manufacture of pulley blocks for the Royal Navy to a specification of Marc Brunel, the father of I. K. Brunel. It has been estimated that the Navy used 100,000 of these blocks annually at the beginning of the nineteenth century, so that any economy in their manufacture was welcome. Maudslay built forty-five machines to mechanize the process almost completely, so that ten unskilled workers could perform work which previously required 110 skilled block-makers, and by 1808 the equipment was producing 130,000 blocks a year. There were actually twenty-two different sorts of machines, although additional machines were necessary to avoid bottlenecks in production and this brought the total up to forty-five. This set of machines is important not only because it comprised in effect the first successful example of mass production, but also because a number of the machines survive in the Naval Dockyard at Portsmouth, where Maudslay originally installed them, and a representative group of eight have been preserved in the Science Museum.[2]

Despite the undoubted significance of this set of block-making machine tools, they did not set a precedent which was immediately applied to other engineering processes. Indeed, it was not until the middle of the nineteenth century, when the engineering industry was developing rapidly in continental Europe and North America, that the next big step was taken towards mass-production techniques by the introduction of standardization. In the United States, in particular, an engineering industry was emerging in which the standardization of parts was so rigorous that it became known as the 'American System'. Agricultural-equipment and small-arms manufacture on this system gave a clear indication of the advantages of machines with completely standardized and therefore interchangeable parts. In place of the 'one-off' practice of most British workshops – each of the 500 or so steam engines made by Boulton and Watt between 1775 and 1800 had been made to individual specifications – the principle of assembling complex machines from mass-produced uniform parts was gradually adopted. Promoted by a chronic shortage of skilled labour in the United States this soon became the general engineering method in the manufacture of sewing machines, typewriters, bicycles, and ultimately of motor cars and aeroplanes. It has been along these lines that the modern engineering industry has developed.

One result of this development, however, has been the diversification of the engineering industry into a number of distinct industries which, although using machine tools that are basically the same, have become so specialized in the manufacture of their own products that it is hardly practicable to regard them as part of the same industry. Admittedly, the professional specialization into civil and mechanical engineering

had already been defined in the first half of the nineteenth century, although a multi-sided genius like I. K. Brunel was still
capable of combining the skills of civil, marine, and mechanical

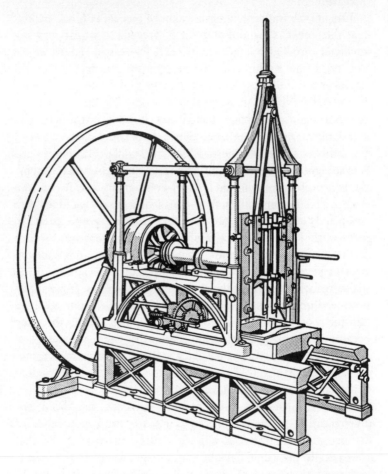

10. Mortising machine. One of the series of machines designed by Marc
Brunel for the block-making equipment at Portsmouth during the Napoleonic
Wars.

engineering, and of excelling in each. But Brunel was outstanding, and since his time no similar polymath figure has appeared in the engineering industry. Nevertheless, his career does help to indicate the increasing diversification of engineering in the middle of the nineteenth century, and to suggest that we need to take a closer look at some of the specialized branches of the engineering industry.

Electrical Engineering

Electrical engineering derives from the pioneer investigations of scientists in the late eighteenth and early nineteenth centuries into the nature of magnetism and static electricity. These researches led to the chemical generation of electricity by Volta in 1800 and culminated in Michael Faraday's perception in 1831 of the relationship between magnetism and current electricity, which showed the possibility of the mechanical generation of electricity and of the electric motor. The exploration and exploitation of these possibilities gave rise to electrical engineering, for they required mechanical skill in the construction of armatures (the coils of tightly wound wire which turn between the poles of a magnet when current passes through them) and accurate moving parts, and thus became a specialized engineering competence from the outset. Mechanical generators, or 'dynamos' as they became known, developed rapidly in the second half of the nineteenth century. At first they were driven by conventional reciprocating steam engines, but Charles Parsons devised the steam turbine in 1884 to increase the speed of generators and thus improve the output of electrical energy. The steam turbine has since become standard equipment for the generation of electrical power, even in the most modern atomic-fuelled power stations, but hydro-electric power has supplemented it in areas where the geography is suitable. From the late nineteenth century, the demand for electrical power became sufficiently great, at first particularly in the main metropolitan centres, but subsequently in all parts of the world, to justify the installation of large generators in 'power stations'. The significance of this development is discussed in the chapter on public services.

Electricity has been used as the source of power in a steadily increasing range of equipment for industry, transport, and the ordinary household, and the manufacture of this equipment has been another important function of the electrical engineering industry. One of the first uses for electricity was as a source of light, produced first by an electric arc. This is most efficient when the light is large, so that it has been used extensively in lighthouses since it was first installed at the South Foreland Light in 1858. Much thought was given by electrical engineers to the problem of 'sub-dividing' the light for domestic use, and during the 1880s both Edison in America and Swan in Britain solved this problem by manufacturing satisfactory incandescent filament lamps. This was made possible by the development of high-vacuum techniques and the discovery of suitable carbon filaments. The evolution of electric lighting through these stages and on through the tungsten filament to the modern gas discharge lamps is a fascinating story, evidence of which can still be discovered by observant industrial archaeologists in the lamps themselves and in the transformation of street furniture which has accompanied it.

Meanwhile, many other applications for electricity have been found, most of them requiring an electric motor. The principle of this had been discerned by Faraday in 1831, as we have seen, and it consists of a generator in reverse in the sense that a current fed through the armature between the poles of a magnet causes the armature to turn. Although electric motors were operating satisfactorily by the middle of the century, they were slow to become popular. There were two main reasons for this. One was the ubiquity of the steam engine, then well tried and tested and enjoying a virtual monopoly of the power business. This was especially the case in Britain, and the lesser hold of the steam engine elsewhere accounts in part for the greater progress of electrical power in Germany, Switzerland, Belgium, and America in this period. The other reason for the slow adoption of electrical power in Britain was the fact that industrialists were reluctant to invest in large-scale generating equipment until there was a well-proved system of electric traction. Only when this vicious circle was broken by the construction of the first power station could electric-powered transport systems like the municipal tram services and the London Underground develop, and this did not happen until the last decade of the nineteenth century. From then onwards, however, the electric engine has been widely adopted, even though it has had to compete with the vigorous development of the internal combustion engine.

There is now scarcely a household in the Western world which is without its electric power supply, providing energy for lighting, cooking, and a staggering range of appliances which have brought about a domestic revolution in the twentieth century. Amongst these, the instruments of the mass media of communication, radio and television, have an important place, and these represent another contribution of the electrical engineering industry to modern life. Professor Clerk Maxwell established the theoretical relationship between electricity and light in 1873, which was demonstrated experimentally by Hertz in 1885 and developed into a viable system of wireless telegraphy by Marconi in the 1890s. The subsequent development of the thermionic valve, the television tube, and the electron-microscope, and the analysis of atomic particles and the disintegration of the atom itself, represent the most momentous achievements of the twentieth century, and the electrical engineering industry has played a leading part in them. Add to this the simultaneous development of electronics, radar, computers, transistors, and microminiaturization, and it becomes apparent that it is difficult to exaggerate the importance of this industry. From the point of view of the industrial archaeologist it is a rich field, but the main problem is the tremendously high rate of obsolescence which has to be taken into account. Early computers, for example, although constructed in the 1950s, are already obsolete, requiring recording and consideration for preservation.[3]

Coach and Locomotive Construction

For all its importance, electrical engineering is only one branch of the complex of engineering industries. Another which pre-dated it and still accounts for a large proportion of the engineering resources of the world is vehicle building, which may be sub-divided for convenience into coach and locomotive construction followed by automobile and aeroplane construction. The coach-makers of the early Industrial Revolution were carpenters, wheelwrights, and other sorts of traditional craftsmen, but they developed highly specialized skills in the course of improving the performance of stage coaches, such as the manufacture of dished wheels (with the spokes curving outwards slightly from the axle hub to the rim) and the design of springs. Coach-making was frequently carried out in large buildings, with the parts being made on the upper floors and assembled at the bottom floor, from which wide doors allowed the finished product to emerge, and some of these buildings survive. It was really the application of inanimate power to locomotion in the shape of the steam engine and the internal combustion engine, however, which converted the traditional skills of the coach-builder into those of modern vehicle engineering.

The railway workshops set up by all the main railway companies to build and maintain their locomotives and rolling stock were true engineering workshops. They are also important, and in some cases urgent, causes of concern to industrial archaeologists, because in the process of the 'rationalization' of the national railway network by British Rail and the transfer from steam to diesel and electric locomotives, the railway workshops are being closed or drastically altered. Towns such as Darlington, Crewe, Wolverton, and Swindon owe much of their present appearance to their growth as railway towns, but in most cases their railway workshops have been at least partially dismantled. In Swindon, for example, only a fraction of the enormous acreage once used by the GWR engineering workshops is still in use, the rest having been cleared to await redevelopment. The old town of Swindon, with its workers' cottages and public buildings arranged on a grid pattern alongside the workshops, remains for the time being intact, and provides the industrial archaeologist with an interesting model of planned development in the middle of the nineteenth century. Also worthy of note are the workshops of the private locomotive manufacturers, of whom only a few of the larger firms remain in business. Hunslet of Leeds, for example, still turn out small shunting locomotives, although these are now all diesel powered.

The locomotives and coaches produced in these railway workshops have been, on the whole, well treated in museums and special collections and it is not necessary to say more about them here. The preservation of representative specimens has been reasonably assured by the great pride and interest taken in them, although it should never be taken for granted that such interest will be maintained from one generation to another. The notorious case of the pioneer broad-gauge locomotive *North Star*, which was preserved at Swindon until 1905, when G. J. Churchward ordered its destruction because it was 'occupying valuable space', [4] should remind us of the uncertain nature of much preservationist effort, even though a replica of the locomotive was lovingly re-created later on for the present railway museum in Swindon. Nevertheless, railway artefacts have been preserved better than most other aspects of the engineering industry, although vehicular transport as a whole has done well. There are many specimens of steam traction engines, for example, carefully preserved by their proud owners for periodical display in traction rallies. Some of the firms which made these are still keenly interested in their preservation: Marshalls of Gainsborough, with its contemporary preoccupation in diesel rollers and other modern engineering products, is a case in point, having one of its own traction engines available to put on steam for visitors.

Automobile and Aeroplane Construction

In the field of the automobile, again, there are immensely active interests, with enthusiasts ready to spend large sums of money on the purchase and restoration of old motor cars, and collections such as that of Lord Montagu at Beaulieu drawing large crowds every year. The production of motor cars by the million has been an epic of the modern engineering industry: in most Western countries automobile manufacture has become the pivotal industry, accounting for a large proportion of national resources and engineering skills. The transformation in scale of operations from the 'one-off' production of the early British manufacturers like F. W. Lanchester to the mass production of the modern car-makers represents an enormous advance in the techniques of production, expressed fully in the 'scientific management' of Henry Ford's assembly-line production. To make this effective, the engineering industry has had to improve the range and quality of its tools, so that motor manufacture has contributed materially to engineering advances in the twentieth century. In the early days of the automobile, in the 1880s and 1890s, manufacturers were able to borrow important innovations from the bicycle (gearing, the use of ball bearings, chain drive, the pneumatic tyre, etc.), which was made easy by the fact that they were often the same manufacturers. But the pressure of large-scale demand soon led the car-makers to introduce important innovations in tools and techniques. The result in Britain has been the growth of the great car-manufacturing empires at Cowley, Longbridge, Luton, Dagenham, and elsewhere, and the flooding of the highways of the country with the products of these factories, and with the street furniture (filling stations, road signs, etc.) which has accompanied the coming of the motor car. Perhaps it is because civilized life in the last third of the twentieth century is still struggling with the attempt to live with the automobile that it is difficult to regard this vast industry and its products seriously as a subject for industrial archaeology, but it is a constantly changing industry and the early phases of its development are certainly in need of recording.

One aspect of the transformation of the motor car from a single 'quality' product such as a Rolls-Royce to the cheap family saloon which became popular in the inter-war years is the social change in spending power and attainable aspirations which it represented. In a rather similar manner, the development of that other outstanding product of the internal combustion engine – the aeronautical engineering industry – has been prompted by the increasing demand for rapid transport made possible by a rising standard of living. Aeronautical engineering started on an even more humble scale than automobile engineering and it was only the pressure of weapon competition in the First World War which enabled it to grow beyond the scale of a 'back-yard' industry. After a rapid growth during the war, it was in serious danger of relapsing until the feasibility of air transport was demonstrated, after which the expansion of the world airlines guaranteed its continued prosperity. The Second World War provided another boost to aeroplane production, and the emergence of the jet engine and other innovations ensured the continuance of the industry as a large-scale process in the subsequent years. Aeronautics has thus become a highly specialized and important branch of the modern engineering industry, with many of its own distinct machines and techniques (such as wind tunnels for testing the performance of different shapes of aircraft). Attempts are already being made to preserve specimens of early aircraft, but there is work for the industrial archaeologist in recording hangars, ground equipment, machinery, and even the early airfields, where these have disappeared under suburban expansion or the farmer's plough.

Marine Engineering

The transport industries do not exhaust the contribution of the internal combustion engine to engineering, for it has been used in a variety of static forms, particularly in the application of the heavy diesel engine to pumping apparatus in public services and other industrial functions. The manufacture of such heavy-duty engines has become itself a specialized branch of the engineering industry. The fact that such engines have been used to power ships introduces another aspect of the engineering industry – shipbuilding. Like coach-building, this was transformed gradually from a traditional craftsman's process to a modern engineering industry by the introduction of the steam engine and the change from wood to metal construction. Both these changes occurred in shipbuilding in the middle decades of the nineteenth century. The first steam-propelled boats to achieve commercial viability did so in the opening decade of the nineteenth century (Robert Fulton's *Clermont* in America in 1807, and the *Comet* on the Clyde in 1812), but it took another quarter of a century for the steam ship to become a satisfactory means of trans-oceanic traffic. The first to do this was I. K. Brunel's *Great Western*, launched in Bristol in 1837. Six years later, in 1843, Brunel launched his second ship, the *Great Britain*, which was the first large iron ship in the world, and the first large ship to be propelled by a screw rather than by paddles. This ship is a unique industrial monument, as it has been preserved by a remarkable series of accidents and was brought back to the dock where it was built in Bristol in the summer of 1970.[5]

In the space of a very few years, the pattern of a new type of shipbuilding industry, based upon iron and steam, was thus established. One consequence of this was that the industry began to move from the southern river mouths (Thames, Solent, Severnside), where it had previously flourished, towards the rivers of the north (Tyne, Mersey, Clyde), where the products of the iron industry were more readily available, together with the skilled labour and the coal supplies which had made these areas the growth-points of the British Industrial Revolution. Brunel's third and last ship – the giant *Great Eastern* – was built at Millwall on the Isle of Dogs, and was one of the last large ships to be built on the Thames. Shipbuilding at Portsmouth, Bristol, and other southern ports either languished or adapted itself to specialized types of smaller vessels. From the 1860s onwards, shipbuilding in Britain became a heavy engineering industry of the northern industrial river mouths and bays, where it has since remained. Jarrow, Clydeside, Barrow, Belfast, and Birkenhead have become the main centres. To rehearse these names is also to list some of the most depressed areas of the inter-war years, for since the 1920s British shipbuilding has been in the doldrums, from which only belated attempts at regrouping and modernization have recently begun to release it. These changes within the industry make it already an urgent priority for the industrial archaeologist, if the physical appearance of the British shipbuilding industry at the height of its prosperity is to be adequately chronicled. The foremen at some Glasgow shipyards still wear the traditional bowler-hats of their office, but in many respects the shipyards are now undergoing rapid change. The deafening clamour of the riveters, for example, has now virtually disappeared, to be replaced by the almost uncanny calm of welding. With the introduction of ever-larger ships, and with vigorous competition from Japan and other shipbuilding nations, it seems likely that the British industry has to enter a long period of change if it is to survive as a major industry.

Engineering Services

In addition to the aspects of the engineering industry described so far, it should be remembered that engineering performs an essential servicing function in many other industries. To mention only a few of these: coal-mining requires the services of specialized manufacturers of coal-cutting equipment; textile machines have become a highly specialized engineering product; paper-making, sugar-refining, hydraulic plastic-pressing machinery, agricultural equipment, and an almost endless range of such specialized processes all contribute to the diversity of the modern engineering industry. The geographical dispersal of these industries tends to follow that of the original engineering work-shops, which after the generation of Bramah and Maudslay moved away from London to the industrial centres of the Midlands and the North to flourish at Manchester, Sheffield, Tyneside, and Glasgow, where they enjoyed the advantage of proximity to the iron and steel industry and to coal and a large labour force. Although the spread of the national electricity grid and the extension of road transport has diminished the advantages of these classic centres of the Industrial Revolution and caused a marked dispersal of the engineering industry – particularly pro-nounced in the location of automobile engineering – many of the engineering industries have remained where they were planted at the time of the Industrial Revolution by a process of industrial inertia. Sugar-refining machinery, for example, is still manu-factured in Glasgow even though sugar is no longer refined in that city, and the original causes of its location there have lost their force. The geographical pattern of the engineering in-dustries has thus become complicated, not to say obscure, and is a subject deserving further study.

The Engineer

The human aspects of the engineering industry are similarly

complicated. The word 'engineer' is used variously in the English language to describe: (a) the professional engineer, (b) the skilled engineering craftsman, and (c) the man who operates the engine. The latter may be regarded as an American usage for the person who is described in Britain as the 'engine driver', whose job in the days of the steam locomotive was the object of every school-boy's aspirations. Both the former senses, however, are used for the description 'engineer'. The professional engineer emerged in the eighteenth century as a result of the boom in civil engineering accompanying the construction of roads and canals. The first generation of these men thus had no qualms about calling themselves 'civil engineers'. Brindley, Smeaton, Jessop, Rennie, Telford, and McAdam were the pioneers of this profession, and when the Institution of Civil Engineers was formed in 1818, Thomas Telford was a natural choice as its first president. Although the 'Civils' have always emphasized their role as a learned society, they have also done much to determine the professional competence and social stature of engineering. Already by the 1830s they had become so choosy that George Stephenson was not accepted as a member (although his son Robert was admitted, and was president in 1856–7). This was one reason for the foundation of the Institution of Mechanical Engineers in 1847: a group of railway engineers, meeting the previous year near the Lickey incline on the Bristol and Birmingham Railway, expressed a common anxiety to honour their founding fathers, so they established the Institution and installed Stephenson as their first president. The 'Mechanicals', indeed, represented a significantly different engineering tradition – that which had sprung from the steam engine and the early engineering workshops and which has been explored in this chapter. The break in 1847, however, marked the formal diversification of the engineering profession, and it has been followed by a spate of other foundations as different groups of engineers have separated themselves off for the representation of their distinct professional

interests. Each of these has contributed to the specialized concerns of its members, but they have served to confuse the overall
role of the professional engineer in society.

The engineering craftsmen formed a distinct and important
part of the working-class community in the nineteenth century.
Theirs was one of the new crafts of the Industrial Revolution,
and there is virtually no evidence of their existence as an
organized group before 1826, when the trade union of 'Journeymen Steam-Engine and Machine Makers and Millwrights' was
formed. In 1851 this amalgamated with other bodies to form the
Amalgamated Society of Engineers, one of the first of a new type
of centralized, co-ordinated, trade union having a full-time
salaried secretary, and the predecessor of the modern Amalgamated Union of Engineering and Foundry Workers. This
organization, which acquired a membership of 21,000 in ten
years, represented the aristocracy of the working class – an elite
of skilled artisans who led the way in pressing for collective
bargaining procedures and the widening of the franchise to
include themselves. At a time when an engineer could hope to
earn between 20s. and 30s. a week, members of the ASE paid a
weekly subscription of one shilling and received in return a
range of benefits which anticipated those later provided by the
welfare state. These men learnt their skill by serving a long
apprenticeship and endeavoured to protect their position by
maintaining such training as a prerequisite of entry to the trade.
Neither engineering employers nor workmen were very receptive
to the campaign for increased technical education until late on in
the century. The ASE established a reputation for hard but
fair bargaining and for a conciliatory attitude in industrial disputes. With the proliferation of the engineering industries, however, other organizations have become involved in labour
representation, and the record of labour relations in the twentieth
century has been somewhat less harmonious than it was a
hundred years ago. Nevertheless, the artisan engineers remain

one of the most highly skilled groups in the modern industrial community, making their indispensable contribution to an industry which, in all its complex ramifications, is of enormous national significance.

6. The Textile Industries

Amongst the most ancient industries known to man is that for the manufacture of artificial fabrics – the textile industry. In temperate climates the need for some form of bodily covering comes second only to the need for food and drink, as without clothing human beings cannot survive the rigours of winter, and once the supplies of animal skins had become inadequate, some man-made means of providing clothes had to be devised. The development of textile-making skills was thus a condition of survival in many prehistoric communities, and there is certainly evidence of an established textile industry amongst the agricultural societies of the Middle East and Europe in the Neolithic period. Since then the industry has had a continuous history. In its early days, it was a small-scale industry, organized within the family amongst the many other duties which the women and children were expected to perform. Gradually, however, it grew in scale and organization, although it was not until the Industrial Revolution that it became a highly concentrated industry. The fact that most of the monuments of the textile industry date from this period tends to obscure the antiquity of the essential processes which comprise it, so that it is useful to recall the long traditions of textile manufacture as a background to the industrial archaeology of the subject.

The Textile Machines

Textiles can be made from a variety of materials – animal, vegetable, and mineral – and with the exception of the mineral sources most of these have been known from antiquity. Whatever the sources of their raw materials, however, there is a close similarity between the processes of the textile industries, and thus of the machines used in them also. The two central processes are spinning and weaving. Spinning consists of the preparation of the yarn by drawing out and imparting a tight twist to the fibres. The process is called 'throwing' in the silk industry, where the emphasis is on twisting together the required number of continuous filaments unravelled from the cocoon of the silk worm. Unlike most other textiles, the 'staple' – that is, the length of individual fibres – is not a limitation on the strength of the yarn, but the fragility of the filaments of silk is a serious problem. The *silk-throwing machines* installed by the Lombe brothers at Derby in 1717 consisted of cumbersome wooden drums which drew out the filaments and twisted them into threads as they rotated.

Silk throwing was a foreign craft imported into Britain, but the spinning of woollen yarn had been carried out in British homes for centuries before the mechanical improvements of the eighteenth century. The oldest method was that of the *spindle and distaff*, a skein being drawn from a hank of fibrous wool held on a distaff, and twisted by attaching it to a rapidly turning spindle, on to which the spun yarn could then be wound. This process was replaced by the *spinning wheel*, which imparted a more continuous rotary action to the spindle and thus increased the productivity of the spinster – not enough, however, to satisfy the demands for yarn in the expanding cotton industry of the eighteenth century, which had adopted the same method of spinning and proceeded to mechanize it. This was done, first, by making a spinning wheel operate a series of spindles (as in Hargreaves' *spinning jenny*);

then by using rollers rotating at different speeds to draw out the skein before it was twisted (as in the *spinning frame* invented by Arkwright, although Paul and Wyatt had earlier been working along similar lines); and then by drawing out the skein by means of a moving trolley (as in Crompton's *spinning mule*). The first of these devices, the jenny, was readily adopted by the domestic cotton industry, being powered by the operators, but both the frame and the mule were extensively adapted to mechanical power. Arkwright's machine, enlarged and improved, became the *water frame* with the application of water power, and later became known as the *throstle* when driven by steam power. The mule underwent considerable development and was very widely adopted, but retained its basic form.

Weaving is the process of webbing the yarn into a continuous fabric of interlocking threads, and is carried out on a *loom*. This consists of frames carrying the longitudinal threads in the fabric – the 'warp' – which can be separated to allow the latitudinal thread – the 'weft' – to be drawn between them and pressed into position. The shuttle carrying the weft was passed across the loom by hand, and the first attempts at mechanizing the process were those concerned with the development of the 'flying shuttle', a device for catapulting the shuttle across the frames of the loom by means of springs operated by the weaver. The conversion of the whole process of weaving to mechanical power was a difficult engineering task, and was not perfected until the improvements in machine construction in the early nineteenth century, although the clergyman Edmund Cartwright had invented the means of making such a *power loom* in 1786. Once developed, the power loom replaced the hand loom, first in the cotton industry and then in wool and other textiles. In the shape of the *Jacquard loom* it acquired a further sophistication, for it became possible to control the weaving of intricate patterns by means of a punched-card system directing the operation.

An alternative to weaving as a method of interlocking threads to make a fabric is the knitting process, in which loops of yarn are linked together rather than being intertwined. One advantage of knitting or crocheting is that only one thread need be used, instead of two which is the minimum required in weaving. William Lee had invented a *stocking frame* for knitting lengths of hosiery in the sixteenth century, and this machine became widely used in the Midland counties. It was subsequently improved, notably by Jedediah Strutt, who invented a device for reversing the loops during the knitting process to form ribs, which he patented in 1758 and which became the foundation of a family fortune in the hosiery industry.

In addition to these central textile processes, there are a number of preparatory processes which precede spinning or throwing, and some finishing processes which follow weaving or knitting. The particular preparatory and finishing processes used in any instance depend upon the type and quality of raw material and the final condition which is required for the fabric. The most common preparatory processes include washing, carding, and combing the fibrous material from which the yarn is to be spun. Carding and combing are alternative methods of pulling out the fibres so that they are all arranged in the same direction in a continuous skein. Both were originally done by hand with 'cards' or 'combs', the former being pieces of board with short metal teeth covering one surface. Arkwright devised a *carding machine* to card cotton continuously using rollers set with teeth: this produced 'rovings' or 'slubbings' of softly twisted cotton which were then ready for the spinning process. Various attempts were made to mechanize the combing process, beginning with a patent by Edmund Cartwright in 1792 for a *combing machine*. This dragged the wool over teeth placed radially inside a rotating circular frame about six feet in diameter, and could do the work of twenty men. The machine was greatly improved in the mid-nineteenth century, but later models mostly retained the circular comb-frame. Combing was an important process in the manufacture of worsted cloth, and was applied only to the longer-stapled wool. Another preparatory process, used with vegetable materials such as cotton and flax, was that of 'scutching', in which the raw material was beaten in order to open out the fibres. Various forms of *scutching machine*, *hackling* (or *heckling*) *machine*, and *chain gill* were devised to speed up this operation, consisting usually of spiked beaters arranged so that they could hit the raw material and be drawn through it.

Finishing processes, after weaving or knitting, are especially important and varied in the manufacture of woollen cloth, although the *printing machine* to apply colours by rollers to cotton fabrics was invented by Bell in 1783. Traditionally the most significant of these woollen finishing processes was that of fulling by *fulling stocks*, of which more will be said in the next section. Others were dyeing, knapping, and shearing, the last two of which were fairly easily mechanized once the need to increase productivity in the finishing department affected the woollen industry in the mid-nineteenth century.

The basic similarity of traditional textile materials has been reflected in the problems of manufacturing them into fabrics and in the machines which have evolved to achieve this, and despite mechanization the processes themselves remain recognizable. The essential twisting operation in the spinning process, for example, can be seen at all stages from the distaff and spindle to the most advanced spinning mule. This cannot be said, however, of the new textiles, produced from mineral sources such as petro-chemicals, in which many of the processes are qualitatively different from those of other textile materials. Thus the preparatory processes bear no resemblance to any of those described above, and spinning is replaced by a process of extrusion. Even the machines producing modern synthetic fibres should not be ignored by the industrial archaeologists, however, as they are undergoing rapid development and the early models are already completely obsolete.

Wool

The English landscape bears eloquent testimony to the importance of the woollen cloth industry, at least since the fourteenth century, with its magnificent village churches in East Anglia and the West Country. Superb buildings like the parish churches of Lavenham and Long Melford in Suffolk or the city church of St Mary Redcliff in Bristol were built from profits made in the woollen cloth trade, and to that extent may be considered as industrial monuments. For centuries before the cloth trade became an important international organization, England had been known as a source of abundant high-quality wool, and there had been a significant trade in the raw material. Although the Domesday Survey of 1086 was not very specific on the location and extent of sheep farming, it seems highly probable that it was already very extensive in late Anglo-Saxon England in those parts of the country which later became associated with the cloth industry, and even that it was the wealth derived from this sheep farming which made the country attractive to the Danish marauders of the tenth and eleventh centuries. Be this as it may, the wool and woollen cloth industries have certainly had deep roots in England. This is shown symbolically in the traditional 'wool sack' which provides a seat for the Lord Chancellor in the House of Lords, and it is shown also in the survival of many common surnames such as Weaver, Webster (a weaver), Walker (a fuller), and Lister (a dyer), which have their origin in woollen cloth processes.

By the fourteenth century, the woollen cloth manufacturing industry was firmly established in East Anglia and the West of England, and the export of English broadcloth (fulled, undyed cloth) had begun to replace the trade in wool as the major source of commercial prosperity. Indeed, the export of raw wool was progressively discouraged as the manufacturing industry grew and consumed the product of the sheep pastures itself. Woollen cloth making had already become an important urban craft by this time, with many guilds devoted to the various branches of the industry, some of them leaving a token of their existence in

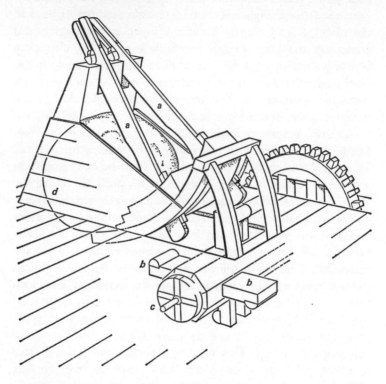

11. Fulling stocks. The heads of the hammers (*a*) are raised by the cams (*b*) on the main driving shaft (*c*), to fall on the cloth being 'fulled' in the trough (*d*).

street names such as Tucker Street in Bristol, from the name sometimes given to the fuller (the word also occurs in the form of 'Tuckingmill' to describe the site of a fulling mill). About this time, however, an important transition took place from the towns like Bristol and Norwich into the adjacent countryside, and this led to the emergence of East Anglia and the West Country as the main areas of woollen cloth manufacture. The transition took place partly because the craft guilds of the urban cloth industry were restrictive and jealous of newcomers to their trades, so that expansion of production was hampered within the areas which they controlled. Of more significance, however, was the appearance of an important technological innovation which has caused the change to be called 'an Industrial Revolution of the thirteenth century'.[1] This was the introduction of mechanical fulling in the crucial finishing process, which converted the loosely woven woollen fabric into a closely matted or felted 'broadcloth' by soaking it in water and 'fuller's earth' and pounding it to shrink the material and make it more compact. This had been a tedious task requiring a lot of heavy footwork, as the cloth had traditionally been fulled by tramping on it. The thirteenth-century invention which changed this and which altered the location of the woollen cloth industry was the use of water power to drive fulling stocks, heavy wooden hammers raised by cams on a shaft from a water wheel and allowed to fall into a trough containing the cloth undergoing treatment in the fulling solution. This was an important labour-saving device because it simplified an operation which had previously distorted and restricted the process of cloth production. The fulling stocks could run all day and night, provided only that water power was available. This meant establishing the fulling mill on a reliable or fast-running stream, such as those which occurred in abundance in the south Cotswolds and, to a lesser extent, in Suffolk and Essex. Having invested capital in such mills, the land-owners and entrepreneurs who were promoting the expansion of the industry in the fourteenth century found it convenient to encourage the other processes to move into the vicinity of the mills. Hence the transition from a predominantly urban craft to the more rural environment of north Somerset, west Wiltshire, south Gloucestershire,

Essex, and Suffolk, and, in Yorkshire, from the urban centres of York and Beverley towards the valleys and streams of the West Riding.

The English woollen cloth industry flourished mightily from the fourteenth to the seventeenth century, enriching the nation through the trade with Flanders, enriching the government through the taxes which it was able to impose on this lucrative trade, and enriching the landscape in the way which has already been described. Although largely a rural industry, it was highly organized by merchants and other middlemen who kept the lines of production moving between carders and spinners, spinners and weavers, weavers and fullers. The industry operated, with the exception of the fulling mills, in the homes of the workers, so that it was a classic example of a 'domestic' or 'cottage' industry. Whereas carding and spinning were regarded usually as the tasks of women and children, weaving was almost invariably a man's job, so that the industry frequently fitted into the economy of the extended family, with the man in the family weaving the yarn produced by his wife and children, and turning his hand to farming or gardening when the supply of yarn failed to keep him fully employed at the loom. The loom was usually installed in a bedroom, which was provided with a long window to maximize the light for the intricate work involved. These long weavers' windows occasionally survive in Cotswold villages and elsewhere where domestic textile weaving became important. The 'spinsters', on the other hand, usually worked in any odd corner and in any spare moment between other household labours: the distaff and spindle, held on a stool in the porch, or the simple spinning wheel in the inglenook by the cottage hearth, became features of the traditional village community. Specimens of these domestic craft tools are frequently preserved in museums, especially folk museums such as the Welsh National Museum at St Fagan's, Cardiff, where, incidentally, a complete working woollen mill has been reconstructed, with all the main processes

of woollen cloth manufacture contained in a single compact
building.

Internal political upheavals and the increasing competition
from continental rivals brought about a prolonged depression in
the English cloth industry in the seventeenth century, one result
of which was the growing leadership of the West Riding as a
centre of the industry. Even before the Industrial Revolution,
the West Riding was proving more resilient to changes in taste
and more adaptable to new processes and materials than the West
Country and East Anglian industries. When Daniel Defoe visited
Yorkshire in 1724 he described with enthusiasm a scene of
impressive domestic industry.[2] By 1760, the West Riding was
already producing about half the national exports of all kinds of
woollen cloth, and the coming of the Industrial Revolution with
its rapidly growing use of coal gave the county a further advantage
over the other manufacturing areas, so that it gradually won a
predominant position in the British woollen cloth industry.
Although the West of England remained throughout the nineteenth century a centre of vigorous cloth production, particularly
in the valleys of south Gloucestershire converging on Stroud,
the West Riding became the outstanding area of production.
Today the West Country industry has dwindled to a handful of
mills at Trowbridge, Stroud, and Dursley, and with the exception
of a scatter of small mills in Wales and Scotland, mostly surviving on the strength of high-quality traditional fabrics, the
industry has otherwise become concentrated in the West
Riding.

Three factors of particular importance to industrial archaeologists in considering the location of the industry and the disposition of its remains should be noted. First, the shift of the
industry towards the West Riding of Yorkshire, like the earlier
transition from the corporate towns to the rural areas of the West
Country and East Anglia, has meant that marks of the industry
have survived in parts of the country now abandoned by it.

Many woollen mills, often converted to other uses but occasionally derelict, survive in areas like the Stroud valleys and the district around Bradford-on-Avon, together with the elegant houses of the cloth merchants and their families. These are well worth careful examination. Secondly, the woollen cloth industry was much slower than cotton to abandon the domestic pattern of organization to which it had become well adjusted over many centuries. Professor Heaton found hand-loom weavers surviving in the West Riding into the second half of the nineteenth century, and told the story in 1920 of one whom he met as an old man of eighty who had abandoned weaving forty years earlier rather than go into a factory where he would have to work alongside women. Instead, he had chopped up his loom and turned to growing cabbages.[3] One consequence of this slow transition (compared with cotton) from domestic to factory production is that woollen districts are frequently disappointing to industrial archaeologists precisely because so much of the traditional enterprise was on a handicraft, domestic basis, and in the nature of things the material framework of such enterprise is less distinguished and less likely to survive in recognizable form than a large mill. For all this, the influence of domestic production survives in important features such as the settlement pattern in the West Riding, where an apparently random scatter of small groups of houses on the hillsides often bears witness to an era of industrial prosperity even before the large mills were established in the bottom of the valleys.

A third interesting feature of the woollen cloth industry is the fact that few entrepreneurs of the Arkwright type entered it in the eighteenth and nineteenth centuries, and the normal scale of units was correspondingly smaller than in the cotton industry across the Pennines. One reason for this was probably the wide range of woollen fabrics which were produced, and the tendency to specialize in particular woollen cloths or worsteds, the latter being made from longer fibres than woollens, combed instead of carded, and not fulled. The mills of Huddersfield, for example, have tended to specialize in high-quality worsted suitings, while those of Dewsbury and Batley have concentrated on producing 'shoddies' from rags and other scrap material. Most of the enterprises, however, have been of small or medium size compared with their counterparts in the cotton industry, and have often remained family concerns: the large-scale operator like Benjamin Gott, the Leeds worsted manufacturer who made a fortune out of supplying the armies of the Allies with clothing during the Napoleonic Wars, was the exception rather than the rule. It is significant that even Gott's great Bean Ing Mill in Leeds, only recently demolished, employed hand-loom weavers and drew on a considerable number of domestic out-workers, so that Professor Heaton described him as 'only an Industrial Half-Revolutionary'.[4] The consequence of this multiplicity and range of manufacturing units is that the West Riding woollen cloth industry presents the industrial archaeologist with a bewildering jumble of material in its mills, forms of motive power, processes, and products, which can only be sorted out by careful field-work and research.

Silk

Silk was a luxury commodity in great demand amongst the well-to-do classes in the seventeenth and eighteenth centuries. From its origins in China the secrets of silk manufacture – particularly the process of making a usable yarn out of the cocoons of silk worms – had been introduced into Europe in the Middle Ages and the industry had taken root first in Sicily and Italy and later in France. British governments were anxious to avoid dependence on foreign producers for this commodity, and attempted to encourage its manufacture at home. The influx of religious refugees from France – the Protestant Huguenots – at the end of the seventeenth century was welcomed as a means, amongst other things, of stimulating a British silk industry, and while James II encouraged the cultivation of mulberry trees in East London (several of which miraculously survive), William III granted monopolies to various producers. Spitalfields in East

12. Handloom weaver's cottage, with characteristic long window to the upper-floor room where the loom was worked.

London became the main centre for the manufacture of the more expensive silken fabrics, the industry being organized on the domestic system, the weavers working in garrets with long 'weavers' lights' above the merchants' houses. Examples of handsome eighteenth-century houses of this type can still be found in Spitalfields, but as the industry became depressed in the nineteenth century in competition with fine cotton fabrics, the centre of production moved eastwards into Bethnal Green, where many rows of poor weavers' cottages survived until a few years ago. The industry also moved into the provinces and was established at, amongst other places, Coventry, Macclesfield, and Stockport, where it became associated with the manufacture of ribbon and hosiery. In time, cotton provided a cheaper substitute for silk in these and other areas of production, but in 1717 the silk industry had the distinction of being the first English industry to possess a fully developed factory in the modern sense of a single building containing a large number of people working on complex processes with machines powered by non-animate means. This was the factory built on an island in the River Derwent at Derby by Sir Thomas Lombe, containing silk-throwing machines the design of which his half-brother John Lombe had procured in Italy. The factory employed about 300 people and used water power from the river to drive the machines, but it is likely that the need for security was as important to Lombe in building the factory as that for mechanical power. The building has undergone fire, partial collapse, alterations and additions, but parts of the original structure can still be seen.[5] But the British silk industry always suffered from its reliance on foreign sources of raw material which were particularly vulnerable at times of European wars, and with rare exceptions such as the factory at Derby it did not become a large-scale industry. Silk mills survive, however, in various parts of the country, Macclesfield in Cheshire possessing some particularly impressive buildings.

Flax, Hemp and Jute

These three fibrous plants all provide valuable textile materials. Hemp and jute are cultivated mainly in India and supply a coarse fibre suitable for rope and sacking respectively; both of these have been important lesser industries, especially as subsidiaries to the shipbuilding industry in the days of sail. Jute, moreover, became the basis of an important factory industry in the mid-nineteenth century in Dundee, which grew more rapidly in that period than any other British town because of the expansion of the jute industry and earned for itself the nickname 'Juteopolis'. Many of the mills erected between 1830 and 1870 survive, and make Dundee a fascinating study for the industrial archaeologist.[6] Jute was often used in conjunction with linen, which is a much finer material produced from flax, a type of plant which has been cultivated in the British Isles for many centuries. The manufactured fabric is called linen because linseed is the seed of flax. Tudor governments had sought to encourage the native linen industry by compelling land-owners to grow flax. As in the silk industry, however, British linen manufacturers lacked the expertise of their continental competitors and were unable to hold their own even in the British market until the advent of Huguenot refugees brought succour to them as well as to the silk industry. But by the mid-eighteenth century British producers could still not supply more than a quarter of the home consumption of linen, and by that time they were beginning to suffer severely from competition with cotton. In time, however, the linen industry did manage to find a stable economic base, although only on a small scale compared with cotton or wool, and restricted mainly to the 'Celtic Fringe'. It is in Eire and Ulster in particular, and also in Scotland, that the industry survives today.

The processes of linen manufacture closely resemble those for cotton, but the preparatory processes are more important, particularly that of 'scutching', for which many small mills known as 'lint mills' were established. (Robert Burns worked in one of these at Irvine in the 1780s.) Scutching was a beating process to break up the flax into a fibrous mass (the 'lint') from which a skein could be drawn. The most distinguished industrial monument of the linen industry south of the border is probably Marshall's Mill in Leeds. John Marshall established his linen business in Leeds early in the nineteenth century, and by the end of the Napoleonic Wars he had made a large fortune for himself. He built an exotic mill embellished with a magnificent façade in Egyptian style and with a large flat roof to give good illumination through sky-lights. The roof was covered in soil to insulate the building against extremes of temperature, and it was found that grass could be grown on the roof and a flock of sheep maintained by grazing it. The business declined under the second generation of the Marshall family and expired in 1886. The building has now been taken over by a large mail-order firm and its main architectural features have been happily preserved. The flock of sheep, however, has long since departed.

Cotton

Like flax, cotton is a plant, but unlike flax the fibrous material from which the textile is manufactured comes from seed-hairs not the stem. The cotton plant is a native of the Middle and Far East, being grown in Egypt and India at the beginning of the seventeenth century when the first cotton fabrics found their way into Europe. Early in the eighteenth century attempts were made to manufacture cotton in Britain, and despite government attempts to hamper its growth in order to protect the ancient woollen cloth industry from competition, it expanded rapidly. Two factors aided its development. One was the highly successful introduction of the cotton plant into the southern British colonies in North America, where it thrived and provided the basis for a large plantation crop of an easily available raw material.

The other factor was the growth, both in the colonies of the New World and in the populations of the large new towns of industrial Britain, of a market for a cheap, general-purpose textile. These factors, moreover, combined to attract the attention of some enterprising capitalists and ingenious inventors who were anxious to seek the maximum advantage out of cotton manufacture by establishing mills and employing new machines. Here were the dynamic ingredients of what became the classic transition of the British Industrial Revolution – the transformation of a small-scale domestic cotton industry into the first thoroughly mechanized and factory-based industry in the world, which took place between 1750 and 1830. Something has already been said about this transformation, in which a series of 'bottlenecks' in production, first in spinning and then in weaving and then in the preparatory and finishing processes, were overcome by enterprising initiative and technological ingenuity. The result was the creation of a vast industrial complex and the dramatic transfiguration of the landscape in south Lancashire and elsewhere. The major locational factor of the British cotton industry was the availability of the raw material, and this meant proximity to the ports which traded with the cotton plantation colonies of the New World. In practice these ports were Liverpool and Glasgow, for although Bristol had many commercial links with North America its citizens showed little interest in cotton until after the main patterns of the industry had been established. It was thus in the hinterlands of Liverpool and Glasgow, and most especially the former, that the industry took root. The siting of the first mills, when the industry began seriously to become mechanized in the 1760s, was determined by the availability of water power, so that the Pennine valleys of south Lancashire and Derbyshire predominated for a time, until the coming of the rotative-action steam engine made convenient its migration to the Lancashire coalfield, with its ready access to the markets and labour force of Manchester and the neighbouring towns.

This development of the industry can be traced in its industrial archaeology. Richard Arkwright's first cotton mill survives at Cromford in Derbyshire. It is in the valley of the River Derwent south of Matlock, although it relied for its water power not on the river but on a stream issuing from old lead workings and brought into the mill by a conduit (first a wooden launder, then replaced by a cast iron trough) over the road. The buildings, which have in any case been much altered over the two hundred years since the first mill was constructed on the site in 1771, are now used for the manufacture of ochre. The name of Arkwright survives in the area in the later mill – Masson Mill – which he built in 1783 and which still operates on the main river a short distance up the valley. Of this red-brick, six-storey building, the original part is that at the north end: it is now owned by the English Sewing Cotton Company. The village of Cromford is still much as it was designed by the original proprietor to accommodate the work force which he had to bring into the area. Other early cotton mills – like Lombe's silk factory a generation earlier – used the Derbyshire Derwent and its tributaries as a source of power. Higher up the valley a mill survives at Calver, and there are mills associated with Arkwright on the River Wye at Bakewell and Cressbrook, and also right in the heart of the Peak District on the River Noe at Edale. Down the Derwent valley there is the site of the famous mills established by Jedediah Strutt at Belper, some of which have now been destroyed, although the North Mill (1804) still stands. The Strutt family, and particularly William, the son of Jedediah, pioneered the construction of fire-proof mills here, and the type of building which they devised, with cast-iron columns supporting the floors, stone or brick vaulting between the columns, and the elimination of timber except in the roof, was widely adopted as a standard industrial practice in the nineteenth century. The oldest surviving building of this type, however, is that designed in 1797 by Charles Bage as a flax mill in Shrewsbury, now a grain warehouse.

Bage appears to have received a good deal of help from William Strutt. Another fine early specimen of fire-proof construction is the Stanley Mill at Stonehouse near Stroud. The Strutts had begun as hosiery manufacturers, using cotton yarn as their basic material instead of the traditional silk, and devising new knitting machines to manufacture hose. The whole of the Midlands between Nottingham, Derby, and Leicester, was involved in this branch of the textile industry, and there are many surviving monuments to the hosiery industry.[7]

The transition of the cotton industry to the coalfield of south Lancashire was marked by the construction of many large mills in the towns around Manchester, each equipped with large engine houses and the inevitable chimneys. As the industry rose to previously unimaginable prosperity in the middle of the nineteenth century, the fact that Cotton was King and that the mill-owners were his Vice-Regents was signified by the erection of monumental chimneys such as that at India Mill, Darwen, which appear grotesque to the modern eye but are nonetheless important clues to the ethos and psychology of this phase of British industrial history. Chimneys, indeed, are significant to the industrial archaeologist not only as virility symbols but for the hints they give about local styles, tastes, and building materials. There was some specialization amongst Lancashire cotton manufacturers; even large mills sometimes concentrated entirely on spinning or weaving. As a general rule of mill construction it should be observed that most multi-storey buildings were for spinning machines: good lighting was so essential for weaving that most looms were installed in single-storey buildings with north-facing sky-lights.

Liverpool was by far the leading port for the trade in cotton, but Glasgow also maintained a substantial trade and a considerable cotton manufacturing industry in and around the city. The most famous mill of the Glasgow hinterland was certainly that at New Lanark, associated with the work of Robert Owen. Pioneer

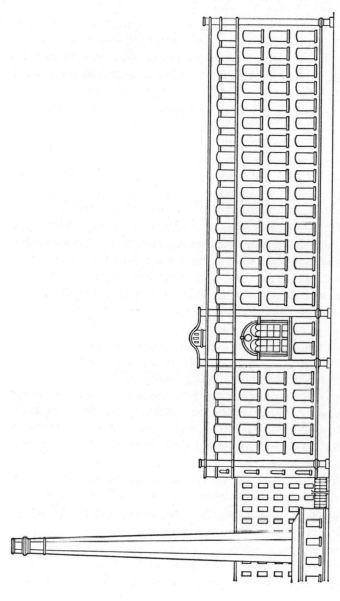

13. Cotton factory (from a drawing by Frank Wightman). A typical Lancashire mill, the Western Mill at Wigan, with a central engine house driving through gears and shafting.

industrialist, co-operator, socialist, atheist, and spiritualist, Owen was one of the most colourful characters ever to cross the stage of British history. In the first decade of the nineteenth century he built up a flourishing business at New Lanark, in conjunction with his father-in-law, David Dale, and established a village for his work-people complete with school, nursery, shops, and dance hall. Wonderfully, this village still survives much as Owen planned it. The tenement blocks are in course of internal modernization by the New Lanark Association, while their façade is being carefully restored, but the factory which functioned in the mill closed in 1968 and it is becoming urgently necessary to find a use for the buildings if they are to be preserved.

Robert Owen was an outstanding reformer with the courage of his convictions, and although not many followed his example of providing social and educational services for workers and their families, there were a few other nineteenth-century textile mill-owners with an eye for social improvement and philanthropy. Saltaire, near Bradford, designed by Sir Titus Salt for the workers in his unusually large woollen factory, survives in very good condition. These and other early exercises in planned industrial development provide instructive material for the social historian and industrial archaeologist.

The British cotton industry had become, by the middle of the nineteenth century, highly concentrated, and also completely converted to mechanized processes carried out in large factories, practically all powered by coal-fired steam engines. In the areas of concentration, the industry dominated the community, producing a generally dreary landscape of terraced houses amidst bleak mills belching out black smoke. The heavy demand of the cotton mills, particularly the spinning mills, for female labour, created strange social distortions with the women frequently finding it easier to get work than the men. Yet it was an oddly law-abiding community, with a reputation for non-violence in its labour disputes, a strong tradition of religious observance in Sunday schools and chapels, and a tendency towards Conservatism in politics. When the great Cotton Famine hit Lancashire in 1862–5 as a result of the American Civil War, the unemployed operatives of the cotton districts bore their deprivation with fortitude mixed with a sense that they were suffering in a good cause, as they were convinced supporters of the North against the slave-owning South. Still, the unemployed had to be fed, and the crisis brought a great boom in public works, financed by private subscription in other parts of the country, the result of which can still be discerned in the civic centres of many Lancashire towns.

Lancashire survived the Cotton Famine and trade returned to its normal course in 1865, but in subsequent years it became apparent that British cotton had passed the peak of its ascendancy. Not only were other industries growing and challenging it in Britain, but also the world trading situation gradually deteriorated as far as British cotton was concerned, with manufacturers in continental Europe, North America, and even in the Far East taking advantage of Lancashire expertise and experience and using more modern machinery, and beginning to compete with it in the world markets. The story of Samuel Slater, an ex-apprentice at Strutt's Belper Mill, who went to the United States of America in 1789 and helped to establish the cotton industry there, is an outstanding example of the way in which the new techniques were transmitted to other countries, but it was not untypical. Incidentally, it is worth noting that an excellent piece of industrial preservation has been performed on Slater's mill at Pawtucket in Rhode Island. The long decline of British cotton was hastened by the world wars of the twentieth century, and it is only by drastic concentration, re-tooling, and protection that it has managed to survive as an important industry. The Lancashire Cotton Corporation, established in 1929, was an important step towards the rationalization of the industry, and in recent decades government grants for modernization have further assisted this process of streamlining. One result has been that many mills have been destroyed or converted to other purposes, and many splendid mill steam engines have been scrapped because they are uneconomical to run in modern conditions. These sweeping changes have given the industrial archaeologist much work to do in south Lancashire and those other parts of the country where cotton once reigned supreme.

Artificial and Synthetic Textiles

The Great Western cotton factory was opened in Bristol in 1838. It was a belated attempt to get Bristol a stake in the industry which had proved to be so lucrative for the rival west-coast ports of Liverpool and Glasgow. It was doomed to be a financial failure, but it limped on over periodic crises until 1925, when the company running it went into liquidation. The premises were then acquired, however, by the Western Viscose Silk Company, which operated in the buildings until it likewise collapsed in 1929. The significance of this four-year period is that it was one of the first attempts to manufacture artificial silk – 'rayon' – on a large scale. In many respects the artificial and synthetic textiles may be regarded as a part of the chemical industry, but in practice they have often acquired buildings from other textile processes and to some extent employ similar machines, especially for weaving. Whereas 'rayon' and other early artificial textiles, first made in 1880, are produced from a cellulosic base (often cotton wool), the newer synthetic textile fibres such as nylon are the products of modern polymer chemistry and the coal and petroleum industries. Early machines for extruding the artificial and synthetic fibres are already museum pieces, and there is a remarkable wastage with such equipment because, its use being so recent, owners frequently fail to understand its technological significance. The development of these artificial and synthetic textiles thus offers considerable scope for the industrial archaeologist.

7. The Chemical Industries

The origins of the modern chemical industry may be traced back to the ancient and honourable crafts of the domestic kitchen. The Neolithic housewife, grinding corn in her quern and using the flour to bake bread in a crude oven, or brewing a fermenting liquid to produce an intoxicating beverage, may be described without unfair exaggeration as the first practical chemist. It was probably as an extension of these crafts that the first pottery was moulded and fired, the first dyes extracted from the juice of plants, and the first animal hides converted into leather. These and a host of other early skills, familiar to quite simple societies, involved processes of subtle alchemy whereby one substance was transformed into another quite different and more valuable material. There was something marvellous or even miraculous about them, made manifest in the womb symbolism of placing the dough in the oven or the moulded clay in the kiln. The persistence of the study of alchemy over many centuries shows the fascination of this magical element, with its promise of transmuting base materials into precious substances. The theoretical understanding of all chemical changes was very primitive and remained so until the nineteenth century, but great practical expertise was achieved in a wide range of chemical processes, and it is appropriate that we should review some of the more important examples of these here because they have frequently left industrial remains of considerable interest. Others, such as tanning, can be considered more suitably in conjunction with agricultural or urban crafts, as they have been little affected by the industrial developments of the last two hundred years.

Salt

One of the most important of ancient chemical processes, and one intimately associated with the kitchen, was the preparation of salt. This vital material had a wide variety of uses, including soldering, leather working, and medicinal applications, but outstanding amongst these was its culinary use in the flavouring and preservation of food. The latter process was essential in order to maintain supplies of food during the winter months, so that every household would try to preserve the carcasses of animals for later consumption by salting them. The growth of population and trade in the Middle Ages made this dependence upon salt increasingly important, especially in the preservation of fish, which, to be successful, had to be performed within a day of the fish being caught. The centres of salt manufacture, or at least its storage, tended thus to be close to the fishing ports. The Domesday Survey recorded 1,195 *salinae* along the coasts between Lincolnshire and Cornwall, the major concentrations being in Sussex (which had 294) and Norfolk.[1] These 'salterns', as they became known in the vernacular, produced salt by boiling seawater which had already been concentrated by evaporation in shallow basins. The English industry was greatly reduced in the fourteenth century as a result of the development of salt manufacture in Brittany, where salt of better quality could be produced with the advantage of more favourable climatic and geographical conditions, so that it became the main saltproducing district for the whole of northern Europe and made most of the English coastal salt enterprises uneconomical. A few survived into modern times, however, and remains of salterns can still be found in various parts of the country.

Between Lymington and Keyhaven, for example, on the low sheltered coastline of south Hampshire, miles of earth banks surrounding the evaporating ponds can still be located, together with fragments of the salthouses, although the salterns here went out of production over a hundred years ago.[2] Inland the competition of French salt was less acute than on the coast, and where alternative methods of producing salt were available the existence of a local market could stimulate enterprise. In parts of the English Midlands a significant salt industry has existed since the Middle Ages, based upon large subterranean deposits of salt removed by leeching – that is, pumping out brine and boiling it to recover the salt – or by mining for rock salt. The 'wiches' – the places ending in 'wich', such as Droitwich or Nantwich – are frequently places which have been associated with this industry at some time, although not invariably so because the Anglo-Saxon suffix could designate any place with a small collection of buildings for a manufacturing purpose.[3] Rock salt has been mined in parts of south Cheshire since the seventeenth century, and the effect of this industry on the primarily agricultural landscape has been to cause irregular subsidence where the salt has been leeched or mined from the underlying strata, and the formation of small ponds or 'meres' in the resulting depressions.

Soap

The Romans had used olive oil as a cleaning agent, and it is popularly supposed to have been the Teutonic invaders who introduced soap to Western Europe during the Dark Ages. A mixture of animal fat and wood ash (containing 'soda' – sodium carbonate – or 'potash', a form of potassium carbonate, both alkaline materials) was boiled to produce a rather unsavoury liquid which was not attractive for personal cleansing but very useful as a means of scouring the fleeces as a preliminary to the woollen textile processes. Like many other chemical processes,

soap manufacture developed to meet the demands of textile production. Soap boiling consumed a lot of fuel, and it is likely that
this was one of the first industrial processes to make use of coal.
Proximity to sources of coal and the existence of a prominent
local textile industry led to the early growth of soap-making in
Bristol, of which town the medieval chronicler Richard of Devizes
wrote in the thirteenth century: 'At Bristol there is no one who
is not, or has not been, a soap-maker'. The introduction of olive
oil in place of animal tallow in the late Middle Ages made a much
more pleasant soap, and with its increasing personal use London
developed a large soap industry, attracted by the great urban
market. So much did London soap-makers prosper that they
were able to obtain a monopoly from Charles I, which caused the
industry to decline in Bristol and elsewhere. As it was generally
a small-scale process with little capital equipment required,
nothing of significance survives from this early soap-making.
But the growth and concentration of soap manufacture since the
Industrial Revolution has led to the absorption of the industry
into large chemical enterprises such as Unilever, in which the
making of soap is only one of many processes. The concentration
is still proceeding, but it is appropriate that one large soap factory
building should survive in Bristol, the early home of the industry,
although it is now converted to other uses. This is the Broad
Plain factory of Christopher Thomas and Brothers, the manufacturers of Puritan soap. The factory was built in the 1880s in
the exotic brick style which has been dubbed 'Bristol Byzantine',
although 'Bristol Florentine' would probably be more suitable
as its inspiration was the architecture of Florence. The industry
is now concentrated in the Merseyside and Tyneside areas, and
towns such as Warrington and Port Sunlight are devoted largely
to soap manufacture.

Dyes

In addition to soap boiling, the growth of the English wool and woollen cloth industry stimulated a range of chemical processes, including the production of bleaches, mordants, scouring materials, and dyes. Bleaching was crudely performed before the Industrial Revolution, depending on exposure to rain, sunshine, sour milk, or urine, until the development of cheap sulphuric acid laid the foundations of the modern chemical industry. Mordants, used for fixing dyes, were compounds of alum, which was worked extensively from deposits in Hampshire (there is an 'Alum Bay' near the Needles on the Isle of Wight) and elsewhere in the Middle Ages. The most important scouring material was fuller's earth, which, as the name suggests, was used in the process of fulling woollen cloth both to scour the fabric and to assist the felting of the threads into the smooth texture of broadcloth. Although the textile use of fuller's earth has declined, other uses have been found for it in industry and in medicinal preparations. It is still worked at several places, including Bath and Redhill. Techniques for manufacturing fast dyes from plants (wood, madder, wood bark, walnuts, etc.) were devised by early textile workers and were refined over many centuries. The expert in procuring and mixing dyes became known as the 'drysalter', and was an important figure in the emergence of the chemical industry. The production of the raw materials for dyes was a significant factor in agriculture until the discovery of aniline dyes from organic chemical compounds destroyed the market for these 'natural' dyes in the second half of the nineteenth century. Many of them disappeared completely, but some natural dye processes survived into the twentieth century, particularly those manufacturing strong colours from tropical trees, which sustained a water-powered logwood mill at Keynsham in Somerset until 1964. This mill contained log-shredding machinery and heavy stone edge-runners (for crushing the wood chips) of a type which must once have been widespread. The large external breast-shot water wheel is still intact.[4]

Pottery

The culinary origin of the pottery industry does not need stressing, but the wide dispersal of pottery shards and their value to archaeologists in dating sites indicates the great antiquity of this industry. All sorts of clays have been worked and fired, with an equal variety of glazes and pigmentation. Analysis of these components has made possible the imaginative reconstruction of prehistoric cultures and trade routes, even though few complete specimens survive of the early pottery manufactures. While the first function of pottery was utilitarian, providing vessels for containing liquids and for cooking purposes, it soon developed a decorative function also, and ceramic works which have survived from early civilizations are frequently objects of great beauty and cultural significance. At some point in the evolution of pottery manufacture an unknown craftsman (or woman) devised the potter's wheel as a way of simplifying the tedious business of moulding clay, and this technique has continued with little modification into the modern pottery industry. The potter's wheel is significant in the history of technology because as a means of converting reciprocating to rotative action it represents an important conceptual breakthrough and is closely related to the origin of the lathe.

For all its longevity, the history of pottery manufacture produced remarkably little development until the sixteenth century, at least in Western civilization where ceramic products were, until that time, still relatively crude and unattractive, even though the wares of some Mediterranean manufacturers (such as 'faience' and 'majolica') were widely traded. The introduction of examples of Chinese porcelain into Europe astounded craftsmen who saw them, for they were utterly unable to imitate this superb, translucent and crystalline material. Still, it stimulated attempts at imitation, and the sixteenth and seventeenth centuries witnessed a great improvement in the quality of European pottery glazes, so that with the opaque white tin glaze of 'Delft ware' they succeeded in manufacturing both attractive and functional commodities. The process was established in England by the mid-seventeenth century, in London at Chelsea and in other parts of the country including Derby, Worcester, and Bristol. It took the organizational genius of Josiah Wedgwood, however, in the second half of the eighteenth century, to convert what was still a small semi-domestic process into a substantial industry; he exploited local sources of raw material and fuel, financed canal construction in order to improve his transport conditions, and, above all, built his factory on a larger scale and with more thought to the utilization of skill and resources than any previous pottery manufacturer. An important part of his achievement was that of establishing a reputation for high-quality products and decoration at one end of the price scale while also succeeding in turning out in bulk mugs and plates for the growing mass market of industrial Britain. The fact that Wedgwood's neighbours were led to copy his methods caused the district of north Staffordshire around Stoke-on-Trent to acquire the nickname it has retained ever since – 'the Potteries'.

Meanwhile, as Wedgwood was building up his pottery factory of 'Etruria' (so named from the imitation Etruscan style adopted for his quality wares) at Hanley, the Chinese secret of porcelain manufacture was being broken by William Cookworthy, a Quaker doctor in Plymouth. In 1768 Cookworthy discovered that a paste composed of the feldspathic material kaolin in the form of 'china clay' and 'china stone', produced by the degeneration of granite and therefore occurring in association with the granite masses of Cornwall and Devon, could withstand the exceptionally high temperature required to obtain the chemical fusion of the ingredients which is characteristic of porcelain. The temperature necessary is in the region of 1,350° C., compared with the 1,150° C. at which high-quality 'stoneware' was customarily fired, or the even lower temperatures for cruder types of pottery. The search for somebody with the industrial resources to convert this discovery into a commercial proposition led within ten years to the beginning of porcelain manufacture in Staffordshire, where it has been made ever since alongside the many other ceramic products.

The industrial archaeology of the pottery industry stretches from the extraction and preparation of the raw materials, through the various manufacturing processes, to the finished articles, although as the latter attract the attention of the fine-art collector and antique dealer they may reasonably be omitted from treatment here. The major extractive process supplying the industry is that of china clay production. For the geological reasons already mentioned, this is confined in Britain to the neighbourhood of the granite masses of Cornwall and Devon. In fact, the extraction of china clay has been heavily concentrated in a district within ten miles of St Austell. There are isolated pockets of kaolin worked on Bodmin Moor and elsewhere in the region, but the St Austell district is by far the most important. The extraction process has consisted traditionally of excavating deep quarries from which the white clay is washed by powerful jets of water, being later recovered in settling basins and then dried and prepared in whatever form it is required for the wide variety of uses to which it is put in addition to pottery manufacture (paper-filling, medicinal, etc.). The waste heaps of the china clay pits, consisting of the white sand washed out of the decomposed granite, provide the bizarre landscape of white 'volcanoes' which characterize this part of Cornwall; and another even less welcome by-product of the industry is the discoloration of the streams, which in some places flow down to the sea like milk. The operation of pumps for the china clay pits was an important function performed for many years by hundreds of Cornish steam engines, all of which have now been replaced by modern engines. Many fascinating features of the industry have been preserved and displayed in the Wheal Martin Museum, a few miles north of St Austell. The china clay industry carries on a thriving export trade, keeping the small harbours at Fowey and Par very busy dealing with the ships which convey the products all over the world.[5]

Although Staffordshire came to depend upon china clay for its better-quality ceramic products, it had originally used local clays of inferior grade, and some such clays are still being worked in various parts of the country such as Poole, particularly for small local potteries producing wares distinctive of their neighbour hood or of an individual craftsman, although even these frequently purchase clay from outside their own region. The manufacture of pottery, however, involves many other materials, depending on the nature and quality of the wares being produced. 'Bone china', for instance, contains a proportion of ground animal bones; and ground flint is a material which has often been employed to stiffen pottery pastes. Such flint was customarily prepared in special mills, using water wheels to drive edge-grinders, and although most of these mills have now disappeared a handsome specimen has been preserved through the initiative of local industrialists at Cheddleton in Staffordshire.

The actual manufacturing process of pottery has created the outstanding visual feature of the industry – the beehive kiln. This is in effect a large oven in which the clay products can be baked at a controlled temperature. Until comparatively recently there were hundreds of these kilns in the north Staffordshire pottery district, all coal-fired and consequently discharging thick smoke periodically. The kilns were made in many varieties of shapes and sizes, but there was little development in their function for a hundred and fifty years. Since the Second World War, however, gas-fired continuous kilns have been installed throughout the country. These keep the clay products moving horizontally, stacked on a conveyor belt, through a kiln which is maintained at a constant temperature so that the wares are subject to exactly the right amount of heat as they pass through it.

14. Staffordshire pottery kilns.

The great virtue of this process is its continuous flow, in contrast with the batch production of the traditional kiln, and it has now been so generally adopted that there has been a terrible carnage of the obsolete beehive kilns. The recording of these, where they remain, is an urgent matter for industrial archaeologists. In at least one case, the Gladstone Pottery in Stoke-on-Trent, a complete unit has been preserved as a tribute to this significant industrial process.

Glass

At first sight, the brick cones in which glass was manufactured from the sixteenth to the nineteenth century resemble traditional pottery kilns. In operation, however, they are quite different, being essentially a convenient way of arranging a large open working area around a central furnace, rather than an enlarged oven like a pottery kiln. Normally a glass cone was larger than a pottery kiln, with a chimney emerging at its apex. There were also larger apertures around the base to provide entrances into the working area of what was, in effect, the glass factory. Knowledge of glass processing is at least as old as early Egyptian civilization, but it remained a very small-scale process until the sixteenth century, by which time the growing urban demand for window glass, bottles, and glass table-ware led to an expansion of the industry and a growth in the units of production. Glass is made by fusing silica (sand) with soda (and other ingredients, depending on the type of glass being produced) at a high temperature, and by pouring, moulding, or 'blowing' the viscous material into the shape required; it may then be finished by cutting or polishing depending on the use intended. 'Blowing' consists of extracting a globule of molten glass from the furnace on the end of a hollow rod or 'blowing iron' through which the craftsman blows in order to produce a bubble, which he can then shape by spinning the rod or flattening it with a wooden bat, eventually cutting the near-solid article from the end. Alternatively, he can blow a large bubble and then slit it and open it out in order to make flat pieces of glass, reheating it to keep it workable in one of the annealing hearths built into the outer wall of the glass cone, which allow the glass-ware to be cooled slowly in order to prevent it becoming brittle.

Many qualities of glass could be produced, and great trouble had to be taken with the raw materials in order to make the best

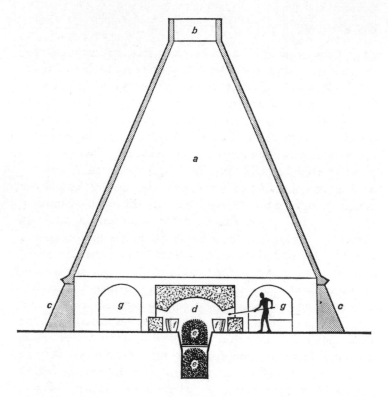

15. Simplified cross-section of an English glass cone. *a* = the cone; *b* = the chimney at the apex; *c* = entrances through arches in the side; *d* = the furnace; *e* = flues to the furnace; *f* = the glass pots holding molten glass; *g* = annealing hearths set in the sides of the cone, with subsidiary heating.

glass-ware. Small metallic additions to the molten glass could produce striking colour effects, and these were used to advantage by the glass manufacturers. Jacobs of Bristol, for example, made superb blue table glass in the seventeenth century, specimens of which are now prized museum pieces. But for the most part, quantity was more important than quality, and most of the glass produced was manufactured in bulk for windows and bottles, with little thought given to clarity, so that the normal material was a sort of cloudy green. The main raw materials of glass manufacture were fairly widely available, so that the major locational factor tended to be proximity to a market, which meant a large urban centre. Most towns of any substance could thus possess a glass cone in the early nineteenth century, and some had quite a cluster of them, but as the century advanced economies of scale began to operate which gave an increasing advantage to the towns of south Lancashire and Cheshire with their proximity to the heavy chemical complex of that region; St Helens in particular emerged as the major centre of glass manufacture in the country. Pilkingtons, the local firm, has continued to expand on this site in the twentieth century, incorporating many novel features such as the 'float glass' process for making large sheets of glass by pouring it upon the surface of molten tin. The firm now occupies large new premises, which contain a fine museum collection devoted to glass technology.

Much of the history of the small local glass manufacturers before the nineteenth century remains obscure, but the most interesting industrial archaeology of the glass industry concerns the glass cones. Only four or five of these stand in Britain in anything like their original form, although a number of substantial fragments survive. One of the most complete is that at Catcliffe, between Sheffield and Rotherham, but others survive at Newcastle, Stourbridge, and Alloa in Scotland. The base of a large cone has been preserved in Bristol, and several other fragments may yet be discovered in other parts of the country.[6]

Paper

Another important chemical process which developed before the Industrial Revolution was the manufacture of paper. This material, produced by pulverizing cellulosic ingredients into a pulp and then pouring the thick liquid into sieves ('moulds') which retained the fibre in the required shape from which it could be pressed and dried, was known in China long before the procedure for manufacturing it was devised in the West. Clerks of the Middle Ages had traditionally used parchment or vellum, carefully prepared from animal skins, but by the close of this period the increasing demand for books and the invention of printing with movable type had so stimulated experiments with new materials that a good-quality paper made from rag pulp had been developed. For long this remained a small-scale manufacturing process, with each operator or his family collecting their own rags, producing their own pulp in a shredding machine known as a 'Hollander', indicating its Dutch origin, and preparing each sheet of paper by hand. The sheets would be stacked between strips of felt and put in a press to extract as much water as possible, and then hung to dry in an airy loft or drying shed.

Paper-making remained an essentially simple craft process until the nineteenth century, when ever-increasing demand led to a mechanical revolution in paper processing, and, in particular, the development of machines which could manufacture paper in a continuous roll instead of individual sheets. This revolution is associated with the inventions of Dickinson and Fourdrinier, who created machines which could make continuously paper or board respectively. The principle of both machines was to pour the pulp on to a continuously moving belt or drum, so that the cellulose web could form and then be dried in a single movement. In modern applications of this principle, such as the *Inverform* machine developed at the St Anne's Board Mill in Bristol, the board (consisting of several layers from different types of pulp) can be manufactured with astonishing speed. Meanwhile, the growing consumption of pulp for paper has far outstripped the supply of rags which kept the early paper-makers in business. Instead, other sources of cellulose have been used, of which by far the most important has been wood pulp, giving a new significance to the lumber industries of Canada and Scandinavia, and also to those of Scotland, where the establishment of a large

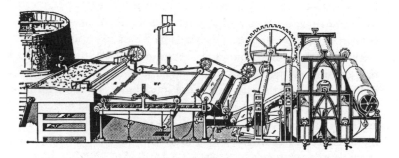

16. Paper-making machine, as illustrated in Tomlinson's *Cyclopaedia* of 1853. Pulp (*left*) is poured on to a moving web (*centre*), from which it is drawn as a continuous sheet and dried on the rollers (*right*).

modern wood-pulp mill near Fort William has recently demonstrated the economic value of this raw material. Another modern development has been the improvement in the quality of paper by additives to provide 'filling' and gloss, this being one of the main uses of china clay in industry today.

As with the pottery and glass industries, the locational factors in the early paper industry were not very strong except for the need to be relatively close to the large urban markets. However, again like these other traditional chemical processes, paper-making has been affected by economies of scale which have led to its concentration in a few large units, which do not as yet offer much scope for industrial archaeology. More rewarding are those areas where the industry flourished until comparatively recently. One necessity of paper-making was a good supply of clean water, so that the industry tended to grow near pure springs and streams on the periphery of the main centres of population concentration, particularly in such places as the Home Counties and north Somerset. Productive units were generally small, although some hand–made–paper firms grew into well established family businesses; and a few have survived because they have specialized in distinctive types of paper (paper for money, Bible paper, etc.). The hand–made–paper mill of Hodgkinsons at Wookey Hole in Somerset has been acquired by Madame Tussaud's and made into an excellent working museum. But most have not survived, and the location of these early paper mills is a useful exercise for industrial archaeologists, with the possibility of discovering valuable information about local specializations and practices, and sometimes surviving machinery. The rag mill at Slaughterford in Wiltshire, for example, was at work only a few years ago and is now a ruin, although its breast-shot water wheel is still intact.[7]

Gunpowder

As in so many other respects, Chinese technology achieved a 'first' with the invention of gunpowder; it was used in China for fireworks although not systematically, it seems, for military applications. The formula was discovered independently by Friar Roger Bacon in the mid-thirteenth century, and its military significance was quickly appreciated in Western civilization. By the sixteenth century, therefore, there was already a considerable gunpowder industry, and it grew in size and importance during subsequent centuries, until more powerful explosives with an organic chemical basis were developed in the second half of the nineteenth century. Gunpowder is a chemical mixture of three ingredients: sulphur, saltpetre (potassium nitrate) and carbon.

The main sources of sulphur in Western Europe were the volcanic deposits of Sicily, in which a considerable trade developed. Saltpetre was recovered by a noxious process of boiling the organic waste material from stables and latrines, until mineral sources of nitrate became available from South America. Carbon was obtained from charcoal, and thus caused less anxiety than the other ingredients to protective governments which placed a high premium on national self-sufficiency in essential commodities. The manufacture of gunpowder consists of mixing the ingredients in the correct proportions, and this is a process which involves some risk as a spark could cause a premature explosion. The results were that gunpowder manufacture was usually carried out in fairly remote places, in order to minimize any danger, and that water power was used wherever possible for carrying out the grinding necessary to consolidate the explosive mixture. This was normally done by edge-runners moving in a circular trough, so that the process could be readily adapted to a water wheel.

When the du Pont family moved to the USA as a result of the French Revolution, they established a flourishing gunpowder (or 'black powder', as they called it) industry on the banks of the River Brandywine in Delaware. Here they built a row of small grinding houses, some of them arranged in pairs with a shared water wheel in between them. Although they were firmly built in masonry on three sides, the fourth side and the sloping roof, directed towards the river, were of flimsy construction, thus minimizing the effects of a possible explosion. Many of these buildings have been preserved on the site of the Hagley Museum, near Wilmington, comprising a fascinating industrial monument. Britain has not been as fortunate with its relics of the gunpowder industry. In addition to natural wastage, some gunpowder mills were deliberately destroyed when they stopped work because it was believed that impregnation of the walls by gunpowder constituted a permanent explosion hazard: the mill at Elterwater in the Lake District is a good example of this, with little surviving on the site. At Faversham in Kent, however, a detailed restoration of one of the largest mills in the country is now taking place.[8]

Heavy Chemicals

All the chemical processes considered so far in this chapter were in existence before the Industrial Revolution, and were modified, but not transformed out of all recognition, by the subsequent acceleration in the forces of industrialization. But in some respects the chemical industry, as a large-scale integrated organization, was created by the Industrial Revolution, and particularly by the discovery of ways of bulk-producing acids and alkalis. These materials had previously been comparatively rare and thus unavailable for large-quantity commercial uses, although substantial amounts of soda (chemically, sodium carbonate) were produced from vegetable sources – wood ash, 'barilla' (from a Mediterranean shrub), and 'kelp' (calcined seaweed). Kelp burning was still practised in the Hebrides and the Isles of Scilly in the nineteenth century, but by that time new sources of supply were becoming available and these earlier processes became victims of the revolution in chemical technology, although in South Uist the kelp burning lingered into the twentieth century as a source of iodine.[9]

The origin of this chemical revolution lay in a combination of elements which occurred in the second half of the eighteenth century. In the first place, the rapid expansion of the textile industry (especially cotton manufacture) in this period was creating an unprecedented demand for bleaching materials, which threatened to become a more intractable 'bottleneck' in production than any of the mechanical problems then being tackled in carding, spinning, weaving, and printing. The traditional bleaches – sunshine, rain, and so on – were too long-acting and inefficient for the expanding cotton industry, and this stimulated experiments with acid bleaches. Secondly, the methods of manufacturing oil of vitriol (sulphuric acid) were vastly improved in the mid-eighteenth century, first by Joshua Ward and then by John Roebuck, as a result of which the latter was able to produce the acid cheaply and in bulk for the first time, and it was then used in the manufacture of chlorine bleaches culminating in 1799 with Charles Tennant's manufacture of a successful bleaching powder (calcium hypochlorite or slaked lime saturated with chlorine). This so much speeded up the bleaching process that cotton goods were being bleached within a week by the 1830s. Thirdly, the increased supply of sulphuric acid provided the French chemist Nicolas Leblanc with the vital material for the process which came to bear his name for producing soda on a large scale. The other raw materials for the Leblanc process were common salt, limestone, and coal, which were readily available in Britain. But the French revolutionary wars delayed the introduction of the process on a commercial scale until the 1820s, when it was established in south Lancashire by James Muspratt and Josiah Gamble. It expanded steadily thereafter, until it was replaced by the more efficient ammonia-soda ('Solvay') process towards the end of the century.

These new processes for the bulk-production of acids and alkalis have become known as the 'heavy' chemical industry, partly because of the great quantity of the materials produced and also because they have become the basic factors in the organization of the modern industry. Traditional chemical processes like soap- and glass-making have been drawn towards the points at which these materials have been produced: the concentration of soap production at Warrington and Port Sunlight, and of glass-making at St Helens, illustrate this trend. As a result of this movement, there are now three major districts of chemical production (excluding, for the moment, organic and petrochemicals), in Merseyside, Clydeside, and Tyneside respectively. The Merseyside district is comprised largely within the triangle formed by St Helens, Warrington, and Widnes. Much of the desolation wrought on the landscape by the Leblanc process, and particularly the problem of getting rid of the noxious black waste material (known as 'galligu'), has been subdued by weathering, although some of the scars remain. The Clydeside district is associated especially with Tennant's highly successful bleaching powder. His St Rollox factory in Glasgow (Springburn) was at one time the largest chemical works in the world and boasted the largest chimney also, although this has now been felled and the works closed. High chimneys are even now frequently clues to the existence of chemical processes, as their height helps to dispel any unpleasant waste gases over a wide area and thus attenuates their impact. Tyneside, between Newcastle and North Shields, is the third area with a concentration of chemical processes, enjoying the convenience of local coal supplies and other raw materials. This became the most important centre of British chemical manufacture in the first half of the nineteenth century, specializing in the preparation of soda crystals and bicarbonate of soda. But by the second half of the century, the Merseyside district had displaced Tyneside from this pre-eminence.

Other materials became closely associated with the heavy chemical industry – ammonia, nitric acid, artificial fertilizers, caustic soda, and suchlike – and in the second half of the nineteenth century the development of the organic chemical industry, based upon the analysis of coal-derivatives and other carbon materials, was drawn towards the same centres. This latter development was closely associated with the application of scientific theory to industrial practice, and there is, indeed, a close correlation between the emergence of the modern chemical industry and the organization of scientific and technological education. The leading chemical scholars in the eighteenth century had been men with a practical turn of mind: one has only to look at the careers and personal associations of men like Roebuck, Priestley, Black, and Tennant to appreciate this point. Leblanc, also, was one of the group of distinguished French chemists around Berthollet and Lavoisier, although it must be admitted that Berthollet, who did so much to make possible the development of chlorine bleaches, was not interested in the practical application of his work. In the nineteenth century, the lead in chemical scholarship passed to Germany, where von Liebig and others undertook the systematic study of organic chemistry. It was Prince Albert's influence which persuaded von Hofmann, another German scholar, to take on the leadership of the Royal College of Chemistry, and it was a pupil of this college, W. H. Perkin, who made in 1857 the first significant application of organic chemistry by producing a synthetic dye. This was the aniline-based dye 'mauve', which quickly proved itself to be better than any equivalent natural dye. It was followed by a host of other synthetic dyes, most of them being discovered and developed in Germany, where the large investment in scientific education began to pay handsome industrial dividends. By the outbreak of the First World War, Germany had established a commanding lead in the production of dye stuffs, high explosives, pharmaceutics, and other important materials. The war has been described as 'a chemists' war',[10] with the Western powers being obliged to develop their neglected chemical industries under emergency conditions. The fact that they managed to do so reflects in part the success of long-delayed but nevertheless effective improvements in scientific and technological education, which had taken place in Britain after the Education Act of 1870 had laid a foundation of national primary education.

In addition to dye stuffs (from coal tar) and high explosives (from compounds of nitric acid and cellulosic material), the organic chemical industry produced two other materials in the second half of the nineteenth century which became of great industrial significance. These were plastics and artificial fibres. Many ways were found of producing both these, so that by the

end of the century materials like celluloid (from camphor and
cellulose nitrate) and rayon (an artificial silk from acetic acid and
nitrocellulose) were already being widely used. By that time, also,
an enormously rich source of raw materials for synthetic chemistry FRACTIO
was already being exploited by the distillation and ~~fraction~~ of - NATIO
crude oil into its many components. The petro-chemical industry
has roots in antiquity, when medicinal preparations were made
from bitumen where this was available as a surface deposit. Not
until the spectacular success of boring techniques in tapping
subterranean reservoirs of crude oil, however, did the modern
large-scale industry emerge. The first successful bore was made in
1859, but the American Civil War delayed exploitation on a large
scale. The demand of the internal combustion engine for some
light, volatile, transportable fuel, converted this growing industry
into one of the greatest success stories of the twentieth century, for
it led to a world-wide search for oil supplies and the dramatic
impact of the automobile and the aeroplane on the landscape and
cities of the modern world. The somewhat less dramatic but still
spectacular effects of this petro-chemical revolution have been
the successes in developing new materials out of oil-derivatives.
These include many new plastics, fibres, insecticides, pharmaceutics, and fertilizers.

Until recently, with the massive investment in the exploitation
of North Sea resources, not much oil has been found in Britain,
although some has been produced in Nottinghamshire since the
late 1930s and assumed significance during the Second World
War. The 'grasshopper' pumps of this extractive industry can
still be seen in fields near Newark. Oil has also been extracted
from oil-shales in Scotland, having begun at Bathgate in West
Lothian in 1851 with James Young's patent for the process, and
mounds of waste ('bing') are plentiful. A single grasshopper
pump is still at work at Kimmeridge in Dorset, extracting oil from
the shale beds which outcrop on the coast at that point. Also,
large deposits of natural gas are currently being explored and

1. Cornish engine house, Tregurtha Down, Cornwall. This derelict building is part of extensive remains of an important tin-mine, now owned by the National Trust.

2. (above left) Engine house, Beamish Colliery, Co. Durham. One of the few surviving vertical steam engine houses, which were once a distinctive feature of Durham collieries.

3. Horizontal steam winding engine, at Washington Colliery, Co. Durham.

4. (above right) The Levant Mine, Cornwall. Ruins of the tin-mine on the clifftops near Land's End.

5. Parys Mountain, Anglesey. Excavations abandoned after the extraction of copper.

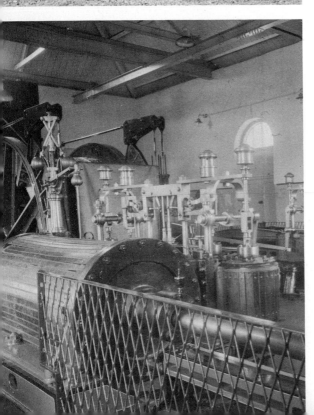

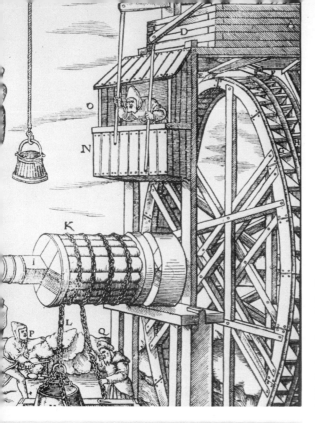

6. (left) Mine winding engine, by Agricola, 1555. One of the series of famous wood-cuts illustrating the processes of mining. It shows a reversible water wheel.

7. Water-pressure pumping engine. An unusual type of engine preserved at Leadhills, Lanarkshire.

8. (right) Annealing oven, Kelston Brassworks, Bath. One of two such ovens surviving on this site, used for re-heating the brass to keep it soft while being worked.

9. Condenser flues at Charterhouse on Mendip, Somerset. Their object was to recover lead from the furnace gases by condensation on the walls of the masonry passages.

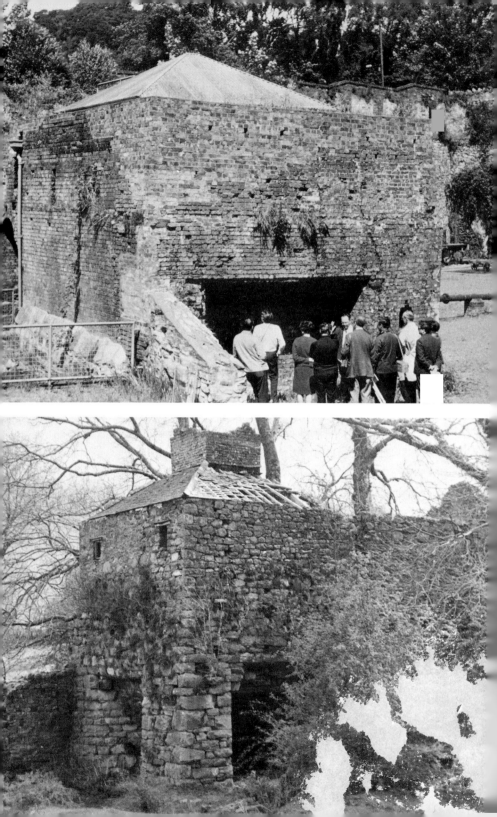

10. (above left) Coalbrookdale furnace. This is the blast furnace where Abraham Darby first smelted iron ore with coke in 1709.

11. Bonawe furnace. An eighteenth-century charcoal-burning blast furnace in the Highlands of Scotland before restoration in 1970.

12. (above right) The Iron Bridge, Telford, Shropshire. The parts for this dramatic bridge were cast at Coalbrookdale and erected in 1779. It was the first cast-iron bridge in the world, and is undergoing extensive conservation work.

13. 'Missionary' cooking-pot. Traditional cast-iron specimen made in Coalbrookdale.

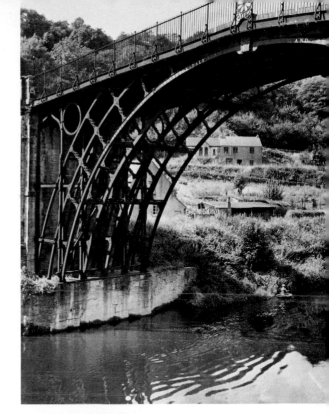

14. (above left) Triphammer and anvil, preserved at Abbeydale industrial hamlet, Sheffield.

15. Hamsterley cementation furnace. An early steel-making site in Co. Durham.

16. (above right) Forge hammer. A water-powered hammer at Wortley Forge, Yorkshire.

17. Crucible furnaces. A battery of crucible furnaces for making high-quality steel at Abbeydale. Each furnace holds one crucible.

18. (left) Pottery kilns. A group of bottle kilns, once a typical feature of the North Staffordshire landscape.

19. (above right) 'An English Glass Works', as illustrated in Diderot's *Encyclopaedia* in the eighteenth century.

20. Glass cone, Catcliffe. One of the handful of surviving glass cones in the country, this has been carefully preserved in the middle of a new housing development in South Yorkshire.

21. (above) Paper mill. Part of the mill at Wookey Hole, Somerset, now a paper-making museum.

22. Hand-made paper. A seventeenth-century engraving showing the activities of the 'vat man', 'coucher', and 'lay man' respectively. Note the stamping mill in the background, for preparing the fibrous material.

23. (above) Brewery. A small town brewery at Tetbury in Gloucestershire, now a laundry.

24. Chemical factory. Disused acid plant at Butler's Tar Works, Bristol.

25. (above left) China clay. Typical landscape of the china clay extraction industry at Greensplat near St Austell, Cornwall.

26. Cheddleton flint mill. Interior of the North Mill as restored to the condition of about 1815. The crushing pan is on the left.

27. (above right) Albert Mill, Keynsham, Avon. Logwood dyes were last manufactured in Britain at this water-powered mill.

28. Edge-runners, Albert Mill. These were used to crush the powdered logwood at Keynsham.

29. (above) New Lanark. A drawing of the famous model factory and community made for a Russian publication early in the nineteenth century.

30. Marshall's flax mill, Leeds. This remarkable Egyptian-style mill was erected in the 1840s.

31. (above) Salt's Mill, Saltaire. This large mill was erected to work alpacca wool by Sir Titus Salt, and is the basis for his model town of Saltaire, Yorkshire.

32. Dunkirk Mill. One of the finest of the surviving woollen mills near Stroud, Gloucestershire.

33. (above) Masson Mill, Cromford. The original part of this mill is the north end, on the left, and was built in 1783. The date on the buildings refers to Arkwright's first mill at Cromford.

34. Bage's Mill, Shrewsbury. The oldest surviving fireproof mill was built by Charles Bage as a flax mill in 1797. It is now used as a malting.

35. (right) Stanley Mill, Stroud. An outstanding specimen of cast-iron fireproof mill construction, at King's Stanley near Stroud, Gloucestershire.

36. (left) Machine tools. A Whitworth vertical slotting machine of 1884, belt driven from a steam engine preserved in the Port of Bristol Authority Workshops.

37. (above right) Workers' housing, Cromford. Arkwright built these houses for his workers in the local mills. They are probably the oldest surviving group built specifically by an industrialist for this purpose.

38. Artisan dwellings, Sheffield. A typical terrace of houses built for workers in the steel industry in Brightside, Sheffield. Each group of eight houses shares a yard at the rear, approached through a tunnel.

39. (above left) Bath Stone. Large blocks of stone extracted from a stone-mine at Box, near Bath. The stone is stacked like this to allow it to harden by weathering.

40. Brick kilns. A battery of disused Hoffman-type kilns at Shortwood, near Bristol.

41. (above right) Portland Stone. One of many small loading bays quarried in the natural stone on Portland Bill.

42. Marble quarry. The disused quarry on Iona, with gas engine, producer plant, and marble-cutting machinery surviving.

43. (above left) Industrial monument. Cast-iron column erected to commemorate the life and work of John Wilkinson, the eighteenth-century ironmaster, near Grange-over-Sands.

44. Applied Science. Figure of 'Science' holding a centrifugal governor, on Holborn Viaduct, London.

SCIENCE

exploited off the eastern coasts of Britain. Despite the general deficiency of the raw material in Britain, however, the petro-chemical industry has made a substantial impression on the landscape of such places as Tees-side and Severnside, where large tankers are able to discharge their cargoes of crude oil into storage tanks to await treatment and fraction into the many valuable materials which can be derived from it. The industry is not one which is visually attractive, and there is as yet little about it to qualify for industrial archaeological attention, although it should be observed that the increasing rate of obsolescence in modern industry is creating a serious problem in ensuring adequate recording and preservation of equipment which is still 'new' by any traditional standards. The early nylon-extrusion machines, for example, like early electronic computers, require sympathetic attention and selective preservation.

The lack of industrial archaeological interest in the petro-chemical industry is an extension of an observation which applies generally to the whole heavy chemical industry as it has developed since the middle of the eighteenth century. Unlike the traditional chemical processes which we considered at the beginning of this chapter, and which provide much to keep the industrial archae-ologists busy, it must be admitted that the processes for manu-facturing acids and alkalis, plastics and fertilizers, dye stuffs and explosives, have not been rich in distinguished industrial monu-ments. Apart from a few gargantuan chimneys, the heavy chemical industry is remembered most for its dismal effects on the land-scape – its discoloration of the streams and its pollution of the atmosphere – even though its enormous commercial value is recognized. In part, the problem of the heavy chemical industry is that it is a process industry in which the processes themselves use equipment of little distinction. For example the lead vessels in which Roebuck first made sulphuric acid on a commercial scale are of little intrinsic interest – unlike an original machine or building which might show significant design details – so that they hardly justify preservation. Most chemical processes are of this nature, being performed with the minimum of machinery (or with machinery which is standard equipment such as the most convenient source of power) and in buildings which are usually at best nondescript and at worst a mess of untidy temporary sheds, so that it is an industry of little visual excitement or archaeological interest.

A good example of this difficulty is the site of the large alkali factory at Netham in Bristol. This flourished in the nineteenth century, before the logistics of economy caused the concentration of the industry in those areas which have already been described. All that remained at Netham was a motley collection of brick-walled sheds without any merit of their own or contents of significance, and much of the site has now been cleared as a store. Yet in its day, like chemical factories elsewhere, this was an establishment of great industrial and commercial importance. The lesson of this observation is that industrial archaeology is not necessarily a good guide to the importance of obsolete industries. The unusual, the distinguished, and the bizarre have a better survival quality than the plain and unadorned. Thus an industry such as that which has produced the essential acids, alkalis, and other vital materials for modern civilization, where the major novelties have been in the processes rather than in equipment and buildings, has created few industrial monuments of any distinction. Industrial archaeologists must be careful to allow for this uneven 'weighting' of industrial monuments when they attempt to assess the significance of an industry.

8. Building, Agriculture, and Rural Crafts

The three industrial groups surveyed in this chapter are alike in that they are all of fundamental importance to the emergence of civilized social life and are thus of great antiquity. In other respects, however, they are very different, and it must be admitted that they do not form a single industrial category such as those reviewed in previous chapters. The grouping is mainly a convenience to accommodate two subjects – agriculture and rural crafts – which deserve some attention from industrial archaeologists but do not warrant full chapters. This accounts for the uneven divisions of this chapter, most of which is devoted to the building industry, because this is one which can be particularly rewarding to the student of industrial remains.

Building

From the point of view of the industrial archaeologist, the most significant aspect of the building industry is that concerned with the preparation of the raw materials – wood, stone, brick, metal, and glass – although the buildings themselves may frequently provide valuable clues regarding these preparatory processes, and, as we shall see, a few prominent types of building have become industrial monuments in their own right. For all the relative permanence of its results, the building industry itself is a highly transitory business, concerned with the organization of particular sorts of labour force and the marshalling of the necessary building materials at a particular site, and it will not concern us here. We will, rather, survey the industry according to the material used in it.[1]

Wood

It is reasonable to suppose that the earliest building material used systematically by man in Western Europe was wood, and certainly wood has performed a function of continuing importance in the building industry even though it is now rarely used as a major structural component in large buildings. Many timber-frame buildings survive in Britain, mostly dating from the sixteenth and seventeenth centuries, and it is useful to be able to recognize them. The simplest and generally the oldest form is the 'cruck' construction, the cross-section of which consists of two massive timber beams so that the insertion of an upper floor makes a shape like a capital 'A'. This can be extended length-wise by the addition of any number of these A-frames, but it cannot be extended upwards or sideways. Hence the superior quality of the 'box-frame' construction, where fresh box-frames of timber beams can be added to the original cube in almost any direction. The 'box-frame' with a variety of cross-members, lath and daub infilling, and a steeply sloping timber-framed roof on the top storey, became widely used for English domestic architecture, with specimens surviving from most parts of the country, but most especially from those parts where timber was abundant and local stone either deficient or unsuitable for building, such as Essex, Warwickshire, Suffolk and Cheshire. Sometimes timber-frame buildings have been covered in plaster or some other coating material in order to protect them or make them more weatherproof. Some villages, however, such as Lavenham in Suffolk, preserve a distinguished collection of buildings in which the timbering is both elegant and well maintained. It should be remembered that, despite its relative decline in importance, wood has remained a vital building material, being

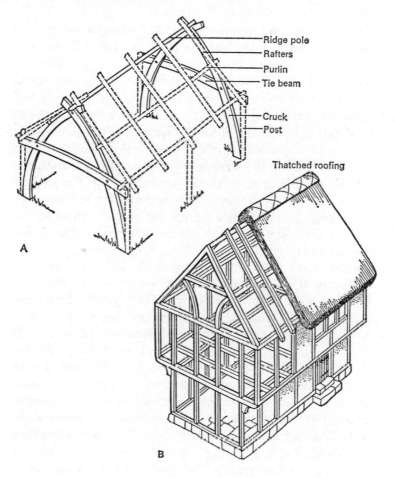

17. Types of wooden-frame buildings. (A) Cruck construction; (B) box-frame construction.

still virtually indispensable for roofing and flooring in most domestic buildings.

Stone

Next to wood, the commonest building material and the one which best displays the 'spirit of place' is stone. The fact that British building varies so widely from district to district is determined mainly by the availability of local stone. Good building stone has to be strong in order to carry weight and resist the effects of atmospheric erosion, but it should not be so hard that it is difficult to work. The best building stones are thus usually those of median age, which is to say that they come from the Jurassic and Carboniferous series of rocks which run roughly south-west to north-east across England. The younger rocks of the south-east rarely produce material strong enough to make good building stone (except for flint, which is an extremely hard form of silica found in nodules or pebbles within the chalk strata, and used for building by being set in a matrix of cement in the form known as 'clunch'); and the older rocks of Cornwall, Wales, north-west England, and Scotland are often too hard to be conveniently worked. Within the median belt of the best building stones, some are limestones (i.e. they have a high content of calcium carbonate derived from shells and other primitive sea-life forms) and others are sandstones (i.e. they consist predominantly of grains of quartz bonded in a matrix which is usually but not invariably of siliceous origin). The best of all the building stones are those which are in strata of sufficient thickness and homogeneity to permit them to be quarried or mined in large lumps and which are then capable of being worked freely in all directions, which is to say that they are 'freestones'. The outstanding British stones to possess these qualities come from the Jurassic limestone series of 'oolites', such as that from the Cotswold quarries, the stone-

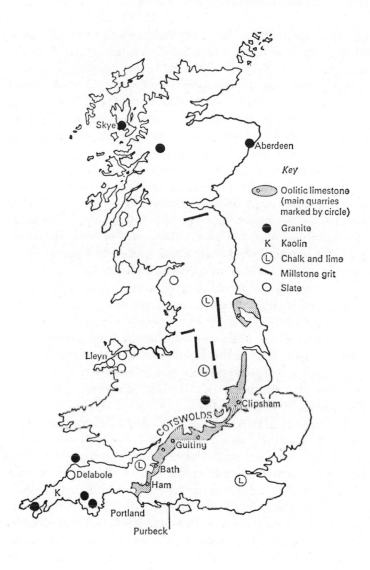

Key

Oolitic limestone
(main quarries
marked by circle)

● Granite

K Kaolin

Ⓛ Chalk and lime

▬ Millstone grit

○ Slate

Skye

Aberdeen

Lleyn

Clipsham

COTSWOLDS

Guiting

Delabole

Bath

K

Ham

Portland

Purbeck

18. Chief building stones and quarries.

mines in the neighbourhood of Bath, and the splendid near-white stone of Portland which Sir Christopher Wren chose for his rebuilding of St Paul's Cathedral in the seventeenth century, taking the trouble of personally selecting the blocks of stone from the quarries then being opened up on the 'island'. But other limestones such as the blue lias of Somerset and the magnesian limestone of Nottinghamshire provide excellent local stone, and the Carboniferous sandstones such as millstone grit (extensively used in Edinburgh and other northern cities) and Pennant sandstone (from the Bristol region) have found similar applications. By and large, sandstones have been found more suitable for the major buildings of industrial cities than limestones because they are chemically inert, whereas limestones are liable to react with the acidic fumes of an industrial environment. The discoloration produced by smoke is also more noticeable on the honey-coloured Bath stone and white Portland than it is on sandstone, although Portland stone discolours unevenly, with the faces receiving most rain-washing usually retaining their white colour while the more shielded parts turn black. The widespread use of this stone in London demonstrates that such selective discoloration need not be unattractive, and Portland stone has certainly proved itself to be a most suitable stone for London.

The weight and bulk of stone has made it a difficult commodity to transport, so that as a general rule it has been used locally. Sufficient stone for a particular building or group of buildings has been quarried as near to the site as convenient deposits could be found, and it is potentially a useful industrial archaeological exercise to locate such quarries in relation to the buildings for which they supplied the material. It is this localization of building stone which makes for the preservation of the 'spirit of place' already mentioned: it would be difficult to imagine anything more harmonious with the warm and gentle Cotswold uplands than a village such as Bibury or Burford in the local stone, or anything more congruous with a bleak Pennine moorland than a squat farmstead roofed and flanked in millstone grit. Only a comparatively few stones have been exploited on a large scale as industrial propositions. These have either been mined, like the Bath stone which has been removed in large quantities from beneath the hills around Bath, or, more normally, quarried, like the Portland stone which has been worked continuously now for three hundred years and is still producing excellent stone. Curiously, this is one of the few stones for which there has been virtually no local demand. Its greatest advantage in the seventeenth century was its accessibility from the sea, making its transport to London a feasible exercise. Whether it is mined or quarried, however, the cutting of stone requires care and skill. Explosives are too wasteful of valuable stone to be generally used, blocks being normally broken from the parent rock and then split by the careful insertion of wedges. One of the advantages of the Jurassic limestones is that they are fairly soft to work, but harden up on exposure to the weather. The weathering of newly cut limestone is an important part of its preparation, and great care has to be taken about it. The extent of the underground workings such as the Ralph Allen stone-mines at Combe Down to the south of Bath was considerable, but it is now virtually impossible to determine the precise extent because of roof falls. The open quarries of Portland offer more scope for a systematic examination. The simple lifting gear, wedges, cutting tools, and transport system in these quarries also provide scope for the industrial archaeologist. It was a special problem of the Bath stone-mines that they occurred at or near the summit of the oolitic limestone hills around Bath, so that the blocks of stone extracted from the mines had to be transported down a steep slope to the river or canal in the valley below. This transport was provided by a number of tramway inclines, of which interesting relics survive.

Certain other rocks have been exploited commercially for

the building industry, such as granite, slate, and marble. Granite is an extremely hard rock which discourages detailed working by the stone mason, although it can take a high polish which makes it suitable for certain decorative purposes. More significant, however, is the great durability of granite, which makes it ideal for such massive engineering works as dams, bridges, lighthouses, and embankments. Granite from Dartmoor was used in 1823–31 for building London Bridge, which has been re-erected block by block in the United States. Penryn (Cornwall) granite was used for Tower Bridge, and granite from Lundy Island for the first section of the Thames Embankment in 1864. Many of the granite quarries worked extensively in the nineteenth century are now derelict, and may profitably be explored by the industrial archaeologist. The Lamorna Cove quarries on the Land's End peninsula, for example, are an interesting site, and the Haytor quarries on Dartmoor show how they tackled their transport problem by the surviving stretches of unique granite-block tramway. Leicestershire also has some features of granite working because of the geological formation of Charnwood Forest, the granite core of which has been extensively quarried; and Aberdeen, as is well known, was built out of a grey local granite which is now practically exhausted.

Slate is another hard and ancient rock. Technically, it is a 'metamorphic' rock: the transformation of shales and other early sedimentary rocks under conditions of great heat and pressure resulted in the occurrence, amongst the ancient rocks of the west and north-west of Britain, of the hard but strongly laminated rock which we know as slate. The laminated structure of slate makes it ideal for splitting into thin sheets as a roofing material, and it is for this use that it has been quarried very extensively in North Wales, the Lake District, and Cornwall. It is also used locally as a building rock, usually – like granite – in a rough-hewn form, and also as a paving material. The most widely used slate is the blue-purple variety quarried in North Wales and transported thence in ready-cut sizes all over the country. There are spectacular quarries, for instance, on the Lleyn peninsula and at various points in Snowdonia, notably around Blaenau Ffestiniog, which is almost surrounded by a remarkable complex of old quarries, few of which are still operating. The Welsh slate industry, indeed, has been afflicted by a change of taste which has made its staple commodity appear unattractive, so that it is undergoing a severe contraction. Other large slate quarries can be found in the Lake District, and at Delabole, near Tintagel, on the north coast of Cornwall. Slate quarries are often worked as a series of steps in order to ensure the systematic extraction of the rock. Some have been so extensive and remote that they have acquired their own transport systems of narrow-gauge railways, of which a number are still at work, while others have been restored by enthusiasts such as those who have put stretches of the Ffestiniog Railway into working order.

Marble, like slate, is a metamorphic rock, caused by the intense heating and crystallization of limestone. There are no large deposits of marble in Britain: the only area to have been exploited is a small quarry on the Island of Iona in the Inner Hebrides, producing a beautiful green-veined stone, but this is now derelict. Some other types of stone, and especially some un-metamorphosed limestones such as the Jurassic limestones of Purbeck, are capable of taking the high polish which makes natural marble so attractive, and they have consequently become known as 'semi-marbles'. Of these by far the most important in Britain is 'Purbeck marble', first discovered near St Aldhelm's Head in Dorset. Like Portland stone, this had the great advantage of sea transport to make it readily available around the coasts of the country. Unlike Portland stone, however, which was not developed commercially until the seventeenth century, Purbeck marble was already being carried to Durham Cathedral by the twelfth century, and it was subsequently used in many of the great Gothic cathedrals of the

Middle Ages. It was almost invariably used for internal decorative features, as it has poor weathering properties.

With the exception of slate, all the types of stone which have been considered here were (and are) transported in rough-hewn blocks to the site where they were to be assembled into a building. Here it was the mason's task to cut them to the required size and shape and to provide any detailed decoration which might be desired. Good-quality freestone would be used as 'ashlar': that is, it would be squared and assembled in level, carefully jointed courses. If the stone was used in irregular sizes and shapes it was known as 'rubble'. The business of cutting and assembling the masonry would constitute a large and intricate organization for any substantial building for as long as the building operation proceeded. Once it was completed, however, all sign of the building process was cleared away and the army of masons, bricklayers, carpenters, plumbers, plasterers, and so on moved on to the next site. Except for the occasional mason's mark which may reward a diligent search on a large masonry structure, this vital stage of the building industry usually disappears without trace. Only the building survives as a monument to this very transitory industry.

Brick and Tile

So far we have considered building in wood and stone. We must now look at another class of building material – manufactured material such as brick and tile. This has become of enormous importance in the modern building industry, and being itself a manufacturing industry it has produced artefacts which are industrial monuments in their own right. Brick has been known in some form or other for many millennia. The first bricks were probably the sun-dried bricks used in Sumeria at the dawn of the first civilizations, although even in these regions they were soon being replaced by fired bricks. Sun-dried bricks are not suitable for the damp climate of North Europe, and it was the Romans who first introduced fired brick to Britain. Roman bricks were normally manufactured in thin 'biscuit' shapes in order to give the inefficient firing technique an opportunity to penetrate the brick, and specimens of Roman brick have survived in many parts of the country. Brick-making languished with the departure of the Romans, and did not revive until the fifteenth century, after which brick became increasingly popular as a building material in the south-east of the country, being used in buildings like Eton College, Hampton Court Palace, Herstmonceux Castle, and some Cambridge colleges. After a vogue at the time of Queen Anne, brick was eclipsed for a while by the switch of taste towards classical models in the late eighteenth century and early nineteenth century, but it came back in a big way from the middle of the nineteenth century with the development of mechanical brick-making, which led to the mass-production of relatively cheap standard bricks.

The great age of brick is thus little more than a hundred years old, and much that it has created in this period has been of doubtful aesthetic quality. As a material for modern industrial building, on the other hand, brick has been invaluable, contributing significantly to the 'functional tradition' of modern industrial buildings. As part of this process, the manufacture of brick (and tile) has become a highly organized industry, and following the general pattern of industrial development over the last hundred years, it has become increasingly concentrated. The economies of large-scale manufacture and the availability of convenient road transport have brought about the growth of large brick firms working in the 'Oxfordshire' clay, running through Oxfordshire and Bedfordshire and thence northwards. The area of the modern industry can be recognized by the crop of chimneys on the landscape and the devastated acres from which the clay has been quarried. But of more significance to the industrial archaeologist are the hundreds of smaller-scale local brick works which have gone out of business in recent decades, frequently leaving intact complete groups of buildings and equipment for his examination. It is an opportunity which should not be missed, as it will be valuable to have a record of all these sites when the developers have moved in, as they inevitably will, and obliterated them.

The three basic processes of brick-making consist of preparing the clay, moulding it into bricks, and baking it. The preparatory

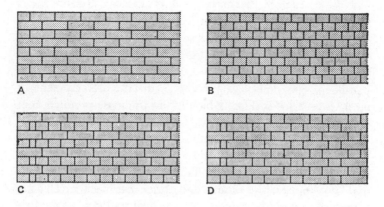

19. Some basic types of brick bonds. (A) Stretcher bond; (B) header bond; (C) English bond; (D) Flemish bond.

process is that of blending clay mixtures to the correct plasticity and firmness. This was traditionally performed by 'treading' the clay, but the 'pug mill' had been an early step towards the mechanization of brick-making. This consisted of a vertical cylinder into which the raw clay was fed at the top, to emerge at the bottom having been pulverized by horizontal blades into a homogeneous dough, the process resembling that of a meat-mincer. The pug mill lent itself to animal power, being driven easily by a horse gin. As part of the mechanization process of the mid-nineteenth century, many pug mills were replaced by steam-powered grinding machines capable of pulverizing less tractable clays than those which could be treated before. The second basic process is that of moulding the bricks. This had remained a hand process, every individual brick being shaped in a wooden mould sometimes called a 'stock', from which the high-quality 'London stock brick' derived its name), until the introduction of mechanical means of pressing the clay into metal moulds in the mid-nineteenth century. Thirdly, the bricks are fired in kilns which developed, like pottery kilns, from methods of 'batch' firing to 'continuous' firing. The invention of the Hoffman kiln in 1858 brought this improvement early to the brick industry, but a careful study of surviving brick kilns will reveal many variations in detail.

The convenient size of a brick has always been determined by what a man might easily handle: it has varied in detail from place to place and from time to time, but the practice has become standardized of making the length twice the width and the width twice the height. This practice has helped to determine the various patterns of brick-laying or 'bonding'. The earliest brick buildings did not use a regular arrangement, but the first such regular pattern to emerge has become known as 'English bond', consisting of alternating layers of 'headers' and 'stretchers' – the former showing the end of the bricks and the latter the sides. 'Flemish bond', which became popular in Britain in the seventeenth century, consists of alternate headers and stretchers in the same layer. Many variations on these basic styles are possible – for example, by 'breaking joint' in 'English cross bond' and 'Dutch bond', so that the stretchers in an English bond formation are displaced half a length in alternating stretcher courses – and the development of the cavity wall has led to the use of stretcher courses alone in many modern brick buildings.

Bricks were almost invariably made on the site in the early days of brick-making, ideally with clay excavated in the course of the works. Even when brick-making developed into an industry in its own right, strong local characteristics remained giving distinctive qualities to the bricks of different neighbourhoods, determined largely by the clays available locally. Thus the grey London brick and the yellow Cambridge brick give – literally – local colour to areas where they are used. Latterly, however, with the concentration of the industry already mentioned, these local variations have been submerged by the general availability of the rather dull red mass-produced brick which can be found now in buildings all over the country. Some blue bricks, also, have a widespread market, because they are prepared from clays in the coal measures which produce a tough sort of brick known as 'engineering brick'. These have been extensively used in railway works, and have sometimes been used with disfiguring effects to repair defective stone in existing buildings. These blue bricks were manufactured largely in Staffordshire, although other areas have been important, such as the Cattybrook brickworks north of Bristol, where about a quarter of the 76 million bricks used in the Severn Tunnel were made.[2]

Baked clay in the form of tile has developed alongside the manufacture of bricks. Indeed, the two have frequently been made in the same kiln, with bricks and tiles stacked so that they take advantage of the different intensities of heat within the kiln. However, although the Romans produced both brick and tile, there is good evidence that the manufacture of tile revived in Western civilization several centuries before that of brick: the name of Wat Tyler, for instance, leader of the fourteenth-century Peasants' Revolt, demonstrates that the craft had become well established by then, and there are references to tiles in documents of the twelfth and thirteenth centuries. The first tiles to be produced were plain rectangular ones which, as they did not overlap horizontally, were obliged to overlap two tiles vertically in order to prevent seepage of water. When pantiles, with their horizontally overlapping lips, emerged in the seventeenth century, they made possible a single vertical over-lap of tiles, with the important result that roofs could be made lighter and cheaper. Pantiles were introduced from Holland in the 1630s, and it is interesting to observe that good-quality brick and tile was at that time finding its way across the Atlantic as ballast in Dutch, Swedish, and British ships, to be used as a precious building material by the colonial settlers. The floor of the old Church in Wilmington, Delaware, is made of bricks imported in this way for the first Swedish colonists in the New World.

Terracotta, Plaster and Cement

In addition to brick and tile, other important building materials have been manufactured, such as terracotta, a fine baked clay used largely for ornamental features on buildings. Also, the production of chimney pots, pipes, sumps, and drains has become an important branch of the building industry, particu-larly with the improvement in sanitary conditions, and the techniques used are largely the same as those of brick-making. Since the Second World War, there has been a spate of new building materials, especially in providing cladding substances for curtain-frame buildings – that is, buildings in which the walls themselves are not the main load-bearing members. Some of these are made of glass or plastic materials, but many are derived from various sorts of concrete mixture. Mortar, generally with a lime base and varying amounts of sand added, has been the traditional way of bonding masonry and brickwork, and architects would go to some trouble to get a mixture of the correct texture and colour for each building. The remains of the lime kilns in which limestone was calcined (i.e. burnt to reduce the stone to a consistent powder of lime) can be found all over the limestone areas of Britain, and are worth the attention of industrial archaeologists. There was a profusion of them, for instance, on the limestone moors of north-west Yorkshire. Mortars varied greatly in quality. The Romans achieved a mixture which was frequently stronger than the masonry that it cemented, so that it has survived the process of erosion better than the stonework on many of their sites. This sort of quality eluded builders in Western Europe until the early nineteenth century, when various 'Roman cements' appeared on the market and were in great demand for 'stucco' – a facing material that gave a fashionably smooth exterior to many Regency buildings at that time. Similar materials were used in 'harling', a sort of rough-cast used to coat many Scottish buildings. The best of these strong cement mixtures was 'Portland cement', patented in 1824 by Joseph Aspdin. The name of the cement reflects the inventor's fond belief that it looked like Portland stone when used as an external plaster. In fact, it has nothing to do with Portland, being produced by firing a mixture of clay and lime at a high temperature (about 1400° C.) and grinding the resulting clinker into a powder. Mixed with water, the powder forms a very strong concrete which has been used extensively in modern building works.[3]

Metals and Glass

To complete this survey of the complex of industries serving the building industry, it is worth mentioning the role of the metal and glass industries. Lead has been used as a roofing material in sheet form since the Roman times, and in the form of pipe it has been used in plumbing for drains and gutters. It was widely used as a church-roofing material in the Middle Ages, but it was generally too expensive to be used in this way for private houses. Undoubtedly, the building uses of lead did much to sustain the lead industry for many centuries, until foreign competition made British mining uneconomic. Copper has also been used for roofing, but its bright green coloration has limited aesthetically the uses to which it could be put, and its cost has been another serious limitation. By far the most important building material has been iron, both as a major structural component and as an ornamental embellishment. In the first role, cast-iron construction began in the late eighteenth century, promoted by the search for safety from fires in textile mills. The fire-proof mill with cast-iron columns supporting arches of brick and paved floors within a brick or masonry shell evolved quickly thereafter, and many specimens of this enormously important type of building survive, although the wastage rate has been high in recent decades. Both cast iron and wrought iron, moreover, were used extensively in the nineteenth century, for bridge and other civil-engineering constructions, and the twentieth century has witnessed an enormous extension in the use of steel in reinforced concrete and the framework of buildings. In the second role, as a decorative feature, the wrought-iron work of traditional smithies is a pleasing feature of many buildings from the sixteenth century, and the charming balconies in Regency squares and terraces such as can be found in Cheltenham illustrate this use nicely. In the mid-nineteenth century there was a vogue for cast-iron balconies, which could be manufactured cheaply in sections as ordered from a pattern book and then assembled in a variety of patterns on the job. The study of these features in relation to local (or distant) foundries and their pattern books is a useful exercise for industrial archaeologists. The same may be said for railings, bollards, gas lights, and the other products of the nineteenth-century iron foundries which found their way towards the ornamentation of buildings and street furniture.

Glass has been used on an ever-expanding scale in the British building industry since the sixteenth century. Beginning with the small panes of glass linked together in a web of lead ('leaded lights'), such as those which still survive in the elegant windows of Hardwick Hall in Derbyshire, glass-makers progressed to manufacturing medium-sized panes of 'crown glass' which, usually assembled in two groups of six in each of the vertically-sliding frames of a sash window, graced the frontages on many eighteenth-century residences in town and country. The fact that the texture of the glass was uneven meant that the light reflected by a set of such windows was never uniform, which gave a particularly charming effect. The advent of techniques for making 'plate glass' in the nineteenth century opened up tremendous new prospects for the use of glass as a constructional material, so that windows tended to become larger and the buildings airier. The effects of this are particularly apparent in the new railway stations, shops, and other distinctive buildings of modern civilization. One unfortunate result of this advance in technique, however, was that many Victorian owners of eighteenth-century and Regency houses were persuaded to replace their multi-paned windows with single sheets of plate glass, the aesthetic effects of which on Regency terraces in Bath, for example, are regrettable. But in general the increasing use of glass has added to the interest and variety of buildings.

Agriculture

The time during which men began to cultivate the ground systematically for food and to keep animals for food and other products marks the transition from the Palaeolithic to the Neolithic period, from the primitive hunting and food-gathering economy of the Old Stone Age to the more settled agricultural society of the New Stone Age. The period of time in question must surely have been long drawn out, probably covering many centuries and occurring at different times in different parts of the world. But the transition certainly took place, and may be regarded as the first great economic–social revolution in the story of mankind, for in this Neolithic Revolution the agricultural industry was born and it became possible to sustain an increasing population and to develop the arts of 'civilization'.

Agricultural techniques developed slowly. The first farming communities in Britain were probably those responsible for the small square plots which can still be traced on many of the chalk and limestone uplands of the south-east and which appear on many Ordnance Survey maps as 'Celtic Fields'. It seems likely that the ground was worked in these places because the soil was thinner than in the forested, clay-soiled valleys, and that the square configuration derived from the need to 'cross-plough' with the primitive hand-plough or digging stick which was the only implement. Again, it seems that plots would have been worked to exhaustion and then abandoned once more.

The first significant improvement in this system of agriculture came with the introduction of a method of crop rotation, whereby fields were cultivated in alternate years, being left fallow in the intervening year. This 'two-year' system was refined further in the Middle Ages by the general adoption in Anglo-Saxon and Norman England of a 'three-year' system, which meant that only a third instead of a half of the cultivatable land was out of production in any period, with a consequent increase in output and also an enrichment of diet because it was possible to grow beans or lentils in one of the two fields under cultivation – in addition, that is, to the staple cereal crop. Another important improvement of this period was the introduction of heavy ploughing techniques, which involved a strongly constructed plough with an iron blade (or at least an iron cutting edge), and a team of draught animals to pull it. These animals were at first oxen, but during the Middle Ages they were gradually replaced over most of Europe by horse teams, which could do the same work much more efficiently and consequently with a further increase in productivity.[4]

The combined effect of these improvements was to make possible the clearance of the forested lowlands of the south-east and Midlands and the farming of the rich clay soils of these areas. A distinctive sort of society, sometimes known as the 'manorial system', emerged in this new environment, typically having a nucleated village in the middle of three large 'open' fields in which each farmer would have rights enabling him to cultivate several 'strips', and surrounded by common land and forest in which the villagers had rights to graze their animals and to collect wood. The strips in the open fields were long and narrow, being normally a furlong in length – the length which a team of horses could be expected to pull without a pause for rest. The deep cut of the heavy ploughshare made cross-ploughing unnecessary, and as each farmer would usually plough his strip so that the cut soil would turn inwards the effect of centuries of this sort of working was to give the cultivated land an undulating appearance. Though much medieval farmland has been put down to pasture, in the Midlands and elsewhere, the indications of this ancient pattern of ploughing are frequently evident in low sunlight or aerial photography, and they have provided useful clues to those archaeologists and historians of the Middle Ages who have in recent years been engaged in the search for 'lost' villages and other settlements. Other archaeological relics of this period of agricultural development include features such as 'strip lynchets' where strips have been farmed on steep hillsides. There is one village in Britain – Laxton in Nottinghamshire – where a nearly complete open-field system has been preserved as a functioning community, and this is well worth the attention of industrial archaeologists. Some parts of the fields have been enclosed, but the visual impression of large open stretches remain, together with the huddle of cottages (all fairly modern), the village church, and the remains of a motte-and-bailey castle. Even with the tractors working in the fields, it is possible to experience at Laxton something of the atmosphere of a medieval farm.[5]

Laxton survives because it was one of the few places in Britain which was not reorganized under the Enclosure Acts. These began as private Acts of Parliament in the eighteenth century, designed to reallocate the property rights in particular village communities. By carving up the open fields and common land into lots, and allocating them according to the size of holdings in the fields which could be legally proved, a number of compact small-holdings was created in place of the manorial community with its shared services and customary duties. This procedure was vicious for the members of these traditional communities who had nothing except ancestral usage and community tolerance to justify their places in them, but from the point of view of the 'legal' property owners it led to a great improvement in the potential efficiency of the farmland, and this incentive proved irresistible. Under the stimulus of rising demand from the urban and industrial markets, agriculture was ready to undertake a great expansion in the eighteenth century, and the interests of property were sufficiently well represented in Parliament at that time to make the legal transition relatively smooth. From a handful of petitions for private enclosure Acts in the early decades of the century, the demand rose to a flood in the second half of the century. In the twenty years 1761–80, for instance, 1,039 private enclosure Acts were passed by Parliament. The procedure was made much easier by the passage of a General Enclosure Act in 1801, and by the middle of the nineteenth century virtually the whole of agricultural England and much of Wales and Scotland had been converted to enclosed farms.

This conversion of the British landscape from one of wide open fields to one of many small farms, each with its own fields surrounded by trees, hedges, or walls, has been regarded as part of an 'Agricultural Revolution', as if this consisted of something separated from the 'Industrial Revolution' which accompanied it. The difficulties inherent in the use of the latter term have already been discussed, and here it must be emphasized that the revolution which has certainly occurred in the agricultural industry since the mid-eighteenth century is only a part, however important, of the whole process of industrialization of the last two hundred years. Without the stimulus of the new markets provided by urban industry, the agricultural reforms would not have begun, and without the techniques of rational organization, scientific method, and mechanization, the revolution in agriculture would not have taken the course which it has in fact taken. The modern agricultural revolution must be seen, therefore, as a product of industrialization, and it can be investigated profitably by industrial archaeologists.

It is rather a shock to look at the 'traditional' English rural landscape for the first time with the realization that it is as much the result of industrialization as an urban textile mill or coal-mine, but it should be so regarded. The field pattern itself, of course, is only the beginning of the story. The Enclosure Acts carried out a legal transfer of property rights and created a new system within which land-owners or tenant farmers could undertake agricultural experiments and innovations which were virtually impossible in the open-field system. First, a four-field pattern of crop rotation was widely introduced, which not only eliminated the need for leaving part of the land fallow and thus unproductive every year, but also facilitated the introduction of new crops such as turnips and clover, both of which provided in turn important animal food and enabled larger flocks and herds to be kept and – even more significant for the diet of the population – kept alive during the winter until they were required as fresh meat. The enclosed farms, moreover, made possible careful breeding of the stock, whereas animals had previously been turned out together on the common pasture. New and more productive breeds of cattle, sheep, pigs, and so on were raised, and in some parts of the country such as Leicestershire many farms devoted themselves entirely to livestock. Much thought was applied to the improvement of estates by the property-owning classes, from royalty downwards, George III ('Farmer George') devoting considerable energy to the development of crown estates such as Windsor Great

Park, and Viscount 'Turnip' Townshend setting an example to the aristocrats. Propagandists like Arthur Young and journals like the *Gentleman's Magazine* applied themselves to the cause of agricultural improvement. The formation of societies like the 'Bath and West of England Society' in 1777 and the efforts of such bodies in organizing shows and awarding prizes demonstrate the application of scientific and influential resources to the agricultural industry in this period.

The result of all this investment of resources and talent was that agriculture developed rapidly in the nineteenth century. It survived the repeal of the Corn Laws in 1846 without any immediate ill effects, although they had been maintained in order to protect the British farmer from continental competition. In the middle of the century, the industry reached the high point of its prosperity. Even marginal land was worth farming, and there was constant pressure to recover more land from the sea in the Fens and elsewhere. In this period, also, the first serious attempts to mechanize farming were made. There had been significant experiments with farming machines since the mid-eighteenth century, but with a few exceptions, such as Jethro Tull's very successful seed-drill, these did not come to anything. So long as farm machines were tied to animal power the scope for mechanization was limited. But in the mid-nineteenth century determined efforts were made to put steam power at the service of agriculture. This was done through the 'steam plough', a stationary engine drawing the plough across the field by a cable; by increasing use of the heavy traction engine for agricultural purposes, often in a stationary form to provide power for threshing machines and other seasonal uses, but also for heavy transport duties; and by the employment of relatively small, compact, stationary steam units to drive agricultural machinery on the farm or in the saw mill. These engines and the machines which they drove provide plenty of scope for the industrial archaeologist.

What did eventually deliver a near-mortal blow to British agriculture was not European competition but the competition of cheap grain from the New World, carried from the North American prairies by railway and steamship, followed by meat in refrigerated ships from Argentina and Australia. The last quarter of the nineteenth century was a black period for British agriculture, and there was no improvement in its malaise, with the exception of a short-lived revival in the First World War, until 1939. Since the Second World War, however, the agricultural industry has received continuous state encouragement, and has undergone a further period of rapid development and change. Indeed, the transformation of the industry in the last thirty years has been such that many of the features of farming hitherto regarded as normal are now disappearing, and deserve the attention of industrial archaeologists. 'Industrialized farming', with its artificial breeding, mechanical milking, controlled grazing, battery hens, bacon houses, artificial fertilizers and insecticides, is having a profound effect on the British farming industry and landscape. There is a move back towards the prospect of the open fields, although now hedges are being bulldozed out and fields thrown together in order to use modern tractors, ploughs and combine-harvesters with the maximum efficiency. Even the 'traditional' English farmstead with its intimate and attractive collection of buildings, its dogs barking, its hens grubbing about in the farmyard, and its own distinctive smells, is becoming obsolete and is going out of existence. Some of these features, such as the barns, which often show local variations in construction and detail that are of considerable significance, urgently require recording while they remain intact.

The agricultural industry, in short, is experiencing the rapid processes of modernization which are affecting other industries and making so many old techniques, buildings, and machines obsolete, only the process is probably more acute in agriculture because of the long period of stagnation for sixty years after 1875, which left more ground to catch up once it became economic and feasible to use electricity, the internal combustion engine, and modern chemical products on British farms. It is certainly an industry which should not be neglected by the industrial archaeologist.[6]

Rural Crafts

Many of the crafts associated with agriculture and the countryside provide fascinating material for the industrial archaeologist. The skill of the craftsman, the ingenious refinement of tools at his disposal, the cultivation of special plants and trees for his craft, and the artefacts of his skill are all valid aspects of inquiry, although being of very localized significance they can only be reviewed briefly here. Rural craftsmen may be divided for convenience into three categories, according to whether they work in wood, metal, or other materials.

Prominent amongst the woodworkers are the wagon-builders: the craftsmen who constructed the sturdy carts, carriages, haywains, and other vehicles used on the farm and in the countryside. These developed many distinctive local varieties, and even the traditional colour schemes for different sorts of wagons changed from one part of the country to another. Many specimens of these now obsolete vehicles fortunately survive, often preserved as casual decorative features by village hostelries, but the wastage rate is high and it is to be hoped that local museums are finding room in their collections for examples of these bulky pieces of equipment which are characteristic of the neighbourhood. Associated with wagon-making was the craft of the wheelwright, who often worked on his own and supplied wooden wheels as required. The cutting of the axle stock, the shaping of the spokes, and the task of assembling these within the section of rim was a highly skilled occupation. The final process of shrinking a red-hot wrought-iron rim on to the wheel would often be performed in co-operation with the village smith. Another class of woodworking is that associated with the

20. Farm wagons. (A) Lincolnshire-style box wagon; (B) Wiltshire-style bow wagon.

processing of 'withies', which are strips of hazel cut, boiled, and manufactured into baskets and other commodities; this has become an important rural craft industry in parts of the Sedgemoor Plain of Somerset. The skills of wood-turning on simple lathes to produce bowls and other utilitarian and decorative items are more generalized, but usually only survive to serve tourist industries.

The outstanding metal-workers amongst rural craftsmen, and also the most picturesque, were the village smiths, although this legendary breed of men has now, for most practical purposes, died out. Until quite recently, however, the smith was the indispensable odd-job man of the rural community, shoeing horses, making and repairing the essential tools of the farmer, making wrought-iron gates, and doing such decorative work as the more affluent members of the local community would pay him to perform, often with rare skill. Some of the metal trades began as rural crafts, but moved by degrees into the towns and became urban industries. The rural origins of such processes as nail- and chain-making, file grinding, edge-tool-making, cutlery manufacture, and pin- and needle-making should be observed, because some of the relics of these processes are still to be found in a rural environment. Nail- and chain-making settled in the small towns of the Black Country, in some of which it is still practised in conditions reminiscent of the village smithy. The remains of tool and cutlery manufacture can still be found where the industry began in the rural valleys around Sheffield: the industrial hamlet preserved at Abbeydale illustrates this point nicely. The ruins of the edge-tool works of the Fussell family around Mells in the heart of rural Somerset are another example. The surviving needle mill at Redditch, the Forge Mill, is now on the edge of a housing estate, but it is hoped that it can be preserved and something of its rural environment kept.[7]

The third category of rural crafts is that comprising the workers in materials other than wood and metal, and includes such crafts as candle-making, peat cutting, kelp burning, the tanning of leather, and the preparation of sheepskins for rugs and clothes. Few of these crafts leave substantial industrial

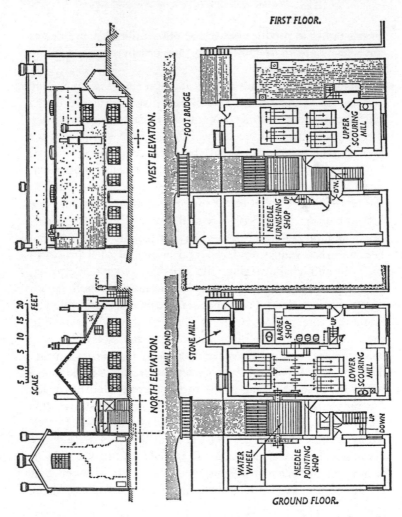

21. Redditch needle mill. These drawings of the Forge Mill, Redditch, are reproduced from *The Needle Mills* by John G. Rollins. The important process of scouring performed in the main part of this mill produced a high polish on the needles by rolling them in coarse cloth with a lubricant and an abrasive powder from the stone-crushing mill, and then rubbing them to and fro on the scouring beds for many hours.

monuments, but the industrial archaeologist should be on the look-out for them, as they add an important dimension to the life of rural communities and occasionally involve local traditions and folk-lore.

9. Consumer Industries and Urban Crafts

A group of industries which are of fundamental importance to human societies are those concerned with food, drink, and clothing. These are described here under the category of 'consumer industries', together with their modern extensions in the shape of such industries as furniture, tobacco, and those catering for leisure, which have grown in importance with the increase in productivity and mass consumption resulting from the Industrial Revolution of the last two centuries. It is convenient to consider with these consumer industries a number of urban crafts which derive from the craft guilds of early town development and survive in some cases as significant industries.

From the point of view of industrial archaeology, these industries are a rather mixed bag. Almost all the consumer industries began, because of their antiquity, as small-scale processes. They were, in fact, domestic industries, practised in the homes of the workers, and however extensive such industries become they leave few industrial monuments, as they rarely have purpose-designed buildings or distinctive machines which might have survived for the benefit of posterity. Much the same is true of the early urban craft industries, the only surviving traces of which are frequently the city churches which they endowed in honour of their patron saints. The foundation of a number of the churches within the City of London occurred in this way. As the consumer and urban craft industries followed the pattern of growth, concentration, and mechanization which has been normal in Western civilization over recent centuries, so they have produced buildings and machines which have survived to tell the tale, for those who care to disentangle it. This is a hitherto little-worked aspect of industrial archaeological studies, but one which is potentially very rewarding.

Grain Milling

As soon as the Neolithic agricultural revolution made grains available in abundance for human consumption, it became necessary to devise ways of grinding the hard seeds of wheat, rye, or other grain into a flour from which palatable food could be manufactured. This grinding was done originally in the home by pounding the grain in a stone trough or quern: the pestle and mortar used by the pharmacist is the modern equivalent of this process. The operation, however, was tedious, and lent itself to the application of mechanical power, so that mills were contrived to perform it. Strictly speaking, of course, this is the only proper use of the term 'mill', denoting the grinding or 'milling' of grain, but the term has come by analogy and general consent to apply to almost any power-using industrial establishment. Watermills were being used to grind corn in the Roman Empire, and windmills were introduced into Western Europe in the twelfth century and were used for the same purposes in areas where water power was unobtainable or was unsatisfactory. The machinery of both water- and windmills is treated separately in a later chapter, but the grinding process, which was essentially the same in all kinds of mill, may be treated conveniently here. Normally, a grain mill consists of three floors. The top floor, to which the sacks of grain are hoisted by a drive taken off the main source of power, is a storeroom, and here the grain is deposited in open-topped bins from which it can be funnelled through chutes to the middle floor. On the

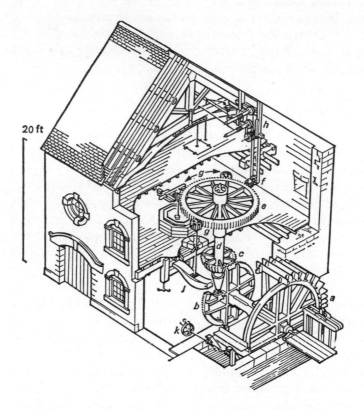

20 ft

22. Brindley's corn mill at Leek. a = the under-shot water wheel (16 ft diameter); b = the pit wheel; c = the wallower; d = the main shaft; e = the great spur wheel (9 ft 11 ins. diameter); f = pinion and pulley driving the sack hoist; g = the stone nuts, the pinions driving the grinding stones; h = the twin sack hoist, with slack-rope drives; j = the tentering apparatus, for adjusting the distance between grinding stones; k = the paddle gear, for controlling water to the water wheel; l = the by-pass sluice.

(The drawing is based on that by C. T. G. Boucher in *James Brindley*, published by Goose & Son, by kind permission of the author.)

middle floor are the circular grinding stones, arranged in pairs.
The bottom stone (the 'bed stone') of each pair is fixed, while
the top stone (the 'runner stone') rotates upon it, being driven

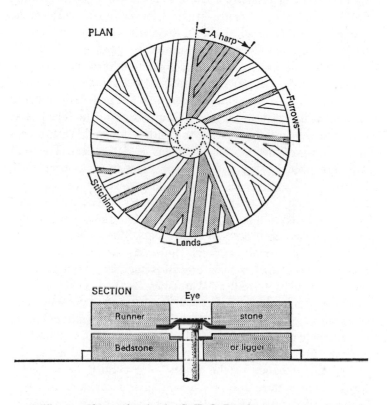

23. Mill stones (from a drawing by C. T. G. Boucher).

from a shaft either from below, passing through the centre of
the bed stone (the usual practice in watermills), or from above
(as in most windmills). The grain is fed in through a 'shoe' into
the centre of the upper stone and is then ground between the

two stones, the carefully cut grooves on the faces of the stones causing the ground flour to move from the centre to the edges, where it is recovered in a box around the stones and led thence by gravity through another chute to the bottom floor. Here the flour can be poured directly into bags for removal. In watermills, the bottom floor also contains the main driving mechanism from the source of power, transmitted by gearing and vertical shafts to the upper mill stone of each pair on the floor above.

Steam power was introduced to assist the grinding process in the last decades of the eighteenth century. The first steam mill, the Albion Mill, was erected on the south bank of the Thames at Southwark in 1784, initially with two Boulton and Watt rotary-action beam engines driving eight sets of stones each. This mill was destroyed by fire within a few years of its construction, but it served as a model for subsequent developments in corn milling, which were towards steadily greater concentration of the process.[1] Bulk milling abandoned the traditional grindstones and performed the process by large rollers. Many of the tradition-al grindstones remain at work, however, although used now mainly for the smaller-scale processes such as grinding animal feed. A small watermill at Waterside, south of Glasgow, still produces stone-ground peasemeal (from imported peas) in small quantities, and is typical of the many mills scattered over Britain in which the traditional grinding processes manage to survive. One of the disadvantages of stone grinding is the skilled maintenance of the stones. These must be regularly 'dressed' to restore the grooves on their faces, and this is a highly skilled craft. Stones do eventually wear out, become too thin to be used, or are discarded for some other reason, and the remains of such abandoned stones can provide significant evidence for the industrial archaeologist. It is useful to be able to recognize the different types. The hardest type of stone, usually preferred for grinding corn, was French stone or 'burr', a freshwater quartz quarried in the Paris basin. These stones were usually built up out of wedge-shaped sections and bound by an iron band shrunk on to them like the rim of a cart-wheel. The fact that they were imported into Britain over many centuries indicates the esteem in which these stones were held, and they were occasionally moved around from mill to mill. Another valued type of stone was imported – blue German or 'cullin' stone, the latter name being a corruption of 'Cologne', which city was at one time involved in the trade in stones. Not so hard as French stone, these were still highly regarded and used widely in Britain for wheat and other grains. British stones did not usually compare well with these foreign products, but they were quarried in many parts of the country, particularly in the Peak District and Anglesey. The former area produced 'Peak' or 'grey' stones from the local millstone grit, and were cut to the required measurements from rough-hewn 'blanks'. Some of these blanks and several uncompleted stones litter the moor under the millstone grit escarpment to the east of Hathersage in Derbyshire. Being relatively soft as mill stones, their life-expectancy was only about ten years, and they were used mainly for grinding animal feed. Of course other uses were found for these Peak stones, in the cutlery and grinding trades of Sheffield and as edge-runners (i.e. rolling on their rims in a trough) to crush dyewoods, cider apples, and for other industrial purposes. Millstone grit and other finer-grained sandstones were widely used in this form. Another type of stone which is common and fairly easily recognized by its texture is 'composition' stone, manufactured as a concrete conglomerate.

Millers were resourceful men, and over the centuries grain milling acquired many refinements which involved minor modifications to the general arrangements described above, and the introduction of many 'Heath Robinson' devices to make the grain flow smoothly from the bin, to control the speed of the stones (the standard 4-foot diameter stones were normally geared to run at 125 rpm), to warn the miller when the bin was empty and to remove stones for recutting when this became necessary. As it was so important to keep the stones running smoothly, moreover, ingenious methods of balancing the runner stone were evolved. Ancillary contrivances such as sieves for separating the chaff from the flour were also frequently incorporated. These are some of the many details of interest which are worth noting and recording when a grinding mill is being surveyed.

The great expansion in the scale of grain milling since the end of the eighteenth century has brought about the decline and disappearance of many local mills, except for certain special products and animal feed. Surviving mills of this kind are thus valuable objects to the industrial archaeologist, because they enable him to reconstruct visually the traditional processes of milling and to appreciate the problems which the miller had to overcome.

Food Production and Preservation

Flour from the mill found its way traditionally to the housewife in her kitchen, where she converted it into bread, cake, biscuit, and other foodstuffs. Culinary archaeology – the use of tools and other equipment (spits, kettles, dog-wheels, etc.) – is a marginal but not insignificant aspect of industrial archaeology, as the perusal of a reconstructed kitchen in any good folk museum will demonstrate. As with so many other processes, however, cookery has been concentrated and mechanized in the last two hundred years, and the history of bakeries and biscuit manufacturers in this period has provided plenty of material for the industrial archaeologist. One firm of biscuit manufacturers, Peak Freans, made an admirable film of the processes of biscuit-making in 1906, which has survived as a unique industrial record.[2]

The growth of the great mercantile empires in Western

Europe from the sixteenth century brought many new food-stuffs into Europe and made possible the enrichment of the diet of the population. Sugar consumption, for instance, increased rapidly in Britain as methods of extracting the material from West Indian cane were discovered. At first, much of the processing was done in the Indies, but gradually sugar refining became established in Britain at the seaport cities such as Bristol where the trade took root. These early refineries were usually small-scale affairs, taking in partially treated sugar and then boiling it in vats, evaporating the resulting syrup to crystallization in pans, and drying it out in 'sugar-loaf' moulds. The equipment used in this process was of little distinction, and in any case, as with other industries, the economies of scale transformed a small-scale domestic industry first into a large local industry and eventually into a highly concentrated national industry, leaving remarkably little evidence of its earlier phases. In Bristol, the large sugar factory of Conrad Finzel flourished in the middle decades of the nineteenth century but had disappeared by the end of the century, so that only a few fragments of this once great concern survive.[3]

Cocoa was another plantation commodity which found a steady market in Britain, developing considerably in the last quarter of the nineteenth century when chocolate confectionery became fashionable and was successfully promoted by some of the first food advertising campaigns. Progress with fruit preserving and the growth of jam factories occurred at the same time. The machines and processes involved in these and other food industries are too numerous to describe, but they deserve attention when they can be studied as a significant aspect of industrial archaeology.

Another vital foodstuff is that derived from animal life, and men have been very ingenious in exploiting this source. Dove-cotes, as means of keeping fresh bird-life ready to hand for the cook, survive as industrial relics of a sort in many parts of the country. Fish-ponds, likewise, frequently made to combine with the functions of mill-pond, have in some cases got long histories. The main source of fish, however, remained the sea, and the problem here was preserving the fish brought home by the fishing vessels. Many fishing ports acquired elaborate facilities for salting and smoking ('curing') fish, particularly herring; this had an important effect on the salt industry and has already been mentioned. Apart from these facilities and dockside equipment, the fishing industry does not have much to show the industrial archaeologist, although certain curious features such as the black-tarred net sheds on the shore at Hastings are well worth observing. Since the beginning of the nineteenth century, great strides have been taken in food preservation by canning, refrigeration, and other more sophisticated techniques such as accelerated freeze drying. Evidence of early canning and refrigerating plant is worth examining.

Milk and dairy products have become essential items in modern diet, and are made available by a complex series of mechanical operations and chemical processes which intervene between the cow and the customer. The equipment for pasteurizing milk, for example, has a significant place in modern social history. Even the humble milk bottle is worth a second glance, for techniques of bottle-making have improved greatly in recent decades, and earlier types and shapes, such as the bottle with a recessed lip to take a cardboard cap (excellent, in my recollection, for skimming in the playground), have long been obsolete.

Drink

Both the pollution of fresh-water supplies and the ancestral partiality of man for alcoholic beverages stimulated the industries devoted to quenching thirst in an agreeable manner. Like food processing, these industries began in the kitchen as domestic crafts: brewing, fermenting, and distilling drinks from a wide range of vegetable substances. By the time of the Industrial Revolution, some of these processes had grown into important local industries, and the subsequent improvement in transport has promoted the concentration of large-scale production which we have observed as a widespread development in modern industry.

This has certainly happened in the manufacture of beer, grouping together those drinks – ale, porter, stout, etc. – which are made by brewing a 'mash' of fermenting 'wort', a liquid produced from treated barley ('malt'), and adding hops or other flavouring matter. Brewing became a significant local industry, particularly in London, Dublin, and other large towns, in the eighteenth century, when the market of potential customers had grown sufficiently large, concentrated, and thirsty to support it. Paradoxically, in view of their later ambivalent attitude towards intoxicating liquor, some of the first capitalists in this expanding business were philanthropic nonconformists anxious to provide a wholesome alternative to gin, the excessive consumption of which had become a serious social problem in the middle of the eighteenth century – a position brilliantly expressed in Hogarth's famous cartoon of *Gin Lane*. Even the great evangelist John Wesley recommended beer to his followers, in preference to both strong spirits and tea, which was still regarded with some suspicion in the eighteenth century. Thus East London firms such as Hanbury Truman & Buxton were launched, and in other parts of the country with good water supplies and, even more important, access to urban markets, large beer-brewing industries developed. Burton-on-Trent became a famous centre in this way, but every town of any size in the country acquired at least one brewery, and the closure of dozens of these in recent years has provided important work for local industrial archaeological groups.[4]

The important processes in beer-making are malting, brewing, fermenting, and bottling (or otherwise dispatching the product to its market). Malting is the process of allowing the grains of barley to begin germination under carefully controlled conditions of temperature and humidity in order to convert their starch content into sugar, and then arresting this conversion by drying the grain in a kiln. This is done by first soaking the barley and then leaving it to germinate on large floors in open rooms through which warm air can be freely circulated. Malting tended to become a specialized activity, because it required more space and time than the average urban brewery could afford to devote to it, and the malt was then delivered ready for use at the brewery. Like the breweries themselves, many of these small local maltings are now going out of business, and require attention and recording while they are still available. J. M. Richards has referred to 'the unmistakable geometry of the brewing industry',[5] in which the pyramidal roofs of maltings with capped vents are an outstanding feature. Many maltings survive in the Home Counties, especially in Hertfordshire, and the Old Maltings in Farnham provide a striking example of an enlightened preservation project. Also, in Kent and elsewhere many hop kilns still flourish as part of this important industry.

When it reaches the brewery, the malt is mixed with water to form the 'wort', which is boiled, other materials such as hops and yeast being added. Fermentation then takes place in large wooden vats, from which the beer is eventually drawn to be kegged or bottled ready for delivery to the market. The bulk of beer made its long-distance transport rare until quite recently. Breweries traditionally maintained their own coopers to make oak barrels, and a fleet of horse-drawn drays (sometimes replaced early in the present century by steam wagons) to deliver the barrels to local public houses. These features have now largely disappeared, together with most local breweries. Beer is now conveyed usually in metal barrels or bottles by orthodox lorries, and is delivered over wide areas from central breweries owning 'chains' of public houses.

One outstanding drink industry which has so far avoided the concentration of production so noticeable in beer brewing is whisky distilling. (The traditional home of this industry, needless to say, is in the Highlands of Scotland, although it is now produced at other places north of the Border also.) There has, admittedly, been a movement towards a concentration of ownership and organization, and the malting process, as in brewing, has become almost completely specialized. But the heart of the whisky industry remains the production of malt whisky, and this is still prepared according to traditional recipes in equipment whose shape is determined by long usage, and – most important of all – using water from particular springs. Connoisseurs of the art of whisky tasting claim to be able to distinguish between the products of neighbouring springs, and as long as tastes remain as finely discriminating as this, and as long as the product continues to make its tremendous contribution to the national export effort, the factors making for the scattered location of the industry will remain strong. Small but flourishing distilleries can thus be found in many parts of the Highlands.

There is a general similarity between the processes of beer- and whisky-making, the most important difference being in the brewing process. In beer-making this is performed in large copper pans or kettles, but in whisky-making the kettle becomes a completely enclosed vessel or 'pot still' from which the vital alcohol is recovered by distilling the vapour from the boiling liquid. The conditions under which this process is performed are minutely controlled, down to such small design details as the angle at which the neck of the still is bent to collect the condensing whisky. Furthermore, malt whisky is not ready for use until it has spent several years maturing in kegs (preferably used previously for sherry, the remains of which impart some colour to the whisky) laid out in a well-ventilated shed. Another difference from beer-making is at the malting stage, where whisky malt is traditionally dried off in a peat fire after the conversion of the starch into sugar, the peat smoke imparting a flavour which is retained through subsequent processes.

Whisky is normally marketed as a 'blend', which is to say that the malt whisky is mixed with 'grain whisky', made from cheap maize by continuous production in much larger stills than those used for malt whisky. A dozen or so grain distilleries,

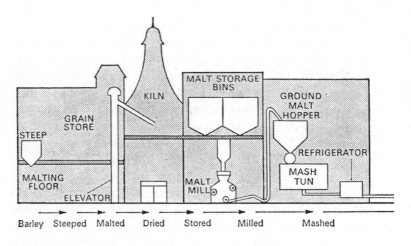

24. Arrangement of processes in a typical malt whisky distillery.

concentrated mainly in central Scotland in and between Edinburgh and Glasgow, produce as much whisky as the surviving malt distilleries, rather over a hundred in number, so that roughly half of each retailed bottle of blended whisky consists of grain whisky. This provides the 'body' of the blend, to which malt whisky contributes the flavour. With the great importance of whisky production, both for the export market and for taxation purposes, the industry operates under close government supervision and has received substantial investment for re-equipment in recent years. Much new equipment has been installed, although apart from the use of electric power traditional patterns and formulas have been carefully copied, so that it is still possible to see whisky being prepared by methods which have been in use for centuries. In many cases, also, the external aspect of the distilleries has been little altered, and they remain as distinctive features of the Scottish

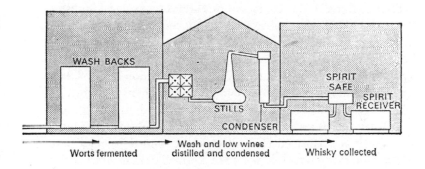

| Worts fermented | Wash and low wines distilled and condensed | Whisky collected |

landscape. The neat little distillery at Glengoyne, north of Glasgow, is a case in point.[6]

Other drinks have provided important local industries, such as cider-making in south-west England. The cider apples were traditionally crushed in stone troughs by edge-runners operated by a horse-gin. A number of these survive on farms and in museums. Part of a cider press is displayed outside a public house in the centre of Avebury in Wiltshire, as an interesting relic of local industry. The ports of southern England have also long traditions of trading in French and Spanish wine: Bristol in particular acquired a reputation for its sherries, but there is little visible evidence of this industry apart from a few bonded warehouses for storing wine. Similarly, bonded warehouses for tea, such as those at St Katharine's Dock in London, provide monuments to another significant national beverage. The mineral water industry, which flourished in the nineteenth century, has left curious relics in the shape of glass bottles with a marble in the neck to seal them.

Clothing

The clothing industry is an important consumer industry, and one which has resisted more successfully than most the concentration of production which is such a general characteristic of modern industry. The personal quality of the end-product and the ever-shifting vagaries of fashion have offset to some extent the pressures to combine and mechanize production. In large parts of Whitechapel in East London, the clothing industry flourishes as what is still essentially a domestic industry in that it is performed in ordinary houses and on a small scale, although the labour relations are normally those of a factory system. In other parts of the country, especially in Leeds and elsewhere in the West Riding, the clothing industry prospers in close relation with the woollen textile industry, but it still remains a pattern of predominantly small-scale enterprises, with individual tailors and seamstresses working with sewing machines, scissors, and hot-irons, often in overcrowded working conditions.

The result of this kind of organization is that the clothing industry has left few industrial monuments, despite its widespread importance and considerable size. Some specialized sections of the industry have shown more tendency to concentration. Hat-making, for instance, has produced some small factories; the shell of one of them survives in the Gloucestershire village of Frampton Cotterell to the north of Bristol. This made felt hats for Christies in the first half of the nineteenth century, but has long been disused. The popularity of silk hats in the second half of the century helped to kill it, which illustrates the importance of fashion in the developments of the clothing industry very clearly. Boot- and shoe-making, also, has become increasingly concentrated since the Second World War, with the introduction of new machines and techniques for welding soles on to shoes. What previously was a widely dispersed domestic industry, with cobblers producing on a small scale for a local market, is rapidly becoming a big factory industry. The growth of Clarks of Street in Somerset and G. B. Birttons of Kingswood in Bristol indicates this trend. Again, however, there is little of industrial archaeological importance, although Brittons have preserved a useful collection of shoes, tools, and documents in a small company museum; and the pattern of small workshops associated with the manufacture of boots and shoes still gives a certain character to parts of Northampton, an important centre for the industry.

Various ancillary industries such as pin- and button-making have shared the general small-scale pattern of the clothing industry. Pins were made in the homes of coal-miners in Kingswood as employment for women: one only needed a supply of brass or steel wire and the minimum of cutting, heading, and pointing equipment. Pin-making did, however, become a small factory industry in this area, and some of the buildings of such factories have survived in the outskirts of Bristol. Button-making has had a similar history in the Birmingham region, where they have for long been made in large quantities.

Furniture

Furniture-making is a luxury consumer industry in the sense that its products can be dispensed with without bringing about complete social collapse. The furniture possessed by families in simple rural communities is primitive in the extreme, and has probably been knocked together by the family itself out of locally available wood, discarded packing cases, and such like. As prosperity increases, however, haphazard woodworking evolves into specialized carpentry, and the craftsman produces chairs, tables, and other articles as the members of the community are able to buy them. The emergence of a wealthy aristocracy encourages the evolution a stage further, so that the carpenter establishes a workshop making high-quality furniture for this market. Furniture produced in this way during the seventeenth and eighteenth centuries now fetches high prices in the antique market, and for sheer functional elegance 'Chippendale' and comparable styles of furniture have never been beaten. But for the mass market which developed in the nineteenth century, quantity became more important than quality, so that cabinet-making and other specialized branches of the trade developed in order to satisfy the demand for large numbers of cheap articles. The furniture industry grew by a proliferation of small units rather than by the concentration of a few, and areas such as Hackney in East London or villages within easy reach of London such as High Wycombe experienced a steady growth in the number of small furniture workshops. When concentration did at last begin, in the twentieth century, with the increasing mechanization of previously handskilled processes, it tended to occur in these areas in the form of one successful business amalgamating with neighbours. In many parts of the country, however, furniture-making still retains a small-scale back-yard character, while in some cases it has been established in the New Towns like Harlow as a suitable light industry. One way or the other, it is not an industry rich in industrial archaeological remains.

Tobacco

Tobacco, whether for smoking, snuffing, or chewing, has become a very important consumer commodity since its introduction from the New World – according to the famous legend, by Sir Walter Raleigh – at the beginning of the seventeenth century. Some of the processes of treating it for the market have become major modern industries, while others such as snuff-grinding and clay-pipe manufacture have become quaint survivals of formerly popular tastes. Storing tobacco, also, has produced impressive commercial architecture in Bristol, Glasgow, and elsewhere, where the imported leaf is kept in bond (i.e. without payment of tax) until it is required by the manufacturers. Tobacco processing and the production of pipe tobacco, cigars, and cigarettes, has stimulated the development of very large factories and a wide range of machines, which have so far received scant attention from industrial archaeologists. Snuff-taking was in fashion during the late eighteenth and early nineteenth centuries – Dr Samuel Johnson was the classic embodiment of the habit – and snuff-grinding developed to meet this demand. The process consisted of grinding the tobacco leaves with edge-runners in pans shaped like inverted cones, other materials such as mint being added in small quantities to impart particular flavours. Water or wind power was normally used to drive the grinders. A few of these snuff mills are still at work, such as the small water-powered mill to the south of Kendal, and one in Sheffield. The remains of many other snuff mills may be discovered by careful inquiry although as many of them were converted from corn-grinding, and frequently resumed this when snuff-taking fell out of fashion, it is sometimes difficult to establish the usage of a particular mill.

For two and a half centuries the most popular way of taking tobacco was by smoking it in a clay pipe, and the manufacture of such pipes became a significant minor industry in several parts of the country such as Glasgow, Chester, Broseley (in Shropshire), East London (the area round Ratcliffe in Stepney), and Bristol. It was a small-scale industry, each manufacturer going his own way with his own family and a few workers. The pipes were cheap and disposable, so that to stay in business a manufacturer had to be able to produce large quantities quickly. Like other small industrial processes it leaves few traces when it disappears, but some of the last clay-pipe factories in the country have been well recorded. The very disposability of the products, however, is of significance, because it means that fragments of clay pipes survive all over the world, and as a large number of British pipes were exported to America in the eighteenth and nineteenth centuries, it is possible to use them as a dating device on sites where documentary evidence is for some reason deficient. This has been done very successfully on some Canadian sites. It is one of the few instances in which industrial archaeology borrows a technique directly from classical archaeology, for ceramic remains have long been a favourite means of dating archaeological material.[7]

Leisure

Modern societies have reaped the benefits of increased industrial productivity, at least partially, in terms of leisure and leisure facilities. In place of the unending cycle of hard labour, sleeping and eating, which has been the normal lot in life for most people for most of the existence of the species, the time spent in work has been reduced by mechanization and other new techniques of production, and a fourth category has been introduced into the life-rhythms of people in Western civilization – recreation and unremunerative activities which may be grouped together under the general heading of 'leisure'.

This has been one of the most significant social changes

brought about by industrialization. For men it has usually taken the form of a steady reduction in the obligatory hours of work and a switch of attention to sport, reading, conviviality, gardening, handicrafts, and other activities. A feature such as a sports stadium could provide a future archaeologist investigating the relics of our civilization with a serious puzzle, although we are familiar with the Roman arena, and it has been assumed that certain strange enclosures excavated by archaeologists in Mexico are associated with some sort of communal activity, probably a form of ball game. The evolution of the public house is another sign of increased leisure, in conjunction with the improved transport system requiring coaching stations, with implications for industrial archaeology. So is the development of the domestic garden. This goes back at least to the large formal gardens provided for the amusement of the comparatively leisured aristocrats and gentry from the sixteenth century onwards, often with lavish expenditure as at Hampton Court and Chatsworth House. The conservatory at the latter, designed by Joseph Paxton, provided the model for his splendid Crystal Palace at the Great Exhibition in 1851. Gardening has now spread from being an exercise in providing a charming environment for a leisured minority to become a form of recreation for anybody who owns or rents a plot of land, and it occasionally involves equipment of industrial archaeological interest. The development of the lawn-mower from rotary shears for trimming woollen cloth, for instance, is an interesting story, suggesting the need for care in scrapping old gardening equipment.

For women, the pattern of the leisure revolution has normally been liberation from the worst features of household drudgery by the application of electricity and other modern conveniences to the home. The domestic revolution, indeed, has been one of far-reaching implications. It began slowly, with the increased supply of pots and pans from the brass and iron industries, and the development of cast-iron stoves and kitchen ranges, all of which now constitute interesting features of domestic archaeology. The revolution gathered momentum with the introduction of piped water, efficient drains, flush toilets (look out for the elegant Victorian cisterns designed by Thomas Crapper with euphonic names like 'Niagara' and 'Cascade'[8]), town gas (for light and cooking) and electricity with its multitude of labour-saving devices; all made housework easier and enabled women to consider professional careers, study, and social services in addition to running the home. The domestic revolution also contributed to social levelling, for it made a vast army of household servants unnecessary just at the time when domestic service was becoming uncongenial. There is thus a wealth of industrial archaeological detail in such features of the household as vacuum cleaners, radio sets, refrigerators, plumbing devices, kitchen equipment and washing machines. To be able to remember such standard items as the mangle, the washing tub, the scrubbing board, the 'posher' (a copper cone on the end of a pole used for pounding clothes in the washing tub), and the flat-iron dates one, while to possess such items is to own potentially valuable museum pieces. It should not be beneath the dignity of industrial archaeologists to observe and record these household items.

Another aspect of the leisure revolution of the last hundred years has been the increase in holiday-taking. The fashionable aristocracy of the eighteenth century withdrew from London during the summer season and gave their patronage to provincial spas such as Bath and Cheltenham, which may claim to have been amongst the first places to provide leisure industries, with their pump rooms, assembly rooms, restaurants, coffee shops, reading rooms, and clubs. The Prince Regent helped to spread such facilities to the seaside resorts by his adoption of the belief that sea air is invigorating and his consequent patronage of Brighton. Increased productivity, improved transport, and the diffusion of the social benefits of better conditions of life to all classes made holidays universally available and very popular. At first it was the day at the seaside by excursion train or special coach, but the practice of granting holidays with pay gradually spread to most forms of employment, and the lodging houses and catering industries flourished at the main resorts to provide accommodation and meals for the seasonal influx of holiday-makers. Seaside resorts can possess much of interest to the industrial archaeologist, both in the pattern of their growth and the provision of services, and in the construction of features such as piers and promenades. The use of cast iron in the Regency Pavilion in Brighton, with its exotic mixture of Eastern styles, is an outstanding example, but most resorts acquired a pier in the nineteenth century, and many of these presented interesting constructional problems. The pier at Clevedon in Somerset is one of the attractive smaller piers, and celebrated its centenary in 1969. The coming of the motor car has added a new dimension to the leisure industries, by making resorts of all kinds much more widely accessible and encouraging new forms of holiday-making by caravan and camping, but most of the resorts which established themselves in the nineteenth century have remained powerful attractions to holiday-makers.[9]

Urban Crafts

Something has already been said about the rural crafts, working in wood, metal, and other materials, which developed in the countryside and remained closely associated with the needs of an agricultural community. Another type of craft industry developed in Western Europe in the Middle Ages within the corporate towns which sprang into vigorous activity at this time. Some of these, like weaving and dyeing, had begun as rural crafts, but found the protection of urban craft guilds more congenial to their development. Some – the textile trades again provide good examples – grew to become major manufacturing industries, and as such have been treated elsewhere in this account. Here it is intended to take note of those purely urban crafts, serving specialized urban needs, which did not grow into major industries.

The craft of cooperage was that of making barrels. Admittedly, this had roots in rural skills, but the main function of the cooper came to be the providing of kegs, barrels, and similar containers for the urban market, for the brewers and the wine merchants, and also in the ports for the ship-owners who had to equip their vessels with fresh water for long voyages. The craft consisted of cutting oak staves to the required shape and fitting them together (usually by shrinking iron bands on to them) so that they made water-tight containers. It is still practised on a small scale, usually in association with breweries and other industries which still find a use for wooden barrels, but it is a dying craft, and it is only a matter of time before the barrels produced by the cooper's skill become prized collectors' pieces.

The workers in precious metals, the goldsmiths and silver-smiths, were distinctive craftsmen in the largest medieval towns. They tended to be amongst the more wealthy of the craftsmen, frequently endowing fine churches and eventually setting up informal banking organizations before specialized banking services emerged. They were also often associated with urban mints, turning out coins under special powers of the King, and the study of coins (numismatics) has discerned the existence of a large number of these small mints even before the Norman conquest. Apart from such coins and the occasional precious antique, however, little of the work of these crafts remains, although the descendants of the craft guilds have sometimes survived as philanthropic societies.

Leather-working is a craft which began in the countryside but became thoroughly urbanized in the Middle Ages. Tanning – the preparation of the animal skins by soaking them in solutions of tree bark and other substances to stiffen and preserve them – often remained in the countryside, conveniently placed for its raw materials, but most of the leather produced was sold to the saddlers, pursers, and other urban craftsmen in leather. The tanning process may still be seen at work in various parts of the country, and a complete tannery has been painstakingly re-erected in the Welsh Folk Museum at St Fagan's. Part of a medieval tannery has recently been excavated in Winchester. Nothing of significance survives, however, of the actual leather-working crafts.

Ports generated a demand for many specialized commodities which supported groups of urban craftsmen. Barrels have already been mentioned. Sail-making and rope-making were other essential port industries. Rope-making eventually became mechanized and grew into a large industry, but it originally involved rope-makers stretching and twisting their fibres along a promenade or 'rope walk', remnants of which sometimes survive and can be located from old town maps. Some good specimens of rope-making machines have been preserved in museums.

Towns bred a galaxy of lesser craftsmen – the butchers, the bakers, the candlestick-makers – who made urban life possible and, to a certain degree, attractive. There is not usually much to remind us of this array of talents in the mechanized bustle of modern town life, but it is as well to be conscious of their one-time existence and importance if we wish to understand the processes of urban evolution by which our contemporary cities have grown. Remnants of these old crafts occasionally survive in street names, street furniture, and shop fronts, all of which are worth the attention of the industrial archaeologist. Certain types of craftsman, for example, had distinctive signs which they placed outside their shops: the only common example of this which is still practised is the red and white pole of the barber, but others were once common, such as the pestle and mortar of the apothecary and the 'black boy' of the tobacconist. They are worth observing as vestigial remnants of once-important urban crafts.[10]

Part 3   Power, Transport, and Public Services

10. Power I – Animal, Wind, and Water

Sources of power provide some of the most attractive features of industrial archaeology, both because of their visual appearance, which is often very elegant, and because of their intrinsic importance in the acceleration of the processes of industrialization during the last two hundred years. Another factor which makes power sources interesting subjects to study is that they are relatively compact and manageable, so that they have received more attention than most industrial monuments as items worth preserving. There has been a great wastage of windmills and water wheels in the present century, but considering their general obsolescence a remarkably large number have been preserved in some form or other. This is not to suggest that enough have been conserved for posterity and that others may be neglected, but only to express gratitude for small mercies.

The Development of Power

The original prime mover in human societies was man himself, and for many millennia he received no animal or mechanical assistance. By the time of the Neolithic Revolution in agriculture, some societies had discovered means of harnessing oxen to draw ploughs and carts, but although there were improvements in tool-making – the use of the lever, wedges, and even gearing – there were few significant advances towards mechanization until the rise of Western civilization in the tenth century. The reasons for this lack of mechanical application in the early civilizations of the Middle East and Mediterranean are a matter of historical controversy, but it seems likely that the most important single reason was the prevalence of the social institution of slavery. The existence of large masses of slaves within a community has two effects, both tending to the same conclusion. On the one hand, it puts at the disposal of the builder and engineer a large labour force which is capable of exercising considerable physical power provided that it is well organized. The Egyptian pyramids, for example, were constructed largely by the skilful deployment of slave power to move the great blocks of stone and to hoist them into position. When more power was needed, more slaves were directed to the operation. Mechanical power was thus unnecessary in such societies. On the other hand, the existence of slavery in a society created a problem of labour utilization: it is essential for the stability of such a regime that the slaves should be kept fully occupied in order to prevent them becoming restive and subversive. Labour-saving devices were thus not only unnecessary – they were positively undesirable. For this reason mechanical innovation was regarded as potentially an agent of social disruption, and was not encouraged.

The prevalence of slavery in the ancient world had another important effect. It made it socially unacceptable for men of means, ability, and education to be associated with any sort of manual work. Such 'menial' work was suitable for slaves and women, but was degrading for anybody who valued his social status. This gave rise to the 'divorce' between science, practised by the minority leisured classes of land-owners and philosophers, and technology, the practical art of making and doing. In some ways this separation is still apparent today: many engineers, at least, feel that they are looked down upon by the 'pure' scientists, who will never condescend to get their hands dirty. Still, the gap is being closed in Western civilization, and it has not had the debilitating effects which it had on previous societies. For it is clear that there was no lack of ingenuity in the ancient civilizations. One cannot fail to recognize the power of the human intellect expressed in the works of Plato and Aristotle, and the imaginative inventiveness of Archimedes has rarely been matched. The 'mechanical' devices of Archimedes, however, were largely engines of war designed to defend his native Syracuse against the Romans, such as the fiendish 'death ray' which attempted (in vain, let it be added) to concentrate the rays of the sun on the canvas rigging of the enemy ships. Some centuries later, another inventive genius, Hero of Alexandria, devised machines which incorporated such 'modern' principles as that of the steam reaction turbine, but it is again indicative of the sort of society in which he lived that these engines were regarded as pleasing toys with little, if any, practical application.

There were exceptions to this general lack of mechanical inventiveness in the ancient world. There was a tradition, to which Archimedes contributed, of military and naval 'secret weapons'. The Iron Age warriors of the first millennium B.C. had, for example, quite literally the cutting edge on their bronze-armed predecessors, and many other inventions were developed for military purposes, including the chariot with or without knife-blades on its axle hubs, the sling, and the catapult. The tread mill was also invented and applied to cranes for building and other purposes. These remained, however, mechanically simple contrivances. The most significant mechanical innovation of the ancient world was the invention of the water wheel. The Roman engineer Vitruvius (using the term 'engineer' in its modern sense) described the construction of water wheels for grinding corn, and towards the end of the Roman Empire under-shot water wheels appear to have been quite widely used for this purpose, and even occasionally over-shot wheels. This, however, was an exception to the general rule that mechanical innovation involving inanimate sources of power remained insignificant until the rise of Western civilization.

The purpose of this historical preamble is to demonstrate the unique character of Western civilization as the only human society which has placed a high premium on means of harnessing inanimate sources of power, and it is worth stressing the change in the social structure which made possible this shift of emphasis, with all the dramatic consequences which stemmed from it. In the first place, the new civilization which emerged from the 'Dark Ages' in Western Europe in the ninth and tenth centuries was one in which slavery played little part. Slaves were present, but never in significant numbers, and they soon disappeared entirely as the new states of Western Europe consolidated themselves between A.D. 1000 and 1500. The fact that the Western mercantile empires deliberately reintroduced slavery in the sixteenth to eighteenth centuries does not diminish the point of this change, because the new slave population was kept at a distance, in the plantations of the New World, to provide vital raw materials for the developing industries in Europe. Secondly, Western Europe was underpopulated as a result of the upheavals of the previous centuries, and with the development of town life and trade there was a labour shortage which encouraged the use of animal and mechanical power. And thirdly, the ethic of what was a strongly Christian civilization, with its implicit rejection of slavery and its explicit approval of the menial crafts, made it possible to start closing the gap which had restricted the spread of technical innovation in the ancient world, between the humble skills of the artisan and the metaphysical speculation of the intelligentsia. More able minds than hitherto applied themselves to the problems of applied science and technical improvement, with results which were to be of profound importance for the future.

The development of new sources of power began gradually in

Western civilization with improvements in the use of animals, but almost simultaneously the application of wind and water as prime movers became important. These grew steadily through the Middle Ages and early modern times, reaching a high pitch of refinement in the nineteenth century. By this time, however, they had been displaced from their position of primacy amongst mechanical prime movers by the steam engine, invented in the seventeenth century and developed in the eighteenth. But such was the crescendo of technological progress that the triumph of steam was short-lived. By the end of the nineteenth century, it was already being strongly challenged by the internal combustion engine and the electric motor, which together have dominated the story of power in the present century. Electricity is not a prime mover, being itself generated either by steam turbines or by water power (HEP, or hydro-electric power), so that the older prime movers survive today. With the development of atomic power, the prospect of virtually limitless energy has begun to open up, but until some more direct and controllable means of harnessing atomic fission and fusion can be devised, this also depends on the production of steam to drive turbines and generate electricity. The story of power is thus full of exciting possibilities, but as modern society looks forward towards these it behoves us to remember the earlier sources of power which have become, or are becoming, obsolete.

Animal Power

Various animals have been employed to provide power for industrial operations, including the goat, the donkey, and the dog – the last in dog-wheels, to keep the spit turning over the kitchen fire. By far the most important, however, have been the heavy draught animals – the ox and the horse – because these could be used to do heavy work such as ploughing, for which the smaller animals were not suitable. The physical structure of the ox made it easier to harness than the horse, because it was possible to place a yoke across the shoulders of a pair of oxen so that they could push against it and pull a plough or carriage. The neck of a horse goes up rather than down, so that a yoke would cut across its wind-pipe and prevent it from pulling, and the horse has other disadvantages such as the tendency of its hoofs to crack when used constantly on wet ground. But weight for weight the horse is a much more efficient animal than the ox, and the story of the successful attempts to harness it, making it in fact 'man's best friend', is a fascinating one, involving the crucial inventions of the horse-collar, the horseshoe, and the stirrup. All were introduced some time in the Dark Ages in Western Europe, and together they revolutionized the part of the horse in economic and military life. Horse power became an important contributory factor to the medieval increase in agricultural productivity, and the mounted knight became the determining factor in medieval armies.[1]

The adaptation of the horse to specifically industrial purposes was a slower process. The way in which this was eventually done was in the form of the 'horse-gin', in which the horse (or ox or donkey, for that matter) walked in a circular track pulling a beam attached to a central axle. This could be used to drive edge-runners for crushing oil seed, dye stuffs, or cider apples, or it could be connected to a drum and used for winding a cable to draw wagons up an incline or to haul men and material from a mine shaft. In yet another form it could be used to drive a continuous chain of buckets to raise water from a mine. Several specimens of these horse-gins survive, although apart from those preserved in museums they frequently require careful searching. A tell-tale feature in many groups of farm buildings up and down the country is a circular or multi-sided 'barn' which in all probability once housed a gin, even if it no longer does so. In some cases the gin-house appears as a semi-circular extension to a large building. These agricultural gin-houses

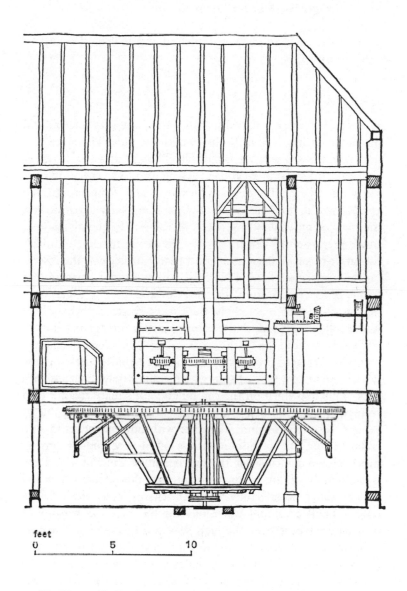

feet
0   5   10

25. The Horsemill, Woolley Park, Berkshire (J. Kenneth Major).

provide the most rewarding industrial archaeological aspect of animal power.[2]

Wind Power

Wind power was harnessed in two forms, one very ancient and the other dating only from the twelfth century. These are respectively the sail and the windmill. The sail appears in representations of ships in Egyptian carvings, and was certainly used on ships by the Phoenicians, Greeks, and Romans. In the ancient world, however, wind power was ancillary to oar power, the oars being wielded by banks of rowers (frequently slaves), sometimes two or even three deep, as in the trireme, although the latter raises certain mechanical problems because the rowers on the uppermost bank must have had to exert a leverage that seems practically beyond the power of a man. The usual practice on such ships was to hoist the square-rigged sail when there was a following wind, while using the oars for moving into or across the wind. One of the outstanding technological achievements of Western civilization during the Middle Ages was the development of a type of ship which could safely dispense with oars. This depended on the combination of square rigging with triangular 'lateen' rigging to produce a versatile ship capable of sailing close to the wind. Together with improvements in ship construction, the invention of the stern-post rudder (giving much closer control over the movement of the ship), and the introduction of the magnetic compass, this created a vessel which was a wonderfully efficient 'energy converter'. Given only a small crew and provisions for them, it was capable of moving anywhere over the high seas and of carrying a worthwhile load of merchandise in the hold vacated by the rowers who had been essential in the early galleys. Such vessels became the essential means of European expansion and the growth of the great mercantile empires from the fifteenth century onwards.

Replicas have been made of several famous sailing ships such as the *Mayflower*, which took the original 'Pilgrim Fathers' to New England in 1620; and a whole port of the American 'colonial' era, complete with ships, has been reconstituted at Mystic Port in Connecticut. A few genuine specimens of sailing ships survive; these are mostly nineteenth-century vessels like the *Cutty Sark*, now moored in permanent dry-dock at Greenwich, although HMS *Victory* at Portsmouth dates from the middle of the eighteenth century, and the Swedish naval ship *Vasa* – incredibly recovered from the sea-bed where she foundered on her maiden voyage – from a century before that. Amongst the oldest specimens of ships to survive are the wonderful Viking long-boats which have been recovered from a condition of natural preservation in deposits of mud and are now displayed in Oslo. These clinker-built ships (i.e. they were made with overlapping planks of timber) were equipped with rowers and a square sail, and roved widely over the North Atlantic ten centuries ago.

With windmills we move into a more specifically mechanical form of energy-conversion, the power of the wind being transformed into mechanical energy and used for a wide variety of industrial purposes. The first recorded account of a windmill in England was in 1191 at Bury St Edmunds, which is only a little later than the date in the 1180s when the first authentic reference to a European windmill is attributed to one in Normandy.[3] There is a legend that the inspiration for the windmill was the prayer wheel used by Tibetan monks, but although the similarity is clear there is no plausible evidence for any such transmission of techniques, so that it cannot be considered as a valid theory to account for the origin of windmills. The first European mills were probably fixed mills, built to face into the prevailing wind and only effective when such a wind was blowing. It was not long, however, before the practice had developed of making the body of the mill movable, by pivoting it on a stout upright

timber or 'post' and providing a long tail-beam by which the mill
could be hefted round to face into the wind. Illustrations of such
post mills survive from the late thirteenth century, and the oldest
mill of this type in existence today is that at Bourn in Cambridgeshire which was erected in 1636. The next development occurred
in the fourteenth century, when the method of fixing the body of
the mill in a permanent tower was introduced, the tower being
usually constructed of brick or masonry and the sails being

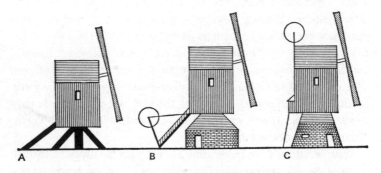

26. The post mill: three variations. (A) Simple post mill, turned into the wind
by the beam on the left; (B) post mill with fantail fitted to the turning beam;
(C) post mill with fantail on the roof.

carried on a cap which could be moved independently of the
mill itself. This was the *tower mill*, which was the sturdiest type
of windmill. Post mills remained popular for smaller mills, and in
those parts of the country where masonry was not easily available, but most surviving windmill remains are those of tower
mills, if only for the practical reason that their strong towers
have a high capacity for survival even when the cap has been
destroyed and the machinery removed.

Post and tower mills are thus the two main types of windmill,
but there are certain variations which should be noted. In parti-

cular, the form of tower mill known as a *smock mill* became important in some parts of the country, and a number still survive. This took its name from its resemblance to the flared miller's smock, produced by the shape of its tapering tower faced with weather boarding or occasionally thatch around a timber frame. Like post mills, smock mills tended to be most popular in districts where brick and masonry were scarce. Another type of

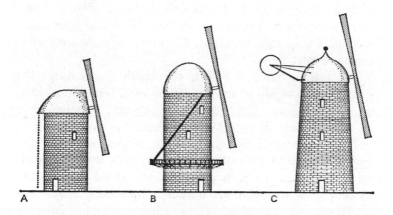

27. The tower mill: three variations. (A) Simple tower mill: cap turned manually by the chain on the left; (B) tower mill with gallery: cap turned manually by beams to gallery; (C) tower mill with fantail: cap turned automatically.

mill, which may be regarded as rather a freak since it was never widely adopted, was the *horizontal mill*, whose sails were in the form of a vertical cylinder with louvres or vanes to make it turn on a vertical axis.

Within these main types of windmill, many variations of construction and detail occur, so that no two mills look exactly alike. The sails of a windmill, for instance, provide plenty of variety. In theory, any number of sails from two to eight is possible, and mills with annular sails (i.e. sails carried round on the arms

– the 'sweeps' – in a continuous circle) have been constructed. But in practice the even numbers are preferred to the odd numbers, because if a single sail is damaged in a mill with an odd number of sails it will be thrown completely out of balance until the damage is repaired, while with an even number it is possible to remove the damaged sail together with the one opposite it, leaving the mill balanced and operational. The normal number of sails is four, and this gives a good balance while remaining fairly manageable, because if the sails are being rigged manually every additional sail involves more work and thus more delay. Examples may still be found, however, of mills with other arrangements of sails.

The type of sails, as well as the number, may vary. The simplest type of sail is an open-lattice work frame attached to the sweep, a canvas sail being rigged individually by the miller on each of these frames. Many windmills survive in Holland, and there almost all have such simple or 'common' sails. The Dutch millers traditionally rigged their sails with differently coloured canvas for each season, which added an attractive element of colour to a flat landscape with many mills. It is an interesting indication of the effects of industrialization and the mechanical revolution that most of the improvements in windmills and their sails were pioneered in Britain in the eighteenth and nineteenth centuries. First came the 'spring sail', patented in 1772, whereby the open frame of the sail was replaced by a set of louvres like those of a Venetian blind. These could be opened and closed by the operation of a lever on the outer end of the sails, thus varying their wind resistance to meet the requirements of the miller. These still had to be worked manually, by stopping the mill with each sail in turn near the ground or platform (the 'stage') around the waist of the mill so that the miller or his assistant could adjust the lever. The next refinement came in 1807 when the 'patent sail' was invented. This was a device for controlling the louvres on the sail by

a rod which ran into the mill along the windshaft carrying the
sails, from where it linked with a lever which the miller could
operate without leaving his position by the grindstones. This
was such a convenient arrangement that it was widely adopted
on the larger British mills.

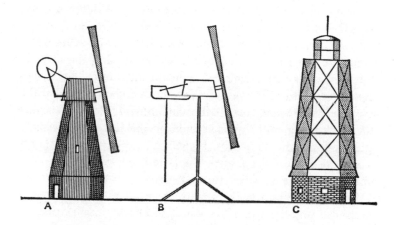

28. Windmills: three less common types (not to scale). (A) Smock mill with
fantail, constructed mainly in wood; (B) hollow post mill, used for pumping
purposes; (C) horizontal mill, one of several experimental designs.

The sails of a windmill are normally fitted into a cast-iron
bracket or 'cross' on the end of the windshaft, which runs back
into the cap or the body of the mill at a downward angle. This
both improves the aerodynamic properties of the mill and makes
it easier to balance the considerable weight of the sails. Inside
the mill, the windshaft carries a large 'brake wheel', so called
because the brake is applied to its rim to stop the sails turning.
Off the inner edge of this brake wheel, spur gears mesh with
teeth on a horizontal wheel – the 'wallower' – which is connected to the end of a vertical shaft transmitting the power down

the body of the mill, either to a 'great spur wheel' on the stone floor, from which a drive can be taken off through 'stone nuts' as desired to whichever grindstones are being operated, or to any other machinery, such as a scoop-wheel (for raising water), for which motive power is required.

Improvements in the mechanical construction of windmills in the eighteenth and nineteenth centuries were not confined to the sails. One very important invention which was adopted on virtually all the larger British mills was the 'fantail'. This was a device for correcting automatically the position of the sails, so that they remained facing the wind at all times. The fantail consists of a set of flat blades set in a circle and all twisted at the same angle so that they turn in the wind rather like a child's windmill. In a tower mill this is erected on the rear of the cap, at right angles to the main sails. If the wind veers round so that it strikes the side of the fantail, the latter will start to spin and engage with gearing which turns the cap on its greased runners so that the sails face once more into the wind, at which stage the fantail will stop moving. If the wind then backs, it will strike the fantail on the other side and reverse the process, turning the cap into the wind once more. In the case of a post-mill, the fantail is usually mounted on the tail-beam and causes the latter to move on wheels in a circular track around the mill. The fantail has rightly been described as an early example of a servo-mechanism or self-regulating device, and it saved the miller a lot of trouble, anxiety, and work. It replaced the earlier methods of hefting a post mill bodily whenever the wind changed, or altering the cap of a tower mill by continuous chains and gearing or, as in many Dutch mills, moving the cap manually by means of beams running down to the stage from opposite sides of the cap.

A rather similar device, in that it anticipated the later development of self-regulating machinery which was first worked out for use in the windmill, was the centrifugal governor, consisting of a pair of weights which were driven off the vertical shaft of the mill and which, as they span, brought into play the braking mechanism, so that the sails were not allowed to turn too rapidly. Alternatively, instead of operating the brake, the governor could be used to ring an alarm bell or to regulate the critical gap between the stones in a grain-grinding mill (a process known as 'tentering'). It seems certain that such governors were being used in windmills before James Watt patented the device for use on a steam engine.

It will be clear from what has been said already about windmills that they could be difficult and even dangerous to operate. The process of rigging common sails or adjusting spring sails, the constant vigilance required by the miller, both towards the internal working of the mill and the behaviour of the weather outside, called for considerable skill and dexterity. A false move in handling the sails could be fatal, as it occasionally was, because the sweeps of a windmill in motion move with great force. Slowness in adjusting to a change of wind, or even a sudden gust forestalling the corrective action of the fantail, could result in tremendous damage to the mill. Moreover, being often perched on exposed hill-tops to catch the wind, windmills were particularly vulnerable to lightning. One way and another, therefore, windmills were capricious instruments with a proneness to damage which made them quick victims of new power sources when these became widely available in the nineteenth and twentieth centuries. Very few windmills thus remain at work, and only a further handful in working order. Quite a number have been preserved, by the action of either a trust, a local authority, or individuals, and these specimens are well worth the attention of industrial archaeologists, preferably before they go on to plot the relics of less fortunate windmills and the sites of the many which have disappeared virtually without trace. For of all industrial monuments, windmills are amongst the most graceful and decorative features of the landscape.

The distribution of windmills follows a clear geographical

pattern. They have flourished in those parts of Europe where water power is not available, either through drought (as in Portugal or Greece) or because the land is so flat and low-lying that the rivers can provide little energy (as in Holland or the Fenlands of Britain). In the latter case, they were especially effective as sources of power for pumping apparatus, and in the polders of Holland in particular they were indispensable in the reclamation of many acres of land from the sea. Drought is not a general problem in Britain, but there are places on dry uplands and islands where water power is sufficiently scarce to have made windmills an attractive proposition. In Cornwall and in the Isles of Scilly, for example, there were some small tower mills with open canvas sails attached directly to the sweeps like many contemporary Portuguese mills. The tower of one such mill survives on St Mary's in the Isles of Scilly. More significantly, similar conditions of semi-drought encouraged the construction of many windmills on the chalk and limestone downland of south-east England, and it is this fact, together with their use in low-lying parts of Lincolnshire, East Anglia, and Somerset, which causes a marked concentration of windmill sites to the east of a line connecting the Severn and the Trent. So many fine specimens still survive that only a handful can be mentioned, to whet the appetite of the industrial archaeologist. At Wrawby in Lincoln-shire, a beautiful small post mill with spring sails but no fantail has been restored to working order by the enthusiasm and skill of two young men. Across the county boundary in Nottingham-shire, a working tower mill has been preserved at North Leverton: it is one of the 'Lincolnshire' type, with ogee-shaped cap painted white on a black tarred brick tower, with patent sails and an elegant fantail. Of smock mills, an outstanding example is that of Union Mill, Cranbrook, described by Rex Wailes as 'the finest in Kent and the finest in England'.[4] Amongst the many smaller mills which have been preserved, Ashton Mill at Chapel Allerton, on the Somerset plain, is now owned by Bristol City Museum and is a neat example of a compact tower mill, with the cap turned manually by means of a continuous chain. Chesterton Mill, Warwickshire, is something of an oddity, as it was designed as an observatory but converted to a windmill, the sails of which have now been restored.

Water Power

The water wheel is not as old as the sail but it is considerably older than the windmill. The first water wheels of which we have definite evidence were those recorded in the later Roman Empire, which have already been mentioned; these were usually under-shot wheels, although it seems possible that the Romans also constructed some over-shot wheels. By the end of the Dark Ages a simple sort of horizontal water wheel was common in Northern Europe, from which fact it derives its usual name of the *Norse mill*. In this type of mill the stream of water is directed on to one side of a horizontally mounted wheel, usually in the form of short vanes set directly into a stubby axle. When the wheel spins it drives the upper of two mill stones placed directly above it by means of a single driving shaft. In other words, no gearing is involved. Although it is still popular in Scandinavia, examples of this sort of mill are now rare in Britain, but they were once used widely in the Scottish Highlands and Shetland.

It is likely that some of the 5,624 mills recorded in the Domesday Survey of 1086 were Norse mills,[5] but it is assumed that by this date the under-shot type of vertical water wheel was well established in England. Certainly it was this type which became most widely used in the country in subsequent centuries. The *under-shot wheel* is a vertically mounted water wheel with flat blades or paddles mounted around its circumference. It may be fixed at the side of an ordinary river or stream, provided that the flow of water is fairly reliable, so that the water passing beneath it will strike the blades and set it in motion. It is usually convenient, however, to place the mill on a 'leat', an artificial water course directing water from the river under the wheel, and returning it to the river through a 'tail-race'. The advantages of this arrangement are that the wheel can be easily isolated by cutting off the supply of water into the leat, and the fall of water can be concentrated into a few feet and funnelled on to the blades of the wheel. But the earthworks associated with an under-shot wheel remain essentially simple, so that this type of wheel is most attractive when there is a reliable source of water to hand and a shortage of other resources. The under-shot wheel is also appropriate in low-lying areas where there is a strong flow of water although only a slight fall of level.

The under-shot wheel is the simplest and oldest of the vertical water-wheel arrangements, but it was gradually superseded for many purposes by the *over-shot wheel* as techniques of mill construction improved during the Middle Ages. In this arrangement, the water is led on to the top of the wheel and fed into latitudinal troughs or 'buckets' set in the rim of the wheel. The weight of water in these buckets sets the wheel turning, rather than the impulse of water striking the circumferential blades as in an under-shot wheel. In technical terms, an over-shot wheel uses the 'potential' energy of falling water, while an under-shot wheel depends upon the 'kinetic' energy of moving water. When an over-shot wheel is moving smoothly, all the buckets on the downward side will be full of water, and the water will fall out into the tail-race on the upward movement. Quite a small supply of water will suffice to unbalance an over-shot wheel and thus set it in motion, but it needs a steady supply, and thus mills using such wheels require careful planning to conserve a water supply in a pond and to convey it as economically as possible on to the top of the wheel. This type of mill is especially appropriate in hilly country where there are many small streams falling considerable heights in a short distance.

Such a stream can be used to fill a reservoir and supply water through a trough or a pipe to the top of the wheel. If, for some local reason, the miller wants his wheel to turn in the opposite direction to that in which an over-shot wheel would operate, the water can be fed on to the up-stream side of the wheel without any loss of energy and set it revolving in the reverse direction. This arrangement is called a *pitch-back wheel*, and it is quite common: it has the advantage over the over-shot wheel of discharging water from the wheel in the same direction that it will flow in the tail-race.

The most sophisticated types of water wheel did not become common until the eighteenth and nineteenth centuries, following the attempts of engineers such as John Smeaton, William Fairbairn, and T. C. Hewes to improve the efficiency of water wheels. Prominent amongst these improvements is the *breast-shot wheel*, in which the water is fed on to the wheel at some point just above the level of the axle (a 'high breast wheel') or just below it (a 'low breast wheel'). The breast-shot wheel has buckets like an over-shot wheel, rather than blades, and is driven mainly by the weight of water in the buckets, although a low breast wheel may also be partially impelled by the flow of water. A breast-shot wheel is usually employed when there is a substantial water supply, carefully culverted and controlled, and often with long leats constructed to maximize the height the water will fall from leaving the main stream to its point of re-entry. Another important improvement in water-wheel design was that made in under-shot wheels by the French General Poncelet in the nineteenth century: in the *Poncelet wheel* arrangement, by controlling the flow of water on to the wheel and by a novel design for the paddles, an efficiency of 65 per cent for a $5\frac{1}{2}$-foot head of water was claimed.[6] Such improvements led directly to the development of the water turbine, of which more in a moment.

Provided that an adequate fall of water is available, the power of a water wheel may be increased by enlarging the diameter or

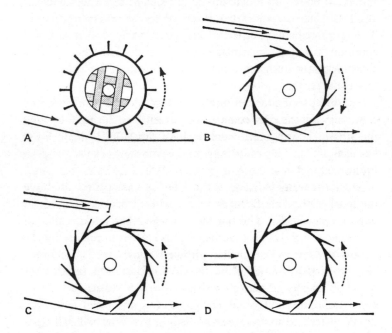

29. Water wheel types: the four main types of vertical wheel. Direction of water flow is shown in black, that of rotation by pecked, arrows.

(A) Under-shot. Falling water strikes the flat boards set in the rim of the wheel, and its momentum is transmitted to the wheel.

(B) Over-shot. Water fed on to the top of the wheel fills buckets, so that the weight of water unbalances the wheel and causes it to turn.

(C) Pitch-back, like the over-shot in construction, except that water fills the buckets on the near side, making the wheel turn in the opposite direction.

(D) Breast. Water is fed into buckets at or near the level of the shaft, causing the wheel to move in the same direction as the pitch-back.

the width of the wheel. The structural difficulty of constructing and mounting a large wheel, and particularly a wide wheel, kept the size of the early under-shot wheels fairly small, and when millwrights did experiment with larger under-shot wheels they tended to increase the diameter rather than the width. Few were made in this country larger than 15–20 feet in diameter, and when techniques of mill construction improved, some broad under-shot wheels were installed such as those at the Claverton pump for the Kennet and Avon Canal, near Bath. The normal under-shot wheel, however, remained a fairly compact affair of about 6–10 feet diameter installed on the outside wall of the mill. The wheel was constructed mainly in wood, and even when parts of the wheel were made of cast iron it was usual to retain wood for the paddle blades, which needed regular replacement.

With over-shot wheels, the supply of water was generally insufficient to fill the larger buckets of a broader wheel, but there was no problem about filling more *small* buckets so that the tendency to increase the power of such wheels by increasing their diameter became pronounced, and some very large wheels were constructed. The great 'Isabella' wheel at Laxey on the Isle of Man, installed to drive pumps in lead-mines, illustrates this point, although it is strictly a pitch-back wheel. It has a diameter of 72½ feet and was built in 1854. Although not quite so large, the big wheels at Killhope in Co. Durham and Foster Beck Mill in Yorkshire make the same point of using a fairly small water supply to maximum efficiency. The problems of constructing and mounting such large wheels were not solved until the eighteenth century, when cast and wrought iron could be employed for the spokes and rims, these being assembled from segments on the site. The buckets were generally made of thin wrought-iron plates, although some small over-shot wheels were constructed entirely of wood. As for mounting large wheels, it was sometimes convenient to carry them on masonry platforms quite separate from the buildings housing the machinery, as at Laxey and Killhope.

Tide mills used either breast-shot or under-shot wheels, and occasionally had one of each to take full advantage of the water supply at different points of the tide. Tide mills have been built in tidal estuaries all round the coast of Britain. They operate by ponding back the water at high-tide level and using this as a head of water as the tide recedes. At most, such a mill can only hope to work for two six-hour stretches in the course of each twenty-four hours, and as the time of these shifts changes day by day tide mills are extremely inconvenient to work. Most have now fallen into disrepair and been demolished, but a few survive, including one at Carew Castle in Pembrokeshire.

The main types of water power have been described here, but the variations within these categories are legion and it is fair to say that of the thousands of watermills constructed for all sorts of agricultural and industrial purposes in Britain, hardly any two wheels were exactly alike. The millwright built each wheel to suit a particular site and purpose, with the materials available to him at the time. Hence the extraordinary richness of this subject for the industrial archaeologist. Few watermills still remain in action, but the relics of literally thousands of them may be discovered, lining every water course of any size (and sometimes of no apparent size at all) in the kingdom. Some have been preserved, and some could still be preserved; but most are derelict and ruinous when they survive in any recognizable form at all, and the investigator must frequently rely on evidence of documents, photographs, and drawings, to establish the existence of a particular site. Enough has been said, however, to indicate that the study of the typology of water wheels is still capable of much development and refinement in detail.

Another important aspect of the watermill which is worth the attention of the industrial archaeologist is the driving method. Power could be taken off the water wheel in a number of ways, but the normal method was by a main driving shaft from the axle of the wheel. In all except Norse mills, this involved the adoption of some sort of gearing to convert the vertical movement of the water wheel into the horizontal movement required for mill stones and many other moving parts. Several types of gearing evolved. The earliest was probably the 'lantern gear', a cylinder of wooden struts meshing with wooden teeth or spurs on the main driving wheel or 'pit wheel' attached to the axle-shaft from the water wheel. The lantern or wheel which received this drive was known as the 'wallower', as in the windmill, and this drove the vertical shaft up the body of the mill to the large horizontal gear wheel which could be engaged as required with the 'stone nuts', the small gears on spindles connected to the upper mill stone. Whereas in a windmill the drive to the mill stones generally came from above, in a watermill it usually came from below. Lantern gears were later replaced by metal gears, sometimes 'bevel gears', in the wallower, usually engaging with wooden teeth in the pit wheel, as metal-to-metal gearing was considered too noisy; and the use of wooden teeth created a point of weaker resistance, like an electric fuse, in case of an emergency when something has to 'give'; it is preferable that it should be some replaceable teeth rather than a more vital part of the mill. This point is neatly illustrated by an accident some years ago in the Claverton pumping station mentioned above: when the water wheel was suddenly jammed by a tree trunk, the momentum of the pumping machinery stripped the apple-wood teeth off a large segment of the pit wheel before it came to rest.

In the case of the power of a water wheel being used for other processes than grinding, the drive could be transmitted by quite different chains of gearing. It was also possible for the shaft off the axle of the wheel to carry cams which engaged with hammers, as in fulling mills, or with crushing rods, as in the case of Cornish ore-crushing hammers, a series of cams at intervals along the drum of the driving shaft raising each hammer or rod in turn and then allowing it to fall. This was, next to the Norse mill, the simplest arrangement of all, as no gearing was required, which may help to account for the early popularity of watermills in the woollen fulling process. Another arrangement which also dispensed with gearing was that for driving a crank off an 'eccentric' (i.e. off-centre) connection on the wheel. The smallest operational water wheel I have ever seen used such an arrangement to drive a number of rods backwards and forwards, each rod being connected to a cable which led to a pump in a nearby farm building. This 'Heath Robinson' contraption was called a 'cucumber pump' and is widely used on the Amish farmsteads of Pennsylvania, where the devices of modern technology are abjured in favour of a more simple and devout life. However, gearing has remained the most widely used and important method of transmitting power, and although the development of gearing cannot be pursued in any detail here it should be observed as an important aspect of most surviving watermills. Another use of gearing in watermills which should be mentioned is that whereby the main drive is taken by gears off the rim of the water wheel rather than off the axle-shaft. This modification allowed large wheels to be built in a free-standing position and reduced the structural strains on the mill building. The larger and more sophisticated wheels were frequently 'suspension wheels' – that is, their thin iron spokes were kept in tension like a bicycle wheel, and the drive was taken off the rim.

Although traditional watermills are now obsolete and mostly derelict, water power is still a going concern. During the nineteenth century, improvements in the water wheel such as those devised by Poncelet, which have already been described, encouraged further thought about the possibility of achieving high speeds of revolution, and led to the *Pelton wheel* (after the British mining engineer Lesley Pelton) and thus to the *water turbine*. These are wheels which are totally enclosed so that a series of carefully shaped cups on the circumference of the wheel can move freely within the surrounding casing. Water, usually from a considerable head, is then directed through a nozzle into the cups, which spin the wheel at high speed. For ordinary mechanical purposes, this sort of prime mover was never very popular because the high speed of the turbine involved a considerable gearing-down to match the speed required for the machinery, but for generating electricity and for a number of specialized purposes the water turbine has come to play an important part in modern industry. Water power itself is thus by no means obsolete. Although the sight and sound of the traditional water wheel, so satisfying to both the eye and the ear, are now things of the past, only to be enjoyed in the few surviving mills and carefully preserved specimens, water power in the form of hydro-electric power from water turbines continues to play its part in modern industry.

11. Power II – Steam, Internal Combustion, and Electricity

One of the outstanding features of modern industrial society is its steadily increasing demand for more power, which has involved the exploitation of ever-widening sources of inanimate energy. This transition from what one American commentator, Professor Cottrell, has called a 'low-energy society' to a 'high-energy society'[1] has taken place gradually over several centuries, but the rate of change has accelerated in the last three hundred years, and a very important stage in the transition was the development of the steam engine, because this represented the first successful attempt to obtain mechanical power from the mineral resources of the world. Animal, wind, and water are 'natural' sources of power in the sense that the energy of the beast of burden or the elements is redirected for human use. With steam and the internal combustion engine, however, power is unlocked from such apparently unlikely materials as coal and mineral oil. The discovery of means of doing this has been one of the greatest achievements of human ingenuity.

Steam Power

The invention of the steam engine derived from the theoretical and experimental work of scientists in the seventeenth century on the nature of the atmosphere and the creation of a vacuum.

The discovery that the atmosphere exerted a pressure led scientists like Robert Boyle in England and Denis Papin in France to experiment with ways of increasing air pressure (as in Papin's pressure cooker) or decreasing it (as in von Guericke's experiment with teams of horses trying in vain to drag apart the two halves of a sphere from which the air had been evacuated). It is unlikely, however, that such scientific considerations alone would have produced the first steam engine. A pressing social need for such a machine had also to be found, and in the conditions of the late seventeenth century just such a need had appeared in the mining industries, where the perpetual struggle against flooding put a severe operational limit on the depth to which shafts could be sunk. This was particularly the case with the coal-mining industry, for in the thriving north-east coalfield the easily available surface coal had already been exhausted and the insatiable demand of the London market for coal stimulated land-owners and merchants to seek ways of sinking deeper shafts. There was thus an urgent need for more efficient pumping apparatus in the coal-mines. The normal devices of the period were continuous chains of buckets or bundles of rag and wadding which soaked up water, driven by animal, wind or water power. It is only fair to add that water power could be used much more efficiently than this, and it was so used in many parts of the Continent, as in the large set of water wheels installed on the Seine at Marly to drive water to the great ornamental gardens at Versailles by means of chains of rocking bars (called *Stangekunsten*) to drive water pumps.[2] Such devices do not seem to have been adopted in Britain, where pump technology remained comparatively primitive until the eighteenth century. As so much industrial archaeology begins, at least metaphorically, with the parish pump, it is worth looking twice at this simple but interesting piece of technology, using a piston in a cylinder to create a partial vacuum and thus to raise water from a well. This is the case with the single 'lift pump' where water is raised by atmospheric pressure, but the 'force' or 'plunger' pump drives the water by the mechanical action of the piston. It was this latter principle which was widely adopted in deep mines and in early fire-fighting appliances.

In the British situation, there was a strong incentive to improve on the existing methods of removing water from coal-mines, so that it is scarcely surprising that the first effective steam engine was named 'The Miner's Friend' by its inventor, Thomas Savery, who took out a patent for it in 1698. Effective it may have been, but efficient it certainly was not. The Savery engine had no moving parts except valves. It consisted of a pair of cylinders into which steam was admitted alternately, and the condensing of the steam in each cylinder in turn created a partial vacuum so that atmospheric pressure forced water up into one and then the other. The wasteful part of the process was that of admitting steam in order to expel cold water from the cylinders, as this involved consuming much more steam than would be necessary to make a vacuum in an empty vessel. Despite its inefficiency and the danger of a boiler explosion inherent in raising the steam pressure sufficiently to inject it into cylinders containing water, the Savery engine appears to have been used in coal-mines in the eighteenth century, but it is difficult to tell how widely. Documentary evidence is frequently misleading, as Savery's name was often associated with that of the Newcomen engine, but there is reliable evidence that these machines were still being used at the end of the century, usually to raise water a few feet in order to operate a water wheel. No examples of a Savery engine are known to survive today.[3]

A new type of steam engine was invented in 1708 by a Dartmouth blacksmith, Thomas Newcomen. This was a novel and robust machine which demonstrated that the problem of draining coal-mines could be reliably solved by steam power, even though its consumption of fuel was too heavy to encourage its use in other mining industries. The first Newcomen engine was erected at Dudley Castle in Staffordshire in 1712. It consisted of a piston moving in a vertical cylinder, connected by a chain with one end of a swinging beam, to the other end of which the pumping machinery was attached. By admitting steam to the cylinder and condensing it with a jet of water a partial vacuum was obtained, which caused atmospheric pressure on the top face of the piston to bring down that end of the beam, thus raising the pumping rod in the mine shaft. On completion of the downward stroke of the piston the vacuum was broken by admitting more steam and the weight of the pump rod made the beam swing back to its first position. Newcomen's skill as a blacksmith enabled him to build an engine which was mechanically sound, but the limitations of engineering technology at the beginning of the eighteenth century were such that great difficulty was experienced in making cylinders of sufficient precision and thus in making the piston fit tightly to maintain a vacuum. Various materials were used to seal the piston in the imperfect cylinder, none with entire success, so this remained a wasteful aspect of the Newcomen engine. Yet the machine was so valuable in the coal-mining industry that it was very widely adopted in the coalfields, and particularly in the north-east field, where there were about a hundred Newcomen engines at work by 1765. Such was the general nature of the wording of Savery's patent, however, that Newcomen was obliged to enter into a partnership with this predecessor in order to license it, and for many years the fame of the inventor was eclipsed by this arrangement. Posterity has been kinder to him, for the 'Newcomen Society for the Study of the History of Engineering and Technology' was named after him in 1919 and survives as the leading British learned society in the history of technology. The Newcomen Society succeeded in salvaging a Newcomen engine in 1964 and resurrecting it in an engine house specially built for the purpose in the centre of Dartmouth, near the site of the inventor's workshop. The engine, which is worth a pilgrimage by any industrial archaeologist, had been last used for pumping water at Hawksbury in Warwickshire for the Coventry Canal, but it had been idle for many years before it was rediscovered and moved to Dartmouth. It is actually a late development of the Newcomen type, having been modified at various points in its history: in its present form it incorporates a 'pickle pot', which is a vessel attached to the cylinder into which the condensing jet of water was sprayed. It thus represents a step towards the separate condenser patented by James Watt. In addition to the Dartmouth engine, a Newcomen machine survives in its original engine house at Elsecar near Sheffield, and several engines have been preserved in museums, the Science Museum in South Kensington having some large specimens.[4]

Newcomen engines were largely made from locally manufactured working parts (although the cylinders were usually cast at a foundry such as that at Coalbrookdale and transported to the site) and each was assembled on the site by a millwright, together with its engine house and boiler room. Because the engine worked at atmospheric pressure, the boiler was rarely more than a glorified kettle for boiling water, and the usual construction was what became known as a 'haystack' or 'beehive' boiler on account of its shape. They were frequently made of wrought-iron plates riveted together. Very few of these boilers survive, and where they do they are museum pieces; but it is worth looking out for others which may have been converted to serve other purposes such as water tanks. These boilers were sometimes encased in masonry, with the furnace flue passing through the centre to increase the heat transference. Newcomen engines were usually known as 'fire engines', which indicates the continuing wonder and puzzlement amongst eighteenth-century people as to what made them move at all. In more sophisticated circles, they have become known as 'atmospheric engines' because they depend for their motion upon the pressure of the atmosphere rather than on the expansive power of steam.

The conversion of the steam engine from a rather rough and ready piece of smithy-work into a product of precise engineering was the achievement of Boulton and Watt in the period of their famous partnership from 1775 to 1800. Something has already been said about the significance of the steam engine in the emergence of the engineering industry, and it is only necessary to repeat here that the two were brought together by the mechanical genius of James Watt and the business acumen of Matthew Boulton at the Soho Foundry in Birmingham in this period. James Watt took out his first patent, for the separate condenser, in 1769. The idea came to him when, as a result of working on a model Newcomen engine owned by Glasgow University, he realized that the heat economy of the engine could be greatly improved by separating the vessel containing the steam (the cylinder) from that in which the steam was condensed (the condenser), and arranging for the steam to be drawn from the former to the latter at the right moment. In the Newcomen engine, the cylinder was alternately heated and cooled by the admission and condensation of the steam. Watt planned to keep the cylinder permanently hot, providing it with a jacket to prevent the loss of heat, and to keep the condenser cool, removing the condensed water by means of a pump driven off the engine beam. The theory was sound but it took Watt six years to convert the idea into a working proposition. His main difficulty was that of finding craftsmen able to manufacture the precisely machined parts which it required, and it was not until he entered into partnership with Matthew Boulton, and was able to take advantage of John Wilkinson's patent for boring cannon in order to make much better cylinders than any which had been previously available, that he was able to make a commercial success of the invention. Then his patent was extended until 1800, so that for the last quarter of the century the Boulton and Watt engine dominated the development of the steam engine. A few relics survive from Watt's early career. The model engine on which he was working in 1769 is still in the possession of Glasgow University. The model of the separate condenser which he knocked together quickly when the inspiration came to him survives in the Science Museum. There are also a few tangible remains of his first attempt to build an engine in association with John Roebuck at Kinneil House in West Lothian.[5]

The separate condenser was the first of Watt's contributions to the improvement of the steam engine. Within a few years of entering into partnership with Boulton, however, he had invented a whole series of improvements, including the parallel-motion device for maintaining the piston rod in a vertical position although attached to the swinging end of the beam; a method of using the steam engine directly to generate rotary action; and the application of the centrifugal governor to the steam engine. The invention of rotary action had the greatest industrial significance, as it enabled what had previously been a pumping machine using a simple reciprocating action to become the means of turning the wheels of all sorts of industrial processes. To achieve it, Watt devised a curious 'sun and planet' gearing because he feared patent trouble if he used a crank, although it was the crank which quickly became the standard form of transmission. The sun and planet gears can still be seen on the Boulton and Watt engines in the Science Museum. The 'planet' was a cogged wheel attached to the connecting rod from the end of the beam opposite the cylinder, and was fixed so that it ran round the circumference of a similar wheel (the 'sun') on the axle of the fly-wheel and driving shaft, to which it transmitted the stroke from the piston.

Boulton and Watt manufactured about 500 engines during the quarter-century in which the initial Watt patent was in force.[6] Each one was designed individually for a particular client and function, and several of these early machines survive as museum pieces. It should be remembered that, although considerable evolution took place in the steam engine during this period,

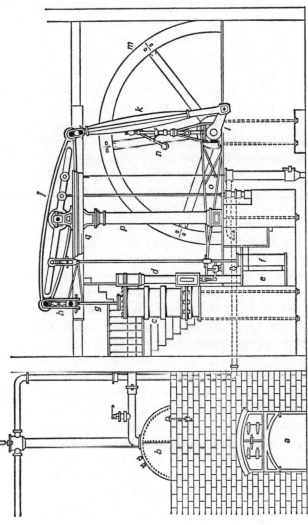

30. Diagram of a steam engine of c. 1800. The main parts are: a = fire-box; b = boiler; c = cylinder (enclosed in steam chest); d = valve chest (admitting steam to the cylinder alternately at top and bottom); e = condenser; f = air-pump (to drain the condenser); g = piston rod (attached to piston in cylinder); h = parallel motion (to keep piston rod vertical); j = beam; k = connecting rod; l = crank and crank shaft to m; m = fly-wheel; n = centrifugal governor; o = valve rods, controlling the valve action by an eccentric bearing on the crank shaft; p = column; q = entablature.

almost all the engines made by the Birmingham partnership before 1800 were beam engines, and that they all used steam at low pressure, only slightly above that of the atmosphere. The early Watt engines, indeed, were atmospheric engines like those of Newcomen, with air pressure acting on the upper face of the piston, but when Watt sealed in the top of the cylinder and lagged it to prevent loss of heat he admitted steam into the cylinder above the piston to make the vacuum produced below the piston more effective. From here it was a simple step to making the engine double-acting: that is, a vacuum was created alternately above and below the piston so that it gave power on both the upward and downward strokes instead of only the downward stroke ('single-acting') as in a Newcomen engine. But Watt resisted the introduction of high-pressure steam on the grounds that it was dangerous, so that in his time the steam engine remained a large and ponderous apparatus, being normally built into its own engine house ('house-built'), from which it could only be removed by a complete reconstruction.

The expiry of the Watt patent in 1800 marked a significant parting of the ways for the steam engine. Experiments with steam at higher pressures than Watt had used had already been made, notably by Richard Trevithick, and early in the nineteenth century Trevithick produced an engine which in addition to being very efficient was remarkably compact. He was quick to appreciate its possible application as a form of locomotion, and constructed his first experimental steam locomotives. Beginning with road carriages in his native Camborne in 1801, he went on to make the first railway locomotive for the Penydarren tramway in South Wales in 1804, and the engine selling trips to daring passengers on a circuit of rail near Euston Square in 1808. A plaque on the wall of University College London in Gower Street commemorates the latter event. While one line of development of high-pressure steam engines led to the very successful career of the steam locomotive, another no less successful, even if less romantic, led to the rapid development of the use of steam in industry. The older steam pumping engines were replaced by the breed of giant 'Cornish engines', called so because they were produced in large numbers in Cornwall by famous engineering firms like Harveys of Hayle. But they were in fact produced elsewhere and they became widely used throughout the world, wherever a pumping engine of great efficiency and reliability was required. The distinctive feature of the Cornish engine was the 'cycle' of events during each stroke, for with high-pressure steam it was possible to use the expansive energy of the steam as well as the vacuum produced by condensing it, and an ingenious arrangement of 'cut-off' levers operated the valves in such a way that enough steam remained in the cylinder to cushion the piston and give it a smoother action. In locomotive steam engines, the condensing action was abandoned completely; they relied entirely upon the expansive power of the steam, but for most stationary engines it was worth retaining.

Cornish engines, although erected all over the world, were thickest on the ground in their native county, where the remains of many large engine houses testify to their value in the metalliferous mining industry. A few of these engines have been preserved by the devotion of a band of enthusiasts in the Cornish Engines Preservation Society, whose work has now been rewarded by the recognition of the National Trust that it should take these 'monuments' into its care. The surviving engines in Cornwall include two in Camborne, one used for pumping (the East Pool engine) and the other adapted for winding (known as a 'whimsy' in Cornwall); another in the works museum of Holmans, the Camborne engineering firm; and a fourth, another whimsy, in its engine house at the Levant Mine, on the cliff tops near Land's End. Yet another machine owned by the National Trust, the Robinson engine, is at present inaccessible because it is adjacent to a working shaft of the South Crofty mine. The most impressive Cornish engines in Britain were the six employed in a single engine house at Sudbrook to pump the water of the 'Great Spring' out of the Severn Tunnel. These were installed in 1886 and demolished in 1968. Fortunately, the Dutch government has taken a more enlightened view and preserved the superb Cruquius Engine, an eight-beamed Cornish giant with annular cylinders (the high-pressure inside the low-pressure), built in 1845 with parts supplied by Harveys of Hayle to pump water out of the Haarlemmermeer, near Amsterdam.[7]

For most industrial purposes, something more compact than a house-built Cornish engine was desirable, and the introduction of high-pressure steam made such an engine possible. Indeed, from 1800 onwards the variation in types of steam engines became so great that it is virtually impossible to find any generally accepted categories under which they may be described. From the point of view of helping the industrial archaeologist to understand, date, and assess a steam engine, it will be most useful to outline some of the main developments which occurred, indicating the sort of features which should be observed.

First, a helpful clue to the age of a steam engine is whether or not it is a beam engine. The beam remained the most popular way of transmitting power from the piston to the main drive until the middle of the nineteenth century. This was partly because of the difficulty in manufacturing sliding-rod connections with sufficient accuracy, but it was mainly because the steam engine was born out of a need for an efficient pumping machine, and the reciprocating action transmitted by the swinging beam was most appropriate for this purpose. Even for pumping purposes, however, the beam could be simplified, and many Cornish engines were manufactured on the 'Bull' pattern, whereby the piston rod from the cylinder was connected directly with the pumping rod. But even as late as 1902 four beam engines were made to pump water from a reservoir at Blagdon, near Bristol (two of which have been preserved), so that beam engines remained operational throughout the history of stationary steam engines.

Another reason for retaining the beam which figured largely in the minds of the early engine-builders was the need to keep the engines vertical. It was believed that a horizontal cylinder would wear unevenly, the weight of the piston bearing more on the lower than on the upper side. This belief was shared by the early locomotive designers, who, except for Trevithick with his Penydarren locomotive, equipped their engines with vertical cylinders until Robert Stephenson experimented first, in the *Rocket*, with diagonal cylinders, and then switched to horizontal cylinders. The experience of locomotive-builders with horizontal cylinders in the 1830s convinced steam engineers generally that this was a convenient and efficient arrangement, so that horizontal stationary engines, which had been introduced by Taylor and Martineau in 1825, became the normal practice in the second half of the nineteenth century.

This transition from vertical to horizontal cylinders provides a basic typology of stationary steam engines, even though it should be remembered that beam engines remained in service for many purposes and that for certain specialized functions new ones were built. It should also be noted that other forms of vertical engine superseded the beam. 'Grasshopper engines', 'table engines', and 'oscillating engines' had been attempts to modify or abandon the beam in the first half of the century, and the 'side-lever engine' had adapted the beam to marine engineering by placing it along the base of the engine instead of above it, thus lowering the centre of gravity of the engine. The requirements of marine engineering, indeed, provided a powerful stimulus to continuing improvements in vertical engines throughout the history of the stationary steam engine, as did the shortage of space in some densely populated districts and the economies of direct connections with pumping apparatus in other cases. The most favoured form of vertical engine came to be the 'inverted vertical', with the piston rod coming out of the bottom rather than the top of the cylinder, and many examples of this type survive. Many of the steam engines which are still at work are of this arrangement, for this was the form adopted by the forced-lubrication enclosed engine built by such firms as Bellis and Morcom.

The second major determinant in the typology of steam engines is the principle of compounding. This is the principle, made possible by the introduction of steam at high pressure, of using the steam more than once at reducing pressures in a series of cylinders. It is a device which adds considerably to the power and economy of a steam engine, so that it has been widely adopted. The first compounding was achieved by modifying the existing beam engines soon after high-pressure steam had become available. It was done, first, by placing a high-pressure cylinder alongside the existing low-pressure cylinder, exhausting the steam from the former directly into the latter. This type was known as the 'Woolf compound' and was both the first and the last method of compounding beam engines, as it was employed in twentieth-century steam pumps such as those at Blagdon already mentioned. It was eclipsed in the middle of the nineteenth century, however, by 'McNaughting', the arrangement patented in 1845 by William McNaught of Glasgow whereby the high-pressure cylinder was placed between the beam pivot and the crankshaft, so that its movements were opposite to those of the low-pressure cylinder and helped to even out the stresses in the engine mounting. With the introduction of horizontal engines, other ways of compounding were devised. Sometimes a high-pressure horizontal engine was coupled to the same driving shaft as a low-pressure beam engine, but most horizontal compound engines were built with the high and low pressure cylinders one behind the other ('tandem') or side-by-side ('cross-compound'). By the second half of the nineteenth century, triple and even quadruple expansion engines were built, especially in the inverted vertical form for marine engines but also in various horizontal tandem arrangements for mill drive purposes. Paradoxically, the 'Uniflow' engine, which may be regarded as the highest development of the steam engine in terms of thermal efficiency, normally reverted to a simple non-compounding arrangement. In the Uniflow, steam is admitted at both ends but exhausted through apertures in the middle of the cylinder, so that the steam does not reverse its movement, thus reducing heat losses.

The third typological feature of the steam engine is its construction, including both the materials used and the form of mounting the engine. The early steam engines were 'house-built', which is to say that they were built into their houses as integral features, the beam – often in some sort of reinforced timber – being mounted on a masonry wall or on a bearing in one of the end walls. Newcomen had made cylinders out of brass castings, but iron castings became the general rule, these being bored with as much precision as engineering skill would allow to give complete regularity to their internal cross-section. From Watt's earliest innovations, however, the practice of lagging the cylinder (or even providing it with a 'steam chest') to keep it permanently warm was adopted, so that the observer rarely gets a chance to see the cylinder itself. The first significant developments in engine construction in the nineteenth century were twofold: the freeing of the engine from dependence upon its house, and the use of cast iron throughout the engine. These went together, for the creation of a free-standing machine depended to a large extent on the increasing use of iron in the construction, as it became necessary for the engine to be self-contained, supporting its own weight and containing its own stresses. The practice developed of providing a substantial casting as the engine bed, and, in the case of beam engines, erecting a frame upon this to carry the beam. This frame could be a single-column, A-shaped, or multi-columned, depending on the size of the engine. In the case of a horizontal engine, the framework was dispensed with, but the need for an engine bed

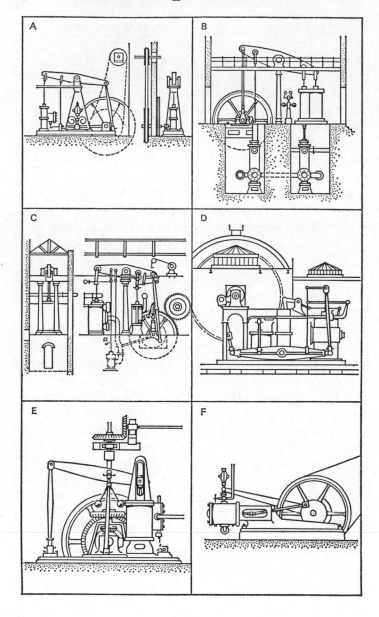

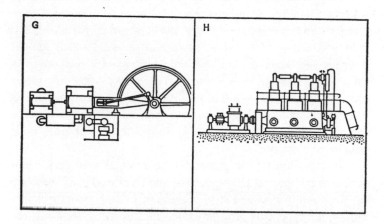

31. Eight types of steam engine, in developmental sequence. (A) A-frame beam engine; (B) Woolf compound beam engine; (C) McNaught compound beam engine; (D) side-lever engine; (E) grasshopper engine; (F) horizontal engine; (G) tandem-compound horizontal engine; (H) Willans inverted vertical triple expansion engine.

(Based on drawings by Frank Wightman in 'Steam Power', written with George Watkins for *Industrial Archaeology*, May 1967.)

remained, and with the development of tandem–compound arrangements these beds sometimes had to be lengthened. Another aspect of the use of cast iron was that it lent itself to decorative features, so that the columns and entablatures of a multi-columned beam engine frequently carried decorative motifs and fluting; and the cross-section of the connecting rod of a cast-iron-constructed beam engine was almost invariably cruciform, this style being replaced in the second half of the century by a smooth-surfaced steel connecting rod, slightly bulbous towards the centre to resist bending stress. The most important feature of the beam engine, however, was the beam itself, and the practice of making this in cast iron, sometimes in large parallel sections, became general in the nineteenth century. The great advantages of metal construction were strength and precision, and the latter factor in particular encouraged the use of sliding cross-head guides, which helped to make the beam engine obsolete for most mill purposes. As mild steel replaced both wrought iron and cast iron for many purposes in the second half of the nineteenth century, it was used increasingly in engine construction, so that the decorative features of cast-iron work tend to disappear from engines built later in the century.

The transitions from vertical to horizontal cylinders, from simple to compound arrangements, and from wood and masonry construction to iron and steel provide main categories for determining the type, date, and function of a steam engine. But there are many ancillary features which, although more detailed, are of considerable significance, such as valves, power transmission, and boilers. Valves developed greatly in the nineteenth century, from the comparatively simple 'slide-valves', in which steam was admitted and exhausted through the same openings, controlled by a moving slide; on to the 'Corliss', with a semi-circular valve turning in a cylinder chamber, and with separate valves for admission and exhaust; and reaching the final sophistication in the 'Uniflow' arrangement described above, or the 'Willans' engine developed in the 1880s to operate at high speeds for electricity generation, with the valves acting through a ported trunk piston rod. These developments took place in order to cope with the increasing steam pressures and to maximize the thermal efficiency of the engine.

In the earliest steam engines, excepting those of Savery's design, power was transmitted directly from the swinging beam to the pumping apparatus. The introduction of rotary action led to the adoption of the fly-wheel to give a smooth movement from what was still a fairly slow-moving beam, and the drive to the machinery was usually taken off this. Various sorts of gearing were used. Many early textile mills, for instance, had lines of horizontal shafting on every floor driven by bevel gearing from a vertical shaft geared to the main shaft or to the fly-wheel of the steam engine. A later practice was to use ropes running in grooves in the rim of the fly-wheel, a large wheel accommodating up to seventy ropes. The ropes connected with driving shafts on every floor of the mill. Again the practice was often adopted, particularly on smaller units, of running the power off a smooth-rimmed fly-wheel by means of a continuous belt. For a specially heavy machine in an engineering shop, a separate steam engine might be installed to drive it directly, but this could not be done so conveniently with steam engines as with internal combustion or electric engines, and the usual mill practice was to install one large engine able to cope with the total load of the factory. A very important development in techniques of power transmission which occurred in the mid-nineteenth century was the introduction of hydraulic systems. These used steam engines to apply pressure to water in pipes: the water under pressure could then be used to drive rams and thus to operate swing bridges, lock gates, cranes, lifts, as well as machine tools and other types of equipment. Remains of nineteenth-century hydraulic systems, often still at work, can be found in docks and other places where many large installations required power intermittently.[8]

Boilers frequently give clues to the careful inquirer about the history of the power installation of a particular plant. The earliest boilers were really glorified kettles, such as the 'haystack' or 'beehive' boilers already described in connection with the Newcomen engine. These were replaced by larger and stronger boilers as steam pressures increased, with various internal arrangements of pipes and flues. Trevithick introduced a single-flue boiler early in the nineteenth century which became known as the 'Cornish boiler' and remained in widespread use, especially for smaller installations. In 1844 William Fairbairn devised the 'Lancashire boiler', with two horizontal flues running the length of the boiler from the fire grates in the front. The

'Galloway boiler' was a development of this type, employing 'Galloway tubes' to increase the production of steam. A considerable variety of vertical boilers were also used, mainly for smaller duties, and a short type of horizontal boiler known variously as the 'Scotch boiler' or 'Economic boiler' was extensively used for marine purposes. Developments of the 'locomotive boiler' and the 'water-tube boiler' also affected steam engine practice, the latter being important in power stations in raising steam for use in turbines.

The stationary steam engine has now been largely superseded, not only by electricity and the internal combustion engine, but also by its own immediate derivative, the steam turbine. Charles Parsons invented the steam turbine in the 1880s, in his search to find a means of increasing the speed of revolution of the steam engine in order to meet the requirements of the incipient electricity supply industry. In the event, he devised a versatile prime mover which not only fulfilled its immediate requirements, but also found a host of other applications in industry and transport, such as marine propulsion, in most of which fields it is still widely used. The reciprocating steam engine, however, is now almost obsolete, after having turned the wheels of British industry for the greater part of two centuries. This is not to imply that steam immediately replaced wind and water once James Watt had invented the rotary-action steam engine, and we have already seen the ingenuity and adaptability applied to these earlier prime movers to enable them to survive as viable sources of industrial power, in some cases throughout the nineteenth century. But the steam engine was the greatest single British invention of the Industrial Revolution period, and it was widely adopted in virtually all industrial processes during the nineteenth century; and such was the engineering quality of these splendid machines that they frequently remained at work into the twentieth century, and long after other considerations of productivity and suchlike dictated conversion to new sources of power which were more economical on operating costs, and particularly on labour. The main disadvantage of a plant operating on steam power in the present century has been not so much the engine as the business of producing steam, which requires a team of boiler-men employed, when solid fuel is being used, on what is still heavy manual labour. Small wonder, therefore, that industrialists and other users have swung gradually to other power sources, and steam has become an increasing rarity. There are still a few mills in Yorkshire and Lancashire operated by steam engines, and steam winding engines remain in use in a few collieries up and down the country. The need to simplify and economize, however, presses remorselessly on the surviving steam plant, and it is usually in the mill faced with closure, the workshop in process of running down, and the unpromising coal-mine that the remaining specimens are still at work. Thus in a few years it is likely that these also will have used steam for the last time.

Steam engines, to sum up, are at the most critical point so far as the interest of the industrial archaeologist is concerned. They have become obsolete and they are disappearing quickly. The task of discovering and recording remaining specimens while they still survive is urgent. If the complex story of the evolution of the stationary steam engine, together with the contribution of the many engineers and their firms to this development and the pattern of distribution and utilization of these prime movers, is ever to be brought together in a single account, much will depend on the success of industrial archaeologists in assembling the essential information for such a narrative. Fortunately, much of this information has been gathered by the diligent researches over many years of men such as George Watkins of the University of Bath. Fortunately, also, several museums have taken an enlightened view on the preservation of selected steam engines, and this together with the labours of bodies such as the Cornish Engines Preservation Society and the Northern Mill Engines

Preservation Society has ensured that a representative selection of engines will be preserved for posterity. But there is so much still to be gathered and checked that this will remain an outstandingly useful task for industrial archaeologists for several years to come.

Internal Combustion

The internal combustion engine is still in its prime, so that it is not yet so ripe for the attention of the industrial archaeologist as the steam engine. Nevertheless, it has already had a considerable history, and it is as well to take note of the potential industrial monuments of the future while they are still fairly plentiful.

The idea of internal combustion was known in the seventeenth century, when there were experiments with gunpowder engines. Gunpowder, however, was not a convenient fuel, and the development of this type of engine, where the power is generated by the expansive force of the burning fuel within an enclosed chamber, had to await the availability of suitable fuels. The provision of town gas brought such a fuel conveniently to wherever it was desired in the towns boasting a gas supply in the nineteenth century, so that thought was once again applied to the problems of internal combustion. Lenoir succeeded in making an internal combustion engine in France in 1859, using an electric spark to ignite coal gas in a horizontal cylinder. The major problems with the early experiments were the difficulties of applying the spark to the fuel ('ignition') and that of achieving a smooth action from the engine. The former was solved by improvements in batteries and eventually by the device of the 'firing plug'. The latter was overcome by using a series of cylinders at different stages of a four-phase cycle, which has been known as the 'Otto cycle' ever since N. A. Otto devised it in 1876, the four phases consisting of injection (of fuel into the cylinder), compression, ignition and exhaust. Gas engines became very convenient for small duties because of the general availability of town gas. Quite a number are still in use in sewage pumping stations and elsewhere, and a selection have been preserved in museums.

The great development of the internal combustion engine came with the application of oil fuels. These not only increased the versatility and convenience of the engine: they also made it mobile, as a supply of petrol or diesel oil could be carried in a tank on a vehicle powered by such an engine, whereas the gas engine was never liberated from dependence upon the gas mains. Gottlieb Daimler used vaporized petroleum to drive an internal combustion engine in 1882, and soon afterwards fixed it to a bicycle to make the first motor cycle. Karl Benz in 1885 used a single-cylinder petrol engine to drive a three-wheeled carriage, making the 'horseless carriage' and the first genuine motor car. The mass of fascinating archaeology resulting from the automobile will be dealt with briefly in relation to road transport. Here it need only be observed that the internal combustion engine has probably contributed more to the twentieth-century way of life and urban landscape than any other single invention. It has achieved this largely through the petrol engine, but also through the diesel engine, developed by Rudolf Diesel in the 1890s to use cruder fuels than petrol for heavier duties in engines for lorries, ships, and industrial purposes; and through the aeroplane, with the sensational revolution in transport which this invention has brought about.

Mention of the aeroplane leads on to the observation that the internal combustion engine underwent a development similar to that of the steam engine when the gas turbine engine was developed for aircraft use (in the first place) during the Second World War. Early gas turbines are now objects of museum value, reminding us of the remarkably high rate of obsolescence by which modern technology constantly renews the material which the industrial archaeologist needs to study.

Electricity

The generation of electricity will be considered later as a public service industry. As a source of power, however, electricity has been a tremendously important agent of technological and social change in the twentieth century. The first electric motors were being produced in the 1850s, but they did not reach the stage of being commercial successes in Britain until the 1890s, when they began to be used extensively in urban tramway services and the London Underground. From there electric power and electric motors have been applied to almost everything requiring power – industrial machines, pumping engines, colliery winding engines, and the vast range of domestic appliances which has been described elsewhere in this account as a domestic revolution. With electric power, the steep 'energy gradient' which restricted the windmills and watermills to the very narrow confines in which they could operate effectively has been flattened out to vanishing point, so that power is now available virtually all over the country at the touch of a switch. The transition was made through steam and the gas engine, both of which were less restricted by locational factors than their predecessors, but provided energy which was less freely distributed over extensive areas than electricity. It is electricity which has brought the most dramatic change in the supply of energy to society in the 'high-energy' communities of Western Europe and North America. The ramifications of this process are of great significance to the study of industrial archaeology, for they throw open a much wider field, both geographically and socially, to the effects of industrialization.

12. Transport I – Ports, Roads, and Waterways

The history of transport is one of spectacular progress in the last two hundred years. Maritime transport, it is true, had already undergone substantial development by the eighteenth century. The evolution of the sailing ship had made possible the voyages of discovery in the fifteenth and sixteenth centuries and the establishment of vast colonial empires. Regular traffic between these new colonies and the mother countries in Europe ensured the continued development of the sailing ship and also the growth of ports to cope with the trade which flowed homewards across the oceans. This growth in maritime activity, however, was not accompanied by a corresponding growth in inland transport, which remained almost indescribably bad until the eighteenth century. Even royalty could not expect a smooth ride over the King's highway before this time, and apart from a few improvements in embankment and flood control to make the rivers more usable as arteries of transport, inland waterways were non-existent. Both road and waterway improvement began in earnest in the eighteenth century, and the subsequent developments have left abundant archaeological evidence. But before dealing with these it will be appropriate to consider ports and harbours, as these had chronological priority in the evolution of the modern transport system.

Ports and Harbours

Certain geographical preconditions are essential for the development of a port. These are, first, the physical features of deep
water giving access to firm flat land edging the water, and
reasonable shelter. Secondly, there are the features of human
geography such as conditions suitable for the growth of a town
and the existence of a hinterland capable of supporting the town
with food and raw materials and providing commodities for
export and a market for imports. A site lacking any one of these
features will never become a large port unless the deficiency is
remedied artificially, as by the construction of a breakwater to
give shelter on an otherwise exposed coast. Some parts of the
coastline of Britain such as the Western Highlands of Scotland
possess the physical features of magnificent ports, but the human
factors are virtually non-existent so that no large port has ever
developed there. Where the human factors are prominent, steps
have often been taken to improve deficient physical features
by engineering works, but the extent to which this can be done
successfully is severely limited.

All the preconditions necessary for the development of a
large port are subject to change. Tidal estuaries can silt up,
depriving such towns as Chester, Romney, and Rye of their
medieval status as important ports. Entirely artificial waterways
such as the Manchester Ship Canal can create a major port in
the heart of a land-locked city. Changes in trade and in the type of
ship can also bring drastic alterations in the adequacy of particular sites to provide good ports. The advent of the steam ship in
the nineteenth century, for example, placed the port of Bristol
at a growing disadvantage in relation to its competitors until it
changed its location to the new dock facilities at the mouth of the
Avon. Conversely, the advent of the mammoth oil tanker has
transformed the fishing village of Milford Haven into an important modern port because its deep-water access to a sheltered

unloading point has changed from being a worthless asset into a significant economic advantage. Ports have thus come and gone during the last thousand years, and the industrial archaeologist should be aware of the continuing flux of environmental factors which have influenced the changing fortunes of the ports of Britain.

It is useful to distinguish four stages in the growth of ports. In the first place, there is the natural haven. This is the sheltered cove or river estuary where ships can be run up on the beach at high tide, to be refloated on a subsequent tide, or moored alongside the natural banks of the river. Most ports begin in this simple manner, providing a stimulant to urban growth which feeds back into the development of the port as the urban market expands. On the other hand, development is frequently arrested at the level of this simple haven, so that it never supports anything larger than a small fishing village. If development does take place, the next stage is that of the improved natural harbour. This stage is reached when the natural advantages of the site are improved by earthworks, the construction of harbour walls, breakwaters, and wharves, and by the initiation of dredging operations to maintain and increase the deep-water access. This stage is normally accompanied by urban expansion and the economic exploitation of the resources of the hinterland. The third stage of development is that of the enclosed dock, when the increasing size of ships and the need for closer supervision of complicated loading and unloading operations make it necessary for a port to provide permanent deep-water facilities free from the disturbance of twice-daily tides. The fourth and final stage consists of the emergence of a major port complex, comprising several enclosed docks and the highly specialized facilities such as grain and oil storage and equipment to handle container traffic which are required by the largest modern ports.

A nation with a long history of maritime activity such as Britain should be expected to have ports and harbours at every stage of development, and this is so in fact. Many natural havens remain around the coast, serving a few houses or a fishing village, but with little of interest to the industrial archaeologist. As soon as the second stage has been reached, however, the existence of harbour walls, breakwaters, and other earthworks supply a fruitful source of material. There are many small harbours at this stage of development. Mevagissey in Cornwall and Watchet in Somerset are two well-known examples. The latter has enjoyed a trading boom recently because of the growth of a large local mill and the increasing convenience of road access to the hinterland, while harbours of similar size in the south-east are benefiting from the same sort of advantages because of their proximity to continental ports. Whitby, on the Yorkshire coast, enjoyed a period of great prosperity in the nineteenth century, based upon the whaling industry, and some remains of this industry can still be found, although the harbour has now declined in importance.

Some large ports are fortunate in having deep-water access to their main wharves at all states of the tide. New York is an outstanding case, and Southampton is a prominent British example. Such ports have only a limited use for enclosed docks, but most ports of any size have found it necessary to equip themselves with dock facilities. Dock construction began in the eighteenth century, when small enclosed basins were made at London (Rotherhithe), Liverpool, and Bristol (Sea Mills). The great era of dock construction began, however, with the nineteenth century, when the 'London Docks' were excavated in Wapping and the West India Dock in the Isle of Dogs. These were the first of the series of large basins made to accommodate the expanding trade of the port of London when the wharves below London Bridge became inadequate to deal with the volume of traffic, and the growing size of ships made it desirable to keep them afloat rather than to deposit them twice daily on the tidal mud. St Katharine's Dock, the highest of these docks on the

River Thames, immediately adjacent to the Tower, was constructed by Telford between 1824 and 1828. The robust but elegant buildings around the basin, mainly warehouses for keeping tea in bond (that is, without customs having been paid on it), make this a site of high interest to industrial archaeologists, although the redevelopment of this obsolete dock has involved more destruction than was envisaged in the original proposals. The other Thames-side docks, going down-river on the north bank,

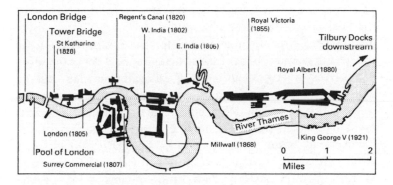

32. The Port of London. Dates against docks show their original construction.

are the London Docks, now also closed, Regent's Canal Dock, the West India and Millwall Docks in the Isle of Dogs, the East India Dock, and the Royal Group of Docks (Victoria, Albert, and George V). On the south bank, the Surrey Commercial Docks have closed, and plans have been discussed to redevelop the whole site as an inner London airport for vertical-take-off aircraft. The future of all these up-river docks is, at best, uncertain, as the main developments in the Port of London are now taking place down-river around Tilbury.

A very similar development has occurred in Bristol. William Jessop, the civil engineer who did much of the early work on the

London Docks, was also commissioned to improve the port of Bristol, and he did this between 1804 and 1809 by the construction of the 'Floating Harbour'. This involved damming the River Avon below the city to provide permanent high-water at the river-side wharves in the city centre. The 'dock' in this case consisted of the traditional river harbour, without the drastic tidal range of about 40 feet which had become a serious inconvenience to the larger ships. The fact that these ships could now float at all states of the tide gave the Floating Harbour its name, and a 'New Cut' was excavated to the south to carry the tidal flow of the Avon clear of the Harbour. This improvement served Bristol, in a fashion, for the greater part of the nineteenth century, but the construction of new docks ten miles down-river at Avonmouth and Portishead caused a gradual shift of trade away from the Floating Harbour. This is now obsolete and is being run down, but it contains much of industrial archaeological interest. The main entrance to the Harbour at Cumberland Basin, for instance, has several surviving associations with I. K. Brunel, and the Port of Bristol Engineering Workshop at Underfall Yard still contains some of the machines installed there in the 1880s, including a Tangye horizontal twin-cylinder steam engine.[1]

The other major ports of Britain, such as Liverpool, Glasgow, and Hull, have all undergone corresponding stages of development. Liverpool is a comparatively new port, having risen to commercial prominence in the eighteenth century when the 'Triangular Trade' in cotton goods, slaves, and raw cotton brought unprecedented prosperity to the city and its hinterland. The port grew rapidly at this time, the Mersey-side wharves being supplemented by ever larger and more convenient enclosed docks. One of these, the nineteenth-century Albert Dock, is now an object of great industrial archaeological importance, because it has become obsolete and is threatened with demolition in the interests of urban development. The warehouses lining the dock, however, are massively constructed in a style of commercial architecture which reflects the confident prosperity of the city in the nineteenth century, and the whole dock deserves the sort of careful consideration which St Katharine's Dock has received in London. Glasgow, on the tidal River Clyde, and Hull, on the estuary of the Yorkshire Ouse, both have long histories, although their development as major ports has been, like that of Liverpool, fairly recent. Both have acquired a medley of docks, wharves, and various fittings which repay careful attention. Cranes, for example, have undergone significant development in the last hundred years, but many specimens of older cranes, steam or hydraulically powered, survive.

Some quite small harbours were equipped with enclosed docks, and many of these survive. Bridgwater Dock in Somerset, for example, is a small basin intended to provide a connection between railway and sea traffic. The future of this dock is at present in question, but it boasted until recently a unique drag- or scraper-dredger designed by I. K. Brunel on the model of the very successful boats of this type which he provided for the Bristol Dock Company. The idea of the scraper was that it pulled a spadeful of mud from the side of the dock into the middle by winching itself across the basin when its spade-blade had been lowered. The mud could then be raised by conventional dredging, or scoured through culverts as in Bristol. The Bridgwater dredger has been given a permanent home in the collection of the maritime museum in Exeter. Other harbours with dock facilities were the coal ports such as Barry Dock, Goole, and Seaham Harbour, which have declined with the collapse of the coal export market but survive as monuments to a once flourishing trade.

The twentieth-century trend towards ever larger ships and increasingly specialized types of cargo and forms of cargo-handling has promoted the fourth stage of port development in

Britain: the emergence of the major modern port complex with specialized storage facilities and sophisticated methods of handling cargo. The model for this development has been the growth of 'Europort' around Rotterdam, but there is now a general tendency to rationalization and concentration of port facilities in Britain which is causing drastic changes in the existing ports and creating, incidentally, some large industrial archaeological problems. The remorseless shift of traffic down-river in the trade of London and other traditional river-side ports has already been described, and although this has been marked by the development of new facilities in the Thames estuary, Severnside, and the mouths of the Mersey, Clyde, and Humber, there has been in recent years a dramatic run-down in the older docks, accompanied by substantial adjustments in the labour force. For the time being, industrial archaeologists in areas where these changes are occurring may usefully concentrate on recording as much as possible of the old docks and their fittings. The future will probably lie with a few large ports offering a range of complicated services, but it behoves us to record the significant past of British ports while the evidence is still available.

Before we leave the subject of ports and harbours, two other items deserve a mention. These are the naval dockyards and lighthouses. The main naval dockyards are now at Portsmouth and Plymouth (Devonport), and both have equipment of interest in addition to such ever-popular features as HMS *Victory* at Portsmouth. Most parts of these dockyards, however, are only accessible with special permission. Other sites associated with the Navy such as Greenwich and Chatham also possess some interesting monuments to this association: Greenwich, for instance, has the naval museum, and it is entirely appropriate that this site should have provided the final dry-dock for the clipper ship *Cutty Sark*, which has become a splendid tourist attraction.

Lighthouses and lightships have featured round our coastline for centuries: there are the remains of a Roman lighthouse at Dover and there are other early examples, although the practice was not systematically organized until the Industrial Revolution

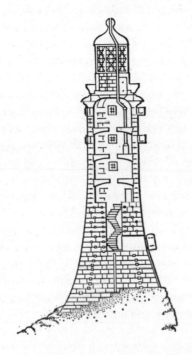

33. Smeaton's Eddystone Lighthouse, conceived like a tree trunk; the granite foundation stones were dovetailed into the rock and each other.

period. Some of the lighthouses constructed in the most dangerous positions have had to be rebuilt on several occasions, the epic story of the Eddystone Lighthouse being an outstanding case. When the present tower was erected at Eddystone, the Smeaton tower which it replaced, dating from 1759, was rebuilt on the Hoe at Plymouth, so that it can be easily visited. Such lighthouses, however, are rarely accessible; but many lights on promontories around the coast can be visited by the casual observer, and it is worth studying them for distinctive features. These may include the material of construction (generally white-washed in order to improve day-time visibility), the height and form of construction, and the nature and quality of the light. Most lighthouses are now electrically powered, sometimes still generating their own power on the premises. The first electric lights used were those at the South Foreland Lighthouse in 1858, when arc-lamps were employed with such success that the Brethren of Trinity House adopted the system in preference to the earlier oil lamps. Nowadays large electric bulbs are normally used, but whatever the source of light it is cast through a fan of prisms to magnify it, and there is a shutter which revolves around the light to produce the regular signal by which the lighthouse can be identified at night. Exactly the same procedure is followed with lightships, which are invariably moored well off-shore and are thus not normally accessible. Lightships have undergone many significant improvements since the first successful installations in the eighteenth century, but it seems likely that they will shortly be replaced by automatic lights attached to buoys, as these have been demonstrated to be reliable and economic devices.[2]

Roads

Wherever men have moved through shrub or forest, across grasslands and alluvial plains, they have made trackways to aid them in their journeys. In the first place these would have consisted of nothing more than clearing and marking the route, but as soon as societies began to acquire the features of a regular civilization steps were taken to improve the quality of their trackways. There has been speculation recently about evidence which suggests that the 'Megalithic' people who built the great 'henge' monuments in the second millennium B.C. constructed trackways in straight lines across the English countryside. Be this as it may, and it is certainly a plausible hypothesis about a remarkable race of whom we know disappointingly little, there is no doubt about the first systematic road-builders in Britain. The Romans built a network of excellent roads, as elsewhere in the provinces which they conquered, covering most of the country. It should be remembered that these were military roads, built to enable the Roman legions to move quickly in order to deal with trouble in any part of the territory on which they had imposed their government by force of arms. Because of this strategic consideration, and because they were not troubled by any obstacles of property ownership, the Roman roads were usually built in straight lines, and it is an interesting possibility that the Megalithic trackways already mentioned were made in straight lines for the same strategic reasons. Roman roads occasionally deviated from the straightest line between towns in order to ease the marching gradient or to take advantage of a particular river crossing, but an aerial view or an Ordnance Survey map still show the general rule that the Romans constructed their roads as straight as possible. The Fosse Way, for example, which ran behind what was for some time the western frontier of Roman occupation, follows an almost straight course from near Axmouth on the south coast to Lincoln, a distance of over 200 miles. Many Roman roads were literally worn away in subsequent centuries, and today when miles of modern road follow Roman alignments the original road has been completely replaced. At those points where a modern road diverges from the Roman route, however, traces of Roman construction can still frequently be discerned, with its distinctive convex 'agger' (the cross-section of the causeway) and well-defined ditches on either side, even though the surface stones survive only rarely.

As far as the history of roads is concerned, the Roman roads provide a justifiable extension of industrial archaeology, and much interest can still be found in retracing a Roman alignment and identifying stretches of remaining road-work. The ironical fact about the Roman roads is that in many instances the excellence of the roads contributed to their own decay, because without adequate maintenance over the 1,200 years following the withdrawal of the legions, culverts under embankments became blocked, to cause flooding in the valleys, and the eventual silting of these artificial ponds left acres of marshland which in time undermined the road embankment and made the valleys more difficult to cross than they had originally been. Little work was done on the British roads throughout the Middle Ages. A fact of general significance about road-making is that it is expensive, calling for large resources of money and labour. The Romans had been able to exact tribute and slave labour from a conquered country, but in the Middle Ages both commodities were in short supply, so that extensive road works were impossible. Towns maintained their own roads, and here and there a particular land-owner would undertake road improvements. But the main trunk roads languished and in some cases disappeared. Not until Tudor and Stuart times was a serious effort made to improve the roads, with strategic arguments again playing an important part in a mercantilist nation which looked to its own defences against possible invasion, and with commercial and industrial arguments in favour of better inland transport also beginning to carry weight. Parish authorities were instructed to maintain the roads in their own jurisdiction, and the result was a mass of local repairs which restricted some of the worst decay but consisted mainly of inefficient and unsuccessful bodging operations like filling holes with loose rubble. The condition of the nation's roads consequently remained bad.

Significant road improvement in Britain began in the middle of the eighteenth century. Again, strategic considerations provided an important stimulus, for the Jacobite Rebellions of 1715 and 1745–6 had underscored the military need for better roads. General Wade had been commissioned to build military roads in the Highlands of Scotland in order to subdue the clansmen after the 1715 Rising, but paradoxically his roads helped the Highland army to assemble in the 1745 Rising and to march successfully on Edinburgh. The alignments of Wade's roads can still be traced in several parts of the Highlands, complete in many cases with bridges. They were replaced in the second half of the eighteenth century and the beginning of the nineteenth by the road system built under the direction of Thomas Telford, in an effort by the government to pacify the Highlands once for all. Many stretches of Telford's roads, although much resurfaced, are still in use, together with dozens of bridges, the Caledonian Canal, and harbour installations which survive from this successful effort of pacification. Telford was also responsible for the other important strategic road of the period – the Holyhead Road to Dublin and the perennial political problems of Ireland. From London to Shrewsbury this followed the line of the old Roman Watling Street, but from Shrewsbury Telford made a new road across the Welsh Marches, up the Dee valley to Bettws-y-coed, and through the valleys of Snowdonia. Many industrial monuments survive along this road, ranging from the set of milestones and occasional toll houses to the superb suspension bridge at Menai which represents a crowning achievement of civil engineering in the period. Telford built the Menai Bridge, opened in 1826, towards the end of his career, when he was the first president of the Institution of Civil Engineers, founded in 1818. It was the first large suspension bridge in the world, incorporating many novel and ingenious features, and despite substantial renovation of the suspension cables and bridge platform it survives today with all its original gracefulness.

Government resources were made available to Telford in

order to build these strategic roads, but for the great bulk of the roads of the country some way had to be devised of recruiting private capital. The solution to this problem was the device of the turnpike trust, a private trust established by Act of Parliament and given a lease on a specified stretch of the King's highway. The trust was expected to repair and maintain the road, in return for which services it was empowered to charge tolls, in accordance with rates stipulated in the Act, on persons and their vehicles using the road. When the initial turnpike legislation was enacted in the seventeenth century little use was made of it, because money was still in short supply for capital investment, and investors who sought an outlet for their savings preferred the stock of the East India Company, which promised lucrative profits, or the National Debt (after 1694) with its gilt-edged guarantee. However, the general rise in industrial and commercial prosperity and the improvement in banking services in the eighteenth century had the effect both of making more money available for investment and of reducing interest rates, so that long-term investments in such undertakings as turnpike trusts began to appear attractive. A few such trusts were formed early in the century, such as the Bath Turnpike Trust in 1707, but the real flood of turnpike legislation came in the second half of the century when hundreds of trusts were formed and many hundreds of miles of road were improved by the turnpike road-builders.

At first, turnpike road-building was a rough and ready affair, not much better than the parochial maintenance which had preceded it. There was no residual road-building expertise in the community, and although road-building had already made good progress in France and other parts of the continent, little of the engineering skill involved in this was available in Britain. Starting virtually from scratch, therefore, British road-builders evolved their own technique. Jack Metcalfe, the blind road engineer who supervised many miles of turnpike road construction in the West Riding of Yorkshire, established the basic principles already worked out in practice by General Wade in the Highlands, that a good alignment was important in order to prevent a road becoming waterlogged, and that careful attention should be given to the foundations and to the provision of adequate drainage. Metcalfe was at work in the 1750s and 1760s, and as his principles became widely accepted the quality of roads improved distinctly, and further thought was given to the techniques of their construction. By the end of the century, as we have seen, Thomas Telford was building fine roads which were meant to last. Telford, the orphan son of a Dumfries shepherd, had the good fortune to be born just north of the Scottish border, so that he had the advantage of an education in the kirk school and served an apprenticeship as a stone-mason. His masonic training is reflected in the monumental character of his civil engineering; the principle of his roads was to lay very solid foundations, upon which he then built up a carefully graded surface of pulverized stone. But Telford built largely for government commissions, and then as now a government con-tractor could usually take a more generous view of expenditure than one working within the meagre budget of a private company. Certainly, Telford's roads were too expensive for most turnpike trusts, so that this monumental technique was little used on ordinary roads.

This was why the method of road-building pioneered by John Loudon McAdam became so popular with the trusts – it was comparatively cheap. McAdam's great achievement was to dispense with the solid foundations provided for their roads by Telford and many other builders. He realized that, given a firm and dry base for a road, all that was necessary was to provide a good surface which would be impervious to the weather. If the sub-soil could be kept dry, it would support any normal road traffic, and having more resilience than solid stone found-ations it actually produced a bonus by making the surface wear better than that of a Telford road. Small wonder, therefore, that 'macadamized' roads became universally popular with the turnpike trusts, and that the services of McAdam and his family were widely sought by the trusts from 1818, when he was appointed Surveyor to the Bristol Roads, to the decline in road-building in the late 1830s. Macadamizing, incidentally, did *not* involve the use of tar. The surface was compacted like that of a Telford road, by laying down stones of standard sizes, graded upwards so that the smallest were on the top, hammered down to form a water-tight mass. The action of horses' hoofs and the metal rims of wheels served to consolidate this surface, so that it would wear without major repairs for many years.

The result of several decades of activity by the turnpike trusts was that Britain achieved, for the first time since the Romans, a respectable network of roads. By the 1820s this was virtually complete, and it had become possible to make journeys from London to Edinburgh in the incredibly short time of forty-eight hours. Such a journey involved using the stage and mail coaches which operated over the main trunk roads, changing teams of horses at regular staging points. These vehicles underwent a rapid evolution from the heavy horse carriages which had been built to survive the ordeal of road travel before the coming of the turnpikes. The new sprung coaches, with slim dished wheels (i.e. the spokes radiated slightly from the hub to the rim, making for a lighter and faster design), appeared in the 1760s and enjoyed a tremendous vogue. The curious thing about them is that the era of the stage coach lasted barely eighty years – they had been made obsolete by the railways by 1840 – yet they have succeeded in establishing themselves as a familiar and romantic phenomenon, for example by being used to embellish Christmas cards, in a way in which the steam locomotive has not managed to do, even though it flourished for twice as long.

The stage coach has disappeared, except for the occasional specimen in a museum or transport gallery, but the era of the turnpike trusts has left many road-side monuments for the observant traveller. There are, first, the toll houses. There has been a great carnage of toll houses in recent years, because their proximity to the highways makes them vulnerable when road-widening is being carried out, and their frequently inadequate services and drainage make them unattractive as modern residences, so that they are often left empty and rapidly become derelict. Still, a great number remain, and are worth noticing. They come in all sorts of shapes and sizes, but the normal pattern is a small, compact house providing accommodation on the job for the toll collector, with windows that give a clear view both ways along the road, and with a board in a niche on the front giving the toll charges. Toll boards are now a rarity, but the blank recess in the wall is a tell-tale indication of a toll house. In a very few cases, the gate or toll-bar which blocked the road survives, sometimes having been used as a garden or field gate.

The most numerous turnpike relics are mileposts. Every trust equipped its roads with sets of posts to indicate the distance from some central reference point or between towns. There is a remarkable diversity of mileposts. Some are very plain, with a number inscribed in stone. Others have metal plates, fixed to stones or walls. Others again are all-metal castings, with letters and figures embossed on or incised in the metal. The style of lettering and numbering, like that of the design of the posts, varied from trust to trust, so that the incidence of particular types of mileposts can be taken as a sure sign of the area of operation of a trust. Some, like the Bath Turnpike Trust, adopted a special 'terminus' post to mark the end of their territory; but usually one has to notice the change from one type of post to another. Almost all the posts were removed during the Second World War as a precaution against airborne invasion, but most county councils have been conscientious about replacing them and maintaining them in good condition. It is, however, useful to remind the authorities from time to time that the preservation of such road-side details, giving character and interest to our roads, is a valued service. The advent of metrication is a special threat to the survival of mileposts.

34. Turnpike trusts: roadside relics. (A) Milepost; (B) terminus post; (C) parish boundary post. These examples are from the Bath Turnpike Trust; they are from drawings by Don Browning.

The turnpike relics also include signposts, although most of these are relatively modern, ornamental finger-posts at important road junctions, and parish boundary stones. The latter were mostly erected in the 1820s, when the trusts were made responsible for marking the points at which their roads crossed parish boundaries. They usually bear the name of the trust and those of the two parishes concerned.

The turnpike trusts declined in the second half of the nineteenth century. Competition with the railways made them less and less remunerative, so that as trusts came up for renewal their proprietors preferred to let them lapse, and in most cases their assets were acquired by local authorities. After the County Councils Act of 1888 these new agencies of local government, the county councils, were given the responsibility for roads in their territory. By this time, the roads were beginning to experience the first stirrings of that sensational revival of fortune which has continued to the present day. It was presaged by the vogue for the bicycle, and gathered momentum with the introduction of the motor car in the 1880s. The motor car increased rapidly in popularity during the following decades, and the modern automobile industry was born in Western Europe and North America in order to cater for the rising demand for vehicles. The road authorities were also galvanized into renewed activity. In 1896 the legislation known as the 'Red Flag Act', which had been passed to restrict the development of steam carriages on the roads by imposing a prohibitive speed limit of 4 mph, was amended. The event was celebrated on 14 November that year by the first London to Brighton rally, which may be taken as the dawn of the motor-car age in Britain.

One of the effects of motor cars with pneumatic tyres on the macadamized surfaces of the roads was a serious deterioration in the quality of these surfaces. The early automobile drivers and their passengers are invariably depicted wearing cloaks and scarves, not so much to keep out the cold as to protect them from the clouds of dust sent up from the roads by their own and other cars. The dust problem became an urgent public nuisance in the twentieth century, and attempts to remedy it led to the development of new types of road surface, which usually involved some form of tar-spraying or tar-mixing, from which the word 'tarmacadam' is derived. Other more radical solutions included the construction of all-concrete roads, which enjoyed a brief popularity in the 1930s when this method was adopted for the German *Autobahnen*, but most have subsequently been covered with tarmac, so that the survival of stretches of concrete road is of industrial archaeological interest.

The road boom of the present century has created a plethora of road-side structures and embellishments, some of which are worthy of the attention of the industrial archaeologist. The development of the petrol pump, for example, is an interesting story, and some early pumps of simple hand-operated design still survive. Again, the changing fashion in road signs is a topic of genuine industrial archaeological concern. Even signs which were in widespread use a few years ago, such as the T-shaped HALT notice, have disappeared from the roads with the advent of the new standardized international code. As we move into the age of the motorways, with their efficient design and functional road signs, it is worth an effort on the part of planners and road-users to preserve the individuality of the lesser roads, and a most pleasing and satisfactory way of doing this is by the judicious preservation of road-side relics from turnpike and other now obsolete periods of road history.[3]

Bridges

One feature of roads, as indeed of railways also, which requires special attention from industrial archaeologists is bridge design. The function of a bridge is 'to provide a passageway . . . where normal surface construction is not practical'.[4] The simplest type of bridge is the *beam* bridge – the stone slabs between stepping stones in the 'clapper bridges' of Exmoor and Dartmoor being early examples. The development of the *arch* in masonry or brick by the Romans placed another structure at the disposal of the bridge builders, and one which has been very extensively used. With the coming of iron as a major constructional material, iron-arch bridges such as that at Ironbridge were constructed, although refinements of the beam-type bridge (various sorts of girder designs such as 'truss' bridges) became the more common use of this material. Another sophistication in bridge building is the *cantilever* structure, in which a beam is extended with one end free of load while the other is counterbalanced to hold it in position. The outstanding bridge of this design is, of course, the Forth Railway Bridge. A type of bridge which has become extremely important in the twentieth century is the *suspension* bridge, in which the load of the platform is carried by cables or chains slung between towers. Simple suspension bridges have existed since man's earliest bridge-making activities, but their use in modern times has depended upon the development of suitable iron chain and steel cable, so that they did not become important until the nineteenth century, when the designs of Telford (Menai and Conway) and of I. K. Brunel (Clifton and Hungerford, London) showed the value of the suspension principle in crossing spaces which would be otherwise un-bridgeable. This type has been widely adopted for large road bridges in Europe and America in the present century. Brunel also devised a *composite* type of bridge, as at his Royal Albert Bridge over the Tamar at Saltash, which is part wrought-iron girder, part arch, and part suspension.

The nineteenth century was a period of intensive experiment in bridge design, and by no means all the types of bridge developed at this time were successful. Amongst the partial successes, however, may be numbered the *transporter* bridge, in which the traffic is 'ferried' across a river on a platform slung from trolleys running over a lattice of girders high above the water level. They were intended for use across river estuaries which required a high clearance for navigation. Two survive in use in Britain, at Middlesbrough and Newport, Monmouth-shire. Finally, modern materials and particularly steel and concrete have made possible further refinements in bridge construction, such as the slender arches and box-girder fly-overs being used at present on urban motorways. Bridges thus provide a wealth of industrial monuments, some of which are outstandingly graceful and valuable, and all of which are worth careful observation.

Waterways

Like road transport, inland navigation was either impossible or hazardous in Britain before the middle of the eighteenth century, except in the tidal reaches of the larger rivers and in the few cases where minimum improvements had made the higher reaches of such rivers accessible to small barges. It is true that there had been some large river-works earlier, at least in the seventeenth century, but these had been concerned with fen drainage and land reclamation such as the great works of the Dutch engineer Vermuyden around the Wash, and had little commercial significance. The Thames had been made navigable, in a fashion, as far as Oxford, in the seventeenth century, using a series of weirs and 'flash locks'. The latter consisted of sections of weir which could be removed, releasing a flood of water which could then be negotiated in a hazardous manner by the barges. Such locks became obsolete with the general adoption of the 'pound lock', but they were once widely used and fragments of them can be found in various parts of the country.[5] The Bristol Avon was made navigable up to Bath in 1727 by the Avon Navigation, which constructed or adapted six weirs and standard pound locks. These improvements, although important for local traffic, by no means resolved the increasingly urgent problem of inland transport, which constricted the development of industry in the large land-locked areas of the country. A more drastic solution to this problem was needed, and the answer was found in the construction of canals.

Canals were complementary to roads in the transport revolution of the period from 1750 to 1830. Whereas improved roads provided for the rapid movement of people, luggage, mail, and small items of freight, the canals were essential for the conveyance of bulky commodities over long distances. Both road and canal building began in earnest in Britain in the 1750s, and both were superseded by the railways in the 1830s. The roads, as we have observed, survived to make a spectacular recovery in the twentieth century, but the decline of the canals which began in the 1830s has continued up to the very recent past, when the growing interest of various amenity bodies is bringing fresh hope to the small fraction of the canal mileage which remains in usable or recoverable condition. An interest in canals is thus a very practical aspect of industrial archaeology,

35. Types of canal lock.

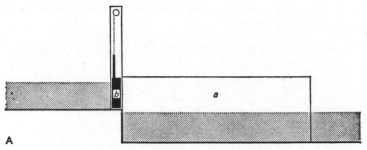

A

(A) Flash lock or 'staunch'. a = Masonry pit or 'half lock'; b = guillotine gate retaining water at the level of the adjacent weir. When the gate is raised, the water flows beneath it and enables boats to pass the weir.

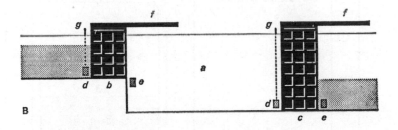

B

(B) Standard pound lock. a = Masonry pit or basin; b = upper gate (open), hinged on right; c = lower gate (open), hinged on right; d = sluice for equalizing water levels, controlled by paddle; e = mouth of sluices; f = beams to swing gates; g = winches to operate sluice paddles.

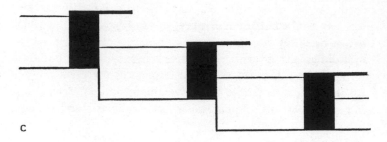

C

(C) Lock staircase. The upper gate of each lock pit is the lower gate of the lock above it in the staircase.

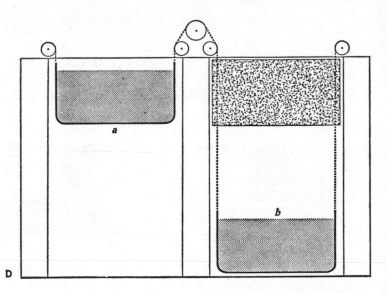

D

(D) Balance lock. *a* and *b* are counter-balanced troughs into which barges can be floated to be raised or lowered.

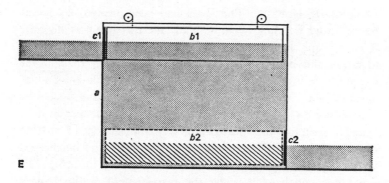

(E) Caisson lock – a form of lift-lock. a = Cistern full of water; b_1 = the caisson or enclosed vessel in its uppermost position; b_2 = the caisson in its lower position; c_1 and c_2 = water-tight doors connecting with the caisson. N.B. Only one caisson lock as illustrated was ever used, and that only experimentally, on the Somersetshire Coal Canal. But it represents a general type of lock in which traffic is raised or lowered in a vessel moved mechanically.

because it offers a real opportunity to assist in the preservation of remaining inland waterways.

There has been much discussion of the claims of various canals to be considered as the first in the country, and it seems likely that the best case has been made for the Sankey Brook Canal in Lancashire constructed in 1755, although the Newry Canal in Northern Ireland pre-dated this by ten years.[6] These were the first British waterways to run for any considerable distance without being merely an improvement of an existing river or stream (like the Welland Navigation and other works which represent a transition from river improvement to independent canals). What can be said with certainty, however, is that British practice was well behind that of many continental countries, where genuine canals with locks were already well established by the eighteenth century, and that the credit for developing canals in Britain belongs largely to Francis Egerton,

Duke of Bridgewater. The Duke had been inspired by continental canal building when he made the traditional aristocratic 'Grand Tour' in his youth, and he returned home determined to apply the principle of artificial waterways in Britain. He happened to own a profitable estate at Worsley, some five miles north of Manchester, where coal was mined and transported by road into the town. Bridgewater planned and financed the first canal in Britain which was completely independent of existing rivers in order to link these Worsley coal-mines with Manchester. Work commenced in 1759 and was completed in 1761. The canal was constructed under the management of the Duke's agent John Gilbert, and the engineer employed to build it was the itinerant and eccentric millwright James Brindley. At the age of forty-three Brindley discovered his vocation as a canal-builder and spent the rest of his life (he died in 1772) in the service of the Duke and other canal promoters, surveying and constructing canals.

The Worsley to Manchester Canal was short and free of locks, but it made a great impression on contemporary opinion. It began in a basin with access for barges into horizontal adits driven into the hillside to join the coal workings, an arrangement which served also both to drain the mines and to supply the canal with water. The route of the canal then followed the contours as closely as possible, except for the point where it crossed the River Irwell by an aqueduct. This aqueduct at Barton was an inelegant structure carrying the canal bed of 'puddled' clay (i.e. it was trampled by the boots of the navvies to make it water-tight), but the sight of water crossing water with barges plying across the river fired the imagination of observers and did much to cause the canal idea to catch on. The Duke of Bridgewater was frequently depicted in prints against the background of this early feat of canal engineering. Perhaps even more significant to contemporary opinion, however, was the fact that the opening of the canal halved the price of coal in

Manchester. The commercial value of the enterprise was thus made abundantly clear, and other investors were persuaded, timidly at first but with increasing eagerness, to invest in canal works. The canal age had begun.[7]

Brindley's aqueduct at Barton has been replaced, but the original canal basin survives at Worsley and is a suitable place of pilgrimage for the industrial archaeologist. The canal can still be traced into Manchester. It was subsequently pushed on to the Mersey at Runcorn and became known as the Bridgewater Canal. Before this scheme was complete, however, plans were already being made, parliamentary sanction was obtained, and capital was raised, for many other canal schemes, in most of which the Duke had an interest and for which Brindley was employed as the engineer. The Grand Trunk Canal linked the Trent with the Mersey, passing through the Potteries in order to suit the convenience of Josiah Wedgwood, one of its leading promoters. The Staffordshire and Worcestershire Canal, authorized in 1766, the same year as the Trent and Mersey Canal, went south from a junction with the latter at Great Haywood through a summit level near Wolverhampton to join the Severn at Stourport. This acquired a link with Birmingham in 1768, when the Birmingham Canal was authorized, and a network of canals spread quickly over the land-locked Midlands around Birmingham in subsequent years, bringing unprecedented prosperity to the Black Country. Having established the links between the Mersey, Trent, and Severn, canal promoters turned to the greatest potential prize, a connection with the navigable Thames and the London market. This was first achieved by the Thames and Severn Canal, from the head of the Stroudwater Canal in Gloucestershire through the Sapperton Tunnel in the Cotswold escarpment to Inglesham near Lechlade on the Thames, opened throughout in 1792. The Kennet and Avon Canal took a more southerly route through Bath and Devizes to Newbury, being opened in 1810. By this time canal construction had made very considerable advances on those of fifty years earlier, and most nineteenth-century canals were substantially larger and less shy of engineering works than their predecessors. The links with London were completed first by the Oxford Canal and then by the Grand Union Canal, from Rugby and Leicester to Stoke Bruerne near Northampton (Stoke Bruerne is at the southern end of the Blisworth Tunnel and is now the home of an excellent Canal Museum) and on via the Watford Gap through the Chilterns to London, eventually linking with the Regent's Canal through the inner suburbs of the metropolis to the Regent's Canal Dock in Limehouse, the last stretch of which was opened in 1820. This is the only one of the routes to London from the North and West which is still operative, although there are hopes that the Kennet and Avon route may yet be reopened to pleasure traffic.[8]

A great deal of geographical in-filling went on during and after the completion of these major routes. Lancashire and Yorkshire, in particular, were equipped with networks of canals, and linked together through the valleys of the Aire and Lancashire Calder by the Leeds and Liverpool Canal. This canal is still open and includes such remarkable engineering features as the lock 'staircase' near Bingley known as 'Bingley Five-Rise' (a 'staircase' differs from a 'flight' in that the locks empty directly into each other without being linked by a side-pond or pound). Two other trans-Pennine canals were built: the Rochdale Canal, through Todmorden to Sowerby Bridge, and the Huddersfield Canal through the Standedge Tunnel, which, at 5,456 yards, was easily the longest canal tunnel to be built in Britain. Shropshire was opened up to water transport by the Shropshire Union Canal and its various off-shoots. The Newport, Monmouth, and Brecon canal system was built to move coal down from the Monmouthshire valleys to the sea, and the upper part of the canal in the Brecon valley is now used extensively for pleasure cruising. In the south-west, the vision of a coast-to-coast waterway linking the English Channel with the Bristol Channel haunted canal-builders, but was never realized. The Grand Western Canal, despite its title, was a modest canal continuing the Bridgwater and Taunton Canal to Tiverton on a route which included some vertical balance locks, and opened in 1838. A fourteen-mile link from a point near Taunton to Chard, the Chard Canal, was even more modest, being designed for tub boats only. Completed in 1842, this was one of the last British canals to be constructed.

Many small canals were constructed in the south-east, but this was not one of the most popular areas for canals because industry was not expanding significantly in this region outside London in the period when canal building was at its height, although a north-south route from the Thames to the English Channel was projected and completed in 1816 as the Wey and Arun Canal. Similarly, the eastern counties remained comparatively undeveloped, and in any case they had the advantage of ample navigable rivers even though they possessed little industry. Even here, however, small canals like the Welland Navigation were of considerable local importance. Short canals were built in the north-east also, to assist the movement of coal to the ports. In Scotland, the major canal was the Forth and Clyde, for which John Smeaton prepared the plans in 1768, although he did not live to see its completion in 1790. The Caledonian Canal along the Great Glen is a substantial monument to the engineering skill of Thomas Telford, completed in 1822, but its value was strategic rather than industrial and it has never become a route of any commercial importance. Nevertheless, the Canal has many outstanding engineering features, such as 'Neptune's Staircase', the set of eight locks at Banavie, and it is still in working order.

This review of canal construction in Britain shows that there is a convenient distinction between the earlier canals, built from the 1750s to the 1780s, and the later canals, built from the 1790s to the 1830s. By and large, the earlier canals were narrow, built by Brindley and engineers who adopted his standard 7-foot wide 'narrow' lock. The main condition under which Brindley operated was the need for economy, with shoe-string budgets from capital which, although large in comparison with most undertakings of the time, was rarely adequate to meet the costs of construction. This consideration governed his choice of the narrow lock, and created the famous breed of 'narrow boats' which were designed for the standard lock. Most of the routes of the canals, of course, were at least wide enough to let two such boats pass, but the locks set the operating limits on the size of boats, and Brindley's standard lock was 72 feet by 7 feet 6 inches. Another consequence of the economics of canal-building was that Brindley and the other early canal engineers sought to avoid major earthworks as much as possible. This led them to adopt tortuous routes which followed the contours of the landscape and thus avoided the need for expensive cuttings, embankments, and locks. When a hill had to be crossed, Brindley preferred to tunnel rather than cut; the Harecastle Tunnel on the Trent and Mersey Canal north of Stoke-on-Trent was his largest operation of this kind. This tunnel was first duplicated and eventually replaced by another tunnel constructed by Telford, and the north and south portals of both tunnels are still worth a visit. Brindley's aqueducts were always very heavy structures like his first over the Irwell, but unlike the prototype many of them are still intact and in use.

The second period of canal-building is associated with a number of notable civil engineers such as William Jessop, John Rennie, and Thomas Telford. By this time capital for canal works had become somewhat more abundant (although proprietors maintained a meticulous control over the expenditure of their engineers) and the engineers had grown more confident as a result of the experience of their predecessors. Although many stretches of short 'feeder' canal were still constructed on the narrow 7-foot gauge, or with inclined planes

and balance locks which were usually restricted to small tub
boats, the normal width for the main trunk canals rose to 14
feet. Locks such as those on the Kennet and Avon Canal were
provided with large side-ponds to act as reservoirs and passing
places. Most important of all, the canals started to move more
directly across the countryside, through deep cuttings and wide
tunnels, and over embankments and lofty aqueducts. Possibly
the most splendid industrial monument in the country is the
Pont Cysyllte Aqueduct over the River Dee near Llangollen,
where Telford carried the Ellesmere Canal branch of the Shropshire Union system through a cast-iron trough over eighteen
masonry piers, rising at the highest point 127 feet from the
river below. It is fascinating to trace the evolution of Telford's
design from the short section of cast-iron trough carried on
iron stilts across the river at Longden-on-Tern near Wellington
in Shropshire, through the Chirk Aqueduct, where his confidence
seems to have failed him so that he enclosed the iron trough in a
high masonry aqueduct, to the final magnificent consummation
at Pont Cysyllte, where the graceful iron trough is unencumbered
by protective stonework. The details of this aqueduct are worth
close examination, particularly the way of slotting and bolting
sections of cast iron together to make the trough. Other distinguished aqueducts of this period which remain as elegant
industrial monuments are the masonry structures built by
Rennie on the Kennet and Avon Canal at Dundas near Bath,
and again at Avoncliffe, and his Lune Aqueduct on the Lancaster
Canal. Rennie also tackled gradients with some remarkable
flights of locks, such as those at Widcombe in Bath (seven locks)
and at Devizes (twenty-nine locks) on the Kennet and Avon
Canal.

Even the great improvements of this second period of canal
construction, however, could not equip the British canal system
to withstand the competition of the railways. Two decades of
sharp rivalry with the expanding railways resulted in a steady

decline in the revenues of most of the canals, so that by the 1850s they were either being bought out by the railway companies and run down, or they came to an amicable arrangement to serve the railway system, as did the Birmingham Canal Navigations. It is an interesting observation that the British canals paid the price of being first in the improvement of transport for bulky commodities by being condemned to early obsolescence. Like other technological 'firsts', they were not able to compete successfully with the more sophisticated systems which superseded them. It was not just a matter of the railways being faster and more convenient than the canals: the viability of many German and Belgian canals, constructed in the midnineteenth century, shows that there is still a place in an industrial landscape for large canals, and the continuing success of the Manchester Ship Canal makes the same point. (The latter, completed in 1894, is the only flourishing commercial canal left in Britain, and the only canal of any size to have been built in the country since 1850.) The trouble with most British canals was that they were too narrow, too shallow, and too tortuous to permit the introduction of the very bulky traffic which would have enabled them to remain in business in a period of rapid industrial expansion, whereas the railways were more flexible and were able to grow and adapt themselves readily to changing transport requirements.

The story of the British canals since 1850 has thus been one of decline, closure, and abandonment, until this process of decay was arrested in the 1950s by the rediscovery of the canal system as an amenity factor of great potential importance. The interests of the boating and fishing fraternities have combined with those of water engineers and planners thinking of 'linear parks' running along the banks of publicly owned canals, to breathe new hope into the dying canals. Many, unfortunately, have already disappeared beyond any prospect of recovery. Large stretches of the Thames and Severn Canal, for example,

have been filled in and built over, including the attractive inland port of Brimscombe, where cargoes were transhipped
from large Severn barges to the smaller canal boats; and hundreds
of miles of canal have vanished in this way. Only a few major
canals in the Midlands and the textile districts of Lancashire
and Yorkshire have maintained any semblance of commercial
activity, but at least they have been kept in existence, and there
is now an excellent prospect of their permanent retention as
pleasure waterways. A few, moreover, are capable of restoration.
The Stratford Canal, for instance, was completely rehabilitated
in the early 1960s when the National Trust, British Waterways,
and a lot of voluntary labour directed their resources and energy
to this objective, and it is now in use once more for pleasure
traffic. The Kennet and Avon Canal Trust confidently hopes that
it can revivify its once important canal, although the process
of degeneration is far advanced, especially at the critical point
near Devizes where the canal ascends Caen Hill by the great
flight of twenty-nine locks. The preservation of canal basins,
warehouses, and repair-sheds at Stourport and Birmingham
Corporation's tasteful restoration of 'Brindley Walk' as a
public amenity in the heart of the city show what a modicum of
imagination and enterprise can achieve in this field. There is
plenty of scope here for the industrial archaeologist to apply
himself to the highly practical task of canal preservation. But
there are also miles of now almost vanished canal to trace, and
many features to explore on the way, in addition to the wealth of
documentary material inviting research on the growth and
decline of particular canals. As an almost completely obsolete
industrial system with promising future prospects as a public
amenity, the British canal network deserves very careful
attention.

13. Transport II – Tramways, Railways, and Other Systems

The revolution which had been achieved in inland transport between 1750 and 1830 proved to be only the first phase in a continuing process of improvement and expansion. The roads and canals which had served the transport needs of the eighteenth century were both eclipsed by the emergence of an even more spectacular transport system in the shape of the railways. Canal traffic in Britain was hardly able to survive the competition of this rival system and declined into a long and lingering death, and although, as we have seen, the road system survived to stage a very successful return to prosperity in the twentieth century, the period from 1830 to 1914 may be fairly regarded as the Railway Era. Since the First World War the railways have themselves been faced by mounting competition, both from the automobile and – for long journeys – from the aeroplane, so that much of the railway system has become obsolete. Despite stringent attempts to modernize the system (electrification, diesel locomotives, freight-liners, tighter schedules, and so on), the fact is that British Rail operates over what is, at least in its civil-engineering features, the largest single collection of industrial monuments in the country. The tension between the need to modernize on the one hand and the industrial heritage on the other has not, indeed, been a happy one, and has brought about some of the *causes célèbres* which have stimulated the study of industrial archaeology. The controversies over the Doric portico at Euston Station, demolished in 1962, and the set of pumping engines on the Severn Tunnel at Sudbrook, scrapped in 1968, are two of the more outstanding examples, and the fact that both these monuments were destroyed in the interests of modernization gives cause for thought about the overall policy of British Rail in relation to the tremendous engineering legacy for which it is responsible. In this chapter we will consider the development of the railway system and that of other transport systems related to it and replacing it.

Tramways

The Railway Era was the product of two distinct lines of development: the growth of tramways and the appearance of the locomotive steam engine. These were first brought together in a tentative manner by Richard Trevithick, who devised a steam locomotive to operate on the Penydarren tramway in 1804. The experiment was not a conspicuous success, because the engine was hard on the cast-iron sections of the track, which broke repeatedly under the treatment. Techniques of both track and locomotive construction rapidly improved, however, so that steam locomotion was able to vindicate George Stephenson's faith in the method on the Stockton and Darlington Railway, opened in 1825; and by 1830 the opening of the Liverpool and Manchester Railway was able to provide a convincing demonstration of the ability of steam power to drive locomotive engines of sufficient efficiency to fulfil all the requirements of the proprietors.

Before this conjunction had been completed in 1830, tramways had already undergone a significant evolution which prepared the way for the subsequent success of the railways. There is a certain difficulty about terminology here, as 'tramway'

and 'railway' were used interchangeably in the late eighteenth and early nineteenth centuries, together with such other
terms as 'dramroad', 'wagonway', and 'plateway'. In this
context, a tramway is understood to denote a track (of any kind)
for carrying wagons under the influence of gravity or by animal
power or by haulage from stationary engines. Writing a recent
account of such tramways, Bertram Baxter traced their origins
from a wooden 'Rayle-way' constructed at Woolaton near Nottingham in 1603.[1] It is probably fanciful to seek an earlier origin in
such features as the grooves for chariot wheels cut in rock during
the Roman Empire at Syracuse in Sicily and on the island of
Malta, and as far as Britain is concerned it may be safely agreed
that tramways began in the seventeenth century. Certainly by
the end of that century they were becoming common in the
colliery areas of north-east England and in the iron-working
districts of Shropshire and their popularity for short-haul
operation, usually in connection with river transport, continued to
increase in the following century. Baxter has suggested a useful
way of classifying tramway development in three phases, according to the type of organization which built them. The first tramways were mostly built by colliery, quarrying, and iron-working
companies to improve the internal transport of their own plant
and to give them better access to available waterways. The
early Tyneside tramroads were of this nature, and one of these,
the Tanfield Tramway, still possesses the remains of the first
'railway' bridge in the world, the substantial masonry structure
of the Causey Arch in County Durham, erected in 1721. Ten
years later, Ralph Allen of Bath opened his Prior Park Tramway
to convey stone mined on his estate to the River Avon in the
valley below, and this model was copied by other stone-mining
enterprises in the region, fragments of whose tramways can still
be discerned. The first 'railway' Act of Parliament was promoted
for a colliery enterprise, being passed in 1758 in order to establish
the Middleton Railway at Leeds. The Penydarren tramway in

South Wales was similarly sponsored by a group of industrialists – in this case ironmasters.

In the second phase of tramway development, they were
promoted by canal companies in order to provide feeders for
the canals or to fill in gaps where canal construction was difficult.
Tramways of this kind were sponsored by the Trent and Mersey
Canal to link Stoke-on-Trent with limestone quarries at Caldon
(opened in 1777), and by the Peak Forest Canal to link with
quarries at Chapel-en-le-Frith (opened in 1796; a branch canal
ran from a junction with the Ashton-under-Lyne Canal near
Marple to Bugsworth, and thence the seven-mile tramroad
ran to Doveholes). A longer link was made to connect the Peak
Forest Canal at Whaley Bridge with the Cromford Canal at
Cromford (twenty-four miles long, opened in 1831, with nine
inclined planes all worked by steam engines, except for one
which was counterbalanced). Many canals had complicated
networks of feeder tramways, such as those in the South Wales
valleys and, on a smaller scale, those built to serve the Somerset
Coal Canal, running westwards from the Dundas Aqueduct on
the Kennet and Avon Canal. Traces of most of these lines
survive.[2]

The Act authorizing the formation of the Surrey Iron Railway Company in 1801 marks the beginning of the third phase
of tramway construction, in which the tramway became the
specific object of a public company instead of being ancillary
to another enterprise or the appendage of a canal company.
William Jessop built the Surrey Iron Railway, covering in the
first place a distance of nine miles from Wandsworth on the
Thames to Croydon (opened in 1803), but it was subsequently
extended to Merstham (in 1805) as the next stage in the construction of a route which was envisaged as linking London and
Portsmouth. Several further Acts were promoted for tramway
construction in the following decade, many of them being in
Wales, including the Oystermouth or Swansea and Mumbles

line, for which it is claimed that in 1807 it became the first line on which passengers were regularly carried. This line was finally closed in 1960 and its remains have only recently been destroyed. There followed a spate of tramway companies' in the 1820s, including the Stockton and Darlington Railway

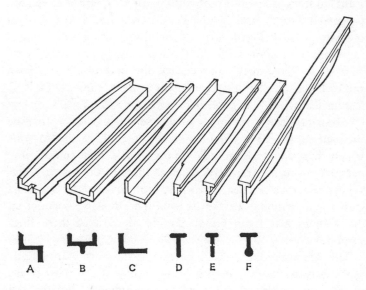

36. Some typical tram-plate sections: (A) Surrey Iron Railway (1803): (B) Silkstone (1809); (C) Coalbrookdale (1814). Some early types of edge rail; (D) Stephenson (1816); (E) Coleorton (1820); (F) Birkinshaw (1825).

(opened in 1825 and partially operated by steam locomotives). There were fifteen Acts in the year 1825–6 alone, and another nine in 1828–9, including the Bristol and Gloucestershire and the Avon and Gloucestershire, after which interest shifted from tramways to railways, although tramway construction continued in the 1830s, and many of them remained in oper-

ation throughout the nineteenth century and in some cases survived into the present century. Many other lines, of course,
were converted into railways, so that it is often difficult to
distinguish the tramway origin of the route.

While tramway organization advanced through these three
phases, the techniques of construction underwent a similar
evolution. The early tramways usually had wooden rails attached
to wooden sleepers, with flanged-wheeled wagons running
over them. The Prior Park stone-quarry tramway was a good
example of this type of construction. With the widespread
introduction of cast iron, however, the practice developed of
making plateways – that is, L-shaped plates with the flange on
the inside edge to hold the flat wheels of the wagons. These
were fastened with metal spikes to stone sleepers set in the
ground, and when the iron rail underwent a further development, becoming a ridge-rail once more to accommodate flanged
wheels, the practice of using stone sleeper blocks was retained
and survived into the early years of railway building, when the
increased weight of engines and rolling stock made necessary the
insertion of a cross-tie, so that the stone sleeper was discarded
in favour of the wooden sleeper carrying both rails. The extent to
which the individual stone sleeper blocks could become displaced over a period of time was brought home to me when,
after some careful field-work on the Avon and Gloucestershire
Railway, I concluded that its gauge was considerably more than
the standard 4 feet 8½ inches, only to be convinced subsequently
by the outcry of the experts and further field-work that the line
was, in fact, of standard gauge. To this cautionary tale may
perhaps be added a further word of warning. In measuring the
gauge of a tramway or railway it is important to take the distance
between the *inside* of the rails and not their centres as marked
by the bolt holes in the stone sleeper by which the cast-iron
'shoe' was attached before the rail was fitted. In these observations it is assumed, as is usually the case, that only the stone

sleepers survive: the industrial archaeologist considers himself fortunate to find even these. The gauge of tramways did, of course, vary, although by the early nineteenth century the 'standard' gauge was being widely accepted as the 4 feet 8½ inches which had been adopted on the Tyneside mineral tramways. The major determining factor was the convenient width of a horse-drawn vehicle.

The quality of the track also underwent great improvement in the hundred years before the Railway Era. Many types of iron castings were tried, including the 'fish-belly' form which was widely used on the later tramways; many sections of it have survived in fencing and other uses even though little if any is still *in situ*. Much may be found alongside the Kennet and Avon Canal, for instance, because the Great Western Railway used the track from the Avon and Gloucestershire Railway, when it obtained possession of this tramway, in order to provide railings and racks for stop-beams by the canal, for which it had also become responsible. 'Fish-belly' rail, incidentally, is rail with an undulating bottom edge, which makes it easy to fix the sleeper shoes at the narrow points while giving greater strength on the stretches between the sleepers. A unique sort of tramway rail which largely survives where it was laid is that of the track which was opened in 1820 to serve the Haytor granite quarries on Dartmoor: not only did this track carry granite, it was also made of granite blocks, carefully grooved with an L-section like a plateway and laid end-to-end, intersections being provided with points operated by a small flange of cast iron.

Finally, in relation to tramways, it should be observed that the engineers responsible for their construction gained a confidence and expertise which served them well when they went on to build railways after 1830. Indeed, the rapid development of the railway system would have been inconceivable without this experience in constructing carefully graded causeways, involving extensive cuttings, embankments, and tunnels. Tramways frequently turned corners at sharper angles than was possible on railways, but in most respects the techniques appropriate to tramway construction could be applied directly to railways, and many of the early British railway engineers had served their practical apprenticeship on tramways, George Stephenson being the outstanding example. The mineral tramways thus performed an essential role in the dawn of the Railway Era, and the fact that so many of their routes can still be traced makes them a fascinating subject for the industrial archaeologist.

Railways

In addition to the development of the tramways, the other essential ingredient in the British railway system was the emergence of the locomotive steam engine. Trevithick had perceived that high-pressure steam made possible the construction of a more compact boiler and the abandonment of the condenser, so that it became feasible to build a steam engine capable of propelling itself efficiently. His experiments with locomotive engines in the first decade of the nineteenth century, however, were not commercial successes, and it was left to other engineers to develop the idea in subsequent decades. The first satisfactory steam locomotives were introduced on the colliery tramways of Tyneside, such as that at Wylam where William Hedley's famous *Puffing Billy* (preserved in the Science Museum) was built in 1813, using the exhaust steam to increase the draught through the fire-box, thus raising the efficiency of the machine. At Wylam, also, George Stephenson was born, so that he was able to observe the experiments with steam locomotives in his home village before he became personally involved in engine construction. He made his first locomotive, the *Blucher*, in 1815, and by 1825 he had built several more, including the *Locomotion* (preserved on Darlington Station) for the Stockton and Darlington Railway, which he had surveyed and constructed. This early experience and that of contemporary locomotive engineers such as Timothy Hackworth had produced a robust form of steam locomotive with vertical cylinders and steam blast which was capable of pulling a 'train' of wagons at speeds of 15-20 mph.

Despite this progress, it was still not certain until 1829 whether or not the locomotive steam engine was capable of fulfilling all the requirements of a passenger-carrying railway system, so that the proprietors of the Liverpool and Manchester Railway were considering the possibility of installing stationary steam engines to help on the severest gradients on their route. The issue was finally determined by the famous Rainhill Trial in October 1829, when the revolutionary locomotive of George and Robert Stephenson, the *Rocket* (preserved in mutilated form in the Science Museum, together with a replica of the original), gave a convincing demonstration of its ability to cope with all sorts of traffic in any likely conditions. The novel features of the *Rocket* included a multi-tubular boiler and cylinders arranged diagonally on the side of the engine. It won the Trial and was adapted for use on the new railway when it opened. At this point in time – 15 September 1830 – the two separate developments of the tramway and the steam locomotive can be said to have combined fully in a time-tabled passenger and goods service to create the first complete railway system in the world. At this point, also, the Railway Era began.

For all its novelty and success, the design of the *Rocket* was essentially transitional, marking the half-way point between the vertical cylinders of the early locomotives and the horizontal cylinders of those which quickly succeeded it as Robert Stephenson improved upon his design and carried the idea through to its logical conclusion by placing the cylinders horizontally between the wheels of the engine, driving on to a cranked axle. As locomotives grew in size, the horizontal cylinders were placed both inside and outside the frame, and a vast number of variations in locomotive design were incorporated as loads, speeds, and safety factors were all increased in the following hundred years. Much of the history of mechanical engineering is bound up with this development of the steam locomotive,[3] and to the differences within British practice must be added those introduced by European and American designers to meet varying local conditions. The whole story, however, is one of such intricacy that it cannot be conveniently told or even adequately summarized here. The best industrial archaeological material on the steam locomotive is in the new National Transport Museum at York, with much smaller but significant collections at Swindon and in the South Kensington Science Museum. Several city museums, such as Birmingham, Liverpool, and Glasgow, have distinguished collections of transport exhibits including locomotives with local connections. Many individual locomotives have been preserved, such as the *Locomotion* and *Rocket* as already mentioned; the *Invicta*, with which the Canterbury and Whitstable Railway was opened in 1830; and the *Duchess of Sutherland*, one of the last great LMSR 'Pacifics', preserved until recently outside Butlin's Camp in Ayr, and now removed to the Bressington Steam Museum in Norfolk. Others have been maintained in working order, such as the privately owned *Flying Scotsman* which is allowed to haul occasional trainloads of enthusiasts over the permanent way of British Rail, and those which pull the trains on the standard-gauge preservationist ventures such as the Dart Valley Railway in Devon and the Keighley and Worth Valley line in Yorkshire. The industrial archaeologist with an interest in steam locomotion will thus find no shortage of material to keep him happy, and there is an almost overwhelming mass of literature on the subject if he should wish to pursue the documentary aspects of the steam locomotive. Various narrow-gauge preservation societies also possess collections of engines and rolling stock, diligently assembled and restored: those in

Wales at Ffestiniog and Talyllyn have pioneered this sort of activity.[4]

Apart from this wealth of mechanical engineering material, it has already been observed that British Rail are responsible for what is probably the largest single collection of civil-engineering monuments in Britain. Following the success of the Liverpool and Manchester Railway, there was a spate of railway construction, coming to a first peak of activity in the late 1830s and, after a brief pause, to a second in the mid-1840s, the so called 'Railway Mania'. The initial objectives were to link London with the Liverpool and Manchester Railway, by the London and Birmingham and the Grand Junction Railways (both approved in 1833), and to link London with Southampton by the London and Southampton Railway (1834) and with Bristol by the Great Western Railway (1835). Further lines were pushed out from London to the south coast and into East Anglia, and work began on the main cross-country routes. These developments were promoted by a large number of railway companies, all of which secured their own parliamentary sanction on the pattern established by the canal and tramway companies, and all of which raised their own capital and carried out their railway building and operation in rivalry with and frequently in direct competition with other companies. The result was chaotic but substantial, with a total railway mileage of some 2,000 miles already established by 1843, and this figure more than doubled to around 5,000 miles by 1849. The fact that such an astonishing rate of growth was accompanied by great financial speculation, and that it provided opportunities for commercial adventurers such as the notorious George Hudson, is hardly surprising. It was Hudson who first demonstrated the effectiveness of railway amalgamations by building up the Midland Railway, and after the first two decades of rapid growth the railways of Britain adopted a policy of discreet amalgamation when the chance arose. By the middle of the nineteenth century, the pattern of the British railway network was almost complete. Later on the Midland Railway acquired its own direct access to London at St Pancras in 1868, and the Great Central Railway opened with its new terminus at Marylebone in 1899, and there was a great deal of in-filling, but the essential features of the network had already taken the shape they still possess.

Speculation in the rapidly growing railway network of the 1830s and 1840s was not confined to commercial aspects of railway building. Although most of the early railway builders followed the pattern adopted by the Stephensons of the conventional Tyneside 'narrow' gauge of 4 feet 8½ inches, the young I. K. Brunel, who was appointed engineer of the Great Western Railway, chose a 'broad' gauge of 7 feet. Brunel's argument that this would lead to greater stability and make possible higher speeds for express trains was valid, but unfortunately it precipitated a vigorous 'gauge war' with increasing embarrassment as the need for transfer of goods and passengers at the 'frontier' points between the narrow and broad gauges grew. Parliament intervened in 1846, ruling that in future all new railways should be constructed to the narrow gauge, but by that time the GWR system, including the Bristol and Exeter Railway and the South Devon Railway, was already well under construction on the broad gauge. Not until 1872 did it begin to compromise by adding a third line to make mixed-gauge operation possible, and only in 1892 was the broad gauge finally extinguished. Relics of the broad-gauge system survive throughout the West Country, the most extensive being the sections of distinctive ⊓ -shaped 'bridge rail' incorporated into fences and used to carry notices. This type of rail was in general use on the broad-gauge system, being bolted to longitudinal timber sleepers through holes in the flat flanges on the rail.

Brunel's wide-ranging genius extended to many other railway improvements as well as the broad gauge. For example, he devised the first large-scale working pneumatic railway in the world by equipping the South Devon Railway between Exeter and Plymouth with this novel system of propulsion, which involved a continuous tube between the rails containing a piston to which each train was attached through a longitudinal flap or valve. When air was pumped out of the pipe on one side of the piston, the latter propelled the trains along the rails. The system had the merits of eliminating the weight of the locomotive and was capable of producing remarkably high speeds, but it ran into considerable operating difficulties at points and stations, and it was soon rendered unusable when frost cracked the leather flap which sealed the valve. The line was thus converted to conventional steam locomotion after only a year of operation in 1848, but remains of the pneumatic system survive in a few fragments of ornate engine house where the powerful stationary pumping engines had been installed, such as that alongside the present main line at Dawlish.[5]

The ill-fated pneumatic railway may be regarded as an exotic fancy (although it is curious how frequently Victorian engineers returned to the idea), but the railway builders tackled the more humdrum problems of crossing valleys and mountains with comparable ingenuity. Following tramway practice, it was the aim of the railway engineers to adopt a smooth gradient, with the added requirement that for the steam locomotive it needed to be as close as possible to dead-level. Long tunnels, great embankments, deep cuttings, and high viaducts were constructed in order to achieve the desired standards, and the permanent way of the British railway network uses all these features, most of which survive and are worthy of careful attention. The story of the construction of the Woodhead Tunnel between Sheffield and Manchester via Penistone, for example, is an epic of determination overcoming formidable engineering problems; that of the Severn Tunnel, the longest railway tunnel in Britain, was an even more stupendous achievement because the workings were completely flooded by the

'Great Spring' which broke in unexpectedly and has ever since poured millions of gallons of water a day into the tunnel. The houses for the battery of engines installed at Sudbrook in Monmouthshire to remove this unwanted water still survive, but they now contain only the efficient but visually unattractive electrical pumps, the splendid set of Cornish steam pumps having been cruelly destroyed.[6]

The engineering monuments on British railways are too numerous to be reviewed here, or even to permit a representative selection. As examples of the industrial archaeological riches of the railway system one has only to mention such features as Robert Stephenson's wrought-iron tubular Britannia Bridge across the Menai Straits, seriously damaged by fire in 1970 and rebuilt to a more conventional design; the great Forth Railway Bridge, which must surely become obsolete one day and present a truly monumental problem of preservation; the splendid viaducts carrying the Midland line to Scotland across the Yorkshire moors north of Settle; and the miles of viaducts and cuttings bringing the main-line railways into the central London area. Amongst the buildings and equipment associated with the railways, the stations provide outstanding monuments, both industrial and architectural. Virtually every town in the country has in its railway station an industrial monument of some significance, and many have more than one. The significance, of course, varies greatly. Fragments of the original Liverpool Road terminus on the 1830 Liverpool and Manchester Railway survive in Manchester, but the oldest main line terminus to survive in recognizable form is Curzon Street in Birmingham, although the remaining pieces of this are now relegated to a goods yard, and only the square masonry office building is of any distinction. Much more complete is the original terminus of the GWR at Temple Meads in Bristol, designed by I. K. Brunel in 1839 with a mock-Tudor façade to the office block on the front of the building and a wide-arched timber beam roof over its elegant train shed. Unfortunately even this has lost its railway lines and been converted into a car park for the more

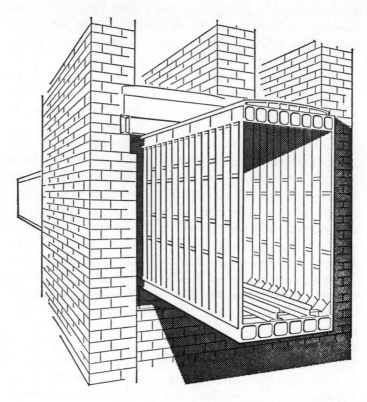

37. Cross-section of the wrought-iron tubular railway bridge over the Menai Straits: the bridge was severely damaged by a fire in 1970.

'modern' Temple Meads station (completed in 1878 although subsequently enlarged and modified) adjoining it. At the other end of the GWR, Brunel designed the graceful palace of Paddington Station (completed in 1854), which still houses one of the busiest termini in the world. The design was influenced by the Crystal Palace. Brunel did not design the hotel at Paddington, which was the work of Philip Hardwick.[7]

Not only Paddington but all the London termini make an interesting subject for the industrial archaeologist. For sheer magnificence, St Pancras deserves the prize. With its Gothic hotel in front (designed by Sir Gilbert Scott) and its superb girder-arch train shed (designed by W. H. Barlow), it is probably the largest and most characteristic of all the industrial monuments of the British railway system. The neighbouring terminus of King's Cross, designed by Lewis Cubitt as the London terminus for the Great Northern Railway and opened in 1852, is positively dull by comparison, but the functional simplicity of its original design as two large train sheds with a clock tower in between is not without architectural merit. Liverpool Street Station, receiving the lines of the Great Eastern Railway from Essex and the Fenlands, rambles amorphously, appearing to be a collection of stations rather than a single unit. Euston retains something of the same indeterminate character, despite the vast efforts made in the last decade to modernize it. Indeed, from the point of view of the industrial archaeologist, this modernization destroyed the most distinctive features of Euston Station when it swept away the Great Hall and Doric Portico with which Philip Hardwick and his son had brought the London and Birmingham Railway – for some years the only rail link between London and the north – to a full-stop in the heart of London. Several of the Southern Region stations – Charing Cross, Victoria, Blackfriars, Cannon Street – were established as termini on the north bank of the Thames, so that they are carried over the river by rather dull bridges, although the one at Charing Cross preserves the brick abutments of the Hungerford pedestrian suspension bridge built by Brunel, the suspension chains from which eventually found their way to Clifton Bridge in Bristol. The largest of the Southern termini, however, was developed on the

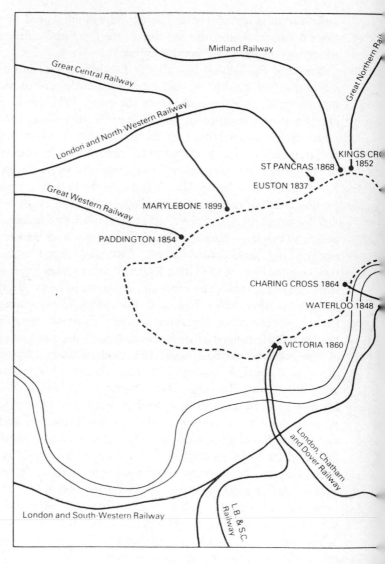

38. London main-line railway termini. Dates against stations sh
(the modern Circle Line) are shown by a dotted line.

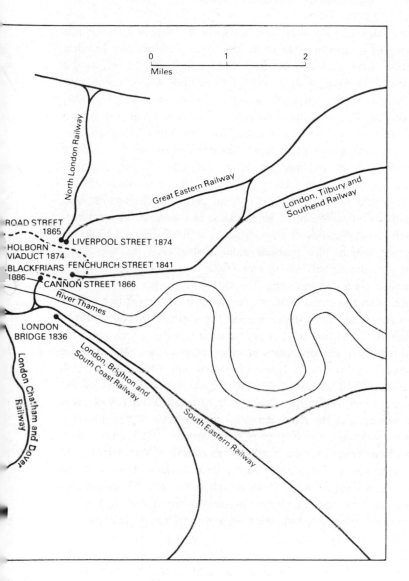

south bank at Waterloo, and bears the indifferent architectural stamp of its modernization in the 1920s. The smaller London termini have a charm of their own: Fenchurch Street, in the heart of the City, with its platforms at first-floor level in order to intercept the viaducts sweeping in across East London; Marylebone, acting as terminus of the last trunk route into London when the Great Central Railway opened in 1899, and with its rather cosy little station dwarfed by the hotel and office buildings in front; and Broad Street, now entirely a goods station next door to Liverpool Street; all are worth attention.

It would be a mistake to assume that only the termini and main-line stations are of significance as industrial monuments. Each railway achieved an individual style of design and architecture which was marked most distinctively in the lesser stations, the signal boxes, and other railside buildings, which provide more opportunity for the reproduction of a 'house style' than the larger edifices, so that it is important to consider the recording and preserving of them while the opportunity remains. Unfortunately, it is just such features which are most vulnerable to the processes of modernization, as stops at lesser stations are removed from schedules and signalling systems are altered. The post-Beeching Report rationalization of the railways has resulted in the closure of many hundreds of miles of railway, and the destruction of much of this sort of material. As an example, the Somerset and Dorset route between Bath and Evercreech may be cited. It was closed in March 1966, and nothing now remains except a few earthworks and the terminus at Green Park Station, Bath, which is being used temporarily as a car park until the redevelopment of the district can be determined. The rails have all been removed along the route, and with them have gone the stations, the signal boxes, and the semaphore signals which retained under British Railways the distinctive details of the Somerset and Dorset Railway. There was plenty of notice of the closure of the line, and it is probably true to say that it was very adequately recorded for posterity on celluloid and on paper before it went out of business.[8] It is much to be hoped that other lines, closed by the same logic of economic forces, will have received similar attention before they disappear.

We are concerned here primarily with the railways as industrial monuments, but it is appropriate to outline the general historical development of the British railway network. The Railway Era began, it has already been argued, with the opening of the Liverpool and Manchester Railway in 1830. It did not come to an abrupt end, but the railways were clearly losing ground to the automobile by the First World War, so that it is not unreasonable to regard the Railway Era as having closed about 1918, just as the motor car, the lorry, and the omnibus were entering their period of immense popularity. The experience of state control over the railways during the war, and the glaring need for a measure of rationalization of the railway network, led to the Railways Act of 1921 and the reorganization of the railways from the first day of 1923. Under this measure 123 existing railway companies were amalgamated into the 'Big Four' – the London, Midland and Scottish Railway (with the London and North-Western and the Midland Railways as its largest constituent groups); the London and North-Eastern Railway (made largely from the Great Northern, the Great Eastern, and the North-Eastern Railways); the Southern Railway (with the London and South-Western and the London, Brighton and South Coast Railways as its main members); and the Great Western Railway, which alone amongst the railways largely retained its original identity with only the addition of the small but important coal railways of South Wales. Although the railways still had plenty of vitality left in them, this move can be seen fairly as a recognition that they had passed their peak of high prosperity, and it was the first of a series of rationalizations which continued through consolidation into the nationalized British Railways in 1948 and on to the Beeching Report of 1963.

The future of the British railway system seems reasonably assured, provided that it concentrates on the provision of fast inter-city passenger services and the speedy transport of containerized cargoes from dockside to customer. In a densely populated country such as Britain the limits to the convenience of the personal automobile are reached sooner than in the United States of America, where the railway system is facing a more catastrophic decline than that of Britain, and the distances here are not generally sufficient to give a sharp advantage to air transport. It may thus be assumed that the main-line network will be with us indefinitely. This still leaves a formidable amount of work for the industrial archaeologist in recording the lesser lines, and those items on the main lines such as old-fashioned signal boxes which are being rapidly replaced. There is also scope for positive preservation, both *in situ* – in the case of outstanding buildings such as Old Temple Meads Station in Bristol – and in museums, and in the form of keeping branch lines open as semi-commercial concerns, being run and maintained by amateurs. The narrow-gauge tramways which have made the Ffestiniog and Talyllyn Railways have already been mentioned, but there is clearly scope for more standard-gauge restoration projects such as the Dart Valley Railway and the Keighley and Worth Valley Light Railway. Not only do they preserve some living history: they are also first-class tourist attractions.

Whatever the future prospects, the past service of the British railway network is beyond dispute. For over a hundred years the railways provided the arteries of the national economic system, carrying an ever-increasing volume of traffic to serve the needs of expanding industries and to provide the facility for rapid movement of people, mail, and goods upon which an advanced society depends for its survival. The interest of the industrial

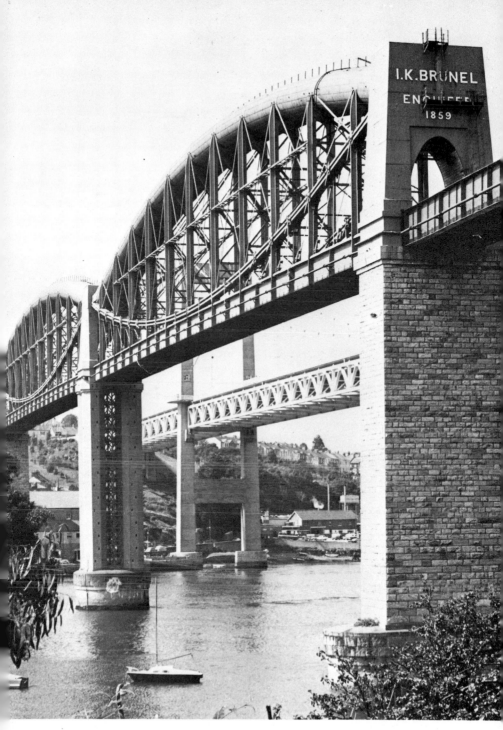

45. Royal Albert Bridge. The railway bridge over the River Tamar at Saltash was the last masterpiece of I.K. Brunel, who died soon after it was opened in 1859.

46. (above left) Smock Mill, with fantail, at Terling, Essex.

47. Post mill, with rear-mounted fantail, at Cross-in-Hand, Sussex.

48. (right) Tower mill, with fantail and eight sweeps, at Hecklington, Lincolnshire.

49. (above left) High-breast water wheel, at Foster Beck Mill, Yorkshire.

50. Over-shot water wheel, at Killhope lead-crushing mill, Co. Durham.

51. (above right) Over-shot water wheel, at Shepherd's Mill, Sheffield.

52. Under-shot water wheel, at Preston Mill, East Lothian, Scotland.

53. (left) Cheddleton flint mill. Two large under-shot water wheels provide power for the flint-grinding machinery.

54. (above right) Laxey, Isle of Man. With a diameter of $72\frac{1}{2}$ ft, the pitch-back 'Lady Isabella' is the largest surviving water wheel in Britain.

55. Horse gin. Horse-driven machinery was widely used for winding purposes in mines until the nineteenth century. The arrangement shown in this drawing was very common.

56. (above left) Elsecar engine.
This engine house at a coal-mine
near Sheffield contains one of the
few surviving Newcomen
engines.

57. Crofton Pumping Station.
Built to pump water into the
summit level of the Kennet and
Avon Canal, this engine house
contains two beam engines, the
older of which, an 1814 Boulton
& Watt machine, is the oldest
engine still under steam.

58. (above right) Lound Pumping Engine. One of two single cylinder grasshopper engines built by Easton & Amos about 1855 and preserved by the East Anglian Water Co. at Lound, Suffolk.

59. Dee Mill, Shaw. A horizontal twin tandem compound engine built by Scott & Hodgson in 1907 for this large Lancashire cotton mill, and now preserved.

60. (above) Stoke Bruerne, on the
Grand Union Canal in
Northamptonshire. The lock in
the foreground contains a
barge-weighing mechanism
preserved as part of the Canal
Museum in the warehouse
behind it.

61. Sapperton Canal Tunnel.
The eastern portal of the Thames
and Severn Canal tunnel at
Coates has long been derelict
but has recently been restored.

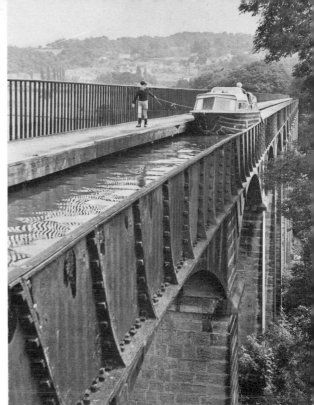

62. (above) Pont Cysyllte Aqueduct. This masterpiece of Thomas Telford carries the Llangollen Canal over the River Dee in a cast-iron trough.

63. James Brindley Walk, Birmingham, showing the sympathetic restoration of this canal basin in the heart of a city, as part of a housing development project.

64. (above left) Causey Arch, Tanfield, Co. Durham. Erected in 1727, this was the first railway bridge in the world.

65. Coal chaldron, Co. Durham. A type of wagon once widely used in the North East Coalfield.

66, 67. (above right) Old Temple Meads Station, Bristol. Opened in 1840, this is the oldest surviving railway terminus in the world. The external view shows the façade on Temple Gate, while the interior view is a lithograph by J. C. Bourne showing the train shed in 1842.

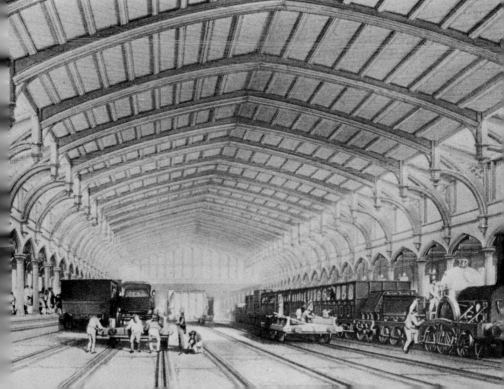

68. (above left) Railway signal box. A standard box, of a type now fast disappearing from British Rail, at Warml near Bristol.

69. Graveyard of steam locomotives. Scrapped engines lined up on sidings at Barry Dock.

70. (right) Narrow-gauge revival. One of elegant locomotives pulling a passenger train on the Talyllyn Railway.

71. (above left) Toll house. A small toll house near Bream in the Forest of Dean.

72. A plateway. A rare photograph, probably taken late in the nineteenth century, of a horse-drawn train using a plateway.

73. (above right) Albert Dock, Liverpool. The preservation of this disused dock-basin, with its fine warehouses designed by Jesse Hartley, has been a matter of national concern in recent years. Its future is still uncertain.

74. Cast-iron bollard, made by Yniscedwyn Iron Works for the Society of Merchant Venturers, on a wharf in Bristol City Docks.

75. Seaham Harbour, Co. Durham, showing a traditional coal drop and the paddle tug *Reliant* which is now in the National Maritime Museum.

76. S.S. Great Britain in Bristol on 19 July 1970, being towed towards the dry dock from which she was launched in 1843.

77. Brunel dredger, restored to her original condition of 1844 in Exeter Maritime Museum.

78. S.S. Great Britain. Detail of her bows, showing progress of the restoration work.

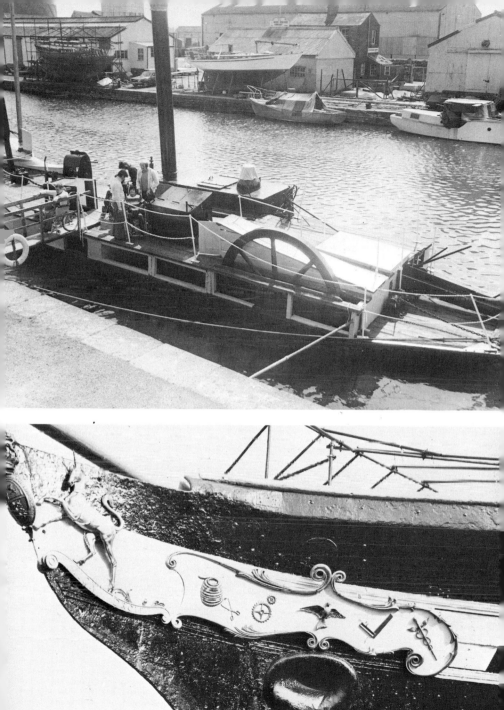

79. (above left)
Nottingham Waterworks.
Papplewick Pumping Station, a
Gothic building housing two
James Watt rotative beam
pumping engines of 1884.

80. Hull Waterworks.
Springhead Pumping Station,
an Italianate building housing a
Cornish beam engine of 1876.

81. (right) Papplewick pumping
engine, showing the intricate
decorative work of the engine
house.

82. Fakenham Gas Works, Norfolk. The gas holder at this small rural gas works which has been preserved.

83. Horizontal gas retorts. The preserved retorts at Fakenham.

84. Electricity generating. This was the first municipal power station in Bristol, now used for storage.

85. Clevedon Pier. Many seaside piers are now decaying and in danger of demolition. This at Clevedon partially collapsed in 1970, and its future remains uncertain.

86. Airship at Cardington in 1930. The huge hangars built to house the R33 and other airships are still in use at Cardington, near Bedford.

archaeologist in the evolution of the railways is grounded thus
not so much in antiquarian enthusiasm – even though it must
be admitted that this counts for something in the study of

39 *North Star*, the first locomotive built for the Great Western Railway.
The original was destroyed, but a faithful reconstruction of 1925 is preserved
in Swindon Railway Museum.

railways – as in the recognition of the outstanding significance of
the railways in British social, economic, and technological history.

Urban Tramways and Transport

The growth of large towns necessitated the provision of urban
transport systems, at least for those who could afford to pay for
the luxury: for the others, the continuing need to be able to
walk to work remained a constricting factor on urban growth
until the second half of the nineteenth century. Only then did a
transport *system* as distinct from a personal service of cabs and

sedan chairs for the well-to-do come into existence. The establishment of cheap workingmen's tickets on the railways, usually
on the first and the last trains of the day, was the first step towards such a system, and it undoubtedly encouraged the suburban expansion of London and other British towns along the
main railway lines. The effort by the Metropolitan Railway to
link the main-line termini on the north side of the Thames was
another important step. This was opened in 1863 between
Paddington and Farringdon Street, having been constructed
just below street level on the 'cut and cover' principle, and as it
was operated by steam engines working in an almost continuous
tunnel it quickly acquired notoriety for its dirt and noise. The
line was subsequently extended, and with the development of
the District Railway, built as a tunnel under the Thames
Embankment, the two lines were linked in 1884 in what is now
the Circle Line. The disadvantages of steam traction made these
underground railways particularly suitable for electrification,
and with the installation of electric locomotives in 1905 the
conditions immediately improved. By that time, however, electric
traction had already demonstrated its value in the deep 'tube'
railways, the first of which, the City and South London Railway
between the Monument and Stockwell, had been opened in 1890
(the Tower Subway, with cable-drawn passenger cars, had
been opened in 1870), and this was followed by the Central
London Railway in 1900 and most of the other 'tube' lines of
inner London in the subsequent decade. Since then all the lines
have been extended at their ends, but the only brand-new lines
have been the Victoria and Jubilee Lines, opened in 1969 and
1979 respectively. Much of the original route of the Metropolitan Railway is still in use, and features of its construction
can be observed from the trains in the open sections of the
route. The keen industrial archaeologist can also find much
of interest on the deep tube lines: differences of design details
between the various lines, both in rolling stock and station

fittings, may still be observed, although they have been directed as a united enterprise since 1913, first in the Underground Electric Railways Company of London and later in the London Passenger Transport Board (from 1933 to nationalization in 1948).

The introduction of electric traction on the London Underground provided a useful lesson in a system which was adopted elsewhere in the form of electric trams. Horse trams had been introduced in London and many provincial towns in the last quarter of the nineteenth century. These were passenger-carrying cars pulled by horses over rails set in the road. It was found that these could conveniently be converted to electric traction, so that the remarkable era of the electric tram began in the 1890s, and within the space of fifteen years virtually every town of any size equipped itself with a fleet of such trams, usually double-deck but occasionally single, together with the paraphernalia of overhead wires and posts (except in the case of central London, where an underground live rail was reached through a slot in the road between the tram lines). The most striking feature of these municipal tramways in retrospect is the shortness of their lives. They lost popularity rapidly in the 1930s, so that by the Second World War many towns had already abandoned them, while others did so either during or immediately after the war. Only a handful of cities such as Glasgow and Sheffield maintained their electric tramway system in good order until the 1950s, but even these places were then persuaded to abandon them in favour of the diesel omnibus, which had been growing in favour since it replaced the petrol bus after the First World War. The British electric tram thus disappeared, with the possible exception of Blackpool and Douglas in the Isle of Man, where they survive as a tourist attraction. In the rush to get rid of their tram services, many towns and cities failed to preserve even a single specimen of their trams, which is a great loss because they frequently represented in their prime great civic pride and local embellishment. Local differences included varying provision for top-deck passengers and different trolley systems for picking up power from the overhead wires. They even spread to different gauges, so towns were sometimes unable to operate over each other's rails, as in the case of several neighbouring municipalities in the West Riding of Yorkshire, although this difficulty was occasionally overcome by fitting trams with variable-gauge axles. Fortunately, a fine collection of working trams has been assembled at Crich in Derbyshire, where some track has been laid down in an old quarry and trams from services all over the country still operate in what is a splendid working museum made possible by a handful of enthusiasts.

Some municipalities abandoned their trams early in favour of trolley buses, which combined some of the flexibility of bus operation with the economic electric power of the tram. Even this improvement did not save electric traction from almost complete eclipse in urban transport systems, however; the flexibility of operation of the diesel omnibus is so much greater that it has been generally adopted since 1945. It is worth observing that, even though this vehicle is now taken for granted, the omnibus has developed greatly in the last twenty-five years, and the earlier types are now obsolete and thoroughly deserve to be considered for museum preservation.

Air Transport

The aeroplane is one of the most astonishing success stories of the twentieth century. The first heavier-than-air flight was made by Orville Wright on 17 December 1903; little more than half a century later, on 21 July 1969, Neil Armstrong set the first human foot on the Moon. Admittedly, the Moon landing depended on the development of rocketry, electronics, and a host of things not strictly derived from aeronautics, but the scope of this technological evolution gives a vivid indication of the development of air transport in the present century. The speed at which the development has taken place means that there is plenty to arouse the interest of the industrial archaeologist. Not only the aircraft themselves – a selection of which has been handsomely preserved in the Science Museum and elsewhere, and in the Shuttleworth Collection at Biggleswade in Bedfordshire, which aims at keeping its exhibits in flying order – but also the aerodromes, hangars, factories, and ancillary buildings which survive in various parts of the country are worth recording. The original buildings of the Bristol Aircraft Company (now part of the British Aircraft Corporation) survive where Sir George White built them at the erstwhile Filton terminus of his Bristol Tramways Company. They are now submerged, however, amongst the extensive modern development, which includes the mighty hangar built to accommodate the ill-fated *Brabazon*, the piston-engined giant of the 1940s which never got beyond its prototype. At Cardington in Bedfordshire two large hangars survive from 1917 and 1927 respectively, when they were built for the construction of airships, culminating in the R.100 and R.101, the latter of which crashed disastrously on its maiden flight in 1931 and brought the development of the British airship to a sudden full-stop. On the outskirts of many cities, early aerodromes have now been entirely covered or partially covered by suburban development, while others just survive for aero club purposes. The Second World War littered the countryside of south and east Britain with RAF aerodromes, very few of which survive in operational use, most having reverted to farmland or remaining only as sets of derelict huts and hangars. Air transport is subject to ever more rigorous control as air space becomes more crowded and the volume of traffic increases, so that the great commercial airports such as Heathrow and Prestwick are no places to look for industrial monuments. But the development of supersonic jet transport and the even more significant switch to vertical take-off may bring surprising changes to even these great airports by the end of the century. In other words, air transport should not be dismissed too lightly as an unlikely subject for the industrial archaeologist.

14. Community and Public Services

Every civilized community makes some provision for public services in order to ensure wholesome social conditions and the smooth functioning of industrial, commercial, and personal relationships. The size and scope of such services has increased with the rapid growth of towns and cities in the last two hundred years, for whereas small towns could manage with only a good supply of fresh water, and whereas many of the services provided in the first flush of urban expansion were performed as commercial ventures aimed at a good profit, in the last hundred years they have come largely under the control of local and national authorities running them in the public interest. In the process, many of them have become very large undertakings and have made substantial contributions to the landscape and industrial environment. They have, in short, come to deserve the attention of industrial archaeologists.

Water Supply

The provision of a good water supply is essential to healthy urban life, and large cities have from ancient times faced the need to bring this vital commodity to their citizens. Roman cities, for example, were usually well provided with water brought in culverts from the nearest springs, and the larger cities such as Rome itself used water brought from considerable distances over spectacular aqueducts, remains of which survive in Italy and South France, but none of any great size in Britain. Medieval cities were somewhat less resourceful, possibly because their occupants made less use of water for personal cleansing purposes than the citizens of the Roman empire. Nonetheless, several cities retain vestiges of water-supply systems from the Middle Ages, tapping springs and wells and carrying the water in stone culverts or elm piping. In Tudor and Stuart times these systems were extended by such enterprises as that of Sir Hugh Middleton, who constructed thirty-eight miles of the 'New River' from Ware in Hertfordshire into a reservoir in London at Clerkenwell, which was completed in 1613. This supply was later modified and augmented by water from the River Lea, but the New River remains today as an important industrial monument.[1] The increasing water consumption of London was further supplemented by supplies pumped directly from the River Thames by water wheels installed in the arches of London Bridge, and the pumping capacity of this installation was raised by the introduction of a Newcomen engine in the eighteenth century. Needless to say, the untreated water pumped to hydrants in the metropolis in this way was not by modern standards fit for drinking, but it could be boiled and used for washing. This system based on direct extraction from the river disappeared with the old London Bridge and the subsequent improvements in water treatment in the nineteenth century, but the bulk of London's water supply is still obtained from the Thames, being extracted from the river above Teddington weir and stored and treated before being pumped into the mains by the Metropolitan Water Board.

By the middle of the nineteenth century, the correlation between fever diseases such as cholera and the existence of poor water supplies had driven many doctors and public administrators to the conclusion that the problem of deteriorating health in the large cities could only be overcome by the systematic provision of pure water. This realization led, in the second half of the century, to a remarkable boom in the construction of reservoirs, the laying of pipes, and the installation of large pumping engines. The piping is normally underground and not available for inspection, but both the reservoirs and the pumping engines provide outstanding items for industrial archaeology. Some of the reservoirs are natural lakes in which the level has been raised and the outflow controlled: the annexation of Thirlmere in the Lake District by Manchester Corporation is a case in point, and has caused a long-standing dispute with amenity societies which object to the restrictions on access to the lake. The acquisition of Loch Katrine in the Trossachs by Glasgow Corporation has had a happier history, for not only is the lake approachable as a picnic area, but a trim little steam ship, the *s.s. Sir Walter Scott*, plies on a regular passenger and pleasure service from one end to the other. Most of the reservoirs serving the great cities of Britain, however, were created by flooding valleys in hilly parts of the country. Sheffield and Manchester had no lack of suitable valleys on the slopes of the Pennines, but as the need for fresh supplies continued to grow, large parts of the Derwent valley in the Peak District were also flooded. Birmingham built large reservoirs in the Elan valley in central Wales, where the high masonry dams are still striking features. Many reservoirs were made with earthen dams, faced with stonework only on the inside. There was some anxiety in the winter of 1969–70 about one of these dams near Maerdy in South Wales which was beginning to leak, and as many reservoirs are now over a hundred years old it is possible that both masonry and earth embankment dams will require extensive maintenance work in order to ensure their continued use. All over the country the existence of reservoirs provides the student of industrial archaeology with an interesting lesson in assessing and interpreting physical evidence and relating it to the water-supply history of particular areas. The ever-increasing demand for water, moreover, is a continuing anxiety to public authorities, and to the important amenity interests, which see valuable farmland and parkland threatened with inundation in the interests of quenching the thirst of the modern cities. It has been argued with some force on this matter that the evolution of a national water conservation and utilization policy is long-overdue in Britain.

The nineteenth-century expansion in water-supply facilities also saw the establishment of pumping stations all over the country, and many of these have become important industrial monuments on account of the now obsolete steam pumping engines which they house. Although most of the buildings are still in use, the installation of electric pumps constitutes such a tremendous saving in space that it has frequently proved possible to preserve part at least of the obsolete steam equipment. The pumps normally serve one or other of two purposes: either they extract water from wells, thus boosting the supply, or they force water already collected in reservoirs to storage tanks at a higher level from which it can gravitate to the customers wherever it is required. A large water authority such as Bristol Waterworks Company has a number of pumping stations of both kinds, and some of them have contained a series of different steam engines of which a few of the more recent ones have survived, including the fine pair of beam engines which once pumped water from Blagdon Reservoir into the storage reservoirs at Barrow Gurney five miles away. There are many impressive but now obsolete pumping stations in the Midlands, such as the Nottingham station at Papplewick, for which there is a well-advanced preservation project, and others elsewhere such as those at Brayton (Selby) in Yorkshire and Ryhope in County Durham. As a general rule for industrial archaeologists it may be said that the water supply of an area is always worth attention. Not only is this of basic importance from the time of the parish pump onwards, but also the fact that modernization and economies of space press relatively lightly on water undertakings means that many of them retain old equipment even if it is not still in use. Amongst such equipment should also be reckoned the methods of water treatment, for there are few places in the country where raw water is of sufficient purity to allow it to be fed directly into the mains. The usual methods of treatment involve large settling tanks and various methods of filtering water through beds of sand and gravel, as well as the addition of chemicals such as chlorine to eliminate harmful bacteria.

Water Drainage

Water drainage is concerned with the problem of surplus water rather than that of water shortage, but as the essential engineering problem in either case is concerned with moving large masses of water, similar devices have been used to achieve both ends. Instead of reservoirs, the water-drainage engineers have erected embankments and endeavoured to control the flow of rivers. Since the work of Vermuyden and other Dutch engineers in the Fens in the seventeenth century, major modifications have been made in the British landscape by successive drainage schemes, and many venerable dikes and ditches can still be traced in low-lying parts of the countryside such as Sedgemoor in Somerset and Humberside as well as the Fenlands. Also, instead of the water pumps already described for water-supply purposes, the drainage engineers have erected large engines to raise water in order to reclaim or maintain land below the natural water level. In the first instance, windmills were used on a large scale, notably in Holland, to perform this function; a vertical shaft down the tower of the mill carried the drive from the sails at the top to a large 'scoop' wheel at the bottom which literally scooped water from a lower level and slopped it out again a few feet higher. The coming of steam power enabled this work to be done more reliably, particularly in countries where there was a good supply of mineral fuel and even in Holland, where the wind-

A   B   C   D

mill remained traditionally dominant until the comparatively recent installation of electric pumps, some large steam engines were built in the mid-nineteenth century. Outstanding as an industrial monument is the Cruquius Engine, the eight-beam Cornish engine made by Harveys of Hayle which has already been described.[2] In Britain, the less spectacular but interesting engine at Stretham, Cambridgeshire, has been preserved as the result of an initiative by the Newcomen Society, and elsewhere other steam pumping plant has been retained where local river board and drainage authorities have engineers who are sensitive to their historical significance. A particularly attractive group of engines has been preserved on the Somerset Plain by the Somerset River Board, which has maintained in good condition some small steam pumps which have been made redundant by electrical apparatus. Most of these units are centrifugal pumps developed by Easton Amos & Co. and installed in the 1860s.[3]

---

40. Chimney types.

(A) Cornish-style chimney, at Tregurtha Down, Cornwall. The traditional Cornish chimney is slightly tapered, constructed in rough-hewn masonry for the bottom two thirds and topped with brick. The coping rim is slightly unusual in Cornish chimneys, and is mainly ornamental.

(B) Bee Mill, Royton, Lancashire. A functional red-brick mill chimney, very typical of the Lancashire textile industry. The 'cap' was designed to prevent downdraught. The name of the mill is picked out in white bricks on the side of the chimney.

(c) Ryhope Pumping Station, Co. Durham. Waterworks architecture was frequently monumental and encouraged modest ornamentation, as in this elegant chimney.

(D) India Mill, Darwen, Lancashire. A splendid surviving example of the exuberant expression of industrial affluence in the shape of huge Italianate chimneys which became popular in the second half of the nineteenth century. A spiral staircase round the shaft of the chimney gave access to two balconies.

Waste Disposal

Towns have not always been greatly concerned about the disposal of their garbage and organic waste: the existence of a fast-flowing river or, even better, a tidal estuary, relieved them of this anxiety until the natural processes of disposal became inadequate to cope with the increasing volume of waste. The fact that a surprisingly large number of British towns and cities still discharge raw sewage into rivers and the sea has become something of a national scandal now that the problems of environmental pollution are at last being taken seriously. Nonetheless, great improvements have been made, and all British towns now make some provision for sewage disposal and garbage collection. London probably led the way, after the Great Fire of 1666, when steps were taken to ensure that the streets were kept reasonably clean, although the Thames remained the convenient receptacle for street sweepings until comparatively recent times. Indeed, when it is remembered that much of the garbage collected in the metropolitan area is shipped down-river and dumped out in the estuary, it is clear that the Thames still carries most of the burden.

The significant improvements in London's sewage disposal came in the mid-nineteenth century. Until that time most organic waste seems to have made its way through a confusing jumble of covered ditches and sewers, most of which discharged into the River Fleet before this joined the Thames. This complex of old drains had a subterranean archaeology of its own, and a knowledge of the labyrinth was turned to good account by the breed of 'toshers' described in Henry Mayhew's account of the London labouring classes in mid-century, who scoured them in search of misplaced valuables. Cholera and urban pride combined, however, in the second half of the century, to reform this non-system, and to replace it by a properly engineered system of feeder sewers linking with main outfall sewers running along both north and south sides of the Thames. The northern trunk sewer was incorporated in the Victoria Embankment and discharges eventually into the river beyond Barking. That on the south side of the river follows a more devious route through Southwark and discharges eventually at Abbey Wood (Crossness), where a fine set of beam steam pumps survives. The construction of this system kept Sir Joseph Bazalgette busy for almost a quarter of a century, during which time, from 1855 to 1875, he was the Engineer to the Metropolitan Board of Works.[4]

The problems of London were exceptional because of their size, but at least the River Thames was available as a sort of tidal sluice to receive whatever was eventually discharged into it. The land-locked cities of the Midlands, however, have had to pay rather more attention to the task of treating sewage so that it can be released in a tolerable condition into rivers which will then flow through other towns and possibly provide part of their water supply. The establishment of sewage farms and treatment centres, involving settling beds and various chemical processes, has thus become an important public service, so that despite their unsavoury associations they are well worth the attention of industrial archaeologists. As with water supply and drainage, the installation of proper sewage systems frequently involves pumping equipment to keep the foul water moving, and so interesting engine houses often survive in connection with sewage works. To take an example almost at random, the seaside town of Cleethorpes in Lincolnshire, which has to deal with various forms of pollution on its beaches, disposes of its sewage in a station to the south of the town which is still equipped with three oil engines and a gas engine by Crossley, installed about 1925.[5]

The processing and removal of garbage and other solid waste presents public authorities with a different set of problems. The systematic dumping of garbage in the Thames estuary already noted is not typical. Most authorities provide for some processing of garbage, so that reusable metal may be extracted and paper products separated for repulping. They also arrange for the incineration of as much as possible. But there is always a residue left for disposal, and the stage will presumably be reached where all available old quarries and gravel pits have been filled in, and some more complete annihilation of the waste will have to be devised. This is without considering the flood of old motor cars, furniture, washing machines, mattresses, and indestructible plastic containers which are presenting a mounting problem of waste disposal. The citizens of modern civilization have been aptly named 'the waste makers', and it is to be hoped that technology will devise more effective ways of reusing the discarded products of old processes in order both to solve the physical problem of waste disposal and the more long-term problem of technological entropy as the world's resources of metals and minerals are converted at an ever-accelerating rate into mounds of useless material. Meanwhile, it behoves the industrial archaeologist in passing to cast a discriminating eye over the scrap heaps.

Gas Supply

The discovery that a gas could be extracted from coal, oil, and other fuels, and burnt as an illuminant, dates back at least to 1688, when a communication to the Royal Society drew attention to these properties.[6] Little progress was made with the idea, because of the inadequate nature of the science of chemistry, until late in the eighteenth century, when renewed interest in the composition of air and the nature of gases led to more experiments with coal gas. The first practical demonstration of its utility is usually attributed to William Murdock, working in Cornwall for the Boulton and Watt Company, who used it to light his home in Redruth in 1792. Ten years later he provided a coal-gas plant to illuminate the Soho factory of his firm at the Peace of Amiens, and this constituted the first of many successful installations for factories and other large buildings. It took another ten years to establish the first general gas company, the London Gas Light and Coke Company, to produce gas for customers within its area in 1812, but other gas companies followed quickly after this, both in the metropolitan area and in the provinces, so that by the middle of the nineteenth century virtually every town of any size in Britain had its own gas works with miles of gas main distributing the product to houses, factories, and street lights around it. The social effects of this tremendous improvement in lighting were very considerable, and gas light became a characteristic feature of Victorian town life.

Attempts were made in several parts of the country in the first half of the nineteenth century to make gas from oil rather than coal, and companies were established for the purpose, but although the quality of oil gas as an illuminant was superior to that of coal gas it proved to be a more expensive process and the oil-gas plant was converted to coal. Oil fuels did, however, eventually come to be widely used, and the range of sources has been further extended by the tapping of natural gas, first in America on a large scale, but now widely applied in Western Europe. This mixture of sources creates a problem of nomenclature for the product of the gas industry, perhaps best resolved by calling the mixture of gases derived from various sources and extensively treated to remove unwanted ingredients as 'town gas' – that is, the 'combustible gases distributed from localized sources of production'.[7] Another confusing feature of the industry is the change in utilization of its product. The first use for town gas was as an illuminant, but in the course of 170 years of production for a wide range of customers the main use has shifted to that of heating, for warmth and for cooking. The lighting function of gas has almost completely disappeared in competition with electric systems, although it survived until comparatively recently for street lighting purposes, so that street gas lamps have now become objects of industrial archaeology.

The first coal gas was made by heating coal in a kettle, and this is the basis of the 'retort' or 'oven' which became the central feature of every gas works. Essentially this is a vessel of iron or fire-clay in which the coal is sealed and then heated, usually to temperatures around 1,000° C. (although lower temperatures may be used for some processes), as a result of which the gas, tar, and other materials are driven off, leaving behind the spongy mass which solidifies as coke. Throughout the nineteenth century it was usual to arrange retorts in horizontal batteries, but as this necessitated a 'batch' production with regular coolings to empty the coke and to recharge the retorts, there was a move first to inclined retorts and then to vertical retorts which could be charged continuously from the top while discharging coke from the bottom.

The gas which is extracted from the retorts is not ready for distribution until it has undergone treatment to remove obnoxious material and to recover various chemicals. This is called 'purification' and may involve gas works in a lot of equipment for condensing, 'washing' and 'scrubbing' the gas before it is pumped into the gas holder to await distribution at a uniform pressure to the customers. The pumping is performed by engines known as 'exhausters' because they help to draw gas from the retorts as well as driving it into the holders, and the need for reliable engines promoted the development of special types of steam-driven pumps, many of which still survive at work in several large gas works as well as the remaining small ones. The rotary-action gas exhauster was developed by Beale in 1848 and improved subsequently by the firms of Donkin and Waller, and these names are worth noting on the plates of surviving steam engines in gas works, although in some cases the exhausters are now driven by internal combustion engines. Further engines were installed in large gas works as 'boosters' to increase pressure in certain mains for long-distance distribution.

The traditional British gas holder became the large 'bell' of wrought-iron plates, sealed in a tank of water through which gas was admitted into the bell, causing it to rise. The capacity of the holder could be greatly increased by telescoping the inner bell within one or more cylinders, and the practice developed of surrounding the holder with a trellis of wrought iron between cast-iron columns, up which the movement of the bell could be guided. Some very elegant frames of this sort survive in various parts of the country. Later holders, however, evolved the self-guiding principle of spiral channels on the outside of the cylinders, and dispensed with the supporting iron work. Several large gas works have installed 'dry' holders in the present century, which replace the traditional means of collecting the gas over water by having a large cylindrical or polygonal shell containing a weighted 'piston' which moves up and down inside the shell according to the amount of gas collected below it.

Coke is an important by-product of the coal-gas industry. As the gas is driven off the coal, coke is left in the retorts and removed thence for sale as industrial or domestic fuel. Some coke is still produced for its own sake, particularly for the metallurgical industries for use in iron and steel processes, and in this case it is the gas which is the by-product and it is frequently piped to local gas works for purification. The coke retorts of a steel works are thus similar to batteries of vertical retorts in a gas works, but they are designed to maximize the quality of the coke produced. Many ruins of old coke plant survive and are worth looking for in association with the coal and metal industries: they sometimes appear like rows of compact ovens, in each of which a batch of coal would be coked by heat from the interlacing flues.

Town gas is distributed from the gas holders along cast-iron mains set below the streets, with branches of smaller-bore piping going into the side streets, from which it is led off to the consumer's meter. Inside a house or other establishment a network of pipes embedded in the walls – known in the industry as 'carcassing' – takes the gas to however many burners are required. The design of gas fittings has undergone great development in 170 years, and these fittings are themselves items of considerable potential interest to the industrial archaeologist. More significant, however, are the surviving features of traditional gas works already described – retorts (horizontal, inclined, or vertical), purification plant, exhausters and other engines, and gas holders – for with the recent modernization programme of the National Gas Boards such features have already become industrial monuments. The mass of small gas undertakings were nationalized in 1949, and ever since then the Boards have been carrying out a gradual process of consolidation, closing many of the smaller works and increasing the efficiency of the larger ones. But since the mid-1960s this policy has been drastically accelerated by the twin decisions to base virtually all the production of town gas on oil fuels at a few gas works pumping gas at high pressure into a national grid, and to exploit the resources of natural gas discovered under the North Sea. The result of this programme has been that even 'modern' coal-gas works equipped with comparatively new batteries of vertical retorts have become obsolete, and there has been a tremendous carnage of such works and their ancillary equipment all over the country. It is doubtful whether much was worth preserving: gas works are notoriously untidy and unattractive visual (and olfactory) features in our urban landscape and apart from the occasional retort house or gas holder of unusual design, few strong cases could be made for preserving them. In any event, most coal-gas works have now been swept away except for their gas holders, which store the gas received from the national grid. Only a few small gas works have been deliberately preserved, the best examples being those at Fakenham in Norfolk and at Biggar in Scotland. These are no longer in production, being preserved as museum features. They are virtually all that remain of a process which has disappeared dramatically within little more than a decade.

Electricity Supply

We have already looked at electricity as a source of power and in its electrical engineering aspects: here we must consider it briefly as a public service. The serious investigation of electrical phenomena had begun in the eighteenth century, but it took the greater part of the nineteenth century to convert increased scientific knowledge into major engineering systems, so that the first British power stations for the generation of electricity for public consumption were those built at Holborn Viaduct and Brighton in 1882, although small generators had been installed to power arc lamps for lighthouses and a small amount of street lighting from the 1850s. The electricity-supply industry can thus claim a mere 97 years of development compared with the 170 years of the gas supply business, but its rate of growth in this period has been prodigious.

The initial problem of electricity supply was that of knowing how to begin. The cost of generating equipment was high, and the functions which it could perform in a society replete with the benefits provided by steam power and gas light were uncertain, to say the least. What was needed was a complete system, consisting of power generation, distribution, lighting, industrial power units, and electric traction, which would break the vicious circle and demonstrate effectively the merits of electricity supply. Ferranti set out to provide such a complete system at Deptford in 1889, and many other enterprises followed once the feasibility of the system had been proved. During the twenty years after 1889, almost every town in Britain was provided with a power station, either by a private company or by the municipal authorities. Many, indeed, found themselves equipped with several power stations, because the new electric traction systems which developed quickly in this period often found it convenient to generate their own power for their electric trams. In London, electric traction proved to be a particular boon because it relieved the passengers on the Metropolitan and other early 'underground' railways of their suffering in dirty carriages and smoky tunnels and, even more significant, made possible the construction of deep tube lines.

The early generating equipment of the electricity supply industry consisted of more or less conventional reciprocating steam engines, although certain new designs suitable for the high speeds needed to turn the dynamos efficiently, such as the Willans central-valve high-speed engines, became widely used. Already by 1884, however, Charles Parsons was developing a steam turbine specifically to meet the requirements of electricity generation, and by the end of the century turbines were beginning to be installed in new power stations; others were converted to turbines in subsequent years. Steam turbines have since become standard equipment for most large generating stations, except those in geographically favoured parts of the country which are able to use water turbines to produce hydro-electric power (HEP). In Britain, HEP has only been developed on a substantial scale in parts of the Scottish Highlands, where it is used in the aluminium-smelting process. There is a large installation, for example, near Fort William. Since nationalization there has been a programme to centralize the production of electricity, so that most of the smaller stations have become obsolete while generation has been concentrated in the giant stations like those along the Vale of Trent or the new coal-fired station at Didcot. Even the newest power stations, however, use steam turbines, including the atomic-reactor stations in which conventional turbines convert the heat from the reactors into electric current, although the scientific possibility of short-circuiting (to coin a phrase) this indirect process may render a vast amount of equipment obsolete by the end of the present century. The possibility of nuclear power stations becoming industrial monuments is intriguing and a little perturbing because it will be virtually impossible to destroy them on account of the radiation hazard, so that they will have to be preserved for an indefinite posterity. Berkeley Power Station, for instance, is likely to outlast Berkeley Castle by many millennia. Indeed, the process can be said to have begun already, with the sealing off of part of the experimental nuclear plant at Windscale in Cumberland after a dangerous leakage of radioactive material into the atmosphere in 1957.

One result of the very rapid expansion from small power stations in the 1890s to large ones eighty years later, and of the attempts at rationalization which began in the 1920s with the introduction of the National Grid and have continued under nationalization since 1949, has been the extremely high rate of obsolescence of electricity-generating equipment and of the buildings containing it. Despite its modernity, therefore, electricity supply has provided a considerable number of industrial monuments, particularly in the shape of old power stations converted to other uses. Few engines survive, because they were frequently changed as the required load increased, and museums rarely saw chunks of steam turbine as attractive features for their galleries so that they were sold for scrap without much complaint from the preservationists. But the buildings are worth locating and noting as a vital part in the history of the public services of a region. Deptford Power Station is a prominent example of a generating plant which, despite modifications, has had a continuous existence since the early days of electricity supply, and now that it has become redundant it has been surveyed by the Greater London Industrial Archaeological Society.

All power stations require a large volume of water as a coolant in order to condense the steam from the turbines for reuse in the boilers. This cooling water itself requires cooling after use, and only those power stations with a readily available supply of water, such as the Thames-side stations at Battersea and Southwark in London, dispense with cooling towers for this purpose. The towers have thus become a very characteristic feature of power stations. They were originally constructed with wooden frames, but the familiar hyperbolic concrete funnel, narrowing to a neck and widening out to its mouth, had evolved by the 1920s, and early specimens of this type of construction survive, notably at Lister Drive Power Station in Liverpool, where four towers were put up in 1924.[8]

Another result of the plethora of local experiments in electricity generation was the great range of distributive systems used. Not only was current distributed in both direct current and alternating current forms, but it has been distributed at many different voltages through many varieties of cable and transformer. Like water mains and gas pipes, electric cables are rarely visible to the industrial archaeologist in built-up areas, but out in the countryside, where the National Grid now aspires to reach even the remotest parts of Britain, the cables cover long distances overground, slung between electric pylons. There is not yet, so far as I am aware, a society for the preservation of electric pylons, but one can almost see it coming as the pressures to place more and more cables underground increase. And seriously, a lot can be learned from pylons by the practised eye regarding the date of construction, the type of current being distributed, and such like, so that the preservation of appropriate specimens need not be an absurd proposition.

Housing and Social Regulation

In a very real sense, the provision of accommodation in the form of houses, cottages, and tenements is a basic public service in our modern industrial society. Every industry needs workers, and as workers require housing for themselves and their families, the factory or work-place has become the natural focus of the industrial community, with houses being provided within easy access either by the industrialist himself or by a commercial speculator.

As many of the early factories developed away from existing centres of population, particularly when they were dependent upon water power, the industrialist had to undertake the whole range of social provision from houses to shops and churches and recreational centres, as at New Lanark or Cromford. Some industrialists made a virtue out of this necessity and designed model industrial villages like Saltaire. With the transition to steam power, however, the more general pattern was to leave the provision of houses to speculative development, often performed with the minimum of control and as cheaply as possible, giving rise to the 'jerry building' which became so typical of British urban housing in the nineteenth century. In the twentieth century much of this shoddy building has been cleared away and replaced by solidly built but aesthetically unexciting 'council housing', both on new estates on the fringes of the great cities and on the inner-city land made available by slum clearance and policies of urban renewal. Since the Second World War, much of this inner-city housing has been made available as flats in high-rise buildings as a means of creating more open space while maintaining population densities, although there has been some revulsion from this policy in recent years.

Even this brief account of the development of industrial housing is enough to demonstrate the very close relationship between places of industrial production and the homes of the workers engaged in this production, so that the extension of industrial archaeological interest to include the housing of industrial workers and their families requires no special justification. In recent years, industrial archaeologists have conducted painstaking inquiries into the domestic conditions of workers in several parts of the country. Some of the best work has been done in South Wales and has already resulted in the publication of informative articles about the range of houses available to different categories of workers.[9] There is clearly much more useful work to be done here, but it will have to be done fairly quickly because distinctive artisan house-types such as the Birmingham back-to-back and the Glasgow tenement are rapidly being replaced by modern houses. It is unlikely that much will qualify for preservation, except in the places like Saltaire already mentioned, so knowledge of this particular form of archaeological evidence about industrial society must be grasped while the opportunity remains.

Amongst the other traditional public services were the provision of markets and fairs and the institutions such as law courts and prisons associated with the maintenance of law and order. Like housing, these features of social regulation occur so inevitably in relation to the growth of industries and industrial communities that it is important for the practising industrial archaeologist to be aware of them and to be prepared to collect clues from them about the general character and quality of a region or a parish. For example, police boxes were once an interesting species of street furniture, but with the growing mobility of the police force these have been abandoned in most parts of the country, so that those which survive are worth noting. The survival of one as the time machine in the TV serial *Dr Who* is perhaps, in the circumstances, not inappropriate.

Civic buildings generally are important items of the urban landscape and integral features of the system of social regulation. Manchester boasted the largest town hall in Europe in 1877, and other cities showed comparable urban pride by the erection of such monumental structures as concert halls, art galleries, museums, libraries, and so on. Many of the Lancashire cotton towns rebuilt their centres with the labour of men made redundant by the cotton famine during the American Civil War, and with the funds raised for the welfare of these unemployed workers by public subscription. Civic buildings frequently bear the stamp of the industrialists – and the industries – which found the money for them, so that no two cities are alike. The solid classical character of Liverpool is distinct from the appropriately (if inaccurately) named 'Bristol Byzantine' of its great commercial rival; the 'little mesters' of Sheffield were parsimonious about civic buildings, while Joseph Chamberlain persuaded those of Birmingham to make a splash. Leeds was determined to demonstrate its dominance of the West Riding textile industry by an array of elegant public buildings, while Manchester asserted its primacy amongst the Lancashire cotton towns by its large squares and public edifices. Cardiff was endowed with a splendid civic centre out of the profits of the coal industry. Most of these developments date from the second half of the nineteenth century, when British provincial pride, based upon solid industrial and commercial achievement, enjoyed a great vogue. Of course they have been subsequently altered, not least by wartime bombing and post-war redevelopment in a uniform style which makes it difficult to tell the centre of, say, Bristol's shopping area, from that of Swansea. But elegant civic buildings are still being constructed, as visits to Birmingham and Sheffield will demonstrate.

An important public service which is also a function of social regulation is the provision of a fire service. These first seem to have been organized systematically in the eighteenth century by insurance companies which, being anxious to safeguard properties in which they had financial interest, equipped themselves with a staff and an engine to protect such buildings. The 'engine' was frequently a multi-handed pump designed to force water from a pond or a hydrant into the fire: several of this design survive on large estates, which once had to make their own fire-fighting arrangements, and in museums. They were later improved by the addition of a steam pump and set on carriages so that they could be moved quickly by horses when an emergency arose. The insurance companies also adopted a policy of marking the houses in which they had an interest, to prevent a waste of labour on other buildings, and the surviving plates of such companies make interesting ornamental features on many of our Georgian and Regency terraces. The later development of fire services, when they were brought under municipal control and equipped with special vehicles to carry pumps, telescopic ladders, and other gear, can also throw some interesting light on local history.

Churches and chapels, and cemeteries and crematoria, are also worth at least a passing observation from the industrial archaeologist. Churches are often built in local stone and in designs with distinctive local details. Two cast-iron churches survive in Liverpool,[10] and a Bristol firm made sectionalized iron churches for export to the colonies in the nineteenth century. Many chapels provided cast-iron balconies for their congregations, and many, again, have frequently been converted to other uses. The ecclesiastical archaeology of South Wales or County Durham has still to be written, and would be an interesting contribution to the industrial archaeology of these regions. The designs of churches and chapels were frequently directed by industrialists who were also responsible for factories, warehouses, and workhouses, so that the architectural similarities are unmistakable and understandable. Cemeteries sometimes contain unexpected delights for the industrial archaeologist, such as the cast-iron tombstones outside the parish church of Broseley in Shropshire. John Wilkinson, the local iron magnate who had a house near Broseley church, aspired to be buried in a cast-iron coffin, but it seems that he outgrew the coffin which he had cast for himself, although he had the posthumous consolation of a cast-iron obelisk erected in his memory near Grange-over-Sands, where he retired in his closing years. The re-introduction of the practice of cremation in 1885 brought another interesting industrial process into the public service of social regulation.

Communications

A vital public service in any advanced industrial nation is the provision of a rapid and reliable communications system, involving, in the first place, an efficient postal service, and expanding to include a telegraph and telephone service and also, in a sense, the modern media of mass communication.

The British postal services improved significantly with the better roads of the eighteenth century, and the voluminous correspondence of industrialists such as James Watt is an eloquent testimony to the importance of this service in the expanding economy of the period. Two Bath entrepreneurs, Ralph Allen and John Palmer, did well for themselves and their society by showing how the 'cross-posts' – the postal services between provincial centres rather than along the main routes out of London – could be improved and made to pay, and a century later the coming of the railways and of Rowland Hill's penny post served to stimulate further the efficiency and utility of the postal service. There is, admittedly, little industrial archaeology surviving from the early days of this service, but from the mid-nineteenth century letter boxes and even pillar boxes (such as the hexagonal pillar boxes replaced outside King's College, Cambridge, and in Pulteney Street, Bath) have survived and, like other street furniture, are worthy of observation.[11]

The first telegraph system in Britain was a semaphore network based upon that of Chappe in France and flourishing, like the French system, during the Revolutionary and Napoleonic Wars. The object was to pass information quickly along a series of observation towers linking London with the south coast at Portsmouth and elsewhere. Each tower was at a suitable vantage point, and was equipped with a set of vertical shutters which could be opened and shut in various combinations to pass coded messages. They were manned constantly during daylight hours, a midshipman being supposed to pass continuously between two telescopes which were kept permanently trained on the adjacent towers. A surprising number of these towers survive, as well as hills retaining the name 'Telegraph Hill'. The system, however, was expensive to maintain, and it was abandoned by 1847.

The electric telegraph was introduced in the 1830s, the first satisfactory system being devised by Cooke and Wheatstone in 1837. This was adapted for railway signalling purposes and installed on the Great Western Railway, being then taken up by

A   B

41. Two unusual pillar boxes. (A) A 'Penfold' type box dating from about 1872; (B) an Edward VIII box of 1936.

other railways. The system was adopted for industrial and commercial purposes in the 1840s and spread rapidly. In 1851 the first cross-Channel link with France was established by a submarine cable, and in America the electric telegraph, with the simplified code devised by Samuel Morse, proved to be a great boon in the opening up of the West. To some extent the telegraph was superseded by the telephone following its invention by

Alexander Bell in 1876, and this has spread ever since to become an indispensable part of the equipment of modern life. Telephone systems, however, have undergone tremendous development in the last hundred years, so that surviving specimens of the earlier receivers, switch-board equipment, and general fittings, have become worth-while items of museum collections and objects of industrial archaeological interest.

Although the so-called 'mass media' of communication are such an important feature of modern life, they are not means of communication in the full, reciprocal, sense of the term, although they can become powerful means of sales promotion, propaganda, and the dissemination of information and ideas. The cinema is the oldest of these media, if one includes its photographic origins, and has fallen on greatly reduced prosperity with the advent of popular television since the Second World War. This is an important fact from the industrial archaeological point of view, because it means that hundreds of cinemas have become obsolete and converted to other purposes, ranging from bingo halls to warehouses, and they are well worth observing in passing for their curious architectural styles as well as for the possibility of their containing interesting equipment.[12]

The development of radio and television is one of the most remarkable achievements of the twentieth century. It is not a subject which has, at first sight, much of interest to the industrial archaeologist, but the early stages of the story contain many fascinating features. Baird's early experiments with mechanical scanning, for example, are worth attention, and it is gratifying that some of Baird's equipment has been preserved on permanent exhibition in the hall of residence named after him in the University of Strathclyde, Glasgow. Old radio and television sets have already become industrial curiosities, and it is to be hoped that somebody will consider it worth-while to preserve a representative selection before it is too late. The same may be said of the phonograph and its development into the gramophone and the tape-recorder. The successful invention of all these means of communication is a complex story, and the artefacts produced in the course of their evolution are very vulnerable and prone to easy destruction. A concern for the recording and preservation of such artefacts is the very proper business of industrial archaeologists.

Part 4 The Progress of Industrial Archaeology

15. The Organization of the Subject

Since the first edition of this book was published in 1972, some significant developments have taken place in the organization of industrial archaeology in Britain. It is now no longer strictly accurate to describe the situation as possessing 'a curiously unorganized quality'.[1] Although local groups and initiatives remain important in the national pattern of industrial archaeological activities and are, indeed, essential to its continued vitality, there have been several innovations in the last decade which have given a structural 'backbone' to British industrial archaeology and which have thus gone a long way towards providing the central co-ordination which the subject previously lacked. From the point of view of the individual field-worker or enthusiast working on his canal restoration or windmill survey little might appear to have changed, except, perhaps, the recognition of a more sympathetic attitude by government agencies through job-creation schemes and preservation grants. But viewed from the perspective of the overall growth of industrial archaeology, these developments are of great importance.

The key factor in this new situation has been the emergence of a viable national organization in the shape of the Association for Industrial Archaeology. The A I A grew out of the series of annual conferences held at the University of Bath between 1966 and 1970. So successful were these conferences in generating a sense of comradeship and common purpose amongst their participants that it was decided to extend them into peripatetic conferences, visiting different parts of the country each year. In September 1972 the conference met at Glasgow, and at an informal business meeting on that occasion Sir Arthur Elton proposed that the conference should transform itself into a permanent society. This was accepted, and the new Association was formally established at the following conference on the Isle of Man in September 1973, with Mr L. T. C. Rolt as its first President. The Association has since grown steadily, both in membership and in the recognition it has received from local industrial archaeologists and from national bodies with whom it has negotiated on matters of industrial archaeological concern.[2]

The creation of the AIA has done much to remedy the deficiencies in the national organization of industrial archaeology which still loomed large in the early 1970s. There is now an information service available to industrial archaeologists through the *Bulletin* of the Association, and the annual conferences have served both as a forum for the regular exchange of experiences and as a means of supporting specific projects. It has been possible, moreover, to organize special conferences and seminars with other bodies like the Victorian Society and the Institute of Town Planning which have explored areas of overlapping interests and made constructive suggestions for further co-operation. Perhaps most important of all, the AIA has promoted a new journal in conjunction with the Oxford University Press which has replaced to a large extent the less satisfactory publications which preceded it. This journal, the *Industrial Archaeology Review*, has appeared three times a year since it was launched in 1976, and has established a good mixture of scholarly papers and articles concerned with aspects of industrial archaeological conservation. The long-term prospects of this journal are the subject of continuing negotiations, and will depend to a large extent on the rate of growth it is able to maintain in its circulation. The rapid rise in production costs in recent years has made the future of many such 'quality' journals precarious, so it must be hoped that a sufficient number of industrial archaeologists will appreciate the value of possessing a first-class journal of their own to take out a subscription and support it.[3]

Important though it has undoubtedly been, the emergence of the AIA and its journal has not been the only significant development in the last few years. For a decade prior to the foundation of the Association, the Council for British Archaeology had an active Research Committee in Industrial Archaeology which, more than any other single body, pioneered the effective legislative protection for industrial monuments. This was done in conjunction with officers from what were then the Ministry of Works and the Ministry of Housing, now combined in the Department of the Environment, who attended the Advisory Panel to the CBA Research Committee which made recommendations to the Ministers concerned for the scheduling or listing of industrial monuments. The most important aspect of this procedure was the fact that, with the sympathetic co-operation of the government departments concerned, it was possible to interpret existing legislation to include industrial monuments without the need for any new laws. The existing legislation consisted of the Ancient Monuments Acts, dating back to 1882, under which industrial monuments could be 'scheduled' as ancient monuments in certain circumstances; and the Town and Country Planning Acts of 1947 and thereafter, which made provision for the 'listing' of historic buildings and which could be extended easily to include historic industrial buildings.

Although no special legislation has been necessary to cover industrial monuments, they have benefited from new laws such as the Civic Amenities Act of 1967, which devised the 'conservation area' whereby whole districts rather than individual buildings are brought under legal protection. The result of all this legislation and its extension to cover industrial monuments has been that a couple of hundred industrial monuments have been scheduled as ancient monuments and several thousand industrial buildings have been listed as historic buildings, while at least a third of the 3,000 conservation areas designated in Britain by the mid-1970s contained industrial buildings. A few conservation areas, indeed, such as the Three Mills Conservation Area in Newham, were designated primarily for their industrial archaeological significance. Of course, it must be realized that legislative protection of any sort does not guarantee the permanent survival of a monument, industrial or otherwise. What the law does is to place constraints on owners in order to make them consider carefully the consequences of destroying a monument or a building. In only a few cases is there provision for taking monuments into the care of the state, although such 'guardianship' protection has been extended to some prominent industrial monuments such as the Iron Bridge at Telford. For the most part, however, preservation of scheduled and listed structures depends on the co-operation of the owners, once they have been alerted to the importance of their property and offered help in keeping it in good condition. Legal protection thus provides a check on unwarranted demolition and controls the rate of unavoidable wastage of the industrial heritage of the nation. It serves to call public attention to the case of industrial monuments deserving special consideration, and enables local societies to monitor proposals to demolish valuable structures.[4]

The principal agency through which the responsible government departments have been notified of industrial monuments deserving consideration for legislative protection has been the CBA Advisory Panel. This has been served by the Survey Officer appointed under the Industrial Monuments Survey, which was established by the CBA in 1963 with the help of a grant from the government. The first Survey Officer was Mr Rex Wailes, the pioneer industrial archaeologist who was already well known for his work on windmills. When Mr Wailes retired in 1971, he was succeeded by Mr Keith A. Falconer, who was based in the

University of Bath. In 1977, the University took over completely from the CBA the administration of the Survey, negotiating a new three-year agreement with the Department of the Environment in order to do this, so that the CBA Panel was replaced by a smaller advisory body nominated directly by the DOE.[5] The main task of successive Survey Officers has been to prepare recommendations for the scheduling and listing of industrial monuments, as the basis of a county-by-county survey. Inevitably they have become involved in other more topical or thematic preservation matters also, and over the years since 1963 an impressive amount of work has been done and a very considerable expertise in the preservation of industrial monuments has been accumulated. Like the painting of the Forth Bridge, the task of the Survey Officer of Industrial Monuments goes on and on: there is a constant flow of new cases requiring attention, and each one of them generates further work of monitoring towards legislative protection and supervision thereafter. It must be hoped that this remarkable achievement can be consolidated and perpetuated by converting the Survey Officer of Industrial Monuments into a permanent officer of the state.

In the early years of the Survey it was a matter of some concern to members of the CBA Advisory Panel to establish the criteria whereby industrial monuments were deemed suitable for preservation. No precise statement of the appropriate criteria was ever formulated, as it became clear with widening experience that to a large extent individual cases had to be judged on their merits because it was difficult to generalize about such a diverse selection of monuments which included milestones, canals, bridges, factories, and so on. But even when monuments are considered on their individual merits it is important to have some agreement about the standards on which a judgement is being made, and six such criteria may be defined.

First is the *degree of uniqueness* of a monument. Strictly speaking, an object either is or is not unique, but as far as an industrial monument is concerned its claim to uniqueness may rest on one of several qualities. It may be the *only* example of a particular type of artefact, it may be the *first* or *earliest surviving* specimen of a type, or it may be the *last* or *latest surviving* specimen. A claim on any one of these grounds constitutes a powerful case for preservation. Secondly, there is the criterion of what might be called *representational distinction*. This is meant to include any claim to consideration based upon the fact that the monument under review represents a distinct regional type, architectural or design style, or has unusual structural properties. It also includes claims to aesthetic qualities and landmark features and claims to belong to complexes of buildings or artefacts possessing such qualities and which require preservation as a group.

Thirdly, amongst the criteria for the preservation of industrial monuments, *size* and *use* must be considered. Every artefact takes up space, and the valuation of this space may be an important criterion in preservation, because there will obviously be more pressure for, say, the land occupied by an old railway station in a city, where land is expensive, than for one in the countryside. Also, the possibility of re-using or converting an industrial building to another use has an important bearing on preservation, for while it is not impossible to maintain a large and historically important building in a condition of dereliction, it obviously aids the case for preservation if it can be demonstrated to possess some functional utility. Fourthly, there is the possibility of *public appeal* and *tourist attraction* to be taken into account. An object like the *Cutty Sark* at Greenwich can provide a welcome leisure and recreational amenity and, incidentally, earn some money for its own maintenance, so that its prospects for preservation are greatly improved. Fifthly, the criterion of *local support* is important, especially if this is shown positively in financial terms. An amenable attitude on the part of local rate-payers, the generous co-operation of the owners, or the interest of a public or private trust, can make all the difference between preservation and destruction. For instance, a site such as an iron forge may be far from unique or possessing representational distinction, but it might be an object of local interest and instruction so that there might be a case for preserving it on that ground alone if support is forthcoming. Sixthly and lastly, the *associations* of the artefact require consideration. To be associated with a famous engineer or an important technological innovation may well constitute a good claim to sympathetic preservation. Thus, a Telford or Brunel association would justify preservation for an otherwise undistinguished relic.

Criteria such as these have been found helpful in deciding about recommendations for scheduling or listing industrial monuments, but it is not possible to lay down categorical rules because of the variety of artefacts covered by the Survey of Industrial Monuments. In any case, it was realized at the outset of the Survey that only a small proportion of monuments would be suitable for preservation, and it was decided to undertake a recording exercise which would produce a definitive catalogue of all sorts of industrial monument, whether suitable for preservation or not. It was soon realized that the compilation of such an index presented formidable administrative problems, so it was separated from the Survey in 1965 to become the National Record of Industrial Monuments (NRIM) at the University of Bath. The record has been compiled since then from entries sent in by field-workers on simple cards designed by the CBA so that they could be easily filled in with details of the nature and location of sites and artefacts of industrial archaeological significance. The procedure has been for the cards to be photocopied and then returned to the people who sent them. Copies are made for the Survey Officer and for the National Monuments Record (which maintains its own collection in Fortress House, Savile Row). The NRIM collection in Bath, however, is the only national record in Britain devoted specifically to information about industrial monuments, classified according to county and industry. Although it now contains some 10,000 entries, the NRIM is still very uneven and patchy in its coverage. The entries vary widely in quality, and some parts of the country have been poorly covered so far. It would thus be unwise to exaggerate the importance of NRIM. It is essentially a preliminary exercise, doing little more than identifying and locating sites of industrial archaeological interest.[6]

Nevertheless, the value of this preliminary exercise should not be ignored. In some respects industrial archaeology is still in the early stages of development, requiring the establishment of a general pattern of information about the material available, and the compilation of a systematic record such as that of the NRIM is an indispensable step in this process. This should in no way discourage field-workers from preparing fuller and more interesting reports for publication, but should instead encourage them to do so because it can help them to assess the relationship between their own work and similar material elsewhere. While regretting the somewhat slow progress of the NRIM in recent years, therefore, and looking a little enviously at some of the excellent recording which has been accomplished in America by the Historic American Engineering Record (HAER),[7] it is worth recognizing that there is a useful foundation here on which a more detailed recording programme could be constructed. In particular, the NRIM is now able to provide county summary lists of sites which have been recorded, and it is hoped that these may soon be made available as a general publication. Meanwhile, industrial archaeological field-workers should still regard the completion of record cards for the NRIM as one of the most useful contributions they can make to the development of industrial archaeology in Britain.

The area covered by the NRIM was determined in the first instance by the regional structure of the CBA, with the result that there are at present no entries devoted to Northern Ireland although the whole of mainland Britain is represented. It is worth noting, in passing, that there are other discrepancies of this nature which should be taken into account. The DOE, for example, is only responsible for scheduling and listing industrial monuments in England and Wales, and even in Wales some of its functions are delegated to regional bodies. In Scotland, a parallel system is operated through the Scottish Office, and there is now a Scottish Survey of Industrial Monuments based at the University of Strathclyde which is the counterpart to the English Survey and which has recently been making strenuous efforts to improve the coverage of industrial recording in Scotland. The Royal Commission on Historical Monuments, which is responsible for the National Monuments Record (NMR), only operates in England, although there are similar commissions covering Scotland and Wales. The record of the Scottish and Welsh commissions, indeed, has shown more sympathy for industrial monuments to date than has the much larger body in England, but these long-standing government agencies would be natural focal points for the development of a detailed recording effort to encompass industrial monuments in their respective areas.

Whatever the shortcomings in recording industrial archaeology over the last few years, the physical conservation of industrial monuments has undergone striking development. This has been accomplished by a combination of agencies, including national and local government, museums, specially constituted trusts, and private individuals. National government has acted directly in industrial conservation, both through the 'guardianship' powers of the Ancient Monuments Board of the DOE, which have already been mentioned, and through various forms of grant given to secure the protection of industrial monuments. One of the more recent additions in this respect has been the introduction in 1973 of the grant administered by the Department of Education and Science (DES) through the Science Museum for the conservation of technological artefacts. There are irksome restrictions on the application of this fund, but it has become a valuable source of financial support for museums and trusts undertaking the purchase, moving, and restoration of the smaller class (as distinct from buildings and other fixed structures) of industrial monument.[8]

Local as well as national government has contributed to the increasing support for industrial conservation. At this level, however, there tends to be a mixture of motives, with a genuine interest in conservation conflicting with other interests such as the restoration of 'blighted' industrial sites and the exploitation of assets capable of development for leisure or tourist purposes. Although often desirable in themselves, these alternative interests are likely to compromise the application of proper archaeological standards to the conservation process, and it is only quite recently that local authorities in some parts of the country have begun to appoint experts in industrial archaeology to advise them in such matters. Many museums, of course, represent local government involvement in conservation projects, and it is through the large regional museums in particular that important collections of technological artefacts have been assembled and displayed attractively. Even more significant, however, has been the contribution of the national technological museums in London (the Science Museum), Edinburgh, Cardiff, and Belfast, as well as that of the impressive Folk Museums like the collection at St Fagan's, Cardiff, and the open-air museums at Beamish, County Durham, and at Blists Hill in Telford New Town. The Ironbridge Gorge Museum Trust, which is responsible for the Blists Hill site as well as the Coalbrookdale Furnaces and other important buildings in Telford, is tackling the task of making a rather decayed industrial area into an exciting heritage complex with great enterprise and imagination.

The large open-air industrial museums were established in the 1960s and were in part a defensive reaction to the forces of redevelopment and urban renewal which were sweeping away so many industrial monuments at the time. They are now growing out of the siege mentality which reckoned on preservation only at the price of removal to the museum, and placing more emphasis on the desirability of preserving structures *in situ*, without attempting to move them. This new attitude has been encouraged both by the more sympathetic attitude towards industrial conservation and preservation which has become widespread over the last decade, and also by the success of many trusts and societies up and down the country in undertaking specific tasks of *in situ* preservation. The National Trust, for example, as the leading conservationist organization in the country, has acquired several mills and steam engines in pursuit of its policy of purchasing and accepting gifts of properties with high heritage value. The Styal Mill estate, near Manchester, came into its possession as early as 1938, and is now being expertly adapted as an industrial museum and public amenity. The Cornish engines at Camborne and St Just have been acquired more recently from the Cornish Engines Preservation Society, but these also are receiving the professional National Trust treatment. More typically, many small new trusts have been created for the preservation of specific industrial monuments such as the Cheddleton Flint Mill and Gladstone Pottery, both in Staffordshire, where enthusiastic individuals have raised money from local industries and government to restore the properties to a semblance of their prime working condition and to make them available to the public for recreational and instructive purposes. The legal device of the trust has proved itself to be a conveniently flexible arrangement for launching a financial appeal and for channelling the money raised into the restoration work. Even with this financial support, most of the successful trusts rely heavily on the devotion of their members who are willing to spend many hours working hard in both skilled and unskilled tasks on the labour of restoration. Such activity remains one of the most distinguished and encouraging characteristics of British industrial archaeology.

Some private companies have established their own trust funds to take care of the physical remains of their past activities or to open company museums. The Bass Brewery Museum in Burton-on-Trent is an interesting example of this sort of enterprise. In some instances, individuals have undertaken their own industrial conservation schemes, particularly those with some engineering experience who acquire old windmills and watermills and then devote all their spare time to restoring the fabric and the machinery to working order. There are now many small mills up and down the country which have benefited from this sort of experience, and have thus had their place in the industrial landscape prolonged for at least another generation. At least one philanthropist, also, deserves to be mentioned for his signal contribution to British industrial preservation. When Neil Cossons and I published our *Industrial Archaeology of the Bristol Region* in 1969 we lamented the fact that 'one of the most remarkable industrial monuments of the Bristol region' lay abandoned in the Falkland Islands.[9] A year later, the splendid rusting iron hull of the steamship *Great Britain* had been restored to the dry dock in Bristol from which it had been launched in 1843, and the main credit for this near-miracle must go to Mr Jack Hayward, the industrialist who largely financed the operation of bringing the ship home.

All this conservation activity, promoted in such a variety of ways, has ensured that the national stock of industrial monuments is now in a much healthier condition than it was a decade ago. There have been losses of irreplaceable buildings and artefacts, many of which could have been preserved with a little more imagination at the time when their fate was being determined. Some outstanding monuments such as Old Temple Meads Station in Bristol and some of the London mainline termini still have shadows over their future. But for the most part, the surviving industrial monuments are in better condition now in 1979 than they were in 1969, and their immediate future at least is secure. Problems will doubtless arise as the personnel of successful preservation trusts changes, as schemes of canal restoration are fulfilled, as preserved railways – both narrow- and standard-gauge – assume increasingly the character of business enterprises. Complex group dynamics affect relationships within the myriad of societies, trusts, and other preservationist organizations and create a momentum for change and fresh experience which maintains conditions of growth. Such groups comprise the vital 'grass roots' of British industrial archaeology, and so long as their vitality remains unimpaired the subject will be in good heart, no matter how diverse and complicated its organization might become.

Not all the groups, both local and national, which are now active in the study of industrial archaeology are products of the boom in interest of the past two decades. Some of the specialist societies go back considerably longer. In particular, the Newcomen Society for the Study of the History of Engineering and Technology can claim to have anticipated this interest by a generation. The Newcomen Society was formed sixty years ago as a result of the James Watt centenary celebrations in Birmingham in 1919. Its object is 'to support and encourage study and research in the history of engineering and technology, and the preservation of records, both technical and biographical'.[10] Over the years, the annual *Transactions* of the Society have brought together a mass of information which is of enormous practical and scholarly value to industrial archaeology. It seemed possible, in the mid-1960s, that the Society might come to perform the role of a national society for industrial archaeology, but it decided that its role was primarily that of a learned society and declined the opportunity of expanding its functions. In view of its character and resources this was probably a wise decision, and in no way weakens the cordiality and mutual respect between the Society and the new industrial archaeological organizations.

Except for the academic study of industrial archaeology, which

is the subject of the next and final chapter, the leading aspects of
the organization of industrial archaeology in Britain have now
been briefly surveyed. In order to complete the sketch, however,
and set it in a wider framework, it will be appropriate to say here
something about the literature on the subject, and its relationship
with industrial archaeology in other countries. The spate of
industrial archaeological publications has subsided somewhat in
the 1970s. The David & Charles series of regional studies on
industrial archaeology ran to some twenty volumes, but it now
appears to have been terminated despite several gaps in the
coverage (most notably, there is no volume for Yorkshire). The
important series of industrial archaeological studies which was
produced initially by Longmans under the editorship of the late
Mr L. T. C. Rolt, and was later transferred to Allen Lane, has
also been wound up after the publication of thirteen volumes.
Other well-established collections like the David & Charles canal
and railway volumes have not grown so rapidly in the 1970s as
they did in the previous decade, but new books have recently
been added to both series. On the other hand, one new series of
industrial archaeological works, providing regional gazetteers
based on the new county structure for Britain, has been launched
by Batsford under the editorship of Mr Keith A. Falconer, and
several regional publishers like Bradford Barton of Truro,
Moorlands Press of Derbyshire, and Moonraker Press of Wessex,
have continued to produce both local studies and scholarly
monographs of national significance. Moreover, the industrial
archaeological coffee-tables have begun to groan under the weight
of finely produced, illustrated volumes such as that by Brian
Bracegirdle: *The Archaeology of the Industrial Revolution* (Heinemann, 1973), and the number of general works on the subject has
been increased by those of Arthur Raistrick: *Industrial Archaeology* (Eyre Methuen, 1972), and Neil Cossons: *The BP Book of
Industrial Archaeology* (David & Charles, 1975). There is thus
an extensive literature now available on industrial archaeology

in Britain, and in addition to the volumes referred to here there are many more specialized publications in related areas of economic, technological, and social history which cannot be mentioned in a brief survey although some of them can be found in the bibliographical notes at the end of this book.

Finally, the organization of British industrial archaeology can be illuminated by comparing it with developments in other countries. One of the most striking developments of the 1970s has been the rapid growth of international understanding in this subject. The Bath Conferences of the late 1960s enjoyed the support of two foreign representatives – Mr Robert Vogel from the USA and Miss Marie Nisser from Sweden. These early international links have developed into a fully-fledged world organization – the International Committee for Conservation of the Industrial Heritage (ICCIH). This was the result of three international conferences – the First International Conference on the Conservation of Industrial Monuments (FICCIM) was held at Ironbridge, Shropshire, in 1973, followed by the Second (SICCIM) at Bochum, in the Ruhr of West Germany in 1975, and the Third (TICCIM) at Stockholm and Grangärde in Sweden in 1978. It was at Grangärde on 4 June 1978 that the decision was taken to establish ICCIH, bringing to a culmination the previous years of negotiation and comradeship. It was also decided not to seek immediate affiliation to any other international body, although it was hoped to establish a formal relationship with UNESCO in order to assist delegates, especially from the Eastern European countries, to attend. Alongside this development in international interest in industrial archaeology, there has been intense national activity in North America (both in the USA and Canada), where the Society for Industrial Archaeology (SIA) has built up a vigorous membership and undertaken several valuable surveys, and in the continental European countries. Amongst the latter, the Deutsches Bergbau-Museum,

Bochum, in Western Germany; the Ecomusée de la Communauté, Le Creusot, in France; and active groups in Belgium, the Netherlands, East Germany, Italy, Poland, and the Scandinavian countries, have all made a contribution. Delegates have also attended from Japan and Australia, so that the world-wide coverage has become remarkably comprehensive. Industrial archaeologists from other countries have until recently tended to look to Britain for leadership, because Britain is both the birth-place of the traditional Industrial Revolution and the place where consciousness of the importance of the industrial heritage first generated the study of industrial archaeology. But with the rise to maturity of the international industrial archaeological com-munity, it is fitting to have an American – Mr Theodore A. Sande – as the first Chairman of I C C I H, and an executive committee on which there is only one British member. Industrial archaeology has thus arrived as a truly international, world-wide, activity with a commensurate organization.[11]

The forecast made in the first edition of this book that there would 'certainly be important changes'[12] in the organization of British industrial archaeology during the 1970s has been amply fulfilled. A vigorous but largely inchoate and amateur activity has been transformed in the last decade into a body with a national and international organization, possessing a well-defined procedure for securing legislative protection for industrial monuments and a versatile mixture of devices for conservation. The opportunities for lay and amateur involvement happily remain wide, as there has been little sign of the emergence of a professional industrial archaeological leadership or secretariat. There is much still to be done to improve the standards of indus-trial recording, and the study of industrial archaeology has still almost everything to do towards establishing itself as a recognized scholarly discipline, as we will see in the next chapter. Never-theless, the developments have been remarkable and encourage the hope that interest in industrial archaeology has tapped some permanent springs of enthusiasm which will enable it to maintain its appeal to a diverse range of people while continuing to deepen its involvement in the conservation and interpretation of the national industrial heritage.

16. The Study of Industrial Archaeology

From the beginning of the growth of interest in industrial archaeology, the subject has benefited from its remarkable interdisciplinary appeal whereby men and women of very diverse professional preoccupations and commitments have met on common ground, each bringing to it some expertise which has helped to illuminate the subject. Thus, architects have brought a knowledge of building construction, engineers have contributed a skill with machinery, and metallurgists have been able to interpret the function of metal-working sites by an analysis of fragments of slag, while historians, geographers, and archaeologists have been able to make comparisons and to establish relationships which have helped in understanding industrial monuments. Even people without specific professional skills have found it easy to identify themselves with aspects of the subject and to make valuable contributions to its development.

This interdisciplinarity is an outstanding quality of the study of industrial archaeology, and must be welcomed without reservation. However, as was observed in the opening pages of this book, interdisciplinarity does pose some problems, and in particular it has probably retarded the emergence of industrial archaeology as a clearly defined academic discipline in its own right. It may be considered that such an objective is not desirable, and that it would be preferable to maintain indefinitely the present amateur or 'hobby' status of the subject. Industrial archaeology has, after all, done quite well over the past twenty years without any professionals except, perhaps, for a handful of museum curators and university extra-mural lecturers. However, it is difficult to see how such a flexible arrangement as that which at present unites the practitioners of industrial archaeology can be sustained without the generation of a disciplinary core which is specific to the subject and which both poses questions for critical analysis and is enriched by the research of people who undertake to answer these questions. Without a core of this nature the subject will never be taken seriously as an academic study. A friendly reviewer of the first edition of this book, considering it in a leading scholarly journal, referred to some of his colleagues who viewed industrial archaeology as a good excuse for taking a girl out on the moors.[1] Other academics, although not ill-disposed to industrial archaeology, have dismissed it as a 'fun subject'. Unless this attitude of scholarly dismissal can be overcome, it seems probable that industrial archaeology will become increasingly fragmented and dispersed, as practitioners drift off into subject areas where their research will receive serious consideration, as it is already doing in the architectural press, historical geography, social and economic history, and in other disciplines which have hitherto fed into the subject a significant academic component.

In order to resist this tendency of industrial archaeological research to become so widely dispersed that it loses its distinctive character and coherence, it is important to recognize that the subject does, in reality, possess a disciplinary matrix, and to identify this as the core of a field of scholarly study which, while retaining the attractive open-endedness of the subject, will enable it to stand as a distinct and important academic discipline. Something has already been said, in the first chapter of this book, about the claim of industrial archaeology to be taken seriously as a branch of historical studies, and several contributions of historical evidence were briefly outlined there. It is now desirable that the broader implications of this claim should be examined. We will do so by considering, first, the theoretical core of industrial archaeology, and secondly, the extent of industrial archaeological studies in Britain at present.

The Disciplinary Matrix

Whatever other disciplines become involved in industrial archaeology, the subject is at its core a historical study. The architect is only likely to become interested in it in so far as he pursues his inquiries into the history of industrial buildings, and the engineer similarly will only find time for it when he becomes interested in the history of the machines and processes with which he is professionally engaged. Similarly, the geographer who studies industrial monuments probably does so because his interest is historical geography. The point may be an elementary one, but it is worth making both because it is easy to lose sight of when welcoming the multidisciplinary input into industrial archaeology, and because it is vitally important in placing the subject where it belongs in the academic pantheon. Industrial archaeology is interdisciplinary and open-ended, in the sense that it is not excluding anybody who shows an interest in its subject matter. But this subject matter is primarily historical.

The historical basis of industrial archaeology is obscured, to some extent, by the use of the word 'archaeology'. The term 'industrial archaeology' has caused difficulties ever since it was coined over twenty years ago, with some practitioners taking the view that, as archaeology involves excavation, only excavatory studies should be included within its scope, with other aspects relegated to 'industrial recording' or some such category.[2] This is an unacceptable distinction because it ignores two facts about archaeology: first, that it does not rely exclusively on excavation, but on many other techniques for examining and interpreting physical remains; and second, that archaeology is itself part of the general study of history, being one of many specialisms amongst the range of historical studies. It is possible that archaeologists, who have only comparatively recently struggled successfully to achieve a large measure of disciplinary autonomy, will not like to be reminded of this fact. Nevertheless, the fact is that archaeology is concerned with the past, and the past is by definition the province of history. The particular contribution which archaeology makes to this broad field of study is an examination and interpretation of the physical evidence. Traditionally, historians have relied heavily on documentary evidence, to such a degree that any period lacking documentation was consigned to 'prehistory', and it was this myopia about any sort of evidence except the written word which allowed archaeology to develop as an independent discipline.

Archaeologists over the last century have made good use of this opportunity. They have systematically exploited the vast reserves of physical evidence available for the early periods of man's existence. They have developed a set of valuable techniques to enable them to extract as much information as possible from this evidence. And they have, moreover, established convincing typologies to account for the stages of human development over long periods of time, from the Palaeolithic or Old Stone Age through the Neolithic to the succession of metal-working techniques in the Copper, Bronze, and Iron Ages. They were able to do this partly because of the tremendous intellectual revolution caused by the discovery, brought about by the study of geology and the development of plant and animal species, that the earth was much older than the six thousand years allowed on the conventional and universally accepted time scale up to the nineteenth century. Into the enormous gap which opened up in our knowledge of pre-literate mankind, the archaeologists were able to move with resounding success. We are all indebted to the contribution made to the knowledge of our past by their achievement.

The very success of archaeology, however, required a reassessment of its relationship with historical studies. It could not be left in the limbo of 'pre-history' as if this had no relevance to the business of historians. It was an archaeologist who made the first serious breach in this artificial distinction, when V. Gordon Childe published his influential survey of *What happened in History*. This was not asking a question but making a statement, and the statement involved demonstrating the continuity between 'pre-history', using physical evidence, and 'history', relying on documentary evidence. Almost simultaneously, R. Collingwood, a philosopher of history and himself an archaeologist of some distinction, published his seminal work on *The Idea of History*, in which he emphasized the multiplicity of sources of history. Collingwood argued that, although all evidence must be converted into 'documents' to be useful to the historian, the source of this evidence could be the oral tradition, the cultural forms of a society, or its physical remains, as well as any available literary evidence.[3]

Over the last thirty years, therefore, the disciplinary gap between archaeology and history has closed. Just as historians have become reconciled to drawing their evidence from a much wider area than surviving fragments of literary evidence, so archaeologists have recognized that the techniques for investigating physical evidence which they pioneered in the period of 'pre-history' are equally applicable in the period of 'history', with the difference that here they can be used to verify or clarify literary sources, or to compensate for gaps in the documentary evidence. Thus the original archaeological typology, with its strong technological basis, has become somewhat attenuated, the 'Iron Age' having been succeeded by 'Classical', 'Roman', 'Medieval', and 'Post-Medieval' archaeology. Some industrial archaeologists have toyed with the notion of 'Post-post-Medieval Archaeology' to fit their subject into this series of successive time periods.[4] But we can do better than that. Leaving aside the question of whether or not it is desirable to limit industrial archaeology to a time period, we suggest that a modification to the basic archaeological typology could accommodate industrial archaeology comfortably. Reverting to the technological categories, it should be observed that we are still in the 'Iron Age', which began around 1000 B.C. But just as it proved convenient to divide the Stone Age between 'Old' and 'New' on the grounds of increasing technological sophistication and social organization, particularly in the so-called 'Neolithic Revolution', so it would seem appropriate to divide the 'Iron Age' between an 'Old Iron Age', when iron technology was limited to comparatively simple bloomery and smithy techniques, and a 'New Iron Age' when these techniques were superseded by blast furnaces, coke-firing, forging, and steel-making innovations which converted iron and steel into cheap everyday materials and made possible the processes of modern industrialization and urbanization. In this scenario, industrial archaeology can be regarded as the study of the New Iron Age.

Industrial archaeology, therefore, is archaeological because its primary concern is with the investigation of the physical remains of industrialization, and this commitment to physical evidence allies it firmly with the archaeological approach to historical studies. However, now that historians of most persuasions have come to accept that physical evidence is a valid source of information for even the more modern periods of history, it may be argued that the time has come to recognize 'Physical History' as a new disciplinary label to subsume archaeology, historical geography, architectural history, and so on. Although this term would make a great deal of sense as an expression of all the aspects of modern scholarship which are converging on a more perceptive attitude towards the physical evidence as a clue in interpreting the past, it is doubtful whether it would be widely popular because it would threaten many academic vested interests. Yet it is a viable suggestion, given sufficient initiative in seeking to combine varying approaches to physical history, and it is one in which industrial archaeology would be well equipped to take a leading role.

As an aspect of physical history, it is possible to distinguish four different levels of analysis at which industrial archaeology can make a significant contribution to the interpretation of the evidence of industrialization. In the first place, useful information can be derived from a study of the landscape in the broadest sense, and from an examination of its topography, geology, soil, minerals, and land utilization. This is large-scale physical evidence, capable of yielding clues about the siting of industries, transport services, water supply, wind and water power – both actual and potential – and a variety of other matters of interest to the industrial archaeologist. For example, a study of the landscape of an old coal-mining area like County Durham or the Scottish Lowlands, through field-work or by maps and aerial photography, can provide plenty of evidence of the development of this industry, regarding both its changing location from exposed coalfields to areas where the coal seams are covered by more recent strata, and its development from primitive 'bell pits' to the sophisticated modern colliery complex with all its ancillary services.

The second level of analysis follows on directly from the first, and is concerned with settlement patterns. Much can be learnt from study of the distribution, size, and shape of human settlement, from scattered farms devoted largely to producing wool in the Yorkshire Dales, to villages, towns, and sprawling modern cities. The latter, of course, are the distinctive settlement configurations of a period of intensive industrialization, so that industrial archaeologists need to understand the processes whereby urbanization is sustained through the location of industries and vital services. Even in the countryside, however, there is much of industrial interest, as will have become apparent to the readers of this book. The example of those physical historians who, in the last quarter of a century, have explored the remains of Deserted Medieval Villages ('DMVs' for short) and have thereby significantly modified our understanding of English rural settlement, is an encouraging instance of the successful application of techniques familiar to the industrial archaeologist. In particular, the use of aerial survey and subsequent analysis of aerial photographs has proved to be very rewarding as a method of acquiring new historical information.[5]

Just as settlement follows landscape, so a study of structures follows settlement as the third level of study. Most structures are buildings of some sort or other, and here the skills of the architectural historian are especially useful. But other structures such as civil engineering works like bridges and tunnels are also important, and require different standards of assessment. Structures vary from large factory complexes to quite simple single buildings, and as we have seen the houses of industrial workers have recently become the subject of intensive study by industrial archaeologists concerned with the social implications of industrialization. Qualities of architectural style and fashion, and of functional efficiency, are involved in the interpretation of structural evidence, so that the variety of skills required at this level is very wide.

Fourthly, physical evidence is concerned at its basic level with artefacts, from fragments of flint tools to the most complicated modern machines, and from easily fabricated materials like glass beads to the sophistication of porcelain or the products of the modern plastics industries. Industrial artefacts, when they are not still in use, find their way quickly to the scrapyard or whatever process of destruction is appropriate to them, although an increasing number are now being acquired for museum collections as a result of the growth of interest in industrial archaeology. The analysis of this evidence calls for an extensive range of skills, including those of the traditional archaeologist, the engineer, and the metallurgist. Once again, the dependence of industrial archaeology upon such associated disciplines must be emphasized, as the task of interpretation can only be successful when all the possible information has been extracted from the physical evidence.

When the process of examination is complete, the subsequent interpretation is a historical one, and it is here that the historical core of the study of industrial archaeology becomes significant. The task is one of integrating the physical evidence, once it has been fully described by the appropriate specialist, with other forms of historical evidence in order to make a full reconstruction of a past event or process. The other forms of historical evidence are primarily documentary, as the modern development of industrialization has generated a spate of records of all sorts of documentary material, and the interpretation of this material is the stock-in-trade of the traditional historian, even though the traditional historian has not shown great interest in many of the forms of documentation which have accompanied rapid industrialization. However, it should be noted that even physical evidence must be converted into documentary evidence in the form of a report or similar literary statement in order to be incorporated in the historical analysis, and this applies also to other forms of non-documentary evidence at the disposal of the historian, such as cultural or oral evidence. Cultural evidence is that derived from the study of the way of life of a society – its organization, customs, taboos, ritual, songs, and so on. Modern anthropological and folklore studies have given rise to considerable interest in evidence of this nature, but like physical evidence it is virtually unusable by the historian until it has been written up into an authentic documentary record.

Oral evidence is hearsay evidence: the information received by word of mouth. This had an important place in early historiography, because there was then a shortage of other evidence. Herodotus relied heavily on tales which he had been told, although he always treated them with a critical caution befitting the world's first historian in the sense of one who undertook a systematic reconstruction of the past on the basis of the best available evidence. Subsequently, however, a great mass of documentary evidence accumulated and historians tended to prefer this to the 'gossip' they received verbally. Such gossip has taken on a new significance for historians of industry and technology in the recent past because, with the rapid obsolescence of industrial processes, particularly old handicrafts, the descriptions of surviving practitioners have become one of the few sources of information about these processes. A commendable attempt is being made, therefore, to secure a record on tape of conversations with people who can describe the processes from first-hand experience, thus securing a permanent record. As with other forms of non-documentary evidence, oral history requires converting to a transcript before the historian can assimilate it, and inevitably the account loses something in accent, dialect, and nuances of meaning by such a conversion. In any event, oral history requires special care in interpretation because it is particularly liable to distortion in the process of telling. It also has a special temporal limitation, in so far as genuine oral history, at the moment when it is gathered, can only hope to recover the recollections of a single life-span. Nevertheless, it has become a source of considerable importance in the field of historical interpretations with which industrial archaeology is concerned.[6]

Whatever uncertainties may remain unresolved about the theory and practice of industrial archaeology, the subject-matter is obvious enough, in the shape of the physical monuments of industrialization, and it should be reasonably clear by now that there is a powerful case for regarding the systematic study of these monuments as a part – and a vital part, at that – of the task of historical reconstruction. In other words, industrial archaeology fits best into the matrix of disciplinary studies if it is regarded as a type of history. As such, it can perform a valuable role in assembling and interpreting the physical evidence regarding the processes of industrialization. Most of this evidence comes, inevitably, from the period of rapidly accelerating industrialization over the last two centuries, and this covers the archaeological time-period we have just called the New Iron Age. But where there is earlier evidence of industrial processes, such as Neolithic flint mining and Roman iron working, it can be regarded as a legitimate extension of the industrial archaeologist's interests to take note of them, even if the bulk of his attention will be concentrated on the modern period. It is here, after all, that he can make his most significant contribution to historical understanding, while evidence of industrialization before the New Iron Age can be brought to the attention of archaeologists equipped with experience in earlier periods.

One criticism which is frequently made of industrial archaeology by historians who should know better is that it is merely a form of antiquarianism. The disparaging implication of this judgement is that industrial archaeology is only concerned with collecting material – the 'bits and bobs' and 'curious objects' of the enthusiastic but undisciplined museum curator concerned with enriching his collection without much discrimination for the significance of the items in it. Without denying the possibility that such an attitude may be found amongst industrial archaeologists as amongst students of most other subjects, it is necessary to say a word in defence of antiquarianism. The great antiquarians, from William Camden (1551–1623) with his enormous curiosity in collecting information about national history for his great work *Britannia*, pioneered the study of physical history by recording topographical and monumental information. As in any systematic or scientific inquiry the first desideratum is to amass a body of information, carefully compiled and classified, so the antiquarians laid the essential basis without which subsequent historical assessments of national history would not have been as comprehensive and satisfactory as they have become. By the same token, industrial archaeology can be regarded as having extended this antiquarian perception to a class of evidence – the industrial monuments – which had previously attracted little attention. In a sense, the study of industrial archaeology is passing through this first and necessary 'antiquarian' stage in the development of disciplinary status. Such, however, should be a matter of congratulation rather than criticism, and industrial archaeologists need not be ashamed to accept the care for fine scholarship which the label of antiquarianism carries with it.

While accepting that the first two decades of industrial archaeology have been greatly concerned with building up the foundations of the subject by accumulating as much evidence as possible about the physical monuments of industrialization, it should also be said that the case for regarding industrial archaeology as a scholarly discipline within the spectrum of historical studies does not rest there. Already much valuable work has been done in interpreting this evidence and thereby contributing to the modification of historical reconstructions achieved on the basis of documentary evidence alone. Unfortunately, much of this work has been published in forms which obscure its identification as industrial archaeology, in various architectural and other professional journals which have provided a suitable forum at a time when the opportunities for publication explicitly as works of industrial archaeology have been very limited. It would be tedious and invidious to give a selection of this diverse work, but the sort of subjects which are currently receiving illumination from the application of physical evidence include the history of iron structures, the internal organization of early factories, the distribution and development of iron furnaces and forges, the history of the non-ferrous metal industries, the social and economic implications of steam technology, the organization of the gunpowder industry, the effects of changing transport systems, and the development of artisan housing. As the study of industrial archaeology has now come to maturity, the scope and significance of such inquiries can be expected to increase. What is being undertaken, indeed, is a complete re-writing of the history of modern industrialization with the physical evidence of the industrial monuments providing an integral part of the reinterpretation.

Having emphasized the role of industrial archaeology within the range of historical studies, and having pressed its claim to be the means of incorporating a particular kind of evidence into the scholarly interpretation of the processes of industrialization, it is appropriate to conclude this survey of the disciplinary basis of industrial archaeology by stressing once again its open-endedness. We have observed that, even in the course of making historical assessments, the service of specialists from a truly remarkable range of disciplines is welcome and, in some instances, essential. This degree of interdisciplinarity is determined by the ready availability of much of the physical evidence of industrialization, and by the very general interest aroused by it. The widespread interest, however, is itself worthy of comment, as it is a comparatively recent phenomenon and reverses an earlier attitude which tended to be dismissive about the remains of industrial processes. To a very great extent, the study of industrial archaeology has shared in and benefited from a world-wide surge of interest in conservation, in turn associated with a concern for ecology and a need to maintain a balance on planet Earth between the resources of food, raw materials, and power, on the one hand, and a rapidly increasing population demanding higher standards of living on the other. In order to secure the right ecological balance, it has become important to conserve the best from the past and to seek to understand the processes by which the present problem has been created. In both these aspects of the ecological programme, industrial archaeology has a part to play, along with many other scholarly disciplines. Its participation in this programme should do much to confirm its disciplinary basis and to ensure its continued interdisciplinarity.[7]

The Teaching of Industrial Archaeology

So far, in this concluding chapter, we have been examining the disciplinary basis for the study of industrial archaeology. It is important that the emphasis should fall on this aspect of the subject, because there has been conspicuous doubt cast on its disciplinary basis, and if only this can be clearly established many other things should follow easily. The treatment of industrial archaeology in schools, colleges, and universities, for example, is bound to reflect the way in which the subject is received into the spectrum of scholarly disciplines, and it is fair to observe that the present patchy appearance of industrial archaeology as a taught subject in our educational institutions does in fact demonstrate the persistent uncertainties about its academic status which we have been attempting to dispel. Nevertheless, some significant progress has been made in establishing industrial archaeology as a subject for pedagogic instruction, so it will be convenient to round off our survey of the study of the subject by considering some aspects of this development and by speculating about whatever future pattern might be desirable.

Perhaps the first thing which should be mentioned in this context is the fact that industrial archaeology has been widely recognized in schools as a teaching aid. This does not mean that the subject has been included in the curriculum along with the three Rs and other traditional school studies, but it has been adopted by many of the more progressive teachers of history, geography, and other subjects, as a means of giving the text books an added dimension and thus making their subjects come to life. There has been a steady rise in the popularity of school visits to museums, and the development in the last decade of large open-air museums devoted to industrial archaeology at Telford, Beamish, and elsewhere has given a further stimulus to this possibility of taking a class of school children for an informative day out. As a school study, such a supportive function is probably the best thing for industrial archaeology, as it can serve to arouse interest without deadening it by submitting the subject to an examination schedule. There is, however, plenty of scope for strengthening this supportive function by the provision of lively and well-illustrated books on industrial archaeology in the school library. And it may be argued that the problem of finding sufficiently interesting and creative work for young people in their final year at school up to sixteen could be solved in part by devising local projects in industrial archaeology.

By far the most successful form of instruction in industrial archaeology over the past two decades has been through university extra-mural courses. All over the country, departments of extra-mural studies have been requested to put on courses in the subject for adult students seeking nothing more than interesting instruction in an attractive field of study. Some departments have responded by appointing full-time tutors in industrial archaeology, thus creating the first genuine professionals in the subject, but more normally they have drawn on local talent in other university departments or elsewhere to take these classes. The classes have been widely successful in terms of numbers of registered students, but naturally it is impossible to keep up any course indefinitely, and some of the best have secured their perpetuation by converting themselves into industrial archaeological societies which have then moved outside the extra-mural programme or remained in it by arranging annual panels of visiting speakers who come to speak to members of the society. Such programmes have now run very successfully for several years in Gloucestershire and Bristol, amongst other places.

There is a well-established pattern in adult education whereby 'vogue' subjects rise in popularity and then tail away as other subjects replace them in the interest of mature students who are looking for a measure of variety and entertainment as well as academic instruction. It is possible that, on this pattern, there will be a falling-off in interest in industrial archaeology in future

years, but it seems likely that the subject has identified itself
sufficiently with local history and other aspects of physical
history and environmental studies to ensure that it will survive
vigorously in this form for a long time. Meanwhile, the problem
of providing some more professional training in industrial
archaeology for those people who see it as an entry to a museum
career or town planning, or some other germane profession, is
being met through a number of diploma courses. One of these
has been established in the Midlands through the University of
Leicester, and there are others being pioneered at Liverpool
College of Higher Education and elsewhere.

While these are all promising developments, there remains a
serious deficiency in the provision of instruction in industrial
archaeology at British universities, particularly at undergraduate
level. There have been a few experiments in offering course units
in industrial archaeology within degree schemes: in Archaeology
at Southampton, in Economic and Social History at Strathclyde,
and in Social Sciences at Bath. The Open University, also, has
drawn up a course unit in industrial archaeology, and at least one
degree validated by the Council for National Academic Awards –
at King Alfred College, Winchester – also allows for a course in
the subject. The response of undergraduates so far to these units –
usually offered as optional courses – has been uneven, and it is
difficult to draw any general lessons from such limited experience.
It is desirable that universities should acquire more experience
in teaching industrial archaeology as an undergraduate study, as
there can be no doubt that the subject can provide a challenging
intellectual experience as well as a vivid insight into important
aspects of recent history. But we are obviously very far from
seeing industrial archaeology being recognized as a major degree
subject, and it is arguable that it would be preferable to develop
it rather as an optional study for a wide range of degree courses
so that the full benefit of its interdisciplinary appeal can
be appreciated. The University of Lancaster is currently

experimenting with such a cross-disciplinary optional course in industrial archaeology, and its progress will deserve watching with interest.

Despite the slight provision for industrial archaeology as an undergraduate study in our universities, there is considerable scope for its development at postgraduate level as students offer to undertake research by thesis in fields involving industrial archaeological investigation, even though they are supervised by Departments of History, Social and Economic History, Architecture, Social Science, and other disciplines. All that is needed in order to make this possible is the existence of a sympathetic member of staff in the relevant department who can be responsible for supervising the project, which can be eligible for the usual sort of postgraduate financial support through the Department of Education and Science, the Social Science Research Council, or internal university scholarships. What *is* lacking at present is a university taught MSc course in industrial archaeology, combining some theoretical and practical instruction in methodology with work on an individual project. The most formidable obstacle to the emergence of such a course is that of financing the studentships. Otherwise, such a scheme could be made quite viable, although like the relationship between the hen and the egg it is difficult to know if it will succeed until it is given a trial. The best possible trial would be for a university to appoint somebody to a Chair in Industrial Archaeology, with the encouragement both to develop appropriate options in undergraduate degree courses and to launch a taught MSc with specific vocational openings into the range of careers in planning, environmental studies, and museum work for which a postgraduate course in industrial archaeology could be a suitable introduction. For the moment, however, no such development seems to be in prospect.

Although industrial archaeology has come to maturity in the last twenty years as a well-defined field of study concerned with a very specific type of evidence, even though its techniques for the interpretation of this evidence retain a delightful degree of interdisciplinarity, it is clear that as a university discipline it is still in its infancy. This should not be the cause either of surprise or dismay, for universities are traditionally conservative institutions which require a lot of persuasion that a new field of inquiry has sufficiently demonstrated its academic credibility to make it worth embarking on as a university study. It took traditional archaeology many decades, after all, to win such recognition, and local history has similarly made slow progress. Universities have at least begun to show interest in industrial archaeology, and provided the momentum of the last few years can be maintained it should not be long before the sort of recognition which we have been envisaging could be achieved. Meanwhile, industrial archaeology has some substantial areas of research to undertake, and in tackling these with the same enthusiasm and persistence which it has demonstrated over the last two decades it will make irresistible its claim to be taken seriously at the highest levels of scholarly achievement.

Part 5   **Regional Survey**

Introduction

In making a regional survey of industrial monuments in Britain it is impossible to avoid being guided to some extent by one's own experiences, preferences, and prejudices. While trying to be as objective as possible, I have certainly not avoided this danger, so that the following review must be regarded as my personal selection of significant monuments, and it is in no sense comprehensive or exclusive. It is hoped, however, that it will provide a reasonable framework to guide an interested investigator approaching one of these British regions, particularly when he is looking at its industrial monuments for the first time.

The regions into which this survey is divided are broad geographical units which can be treated as convenient categories, even though all of them can be broken down into sub-regions for more intensive investigation. Each section has a map showing the most prominent industrial monuments or those mentioned in the text of this book, a list giving grid references for the monuments shown, where appropriate, a general account of the region, and a brief bibliography of industrial archaeological works on the region. Grid references are given in 2-letter and 6-figure form (e.g. ST 565 731), but where it has not been possible to be very precise the third and sixth figures have been given as zero.

One omission needs a word of explanation. Eire can be legitimately excluded from a survey of British industrial archaeology, but strictly speaking there should be some treatment of Ulster,

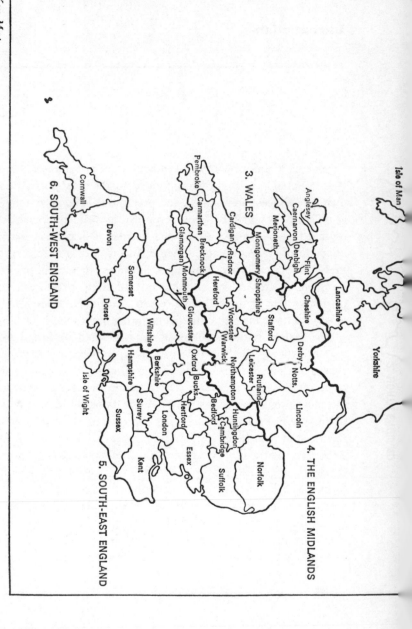

Isle of Man

Anglesey
Caernarvon Denbigh
Merioneth
Flint

3. WALES

Pembroke
Carmarthen
Cardigan Radnor
Brecknock
Glamorgan Monmouth
Hereford
Montgomery Shropshire

Cheshire

Lancashire

Yorkshire

4. THE ENGLISH MIDLANDS

Stafford
Derby Notts.
Leicester
Rutland
Lincoln
Worcester
Warwick
Northampton Huntingdon
Bedford Cambridge
Suffolk
Norfolk

6. SOUTH-WEST ENGLAND

Cornwall

Devon

Somerset

Dorset

Wiltshire

Gloucester

Oxford Bucks.

Berkshire

Hampshire

Isle of Wight

Surrey

London

Hertford

Essex

Kent

Sussex

5. SOUTH-EAST ENGLAND

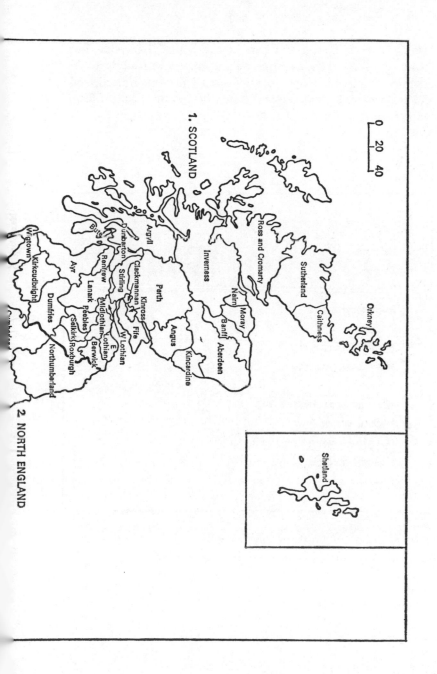

1. SCOTLAND

2. NORTH ENGLAND

0 20 40

Orkney

Shetland

Caithness

Sutherland

Ross and Cromarty

Inverness

Nairn

Moray

Banff

Aberdeen

Kincardine

Angus

Perth

Kinross

Fife

Clackmannan

Stirling

W. Lothian

Midlothian

E. Lothian

Berwick

Peebles

(Selkirk)

Roxburgh

Lanark

Renfrew

Dumbarton

Argyll

Bute

Ayr

Dumfries

Northumberland

Kirkcudbright

W'gtown

which is both British and part of the United Kingdom. But whereas I have at least a passing acquaintance with all the other regions described, I have never visited Northern Ireland, and for this reason I decided that it would be best to exclude it from this regional survey.

Roads	━━━━━━━━━
Railways	<u>London and North-Western</u>
Canals	Thames and Severn
Tramways (and light or narrow-gauge railways)	••••••••••••••••••
Major conurbations	⬭
Ports	▨
Bridges and aqueducts	⏢
Metalliferous industries	▢
Industries	COAL : JUTE etc.
Sites mentioned in notes or text	⊙
Water supply	⊚
Quarrying—stone etc.	⊠
Industrial museums	▲
Folk museums	△

Key to the Maps

Region 1 Scotland

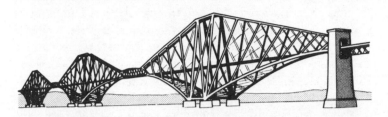

Forth Railway Bridge

The main industrial area of Scotland is the belt of the Central Lowlands between the Firth of Clyde and the Firth of Forth. This was the most hospitable part of the region when an agricultural economy predominated, and the development of commerce through the two great estuaries reinforced the economic advantages of the Lowlands and established Edinburgh and Glasgow as the twin foci of urban growth in Scotland. When the coalfields of Scotland came to be exploited, the position of the Lowlands was strengthened even further by the geological fact that all the main coal resources of the region are concentrated in this area. In addition, the comparatively easy terrain of the Lowlands made them suitable for canal and railway transport, so that the major transport network of the region was established here. The net result of this combination of advantages is a heavy concentration of Scottish industry and industrial remains in the Central Lowlands, from the coalfields of Lanarkshire and Ayrshire in the west through to those of Fife and Midlothian in the east; from the complex of industries around the Clyde in the west to the great chemical, metallurgical, and naval enterprises on the Forth in the east. Outstanding as a subject for industrial archaeological investigation in the west is the linear metropolis of Glasgow, stretching for some forty miles along the Clyde and its estuary, and providing a home for a diverse range of industries. In the east, a less continuous string of towns stretches along both sides of the Firth of Forth, from Stirling through Falkirk to Edinburgh on the south side, and through Alloa to Dunfermline and Kirkcaldy on the north side. On a smaller scale, a similar development has occurred around the Firth of Tay, also on the east coast, between Perth and Dundee, and both these eastern Firths presented challenges to the railway-builders which produced significant and beautiful bridges.

This economic superiority of the Central Lowlands has given them a disproportionately large importance in the social and political history of Scotland, and they account for most of the population of the region at present. Nevertheless, the other two areas of the region – the Southern Uplands and the Highlands – are not devoid of industrial archaeological interest, despite their thin population and more tenuous transport systems. The Southern Uplands are deeply penetrated by river valleys which, on their northern slopes particularly, provided water power for the cotton textile industry. The surviving industrial community of New Lanark is a remarkable monument to this activity, although the preservation of the factory buildings of Robert Owen's mill is at present causing deep concern. The Southern Uplands have also supported important metalliferous industries, of which there are significant remains at Leadhills, a name which speaks for itself, and at Dalmellington.

North of the Highland Line, the wide empty moors of the traditional Scottish Highlands remain as what has been described as the largest wilderness in Europe, a quality which gives the area an ever-rising value as a tourist attraction. Even here, however, there are signs of industrial activity. The primitive farming communities of the clans were disrupted by the Jacobite Rebellions of the eighteenth century and the subsequent 'clearances' of the Highlands, but a simple 'crofting' economy survives in Skye and parts of the Western Highlands, while hand-woven tweed is still made in the Hebrides, and a small amount of kelp-burning is also carried on. In remote Highland isles and glens, malt whisky distilleries produce the magic liquor which does wonders for the nation's balance of payments. Elsewhere, at Bonawe and Furnace, survive impressive monuments to the charcoal smelting of iron in the eighteenth and nineteenth centuries. Again, throughout the Highlands survive fragments of the military roads built by General Wade and his successors, together with specimens of the more substantial roads and bridges built under the direction of Thomas Telford; and the same distinguished engineer's Caledonian Canal still functions through the Great Glen. In the twentieth century new industry has come to the Highlands in the shape of hydro-electric-power installations and the aluminium-smelter factories which consume this cheap form of energy in abundance, and also in the shape of paper-processing around Fort William and atomic power at Dounreay in the far north of Caithness. Nevertheless, the role of industry in the Highlands remains diminutive, so that its presence is rarely oppressive and the relics of old processes and transport systems may be sought with pleasure.

Bibliography

John Butt: *The Industrial Archaeology of Scotland*, David & Charles, Newton Abbot, 1967
John Butt, Ian L. Donnachie, John R. Hume: *Industrial History in Pictures – Scotland*, David & Charles, Newton Abbot, 1968
David L. Smith: *The Dalmellington Iron Company*, David & Charles, Newton Abbot, 1967
Jean Lindsay: *The Canals of Scotland*, David & Charles, Newton Abbot, 1968
John Thomas: *Scottish Railway History in Pictures*, David & Charles, Newton Abbot, 1967
An Comunn Gaidealach: *Highland Communications*, and other pamphlets in

a series obtainable from Abertarff House, Inverness, and 65 West Regent Street, Glasgow C2

Ian Donnachie: *The Industrial Archaeology of Galloway*, David & Charles, Newton Abbot, 1971

John R. Hume: *The Industrial Archaeology of Glasgow*, Blackie, Glasgow, 1974

John R. Hume: *The Industrial Archaeology of Scotland, Vol. 1: The Lowlands and Borders, Vol. 2: The Highlands and Islands*, Batsford, 1976 and 1977

List of numbered sites shown on map, pages 402–3:

1. Brora colliery (NC 900 040)
2. Strath Kildonan – site of a gold rush in 1869 (NC 910 210)
3. Skye crofts preserved as museums (NG 215 485 and NG 395 718)
4. Perth Water Works (NO 121 232)
5. Caledonian Canal: Fort William to Inverness: Neptune's Staircase Banavie (NN 114 770)
6. Bonawe – charcoal iron furnace and buildings (NN 010 317)
7. Furnace – charcoal iron furnace (NN 026 001)
8. Highbridge (General Wade's bridge at Spean Bridge) (NN 200 821)
9. Iona marble quarry (NM 275 223)
10. Crinan Canal: Lochgilphead to Crinan (west end – NR 789 944)
11. Loch Katrine: Glasgow water supply (east end – NN 495 073)
12. Carron Ironworks (NS 880 825)
13. Alloa glass cones (NS 880 924)
14. Tay Railway Bridge (south end – NO 390 260)
15. Firth of Forth Railway and Road Bridges (*circa* NT 130 800)
16. Glengoyne Distillery (NS 528 825)
17. Glasgow: Port Dundas (NS 588 667) – Forth and Clyde Canal, warehouses, etc.
18. Kinneil House Watt engine (NS 982 806)
19. Preston Mill, East Lothian (National Trust watermill) (NT 595 779)
20. Lady Victoria Colliery, Newtongrange, Midlothian (NT 333 639)
21. New Lanark mills and buildings (NS 880 426)
22. Leadhills, lead workings (NS 885 153)
23. Wanlockhead, lead workings (NS 874 130)
24. Dalmellington, iron workings (NS 480 060)
25. Kingussie, Inverness-shire: Highland Folk Museum (*circa* NH 750 010)
26. Prestongrange, East Lothian (coal industry historical site) (NT 374 737)
27. Biggar Gas Works (NT 038 377)
28. Strathalan Aero Museum (NN 923 165)
29. Dumbarton Napier engine (NS 395 753)
30. Orkney Click Mill (HY 290 200)

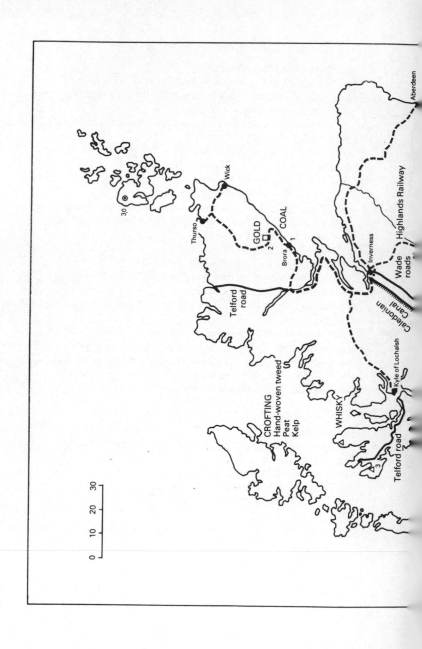

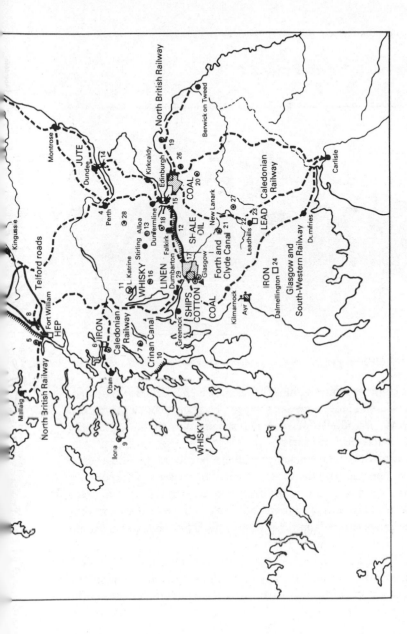

Region 1 : Scotland

Region 2 North England

Lune Aqueduct

The counties of this region are those in which the British Industrial Revolution made its greatest impact, bringing about a spectacular increase in population and industrialization in the eighteenth and nineteenth centuries, but slowing down in the present century with the need for adjustment in the staple industries of the region and with the development of other parts of the country. In no other region, it is probably true to say, are there so many industrial remains, although their very abundance does not serve to enhance their claim for preservation. There is much work for the industrial archaeologist here.

There are four large industrial districts in the region. The first to develop was that based on the coalfield of Northumberland and Durham, with its relatively easy access to the tideways of the

Tyne and Wear permitting the export of coal to London and other fuel-starved areas from at least the sixteenth century. This district, with its southern extension in the Tees-side industrial development, became in time the home of large iron and steel and chemical industries, shipbuilding, and engineering workshops. The relics of the earlier stages of these industries lie thickly strewn on the landscape of the north-east. An ambitious scheme to preserve a representative selection of these remains has now been launched in the North of England Open-Air Museum at Beamish in County Durham.

Across the Pennines, the smaller and less important coalfield of Cumberland supported an industrial area on the fringes of the Lake District which was of considerable national significance. Iron worked in Furness was being sent up to Bonawe in Scotland for smelting in the mid-eighteenth century, but later on much of it was smelted locally and used in Barrow for shipbuilding and other industries. The picturesque National Park of the Lake District itself hides interesting industrial remains of gunpowder works at Elterwater, and various mineral workings scattered over the fells.

The other two industrial districts of this region also straddle the Pennines. These are the coal–wool–iron and steel–engineering complex of the West Riding of Yorkshire, and the coal–cotton–chemicals–engineering complex of south Lancashire. The West Riding woollen and worsted cloth industry continues to flourish, despite changes in fashion and the loss of some of its original advantages, in the towns set in the eastern Pennine valleys with Leeds as their natural focal point. Overlapping with the area of woollen textiles, and further to the south, is the large coalfield of West Yorkshire between Barnsley and Doncaster, and stretching southwards into Derbyshire and Nottinghamshire. This has access to the sea through Goole and Hull, the latter being the main eastern port of the region. Overlapping, again, with the coalfield in the southern part of the region is the heavy iron and steel and engineering group of industries concentrated largely in the Don valley between Sheffield and Rotherham, but active also in the neighbouring valleys, where the world-famous cutlery industry originated and where several distinguished relics of this early activity may be found, such as the edge-tool manufacturing hamlet of Abbeydale on the edge of Sheffield, which has now been handsomely restored.

The counterpart of Hull on the western coast of the region, and the largest port in the kingdom after London, is Liverpool, serving the industries concentrated in south Lancashire. Of these, the first in historical significance is the cotton textile industry, the raw cotton for which is brought in through the port and distributed for processing to the ring of mill towns around Manchester and between Preston and Burnley to the north. The days of King Cotton are over, and this once-dynamic industry is now fighting for survival by contracting and diversifying in artificial fibres, so there is a great deal of industrial archaeology here. One of the advantages of south Lancashire in the Industrial Revolution was the convenience of the local coalfield, with Wigan as one of the main mining centres, and this served to attract various chemical processes to the region, resulting in the heavy industrial development in the triangle formed by St Helens, Widnes, and Warrington (glass, soda, soap, etc.). It should also be remembered that this district provided the first successful canal in Britain (the Worsley branch of the Duke of Bridgewater's Canal, 1760) and the first complete railway (the Liverpool and Manchester Railway, 1830), as well as giving a home to many great engineering enterprises (e.g. Whitworth's factory in Manchester).

It is convenient to include in this region the Isle of Man, with its long history of metal working. Nineteenth-century mining for lead on the slopes of Snaefell has left one very distinguished industrial monument in the shape of the Lady Isabella water wheel at Laxey – the largest water wheel in the British Isles.

Bibliography

Owen Ashmore: *The Industrial Archaeology of Lancashire*, David & Charles, Newton Abbot, 1969

Michael Davies-Sheil and J. D. Marshall: *The Industrial Archaeology of the Lake Counties*, David & Charles, Newton Abbot, 1969

Frank Atkinson: *The Great Northern Coalfield 1700–1900*, Durham County Local History Society, 1966

A. Raistrick and B. Jennings: *A History of Lead Mining in the Pennines*, Longmans, London, 1966

R. T. Clough: *The Lead Smelting Mills of the Yorkshire Dales*, published by the author, Keighley, 1962

Quentin Hughes: *Seaport – Architecture and Landscape in Liverpool*, Lund Humphries, London, 1964

Frank Atkinson: *The Industrial Archaeology of North East England*, David & Charles, Newton Abbot, 2 vols., 1975

K. C. Barraclough: *Sheffield Steel*, Moorland, Hartington, 1976

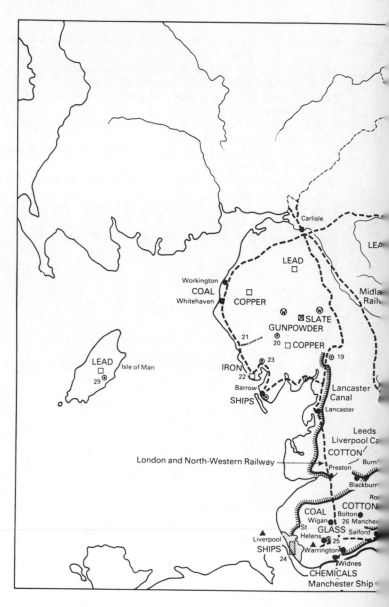

Region 2 : North England

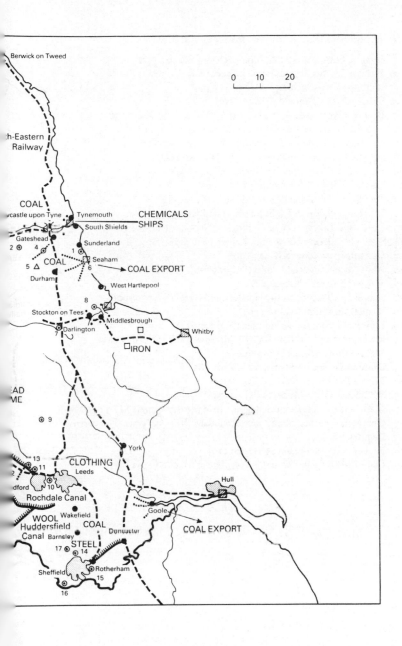

Berwick on Tweed

0   10   20

h-Eastern
Railway

COAL
vcastle upon Tyne   Tynemouth   CHEMICALS
                South Shields   SHIPS

Gateshead
2 ⊙   4 ⊙   1 ⊙   Sunderland

5 △   COAL   ⬚ Seaham
Durham   6   ➤ COAL EXPORT

                West Hartlepool
                8
Stockton on Tees   ⬚
                Middlesbrough
7   Darlington   ⬚   ▨ Whitby

                ⬚ IRON

AD
ME

⊙ 9

                York

13
11   CLOTHING
2   Leeds   Hull
dford   10
Rochdale Canal   Goole
WOOL   Wakefield   Goole
Huddersfield   COAL
Canal   Barnsley   Doncaster   COAL EXPORT
        STEEL
17 ⊙   ⊙ 14
Sheffield   ⊙ Rotherham
            15
⊙
16

List of numbered sites shown on map, pages 408–9:

1. Ryhope Pumping Station, Co. Durham (NZ 404 525)
2. Hamsterley steel cementation furnace (NZ 131 565)
3. Killhope lead-crushing mill (NY 827 429)
4. Causey Arch, Tanfield (NZ 201 559)
5. Beamish North of England Open-Air Museum (NZ 220 537)
6. Seaham Harbour – coal drops and chaldrons (NZ 433 495)
7. Darlington Station – *Locomotion No. 1* (NZ 295 140)
8. Middlesbrough transporter bridge (NZ 500 213)
9. Foster Beck Mill, Pateley Bridge (SE 148 664)
10. Leeds: Marshall's flax mill (SE 295 326)
11. Bradford: Saltaire industrial village (SE 140 381)
12. Keighley–Haworth Light Railway (standard-gauge)
13. Leeds and Liverpool Canal: Bingley Five-Rise (SE 108 400)
14. Sheffield: Elsecar Newcomen Engine (SE 388 000)
15. Catcliffe glass cone (SK 425 886)
16. Abbeydale industrial hamlet (SK 325 820)
17. Wortley Forge (SK 294 998)
18. Standedge Tunnel on the Huddersfield Canal (SE 030 100)
19. Kendal snuff mill (SD 513 903)
20. Elterwater gunpowder mill site (NY 327 047)
21. Ravenglass and Eskdale Railway (narrow-gauge) (SD 085 965)
22. Millom ironworks (SD 180 800)
23. Duddon Bridge iron furnace (SD 197 883)
24. Liverpool: Albert Dock (SJ 342 897)
25. St Helens: Glass Museum (SJ 449 946)
26. Manchester: Worsley canal basin, Bridgewater Canal (SD 749 005)
27. Dee Mill Engine, Shaw, near Rochdale (SD 945 093) (Northern Mill Engines Society)
28. Higher Mill, Helmshore (SD 780 210)
29. Lady Isabella water wheel, Laxey, Isle of Man (SC 432 851)

Region 3 Wales

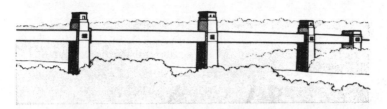

Menai Tubular Bridge

The Principality of Wales has had a long history of industrial activity. In the first place, it has been exploited as a source of metals since Roman times at least. There are well authenticated Roman gold-mines in Carmarthenshire, and in several parts of the region there has been extensive mining and working of metals, from the Parys Mountain copper-mine in the north of Anglesey to the non-ferrous-metal smelting and tin-plate works in the Swansea Valley in the south. Tintern, on the Monmouth-shire side of the River Wye, was the place where brass was first made in Britain, in 1568, by alloying copper with zinc. Then there has been large-scale quarrying of slate in several parts of North Wales, which, although it is now reduced to a shadow of its nineteenth-century prosperity, accounts for some substantial landscape features at Blaenau Ffestiniog and on the Lleyn Peninsula. Between them, metal-working and slate-quarrying account for most of the narrow-gauge railways, several of which have been resurrected as very successful tourist attractions.

When coal became an important industrial resource it was soon realized that Wales possesses substantial coalfields, particularly in the south but also in the north in Flint and Denbighshire.

The coalfield of South Wales, cut through by deep valleys which provided relatively easy access and convenient means of transport, became one of the major coal-producing areas of Britain, supplying large quantities of high-grade steam coal through the wharves of Cardiff, Newport, and Barry Dock, for a vast export business. In the urgent need to convey coal down to the ports these valleys received a network of tramways, canals, and railways, large sections of which survive today for the attention of the industrial archaeologist. A belt across the northern edge of the South Wales coalfield, along the 'Heads of the Valleys', sustained a large iron and steel industry in places like Blaenavon in Monmouthshire and Merthyr Tydfil in the Taff valley. In the present century, this industry has largely migrated to the coastal plain, where several modern iron and steel factories are established between Swansea and Chepstow. The remains of the iron furnaces at Blaenavon, the subject of a current preservation attempt, and the web of tramways across the neighbouring Blorenge mountain, survive as a classic study in industrial archaeology.

The mountainous character of much of Wales has been a problem to successive generations of transport engineers, the two main routes from the Middle Ages being those along the north and south coasts which King Edward I defended with his series of magnificent castles. Telford chose the Dee valley as the route for his Holyhead Road, however, ensuring speedy communication between London and Dublin over many miles of carefully graded road and the superb suspension bridge at Menai, completed in 1826. With a main span of 579 feet, carried 100 feet above high-water level to meet the requirements of the Admiralty, the bridge was by far the largest suspension design to have been built at this date, and it has well justified Telford's meticulous attention to its construction. The same engineer was responsible for the Pont Cysyllte Aqueduct over the Dee near Llangollen on the Ellesmere Canal, and this is undoubtedly one of the outstanding industrial monuments in the world. Telford's bridge óver the Menai Straits was 'paired' in 1850 by Robert Stephenson's wrought-iron tubular railway bridge, carrying the London and North-Western Railway over to Holyhead. This 'Britannia Bridge' was sadly mutilated in 1970 by an accidental fire, and the importance of the route has necessitated the partial replacement of the bridge, but for over a hundred years the two bridges have stood side by side as most elegant and eloquent industrial monuments.

The most distinctive industries of Wales, however, are its rural crafts, some of which survive although in a rather diminished form. Hill farming, hand-woven woollen cloth, dozens of small water mills grinding corn or driving spinning mules and looms, and coracle fishing on the Teifi at Cenarth and elsewhere are all colourful survivals of interest to the industrial archaeologist. Some of the leading aspects of this Welsh 'folk life' have been painstakingly re-created in the open-air museum at St Fagan's on the edge of Cardiff. The region continues to sustain heavy industries in the south, large water undertakings to quench the ever-increasing thirst of Midland cities and, with the installation of a deep-water oil terminal at Milford Haven, there is a promise of new industrial development in the south-west of Wales.

Bibliography

D. Morgan Rees: *Mines, Mills and Furnaces*, H.M.S.O., London, 1969
W. J. Lewis: *Lead Mining in Wales*, University of Wales, 1967
J. Geraint Jenkins: *The Welsh Woollen Industry*, National Museum of Wales, Cardiff, 1969
Charles Hadfield: *The Canals of South Wales and the Border*, David & Charles, Newton Abbot, 1967
D. Morgan Rees: *The Industrial Archaeology of Wales*, David & Charles, Newton Abbot, 1975

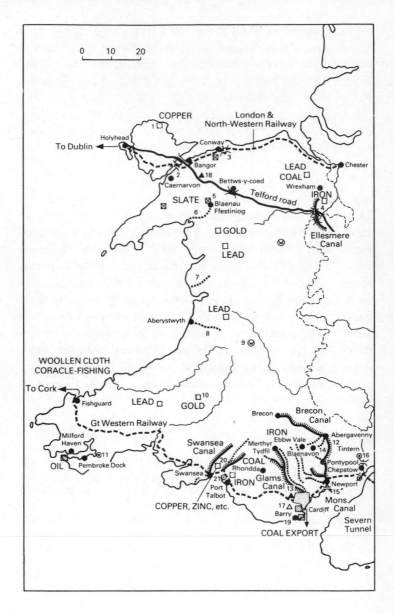

Region 3 : Wales

List of numbered sites shown on map, page 414:

1. Parys Mountain – copper-mining (SH 450 910)
2. Menai Bridges (road, south end SH 558 712; rail, south end SH 543 708)
3. Conway Bridges (road and rail, west end SH 783 774)
4. Pont Cysyllte Aqueduct – Ellesmere Canal (SJ 270 410)
5. Blaenau Ffestiniog – slate quarries (SH 700 460)
6. Ffestiniog Railway (narrow-gauge) from Portmadoc up the Vale of Ffestiniog
7. Talyllyn Railway (narrow-gauge) from Towyn to Abergynolwyn
8. Rheidol Valley Railway (narrow-gauge), British Rail, from Aberystwyth to Devil's Bridge
9. Elan Reservoirs – Birmingham Waterworks (SN 920 630 and neighbour-hood)
10. Dolaucothi gold-mines (Ogofau) (SN 670 410)
11. Carew Tide Mill (SN 046 038)
12. Llanfoist Wharf – Brecon Canal (SO 280 130)
13. Melingriffith water pump, Cardiff (ST 142 801)
14. Blaenavon iron furnaces and buildings (SO 250 090)
15. Newport transporter bridge (ST 318 862)
16. Tintern – site of first brass works (SO 532 001)
17. Cardiff: St Fagan's Folk Museum (ST 119 771)
    Cardiff: Welsh Technological Museum, Cardiff Docks (ST 192 745)
18. Dinorwic Slate Museum (SH 586 602)
19. Barry Docks (entrance – ST 123 667)
20. Swansea Valley (north from Swansea)
21. Ynyscedwyn Steel Works (SN 785 095)
    Neath Abbey Iron Works (SS 738 976)

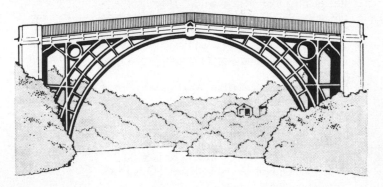

The Iron Bridge

It must be admitted that this is not in any sense an integrated geographical region, although it is convenient to regard it as such for the purpose of this survey. In fact, it may be broken down into six districts, each of which has had a quality and pattern of industry of its own. First amongst these, in the evolution of the British Industrial Revolution, was the westernmost district, with its focal point at Coalbrookdale and appropriately symbolized by the Iron Bridge of 1779, the so-called 'Stonehenge of the Industrial Revolution'. It can be claimed with justice that Abraham Darby's iron furnace here was the cradle of the modern iron and steel industry, and the area now being developed by Telford New Town is littered with the remains of this early industrialization, many of them now included in the open-air industrial museum at Blist Hill. The Iron Bridge itself has received extensive treatment to ensure its stability.

The very success of Darby's coke-smelting process caused the heavy iron and steel industry to move eastwards, to the developing coalfields and growing population centres of what has become known as a result of the association with the industry as 'the Black Country', so this is the second district requiring attention. Criss-crossed by an elaborate system of canals, many of which are still open, and sustaining a remarkable range of industries, this area in and around the Birmingham conurbation is full of historical interest, and the activity of bodies such as the Black Country Society and the Corporation of Birmingham, which has carried out a sympathetic piece of canal-side redevelopment at Brindley Walk in the heart of the city, gives hope that industrial monuments here will receive adequate attention.

The third Midland district is that in the north-west of the region, including the salt-working area of Cheshire but centred primarily on 'the Potteries' of Staffordshire. The original 'Five Towns' have now merged in the conurbation of Stoke-on-Trent, and most of the beehive kilns which were once the uniquely dominant feature of the landscape have also disappeared, but the district retains many features of its long-standing association with the ceramics industry. It was here that Josiah Wedgwood established his industrial empire in the mid-eighteenth century, and arranged for it to be served by the Grand Trunk (Trent and Mersey) Canal, with Brindley's novel tunnel – the first in canal engineering – at Harecastle still visible, although long since made redundant by the parallel bore of Telford's replacement tunnel.

Along with Coalbrookdale, Cromford on the River Derwent just south of Matlock has a legitimate claim to be considered as one of the birthplaces of the Industrial Revolution. Here Arkwright established the first water-powered cotton-spinning factory in the 1760s, to be followed by others up and down the Derwent, and spreading into the Vale of Trent around Derby and Nottingham, for long the centre of the hosiery industry in Britain. This area constitutes the fourth sub-district of the region.

Many relics of the Arkwright era survive in and around Cromford, although the remains of the original mill have been much mutilated. However, some of the early fire-proof mill buildings constructed by the Strutts at Belper still stand, as do sections of the Cromford Canal and the alignment of the High Peak Railway. These two transport systems linked the Derwent valley with the once flourishing lead industry of Derbyshire to the west, and the heavy iron and steel and engineering industries of the Derbyshire and Nottinghamshire coalfield to the east.

The other two Midland sub-districts are the Northampton iron-quarrying area and the Lincolnshire–Fenland agricultural area. The latter has never sustained any major industry except farming, but it possesses one of the finest collections of surviving windmills in the country. There are also well-established engineering firms at Gainsborough and Lincoln, and in Grimsby the district has an important port. The Northampton area along the southern edge of the region has been quarried extensively for ironstone in the present century, and new smelting plant has been established at Corby (and also at Scunthorpe in Lincolnshire) to deal with this low-grade jurassic iron. Engineering industries have long been based at Rugby and Coventry, though here the district merges into that of Birmingham and the Black Country. Northampton itself is a famous centre of the boot and shoe industry, much of it still practised on a small scale, and the town is linked with the Grand Union Canal a few miles to the south. Indeed, it is worth remarking that the whole Midland region is crossed by a transport network of roads, canals, and railways radiating from London. Some of these have very interesting relics such as those assembled in the Canal Museum at Stoke Bruerne, or, still in use nearby, the Kilsby tunnel on the London and Birmingham Railway, completed at prodigious expense in 1838. Fragments of the Birmingham terminus of this Railway, incidentally, survive at Curzon Street in the centre of the city.

Bibliography

David M. Smith: *The Industrial Archaeology of the East Midlands*, David & Charles, Newton Abbot, 1965

Frank Nixon: *The Industrial Archaeology of Derbyshire*, David & Charles, Newton Abbot, 1969

Stanley D. Chapman: *The Early Factory Masters*, David & Charles, Newton Abbot, 1967

Nellie Kirkham: *Derbyshire Lead Mining*, Barton, Truro, 1968

Arthur Raistrick: *Dynasty of Ironfounders: The Darbys of Coalbrookdale*, Longmans, London, 1953

Charles Hadfield: *The Canals of the West Midlands*, David & Charles, Newton Abbot, 1969

Charles Hadfield: *The Canals of the East Midlands*, David & Charles, Newton Abbot, 1966

Helen Harris: *The Industrial Archaeology of the Peak District*, David & Charles, Newton Abbot, 1971

Fred Brook: *The Industrial Archaeology of the West Midlands*, Batsford, 1977

Barrie Trinder: *The Industrial Revolution in Shropshire*, Phillimore, 1973

I. J. Brown: *The Mines of Shropshire*, Moorland, 1976

Neil Cossons and Harry Sowden: *Ironbridge – Landscape of Industry*, Cassell, 1977

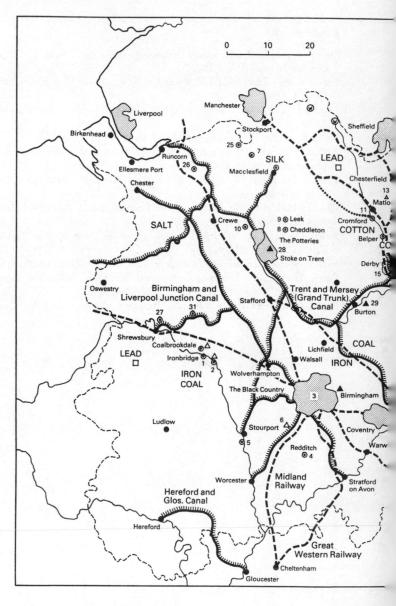

Region 4: The English Midlands

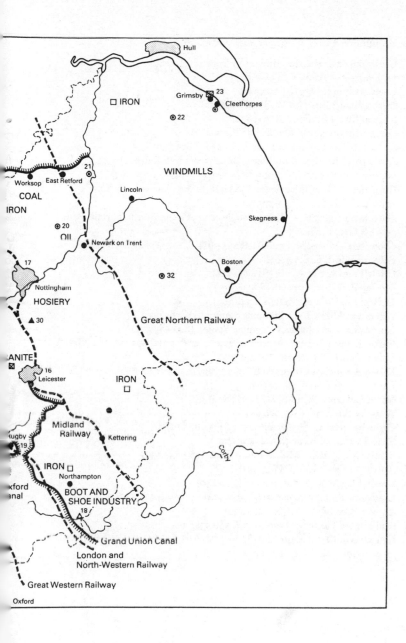

Hull

Grimsby 23
Cleethorpes

◉ 22

□ IRON

WINDMILLS

21
Worksop East Retford

COAL

IRON

Lincoln

Skegness

◉ 20

OIL

Newark on Trent

17

Boston

Nottingham

◉ 32

HOSIERY

▲ 30

Great Northern Railway

ANITE

16
Leicester

IRON
□

Midland
Railway

Kettering

Rugby

19

Corby

xford
nal

IRON □
Northampton

BOOT AND
SHOE INDUSTRY

18

Grand Union Canal

London and
North-Western Railway

Great Western Railway

Oxford

List of numbered sites shown on map, pages 420–21:

1. Coalbrookdale: the Iron Bridge (SJ 673 034)
   1a. Darby iron furnace (SJ 668 047)
2. Coalport iron bridge (SJ 702 021)
3. Birmingham: Brindley Walk (SP 060 870)
   Curzon Street Station (SP 085 873)
4. Forge Mill (needles), Redditch (SP 050 680)
5. Stourport canal basins and warehouses (SO 820 730)
6. Avoncroft Museum of Buildings, Bromsgrove (SO 950 680)
7. Nether Alderley Mill, Cheshire (National Trust) (SJ 840 765)
8. Cheddleton Mill (flint grinding) (SJ 973 526)
9. Brindley Mill, Leek (SJ 977 570)
10. Harecastle Tunnel – Trent and Mersey Canal (north portals Kidsgrove SJ 840 540)
11. Cromford – village and mills (SK 295 566)
12. Belper Mills (SK 346 480)
13. Crich Tramway Museum (SK 346 548)
14. Morley Park iron furnaces (SK 380 492)
15. Derby: Lombe's silk mill (SK 340 360)
16. Leicester: Abbey Lane Pumping Station (SK 585 060)
17. Nottingham: Papplewick Pumping Station (SK 583 521)
18. Stoke Bruerne Canal Museum: Locks and buildings on the Grand Union Canal, Towcester (SP 740 500)
19. Kilsby Tunnel (north portal SP 565 715)
20. Laxton – open-field village (SK 725 675)
21. North Leverton Windmill (SK 775 820)
22. Wrawby Windmill (TA 026 088)
23. Grimsby: port and hydraulic tower (TA 280 110)
24. Shardlow Canal Basin (SK 444 304)
25. Styal: Quarry Bank Mill (National Trust) (SJ 834 830)
26. Anderton Canal Lift (SJ 647 753)
27. Bage's Flax Mill, Shrewsbury (SJ 500 140)
28. Gladstone Pottery, Longton (SJ 912 434)
29. Burton Beer Museum (SK 230 230)
30. Ruddington Hosiery Museum (SK 580 330)
31. Longden-on-Tern Aqueduct (SJ 617 156)
32. Heckington Windmill (TF 150 430)

Region 5 South-East England

Tower Bridge

London is at the heart of the industrial region of South-East England. It should never be forgotten that the metropolis of Greater London is the largest industrial centre in the country and that it possesses the largest port in Britain. The port of London, with its pronounced tendency to move down the Thames from the traditional wharves immediately east of London Bridge, and with Tower Bridge providing an entrance to the Pool of London, is a good starting place for studying the archaeology of this highly concentrated area of industrialization. Many of the up-river wharves, together with St Katharine's Dock and the London Docks, have now been abandoned by the port, and old London Bridge itself has been moved stone by granite stone to become a permanent industrial monument in America.

It seems likely that Tower Bridge, with its large engines to raise the bascule arms, will also become redundant in the not too distant future.

After the port, another key to the industrial pattern of London is provided by the ring of main-line railway stations which encircle the capital, all of them worthy of the attention of industrial archaeologists (see Chapter 13). From London the railway network spreads in all directions, passing through the built-up area by tunnels, cuttings, and viaducts. Within the metropolis, the industries are too numerous to particularize, but amongst many others the furniture industry of Hackney, the now dead silk industry of Spitalfields, the naval establishments at Greenwich and Woolwich, and the many engineering factories of South London have all contributed to the varied industrial landscape, and are well worth systematic study. So are the various service industries, providing water, gas and electricity, removing the garbage and pumping the sewage, and maintaining the desirable conditions of life in this, the industrial and commercial as well as the political capital of Britain.

The South-East region may be usefully interpreted as a series of concentric zones with London at its centre. Immediately adjacent to Greater London itself is the ring of the 'commuter belt', with suburban development obliterating both farmland and the remains of ancient industrial sites on the slopes of the Chilterns and North Downs and in the Weald of Surrey and Kent. Traditionally, this zone has been concerned with supplying the metropolis with food and drink: hence the profusion of maltings in Hertfordshire and neighbouring counties, preparing barley for the large urban breweries. In the next of the concentric belts, farming and a predominantly agrarian pattern of life survive, for the time being at least, as long as the concept of a 'green belt' is retained by the planners, and on the north-east side of London this belt extends deep into East Anglia and the Fenlands. Here in particular, and in the South-East region in general, is the finest collection of windmills surviving in Britain, only a few of which can be shown on the accompanying map. Within this belt also, in the southern Weald, a few tantalizing remnants of the famous charcoal iron industry may still reward the careful searcher.

On the outer edge of the South-East region, and especially well-defined to the south and west, there is another zone of urban and suburban development. This has been partly the result of the conscious placing of 'New Towns' around London, but it has been mainly the product of haphazard growth. Along the south coast, the forty-mile stretch from Hastings to Bognor Regis, with only a short break at Beachy Head, is now almost entirely built up, largely in the course of providing leisure amenities which produce their own crop of industrial monuments such as the seaside piers at Brighton and elsewhere. Further west is the port, dockyard, and industrial complex of Southampton and Portsmouth, while to the east the Kent coalfield has stimulated the development of a new industrial area in the twentieth century; and inland from London new industries have grown rapidly in the outermost zone of the region at Reading, Oxford, Luton, Bedford, and Cambridge. The region as a whole has benefited from the pronounced shift of population towards the South-East in the present century, as this has brought prosperity and a continuing boom in building. This very prosperity, however, is a warning to industrial archaeologists that much of the rich heritage of the region in windmills, water mills, and small semi-rural industrial sites is at risk as a result of rapid redevelopment.

Bibliography

Aubrey Wilson: *London's Industrial Heritage*, David & Charles, Newton Abbot, 1967
P. G. Hall: *The Industries of London*, Hutchinson, London, 1962
London Transport: *London's Industrial Archaeology* (pamphlet), 1970

John Ashdown, Michael Bussell, and Paul Carter: *A Survey of Industrial Monuments of Greater London*, Thames Basin Archaeological Observers' Group, 1969

Metropolitan Water Board: *The Water Supply of London*, 1961

T. C. Barker and R. M. Robbins: *The History of London Transport*, Allen & Unwin, London, 1963

W. Branch Johnson: *The Industrial Archaeology of Hertfordshire*, David & Charles, Newton Abbot, 1970

Peter Laws: *Industrial Archaeology in Bedfordshire*, Beds. C.C., 1967

Charles Hadfield: *The Canals of South and South East England*, David & Charles, Newton Abbot, 1969

P. A. L. Vine: *London's Lost Route to Basingstoke*, David & Charles, Newton Abbot, 1969

P. A. L. Vine: *London's Lost Route to the Sea*, David & Charles, Newton Abbot, 1965

John Booker: *Essex and the Industrial Revolution*, Chelmsford, 1974

A. Haselfoot: *Industrial Archaeology of South East England*, Batsford, 1978

List of numbered sites shown on map, pages 428–9:

1. London: London Bridge (TQ 328 805)
   Tower Bridge (TQ 337 802)
   St Katharine's Dock (TQ 339 805)
   London Docks (TQ 350 801)
   Regent's Canal and Dock (TQ 363 810)
   Cutty Sark and *Gypsy Moth*, Greenwich (TQ 383 781)
   Abbey Mills Pumping Station (TQ 388 833)
   Kew Bridge Pumping Station (TQ 188 780)
   Deptford East Power Station (TQ 375 779)
   Fulham Gas Works (TQ 260 768)
   St Pancras Station (TQ 301 828)
   King's Cross Station (TQ 303 830)
   Paddington Station (TQ 266 813)
   Chalk Farm 'Round House', Camden (TQ 283 843)
   Morden snuff mills, Merton (TQ 262 686)
   Brixton Windmill, Lambeth (TQ 305 744)
2. Fakenham Gas Works, Norfolk (TF 919 292)
3. Cambridge: Cheddars Lane Pumping Station (TL 465 593)
4. Stretham Engine (steam-powered scoop-wheel) (TL 517 730)
5. Bourn Windmill (oldest surviving post mill) (TL 312 580)
6. Cardington airship hangars, Beds. (TL 090 480)
7. Shuttleworth Aeroplane Museum, Biggleswade, Beds. (TL 190 440)
8. Farnham maltings (SU 850 470)
9. Southampton: Docks (SU 420 110)
10. Portsmouth: Dockyard, HMS *Victory*, and block-making machines (SU 630 001)
11. Cort's iron forge, Fareham (SU 550 070)
12. Ashburnham iron-working site, Sussex (TQ 687 161)
13. Dover: Roman lighthouse (TR 330 420)
14. Cranbrook Windmill, Kent (TQ 779 360)
15. Faversham Gunpowder factory (TR 009 613)
16. Saxstead Green Windmill, Suffolk (TM 253 645)
17. Montagu Motor Museum, Beaulieu (SU 380 030)
18. Woodbridge Tide Mill (TM 277 488)
19. Colchester: Bourne Mill (TM 006 238)
20. Marlow: Suspension Bridge (SU 850 850)
21. Harwich: Treadmill Crane (TM 262 325)
22. Bressingham Steam Museum (TM 075 810)
23. Forncett St Mary Steam Museum (TM 166 942)
24. Caister Motor Museum (TG 504 123)
25. Wealden Open-Air Museum (SU 875 130)
26. Bluebell Railway (TQ 404 237)

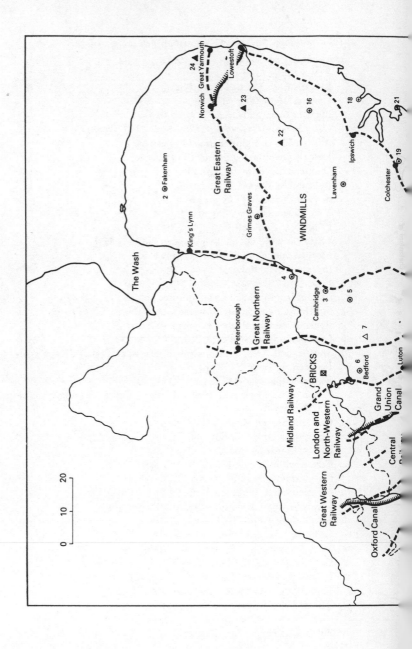

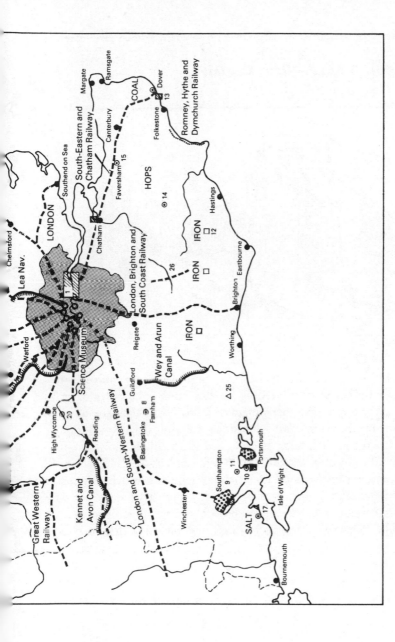

Region 5: South-East England

Region 6 South-West England

Clifton Bridge

At first sight, the counties of the south-western peninsula of Britain do not seem rewarding for the industrial archaeologist, as they have probably been touched more lightly than any other region by the harsh development of the Industrial Revolution period. When the region is examined more closely, however, it is found to possess several ancient industries as well as a significant amount of modern industrial development, which together have left an extremely interesting range of industrial monuments.

Tin-mining in Cornwall can probably claim to be the earliest British industry of which we have any record, although it is impossible to be certain that the 'Tin Isles' of the Phoenician merchants several centuries before Christ can be identified with Cornwall. What *is* certain is that tin has been mined in Cornwall, together with copper and to a lesser extent other minerals, throughout the recorded history of Britain. Even though the industry has been reduced in the twentieth century to a pale shadow of its former glory it has never completely expired. One result of the decline of the industry has been the rash of extraordinarily picturesque ruined engine houses which can be found in many parts of Cornwall. Another prominent industry of the Duchy, which is currently enjoying a boom and which has contributed substantially if not beautifully to the landscape of the St Austell district, is the extraction of china clay. Granite has also been quarried extensively in Cornwall, as in neighbouring Devon on the fringe of Dartmoor, although little is being worked at present. On the border of the two counties, the River Tamar provided a waterway for the once-prosperous metal-working district of the Tamar Valley, which is now derelict. The mouth of the river is crossed spectacularly by I. K. Brunel's Royal Albert Bridge of 1859, carrying a single-track railway.

Passing from one end of the region to the other, the city of Bristol has been the dominant economic and political influence in the South-West since its establishment about a century before the Norman conquest. It has been claimed, indeed, that Bristol is the 'metropolis' of the South-West, and it is a claim which can be powerfully maintained, particularly for the centuries of the Middle Ages and early modern times. As a port, Bristol has served a wide hinterland with many and varied industries, including the West of England woollen cloth industry which enjoyed great economic importance from the fifteenth to the eighteenth centuries, and even thereafter flourished in the valleys around Stroud, which bear eloquent testimony in stone and mortar to the prevalence of this industry. Adjacent to a small but productive coalfield, Bristol was able to find the fuel for many industrial processes such as soap-, glass-, and brass-making. The city also became a natural focal point for road, canal, and railway traffic, so that the Great Western Railway began in Bristol with I. K. Brunel as its first engineer, pioneering his famous broad-gauge track. Although it was affected less drastically than the towns of the Midlands and the North by the dynamic influences of the Industrial Revolution, Bristol has been gradually transformed in the last two hundred years, acquiring new industries based largely upon its imports (tobacco, sugar, cocoa, etc.) and also new engineering enterprises. Its port has been repeatedly enlarged and modified, to such an extent that the traditional harbour in the heart of the city is about to become obsolete. Bristol is now poised hopefully on the brink of further growth in association with the new industrial development of Avonmouth and Severnside.

In between Cornwall and Devon in the south and Bristol and its hinterland in the north, there is a broad belt of still predominantly agricultural land stretching through Somerset into Dorset and Wiltshire. The lead-mines on the Mendip Hills, worked by the Romans, closed down completely at the beginning of the present century, by which time the neighbouring calamine deposits, worked for the Bristol brass industry, had also expired. Similarly, the coalfield of north Somerset is falling into oblivion. Nonetheless, this central belt of the region possesses industrial remains of some interest, in the pumping engines which have drained the Somerset Levels, in waterworks pumps such as those at Blagdon, in canals such as the Chard Canal and the Somersetshire Coal Canal, and in stone quarries such as those at Portland, Purbeck, and around Bath, from which so much material has been removed to beautify the towns of the region and elsewhere.

Bibliography

D. B. Barton: *A History of Copper Mining in Cornwall and Devon*, Barton, Truro, 1966

D. B. Barton: *A History of Tin Mining and Smelting in Cornwall*, Barton, Truro, 1967

D. B. Barton: *The Cornish Beam Engine*, Barton, Truro, 1965

R. M. Barton: *A History of the Cornish China-Clay Industry*, Barton, Truro, 1966

W. E. Minchinton: *Industrial Archaeology in Devon*, Dartington Amenity Research Trust, 1968

R. Sellick: *The West Somerset Mineral Railway*, Phoenix House, London, 1962

Kenneth Hudson: *The Industrial Archaeology of Southern England*, David & Charles, Newton Abbot, 1965

Frank Booker: *The Industrial Archaeology of the Tamar Valley*, David & Charles, Newton Abbot, 1967

Helen Harris: *The Industrial Archaeology of Dartmoor*, David & Charles, Newton Abbot, 1968

W. G. Hoskins, *Old Devon*, David & Charles, Newton Abbot, 1966

Robin Atthill: *Old Mendip*, David & Charles, Newton Abbot, 1964

Charles Hadfield: *The Canals of South West England*, David & Charles, Newton Abbot, 1967

R. A. Buchanan and Neil Cossons: *The Industrial Archaeology of the Bristol Region*, David & Charles, Newton Abbot, 1969

R. A. Buchanan and Neil Cossons: *Industrial History in Pictures – Bristol*, David & Charles, Newton Abbot, 1970

J. W. Gough: *The Mines of Mendip*, Oxford University Press, 1930; David & Charles, Newton Abbot, 1967

Jennifer Tann: *Industrial Archaeology – Gloucestershire Woollen Mills*, David & Charles, Newton Abbot, 1967

Kenneth R. Clew: *The Kennet and Avon Canal*, David & Charles, Newton Abbot, 1968

Kenneth R. Clew: *The Somersetshire Coal Canal and Railways*, David & Charles, Newton Abbot, 1970

Humphrey Household: *The Thames and Severn Canal*, David & Charles, Newton Abbot, 1969

E. T. MacDermot: *History of the Great Western Railway*, revised by C. R Clinker, Ian Allan Ltd, Shepperton, 1964

A. C. Todd and Peter Laws: *The Industrial Archaeology of Cornwall*, David & Charles, Newton Abbot, 1972

Kenneth Rogers: *Wiltshire and Somerset Woollen Mills*, Pasold, Edington Wilts., 1976

M. C. Corfield (ed.): *A Guide to the Industrial Archaeology of Wiltshire*, Wilts., County Council, 1978

W. Awdry (ed.): *Industrial Archaeology in Gloucestershire*, G.S.I.A., 1973

C. Hart: *The Industrial History of Dean*, David & Charles, Newton Abbot, 1971

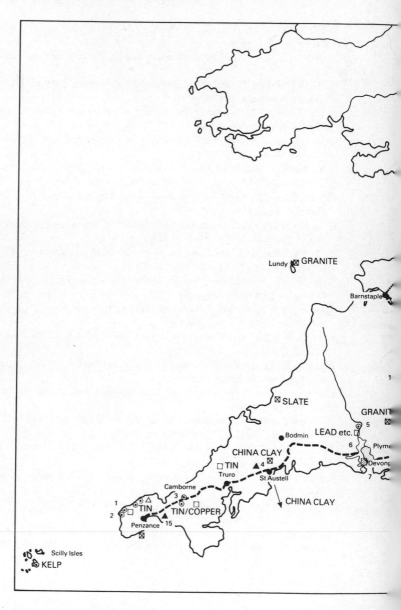

Region 6: South-West England

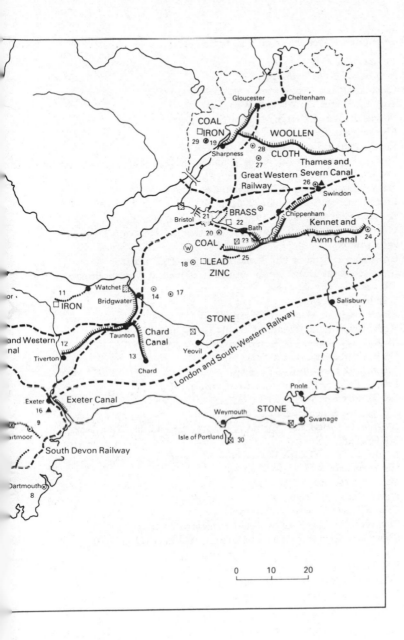

Gloucester　　Cheltenham

COAL
☐IRON
29 ⊙19　　WOOLLEN
Sharpness　⊙ 28　CLOTH
⊙
27　Thames and
Great Western Severn Canal
Railway　26 ⊙ ▲
Swindon

☐ 21　BRASS ⊙
Bristol　　Chippenham
☐ 22
20 ⊙　Bath　　Kennet and
Ⓦ COAL　⊠ 23　Avon Canal 24 ⊙
18 ⊙ ☐LEAD　　25
ZINC

Watchet ⊠
11　　⊙　⊙ 17
☐IRON　Bridgwater　14
STONE　　Salisbury

and Western　Taunton　Chard
nal　12　　Canal
Tiverton　　13　⊠
Chard　Yeovil
London and South-Western Railway

Exeter　Exeter Canal
16 ▲
Poole
⊠⊠　9　　STONE
artmoor　Weymouth　⊠ Swanage
Isle of Portland ⊠ 30
South Devon Railway

Dartmouth⊙
8

0　　10　　20

List of numbered sites shown on map, pages 434–5:

1. Levant Mine (SW 369 346)
2. Botallack Mine (SW 362 337)
3. Camborne: East Pool engines (National Trust) (SW 674 415 and 675 419) and Tolgus Tin Works (SW 690 441)
4. St Austell: Wheal Martyn Museum (SX 004 557)
5. Morwellham, Tamar Valley (SX 442 695)
6. Royal Albert Bridge, Saltash (SX 440 580)
7. Plymouth: Smeaton's Eddystone lighthouse (SX 475 538)
8. Dartmouth: Newcomen engine (SX 878 514)
9. Haytor granite railway (SX 762 778 and elsewhere)
10. Finch Foundry, Sticklepath (SX 641 941)
11. Brendon Hills mineral railway (ST 023 345 and elsewhere)
12. Grand Western Canal: Taunton to Tiverton (lift-locks at ST 145 218 and elsewhere)
13. Chard Canal: Crimson Hill Tunnel (north portal ST 312 220)
14. Somerset River Board steam engines (preserved at Burrow Bridge – ST 357 306 – and elsewhere)
15. Wendron Forge Museum (SW 683 315)
16. Exeter Maritime Museum (SX 921 921)
17. High Ham Windmill (National Trust) (ST 433 305)
18. Mendip lead workings: Charterhouse (ST 505 557)
19. Dark Hill Steel Works (SO 590 088)
20. Albert Mill, Keynsham (ST 656 679)
21. Bristol: Floating Harbour – s.s. *Great Britain* (ST 578 723)
    Old Temple Meads station (ST 595 724)
    Clifton Suspension Bridge (ST 564 731)
22. Avon and Gloucestershire Railway (Mangotsfield to the River Avon at ST 662 698)
23. Kennet and Avon Canal: Widcombe flight, Bath (ST 756 642)
    Claverton Engine House (ST 791 644)
    Dundas Aqueduct (ST 784 626)
    Devizes flight (ST 980 620)
24. Crofton Engine House (SU 264 625)
25. Somersetshire Coal Canal: Combe Hay locks (ST 742 603)
26. Swindon: railway workshops and Railway Museum (SU 146 848)
27. Stroud: Dunkirk Mill, Nailsworth (SO 844 005)
28. Stanley Mill (SO 812 043)
29. Coleford iron furnace (SO 577 100)
30. Portland stone quarries (SY 690 720)

Notes and Bibliographical References

For references to source material for particular regions, the reader should consult Part Five in the text

Part One

Chapter 1: Definitions and Techniques

A pioneer work, promoted initially by the Council for British Archaeology, was Kenneth Hudson's *Industrial Archaeology* (John Baker, 1963), but the rapid development of the subject has made this out of date despite attempts to revise it in later editions. Other general accounts of the subject will be found in Neil Cossons, *The BP Book of Industrial Archaeology* (David & Charles, Newton Abbot, 1975), and Arthur Raistrick, *Industrial Archaeology : An Historical Survey* (Eyre Methuen, 1972), although the latter takes a too narrowly 'archaeological' view of the subject-matter. There have been some rather fine 'coffee-table' productions, of which the best are Brian Bracegirdle, *The Archaeology of the Industrial Revolution* (Heinemann, 1973), and Anthony Barton, *Remains of a Revolution* (André Deutsch, 1975). On the practical aspects of field-work, see J. P. M. Pannell, *The Techniques of Industrial Archaeology* (David & Charles, Newton Abbot, 1966). This, however, tended to place too much emphasis on professional techniques of measuring, surveying, and drawing, and it was improved in a later edition by J. Kenneth Major, whose own handbook on this aspect of the subject, *Fieldwork in Industrial Archaeology* (Batsford, 1975) is an excellent summary.

The study of industrial archaeology is deeply rooted in the history of technology, on which subject the outstanding authorities are: C. Singer, E. J. Holmyard, A. R. Hall, and T. I. Williams (eds.), *A History of Technology* (5 volumes, Oxford University Press, 1954–8); T. K. Derry and T. I. Williams, *A Short History of Technology* (Oxford, 1960); Melvin Kranzberg and Carroll W. Pursell, Jr (eds.), *Technology in Western Civilization* (2 volumes, New York and Oxford, 1967); and Eugene S. Ferguson, *Bibliography of the History of Technology* (M.I.T. and London, 1968).

A compact introduction to the general historical and technological background of industrial archaeology is available in R. A. Buchanan's *Technology and Social Progress* (Pergamon, Oxford, 1965). The artistic aspects of industrialization, with illustrative material of great value to the study of industrial archaeology, have been excellently treated in Francis D. Klingender's *Art and the Industrial Revolution*, edited and revised by Sir Arthur Elton (Evelyn, Adams & Mackay, London, 1968).

Chapter 2: The Historical Framework

The nature of the Industrial Revolution continues to be a subject of lively debate amongst economic and social historians. A useful summary of some of the main issues will be found in R. M. Hartwell (ed.), *The Causes of the Industrial Revolution in England* (Methuen, London, 1967). For a factual survey, the best introduction is still T. S. Ashton's *The Industrial Revolution 1760–1830* (Oxford University Press, first published 1948). The excellent chapter by Professor David S. Landes, 'Technological Change and Development in Western Europe, 1750–1914', in *The Cambridge Economic History of Europe* Volume VI (Cambridge University Press, 1965), has since been published separately as *The Unbound Prometheus* (Cambridge, 1969).

1. This quotation is from the first paragraph of Engels' treatise as in the English translation, Marx and Engels *On Britain* (Moscow, 1953), p. 35. The book was originally published in German and did not become well known in Britain until the end of the nineteenth century.

2. For these important suggestions, see J. U. Nef, 'The Progress of Technology and the Growth of Large-scale Industry in Great Britain' in *Economic History Review* V, 1934, 1, and E. M. Carus-Wilson, 'An Industrial Revolution of the Thirteenth Century' in *Economic History Review* XI, 1941, 1.

3. H. Perkin, *The Origins of Modern English Society, 1780–1880* (Routledge, London, 1969), has a useful analysis of social changes in Britain during this period. For an insight into the scientific interests of the eighteenth-century industrial classes in Britain, see more particularly A. E. Musson and Eric Robinson, *Science and Technology in the Industrial Revolution* (Manchester University Press, 1969). Prof. Musson has also collaborated in W. H. Chaloner and A. E. Musson, *Industry and Technology* (Vista Books, London, 1963), delightfully illustrated with pictures of great interest to industrial archaeologists.

4. Much scholarly work has been done in recent years on demographic changes in the Industrial Revolution period. It has been well summarized

by H. J. Habakkuk, *Population growth and economic development since 1750* (Leicester, 1971).

5. The famous model of Professor W. W. Rostow was set out in his article 'The Stages of Economic Growth' in *Economic History Review*, 2nd series, XII, No. 1, 1959. It has been the subject of much subsequent discussion and comment in the economic history journals and elsewhere.

Part Two

Chapter 3: The Coal-Mining Industry

The best general work on the history of the British coal industry is still J. U. Nef's *The Rise of the British Coal Industry* (Routledge, London, 1932), 2 volumes. Another standard work is T. S. Ashton and J. Sykes, *The Coal Industry of the Eighteenth Century* (Manchester, 1929). An even older work, R. L. Galloway's *A History of Coal Mining in Great Britain* (London, 1882), has recently been republished (David & Charles, Newton Abbot, 1970). Public opinion became increasingly anxious about the depletion of the national coal resources towards the end of the nineteenth century, and this led to various inquiries, the reports of which make interesting reading. The Report of the Royal Commission 'appointed to inquire into the several matters relating to coal in the United Kingdom' in 1871 is a particularly valuable survey of the coalfields of Britain at that time. A very good survey of the north-east coalfield has been made by Frank Atkinson: *The Great Northern Coalfield 1700-1900* (Durham County Local History Society, 1966). On geological aspects of the coal-mining industry I have relied heavily on the excellent collection of essays edited by Sir Arthur Trueman, *The Coalfields of Great Britain* (Arnold, London, 1954), and especially on the introductory essay by Sir Arthur himself. For a recent Industrial archaeological appraisal of the coal industry, see A. R. Griffin, *Coalmining* (Longmans Industrial Archaeology series, 1971).

1. Nef, op. cit., p. 20.
2. Trueman, op. cit., p. vii.
3. Nef, op. cit., p. 3.
4. T. S. Ashton, *The Industrial Revolution 1760-1830* (1948), p. 37.
5. Ashton, op. cit., p. 65.

Chapter 4: The Metal Industries

The metal industries have been fairly well served by historians, so that there is no lack of suitable reference material for the industrial archaeologist. A few of the main sources are given below in relation to the appropriate metals. For general information about metal-working techniques, the superb illustrated volume by Georgius Agricola, *De Re Metallica* (first published 1556; the Hoover edition published by Dover, New York, 1950), is well worth study, and on medieval metal working in Britain the account in L. F. Salzmann's *English Industries in the Middle Ages* (Oxford, 1923) is invaluable. For up-to-date comment on the subject, the publications of the Historical Metallurgy Society maintain a consistently high level of meticulous scholarship.

1. A good general history on tin- and copper-mining is E. S. Hedges, *Tin in Social and Economic History* (Arnold, London, 1964). As tin has been mined almost exclusively in Cornwall, and copper extensively so, much of the best material is in the regional literature, and particularly that written and published by D. Bradford Barton of Truro: *A History of Tin Mining and Smelting in Cornwall* (1967) and *A History of Copper Mining in Cornwall and Devon* (1966; 2nd ed. 1968). Also his *Essays in Cornish Mining History*, Vol. I (1969).

2. There is an extensive literature on lead-mining, of which the following is an introductory selection. J. W. Gough, *The Mines of Mendip* (Oxford, 1930, 2nd ed. David & Charles, 1967); Nellie Kirkham, *Derbyshire Lead Mining through the centuries* (Barton, Truro, 1968); W. J. Lewis, *Lead Mining in Wales* (University of Wales, 1967); and A. Raistrick and B. Jennings, *A History of Lead Mining in the Pennines* (Longmans, London, 1966).

3. The standard work on brass is H. Hamilton's *The English Brass and Copper Industries* (republished by Cass, London, 1967). See also Joan Day, *Bristol Brass: The History of the Industry* (David & Charles, Newton Abbot, 1973).

4. Not so well covered as yet. But for gold-mining in Wales, see D. Morgan Rees, *Mines, Mills and Furnaces* (H.M.S.O., London, 1969).

5. The best introduction to the technical aspects of the iron and steel industry is to be found in the works of W. K. V. Gale: see his *The British Iron and Steel Industry* (David & Charles, Newton Abbot, 1967) and *Iron and Steel* (Longmans Industrial Archaeology series, London, 1969). The earlier history is well covered by H. R. Schubert's *History of the British Iron and Steel Industry from c. 450 BC to AD 1775* (Routledge, London, 1957). On the economic history side, the early work by T. S. Ashton, *Iron and Steel in the Industrial Revolution* (Manchester, 1924), is still worth reading. W. E. Minchinton's *The British Tinplate Industry* (Oxford, 1957) covers an important aspect of the story. Raymond Lister's *Decorative Cast Ironwork*

in Great Britain (Bell, London, 1960) and *Decorative Wrought Ironwork in Great Britain* (Bell, London, 1957) are full of information of great interest to industrial archaeologists. K. C. Barraclough, *Sheffield Steel* (Moorland, 1976) contains a lucid exposition of technical processes and is very well illustrated.

Chapter 5: The Engineering Industries

A good general account of the engineering industries can be found in Derry and Williams, *A Short History of Technology* (see p. 443 above). On the social aspects of the subject, W. H. G. Armytage's *A Social History of Engineering* (Faber, 'Technology Today and Tomorrow' series, London, 1961) is a useful introduction, and in the same series are A. F. Burstall, *A History of Mechanical Engineering* (Faber, 1963), and P. Dunsheath, *A History of Electrical Engineering* (Faber, 1962). Works on machine tools include: W. Steeds, *A History of Machine Tools, 1700–1910* (Oxford, 1969); K. R. Gilbert, *The Machine Tool Collection* (Science Museum Catalogue of Exhibits with Historical Introduction, H.M.S.O., London, 1966); L. T. C. Rolt, *Tools for the Job – A short history of machine tools* (Batsford, London, 1965); and the monographs by Robert S. Woodbury: *History of the Gear-cutting Machine* (Cambridge, Mass., 1959); *History of the Grinding Machine* (Cambridge, Mass., 1959); *History of the Milling Machine* (Cambridge, Mass., 1960); and *History of the Lathe* (Cleveland, Ohio, 1961).

1. K. R. Gilbert, op. cit., p. 1.
2. There is an excellent account of these block-making machines by K. R. Gilbert: *The Portsmouth Blockmaking Machinery* (Science Museum Monograph, H.M.S.O., London, 1965). He observes that Rees mentioned only forty-three machines in his *Cyclopaedia* of 1819, but this was probably because he did not include all the duplicated machines.
3. Dunsheath, op. cit., is the best general source on electrical engineering. On lighting, however, see also W. T. O'Dea, *A Short History of Lighting* (H.M.S.O., London, 1958).
4. See L. T. C. Rolt, *Isambard Kingdom Brunel* (Longmans, London, 1957, p. 317; Pelican, 1970), for a brief account of this incident.
5. See Ewan Corlett, *The Iron Ship* (Bradford-on-Avon, 1975).

Chapter 6: The Textile Industries

The textile industries have figured prominently in accounts of the British Industrial Revolution, and the effects of technical innovation on them have been widely discussed. See, for instance, such general accounts as Paul Mantoux, *The Industrial Revolution in the Eighteenth Century* (first published in Britain 1928; revised edition Cape, London, 1961), and, more recently, S. G. Checkland, *The Rise of Industrial Society in England, 1815–1885* (Longmans, London, 1964). Two new books are of particular value to industrial archaeologists on this subject: W. English, *The Textile Industry* (Longmans Industrial Archaeology series, London, 1969); and Richard L. Hills, *Power in the Industrial Revolution* (Manchester University Press, 1970). Both of these contain instructive descriptions of the textile machines and the way in which they developed.

1. See E. M. Carus-Wilson, 'An Industrial Revolution of the Thirteenth Century' in *Economic History Review* XI, 1941, 1.
2. Daniel Defoe, *A Tour Through Great Britain* (London, 1724), Vol. III.
3. Herbert Heaton, *The Yorkshire Woollen and Worsted Industries* (1st ed. 1920; 2nd ed. Oxford, 1965), pp. xx–xxi: one of the many colourful details in this lively and still authoritative history.
4. ibid., p. xix.
5. Frank Nixon, *The Industrial Archaeology of Derbyshire* (David & Charles, Newton Abbot, 1969), pp. 180–84 and plate on p. 143. Nixon considers that an earlier silk mill on the same site and incorporated into the Lombe factory deserves to be considered as the 'first factory': this was built in 1702 by Thomas Cotchett, the millwright being George Sorocold, who was also employed by Lombe.
6. John Butt, *The Industrial Archaeology of Scotland* (David & Charles, Newton Abbot, 1967), pp. 22, 25, 60–61, and on the textile industries in general north of the Border.
7. For the Midlands textile industries, see Nixon, op. cit. (pp. 188 and 241 on Cromford); David Smith, *The Industrial Archaeology of the East Midlands* (David & Charles, Newton Abbot, 1965); and Stanley D. Chapman, *The Early Factory Masters* (David & Charles, Newton Abbot, 1967). See also Jennifer Tann, *The Development of the Factory* (Cornmarket, 1970).

Chapter 7: The Chemical Industries

Amongst the general works on the chemical industries, the most scholarly are A. and N. L. Clow, *The Chemical Revolution* (Batchworth, London, 1952), and L. F. Haber, *The Chemical Industry during the Nineteenth Century* (Oxford, 1958). A very readable account is S. A. Gregory's *Chemicals and People* (Mills & Boon 'Science and Society' series, London, 1961). Chemical processes are well covered in Derry and Williams, *A Short History of Technology* (see p. 443 above). See also W. A. Campbell, *The Chemical Industry* (Longmans, 1971).

1. A. R. Bridbury, *England and the Salt Trade in the Later Middle Ages* (Oxford, 1955), Chapter 1, gives these figures.
2. See the article by D. A. E. Cross, 'The Salt Industry of Lymington' in *Journal Industrial Archaeology*, Vol. 2, No. 3, October 1965, p. 86.
3. See P. H. Reaney, *The Origin of English Place Names* (Routledge, London, 1960).
4. See the article by Joan Day, 'The Last of the Dyewood Mills' in *Journal Industrial Archaeology*, Vol. 3, No. 2, May 1966, p. 119.
5. For a survey of the industry and its monuments, see R. M. Barton, *A History of the Cornish China-Clay Industry* (Barton, Truro, 1966).
6. On the Catcliffe cone, see the article by G. D. Lewis, 'The Catcliffe Glassworks' in *Journal Industrial Archaeology*, Vol. 1, No. 4, January 1965, p. 206.
7. See the article by J. K. Major, 'A Survival of the Wiltshire Paper Industry' in *Journal Industrial Archaeology*, Vol. 1, No. 1, May 1964, p. 17; and Brian Attwood, 'The BIAS paper mill survey' in *BIAS Journal 3*, 1970. The standard history on the paper industry is D. C. Coleman's *The British Paper Industry, 1495–1860* (Oxford, 1958).
8. See the articles by A. Percival, 'The Faversham Gunpowder Industry' in *Journal Industrial Archaeology*, Vol. 5, Nos. 1 and 2, February and May 1968.
9. See W. Douglas Simpson, *Portrait of Skye and the Outer Hebrides* (Hale, London, 1967), pp. 140–42 and plate opposite p. 160.
10. W. H. G. Armytage, *A Social History of Engineering* (Faber, London, 1961), p. 251.

Chapter 8: Building, Agriculture, and Rural Crafts

An outstanding book on building materials is Alec Clifton-Taylor's *The Pattern of English Building* (Batsford, London, 1962). Also of great value to the industrial archaeologist is J. M. Richards, *The Functional Tradition in Early Industrial Buildings* (Architectural Press, London, 1958; reprinted 1968). Another handsomely illustrated book is Norman Davey, *A History of Building Materials* (Phoenix, London, 1961). There are no comparable works on agriculture, although the subject has been well covered from the point of view of economic history. See, for instance, J. D. Chambers and G. E. Mingay, *The Agricultural Revolution, 1750–1880* (Batsford, London, 1966).

On the rural crafts, Norman Wymer's *English Country Crafts* (Batsford, London, 1946), although printed on utility paper, is informative and well illustrated.

1. In this section I have adopted the framework used by Mr Clifton-Taylor in his excellent work cited above, as I can see no way of improving upon his logical structure.
2. Cattybrook accounted for about a quarter of the 76,400,000 bricks used in the construction of the Severn Tunnel and adjoining bridges etc., completed in 1886: see Thomas A. Walker, *The Severn Tunnel* (1888; facsimile edition by Kingsmead Reprints, Bath, 1969), p. 222.
3. See P. E. Halstead, 'The Early History of Portland Cement' in *Transactions of the Newcomen Society*, Vol. 34, 1961–2, p. 37.
4. On the significance of the horse in medieval agricultural technology, see the stimulating work of Lynn White, Jr, *Medieval Technology and Social Change* (Oxford, 1962).
5. For an account of Laxton, see C. S. Orwin, *The Open Fields* (Oxford, 1938); on a related aspect of agricultural archaeology see M. W. Beresford, *The Lost Villages of England* (Lutterworth, London, 1954).
6. There are some good museum collections of agricultural implements (notably that at Reading) which are worth the attention of industrial archaeologists. Note also J. G. Jenkins, *The English Farm Wagon* (Oakwood and University of Reading, 1961), and G. E. Fussell, *Farming Technique from Prehistoric to Modern Times* (Pergamon, Oxford, 1965).
7. For the Somerset Fussells, see R. Atthill, *Old Mendip* (David & Charles, Newton Abbot, 1964). For needle-making, see John G. Rollins, 'The Forge Mill, Redditch' in *Journal Industrial Archaeology*, Vol. 3, No. 2, May 1966, p. 84.

Chapter 9: Consumer Industries and Urban Crafts

This is a group of industries which has been treated rather indifferently by historians and industrial archaeologists, although there are good books and papers on particular themes and there is much physical material of great potential interest.

1. On the Albion Mill, see John Mosse, *Transactions of the Newcomen Society*, Vol. 40, 1967–8, pp. 47–60.
2. The film has recently been reissued by the firm. It is a fine example of the value of film as a visual record of processes which have since disappeared, and it contains incidentally some interesting social history.

3. See Robin Stiles, 'The Old Market Sugar Refinery 1684–1908' in *BIAS Journal 2*, 1969, pp. 10–17, although this is not primarily concerned with the Finzel enterprise.

4. A valuable historical introduction to the brewing industry is Peter Mathias's *The Brewing Industry in England, 1700–1830* (Cambridge, 1959).

5. J. M. Richards, *The Functional Tradition* (cited on p. 449 above), p. 135.

6. The Glengoyne Distillery was visited by the Newcomen Society on its summer meeting in Scotland in July 1969. There is a useful summary of the whisky industry in Scotland in J. Butt, *The Industrial Archaeology of Scotland* (David & Charles, Newton Abbot, 1967), pp. 46–53.

7. This technique is explained by Iain C. Walker, 'Statistical Methods for Dating Clay Pipe Fragments' in *Post-Medieval Archaeology*, Vol. 1, 1967, pp. 90–101. For the clay-pipe industry in Britain, see A. Oswald, 'The Archaeology and Economic History of English Clay Tobacco Pipes' in *Journal of the British Archaeological Association*, 3rd series, Vol. 23, 1960, pp. 40–102.

8. See the light-hearted account by Wallace Reyburn, *Flushed with Pride – The Story of Thomas Crapper* (Macdonald, London, 1969).

9. The leisure industry is beginning to attract the attention of geographers and economic historians. See, for instance, the geographical and statistical survey by J. A. Patmore, *Land and Leisure in England and Wales* (David & Charles, Newton Abbot, 1970). Also Bryan J. H. Brown, 'Clevedon Pier' in *BIAS Journal 2*, 1969. Sad to relate, two spans of the Clevedon Pier collapsed in the autumn of 1970 and at the time of writing its future is uncertain.

10. See Norman Wymer, *English Town Crafts* (Batsford, London, 1949).

Part Three

Chapter 10: Power I – Animal, Wind, and Water

Power machinery provides some of the most visually attractive and interesting industrial monuments, so that the subject has received plenty of attention in standard works on windmills and water wheels, and in the various regional studies. There are no specifically industrial archaeological treatments of the subject as a whole, but two good studies of the social implications of power technology are Fred Cottrell, *Energy and Society* (McGraw-Hill, New York, 1955), and A. R. Ubbelohde, *Man and Energy* (Pelican, London, 1963). The visual quality of the subject has been delightfully expressed by John Reynolds, *Windmills and Watermills* (Hugh Evelyn, London, 1970).

1. See Lynn White, Jr, *Medieval Technology and Social Change* (Oxford, 1962), for a fascinating account of this factor.
2. Some valuable field-work on these agricultural gin-houses has been done by J. Kenneth Major, who has deposited record cards on the subject in the National Record of Industrial Monuments (NRIM). See also H. Brunner and J. Kenneth Major, *Water Raising by Animal Power* (Reading, 1972) and J. Kenneth Major, *Animal-Powered Engines* (Batsford, 1978).
3. See Rex Wailes, *The English Windmill* (Routledge, London, 1954), p. 149. Like everybody who attempts to write on this subject, I am greatly indebted to Mr Wailes, who is the outstanding authority on windmills.
4. op. cit., p. 34.
5. This figure is given by Leslie Syson in *British Water-mills* (Batsford, London, 1965), p. 33.
6. Syson, op. cit., pp. 79–80. For comparison, Smeaton had earlier demonstrated that whereas an over-shot wheel was capable of a maximum mechanical efficiency of 63 per cent, an under-shot wheel could achieve only 22 per cent (p. 54).

Chapter 11: Power II – Steam, Internal Combustion, and Electricity

Steam power has received a lot of attention from historians of technology, but the subject is by no means exhausted yet. The biggest gap until recently has been the lack of a visual record of stationary steam engines, but this is now in process of being remedied by the superb books of photographs compiled by George Watkins, working in the Centre for the Study of the History of Technology at the University of Bath. These are of particular value to industrial archaeologists because they help to identify and explain the remaining engines to people who are not familiar with them. The first book in the series was *The Stationary Steam Engine* (David & Charles, Newton Abbot, 1968), followed by *Textile Mill Engines* in two volumes, published in 1970 and 1971 respectively. Further volumes are projected on colliery winding engines, rolling mill engines, and steam engines in the public services. See also R. A. Buchanan and G. Watkins, *The Industrial Archaeology of the Stationary Steam Engine* (Longmans Industrial Archaeology series, Allen Lane, 1976).

1. Cottrell, *Energy and Society* (McGraw-Hill, New York, 1955). See particularly the introductory statement of the thesis of the study, and the summary of the low-energy society on pp. 201–2.
2. These are described by Eugene S. Ferguson, 'The Steam Engine before 1830', in Melvin Kranzberg and Carroll W. Pursell, Jr (eds.), *Technology*

in Western Civilization (New York and Oxford, 1967), Vol. 1, Chapter 15, p. 263.

3. The case for the survival of the Savery engine throughout the eighteenth century has been well argued by A. E. Musson and Eric Robinson, *Science and Technology in the Industrial Revolution* (Manchester University Press, 1969), Chapter XII. But most of their evidence concerns small engines returning water to the head of a conventional water wheel.

4. Thomas Newcomen and his engine have understandably attracted much attention from members of the Society named after him. See, for instance, A. K. Clayton, 'The Newcomen-type engine at Elsecar, West Riding' in *Transactions of the Newcomen Society*, Vol. 35, 1962–3, p. 97. See also the biography by L. T. C. Rolt, *Thomas Newcomen: The Prehistory of the Steam Engine* (David & Charles and Macdonald, Dawlish and London, 1963). This has been edited and extended by J. S. Allen as *The Steam Engine of Thomas Newcomen* (Moorland, Hartington, 1977).

5. There are several good works on Watt. See especially H. W. Dickinson, *James Watt – Craftsman and Engineer* (Cambridge, 1935).

6. See H. W. Dickinson, *A Short History of the Steam Engine* (first published 1938; republished by Cass, London, 1963, with a new introduction by A. E. Musson), p. 88.

7. For an account of this remarkable engine, see Richard L. Hills, 'The Cruquius Engine, Heemstede, Holland' in *Journal Industrial Archaeology*, Vol. 3, No. 1, February 1966.

8. See Ian McNeil, *Hydraulic Power* (Longmans Industrial Archaeology Series, 1972).

Chapter 12 : Transport I – Ports, Roads, and Waterways

As with power machinery, the history of transport has attracted a lot of attention, although surprisingly little has concentrated on the technological and industrial archaeological aspects until quite recently. The monumental work by W. T. Jackman, *The Development of Transportation in Modern England* (1st ed. 1916; 2nd ed. 1962), is still useful, and there are a number of standard works on canals such as the regional surveys, *The Canals of the British Isles*, edited and largely written by Charles Hadfield and published by David & Charles; and also the initial volume in the Longmans Industrial Archaeology series, L. T. C. Rolt, *Navigable Waterways* (Longmans, London, 1969). The volume in this series on roads by Anthony Bird, *Roads and Vehicles* (Longmans, 1969), is better on vehicles than roads, but it is useful so far as it goes.

1. See R. A. Buchanan and Neil Cossons, *The Industrial Archaeology of the*

Bristol Region (David & Charles, Newton Abbot, 1969), Chapter 2, and
also Angus Buchanan, 'The Cumberland Basin, Bristol' in *Journal
Industrial Archaeology*, Vol. 6, No. 4, November 1969, p. 325.
2. On lighthouses, the outstanding work is Douglas B. Hague and Rosemary
Christie, *Lighthouses: Their Architecture, History and Archaeology*
(Gomer, Dyfed, 1975).
3. See Donald Cross, 'The Development of Traffic Signs' in *Journal
Industrial Archaeology*, Vol. 5, No. 3, August 1968, p. 266.
4. Derrick Beckett, *Great Buildings of the World – Bridges* (Hamlyn, London,
1969), p. 7. This is a stimulating and delightfully illustrated book.
5. See the useful survey by M. J. T. Lewis, W. N. Slatcher, and P. N.
Jarvis, 'Flashlocks on English Waterways' in *Journal Industrial Archaeology*, Vol. 6, No. 3, August 1969.
6. See T. C. Barker, 'The Beginnings of the Canal Age in The British Isles'
in L. S. Pressnell (ed.), *Studies in the Industrial Revolution* (Athlone,
London, 1960).
7. See Hugh Malet, *The Canal Duke* (Phoenix, London, 1961) for a concise
account of the Duke of Bridgewater's contribution to canal building.
8. The Kennet and Avon Canal Trust is a body of enthusiasts devoted to the
project of reopening a navigable channel between Bath and Reading. The
problems are formidable, but the Trust has achieved some substantial
successes such as the restoration of the Widcombe flight of locks at Bath
and the distinguished steam pumping engines at Crofton.

Chapter 13: Transport II – Tramways, Railways, and Other Systems

The literature on railways is vast, and it would be inappropriate to try to
summarize it here. An excellent general survey of the development of the
British railway system may be found in J. Simmons, *The Railways of Britain*
(Routledge, London, 1961); and a useful series of monographs on the
histories of individual railways has been published by David & Charles. For
a more detailed investigation, the serious student may be referred to George
Ottley, *A Bibliography of British Railway History* (Allen & Unwin, London,
1965), a very painstaking compilation. On tramways, a good account was
provided by Bertram Baxter, *Stone Blocks and Iron Rails* (David & Charles,
Newton Abbot, 1966). Baxter spent many years collecting the material for
this book, and died shortly after its publication. Since then, a more academic
and particular treatment has appeared in M. J. T. Lewis, *Early Wooden
Railways* (Routledge, London, 1970). The electric tramcar has received a
sentimental valediction from Charles Klapper: *The Golden Age of Tramways*

(Routledge, London, 1961). The best general account of aeroplane history is Charles H. Gibbs-Smith, *The Aeroplane – An Historical Survey* (H.M.S.O., London, 1960).

1. Baxter, op. cit., p. 20.
2. Several of these lines have been the subjects of intensive study by industrial archaeologists. Brian Lamb of Stretford, for instance, has done a superb set of record cards on the Peak Forest Canal tramways for the National Record of Industrial Monuments. See also Kenneth Clew, *The Somersetshire Coal Canal and Railways* (David & Charles, Newton Abbot, 1970).
3. See Chapter 5 above.
4. A handy pocket-book for the industrial archaeologist looking at steam locomotives preserved in museums and elsewhere is O. S. Nock's *British Steam Locomotives* (Blandford, London, 1964).
5. See Charles Hadfield, *Atmospheric Railways* (David & Charles, Newton Abbot, 1967).
6. See Thomas A. Walker, *The Severn Tunnel* (cited on p. 450 above) for an account of these engines.
7. See L. T. C. Rolt, *Brunel* (cited on p. 447 above), pp. 231–2, and Simmons, op. cit., p. 92.
8. See the attractive monograph by Robin Atthill, *The Somerset and Dorset Railway* (David & Charles, Newton Abbot, 1967), now supplemented by a *Picture Book* by the same publishers (1970).

Chapter 14: Community and Public Services

There is surprisingly little readily accessible literature on this important group of industries, which suggests that there is still plenty of scope here for industrial archaeologists. The best sources are usually pamphlets and regional studies, referred to below as appropriate.

1. There is a good description of the New River in W. Branch Johnson, *Industrial Archaeology of Hertfordshire* (David & Charles, Newton Abbot, 1970), pp. 97–101.
2. See Chapter 11 above.
3. These engines have been tastefully preserved because of the interest and enthusiasm of Mr E. L. Kelting, Engineer to the Somerset River Board.
4. I am grateful to Mr George Watkins for advice on the London pumping stations. The Greater London Industrial Archaeological Society has

begun detailed work on some of these sites: see *GLIAS Newsletter* special publication, 'Beam Engines in Greater London', January 1970, with a drawing of the set of engines at West Ham.

5. The Newcomen Society visited this site during the course of its summer meeting in 1966: see *Newcomen Bulletin*, No. 78, July 1966.

6. It was from the Revd John Clayton: see E. C. Stewart, *Town Gas* (H.M.S.O., Science Museum pamphlet, London, 1958).

7. This is the definition in Stewart, op. cit., p. 1.

8. I am grateful to Mr Neil Cossons for this reference.

9. See J. N. Tarn, *Working Class Housing in 19th Century Britain* (Architectural Press, 1971).

10. Mr Neil Cossons, again, drew my attention to these churches, described in Quentin Hughes, *Seaport – Architecture and Townscape in Liverpool* (Lund Humphries, London, 1964). The two churches have a cast-iron frame and interior, although both are clad in masonry. They are St George's, Everton, and St Michael-the-Hamlet, designed by Thomas Rickman and built by Thomas Cragg in 1814.

11. The hexagonal boxes mentioned are known as 'Penfolds': see Jean Young Farrugia, *The Letter Box* (Centaur, Sussex, 1969).

12. See C. W. Ceram, *Archaeology of the Cinema* (Thames & Hudson, London, 1965).

Part Four: The Progress of Industrial Archaeology

Chapter 15: The Organization of the Subject

For a summary of the museums, societies, and other bodies involved in industrial archaeology in Britain, a useful starting point is Neil Cossons and Kenneth Hudson (eds.), *Industrial Archaeologists' Guide 1971–73* (David & Charles, Newton Abbot, 1971). Although improved in some respects in Neil Cossons, *The BP Book of Industrial Archaeology* (David & Charles, Newton Abbot, 1975), it is impossible to be completely up to date in any such compilation. Many of the organizations listed in these works produce their own publications, to which reference should be made for more detailed information.

1. See the first edition of this book, p. 50.

2. The official address of the Association for Industrial Archaeology is:
   Ironbridge Gorge Museum Trust
   Ironbridge
   Telford
   Salop   TF8 7AW

3. The *Industrial Archaeology Review* is published by the Oxford University Press in conjunction with the AIA. The Editor is now Dr Stafford Linsley of the University of Newcastle-upon-Tyne. Subscriptions are dealt with through the AIA office at Telford.

4. The legislative provision for industrial monuments has been summarized in papers by P. R. White and Keith A. Falconer to the First International Congress on the Conservation of Industrial Monuments, 1973: see *FICCIM Transactions*, (Ironbridge Gorge Museum Trust, 1975).

5. The Survey of Industrial Monuments is based at the University of Bath, Claverton Down, Bath BA2 7AY. The Survey Officer is Mr Keith A. Falconer. The Council for British Archaeology is still responsible for the Research Committee on Industrial Archaeology. The CBA address is now:
The Council for British Archaeology
112 Kennington Road
London SE11 6RE

6. The National Record of Industrial Monuments (NRIM) is based, like the Survey of Industrial Monuments, at the University of Bath, Claverton Down, Bath BA2 7AY. It has been the responsibility of Dr R. A. Buchanan as Director of the Centre for the Study of the History of Technology since 1965. The record card used is one designed for and distributed by the CBA (see note 5 above).

7. The Historic American Engineering Record was set up in 1969 under the National Park Service, United States Department of the Interior, Washington DC 20240, USA. The Director is Douglas L. Griffin. Several detailed regional reports have already been published, incorporating the admirable measured drawings made by HAER.

8. The Technological Preservation grant is administered by the Science Museum, South Kensington, SW7, through the Director, Dame Margaret Weston, and a small committee. The officers of the Science Museum responsible for the grant are at present Dr J. Wartnaby and Mr J. Robinson.

9. R. A. Buchanan and Neil Cossons, *Industrial Archaeology of the Bristol Region* (David & Charles, Newton Abbot, 1969), p. 49. See also above, p. 110.

10. This statement of aims is from the summary of the Society's functions in the annual *Transactions*. The headquarters of the Newcomen Society are in the Science Museum, South Kensington, London SW7.

11. Amongst the growing number of industrial archaeological studies in other countries, the following works may be noted: Theodore A. Sande, *Industrial Archaeology – A New Look at the American Heritage* (Vermont,

USA, 1976); Bengt Holtze, Ake Nisbeth, Rolt Adamson, Marie Nisser (eds.), *Swedish Industrial Archaeology – Engelsberg Ironworks, A Pilot Project* (Stockholm, 1975); Rainer Slotta, *Technische Denkmäler in der Bundesrepublik Deutschland* (Bochum, 1975; and Vol. 2, Bochum, 1977). See also *SICCIM – Second International Congress on the Conservation of Industrial Monuments, Transactions* (Bochum, 1978).
12. See the first edition of this book, p. 64.

Chapter 16: The Study of Industrial Archaeology

This final chapter examines the case for regarding industrial archaeology as an academic discipline. It is inevitably somewhat more speculative than previous chapters, and there are no obvious reference books on the subject. Nevertheless, the discussion has already provoked some interesting comments in the periodical literature.

1. N. B. Harte in *Economic History Review*, second series, Vol. 26, No. 4, November 1973, pp. 696–7. Mr Harte was quoting 'a distinguished professor of economic history' who said cynically of industrial archaeology: 'It's all right if you can't think of a better reason to get a girl up in the Pennines on a sunny day'.
2. See A. Raistrick, *Industrial Archaeology – An Historical Survey* (Eyre Methuen, 1972), p. 13, p. 300 and elsewhere, for an exposition of this point of view. My disagreement with Dr Raistrick on this fundamental interpretation of industrial archaeology led me to review his book severely in *Antiquity*, Vol. 46, No. 183, September 1972, pp. 247–8.
3. See V. Gordon Childe, *What happened in History*, (Penguin, 1942) and R. G. Collingwood, *The Idea of History*, (Oxford, 1946).
4. The title 'Post-post-medieval Archaeology' was given to an article in *Antiquity*, Vol. 47, 1973, pp. 210–16, by Philip Riden.
5. The best recent summary of work on Deserted Medieval Villages is M. Beresford and J. G. Hurst, *Deserted Medieval Villages* (Lutterworth, Guildford and London, 1971).
6. On oral history, there is a new scholarly treatment by P. Thompson, *The Voice of the Past: Oral History* (Oxford, 1978).
7. For other treatments of academic aspects of industrial archaeology, see J. R. Harris, 'Industrial Archaeology and its Future', in *Business History*, Vol. 12, 1970, pp. 129–34; and R. Symonds, 'Preservation and Perspectives in Industrial Archaeology', in *History*, Vol. 57, 1972, pp. 82–8.

Index

Abbey Lane Pumping Station, 422
Abbey Mills Pumping Station, 427
Abbeydale, 91, 406, 410
Aberdeen, 170
Aeroplanes: *see* Air transport
Agricola, G., 76, Plate 6
Agriculture, 37, 112, 180–87, 193, 413, 418, 424, 432
Air transport, 265, 324–6
    aeroplanes, 43, 101, 108–10, 160, 265, 324–6
    airfields, 109–10, 325–6
Aire, River, 298
Albert, Prince, 159
Albert Bridge, 436
Albert Dock, 271, 272, Plate 73
Albert Mill, Keynsham, 436, Plate 27
Albion Mill, 196
Alcoholic beverages, 200–206, 399, 424
Allen Ralph, 169, 302, 305, 349
Alloa, 151, 398
Alum, 143
Alum Bay, 143
Aluminium, 83, 342, 398, 401
Amalgamated Society of Engineers, 114
Amalgamated Union of Engineering and Foundry Workers, 114

America, North, 38, 101, 131, 137, 186, 210, 227, 266, 285, 287, 309, 350, 369
    See also United States of America
America, South and Central, 40, 47, 51, 155
Amish sect, 242
Amsterdam, 254
Ancient Monuments Acts, 357
Ancient Monuments Board, 363
Ancient world, 172–3, 221, 226
    See also Egypt; Phoenicians; Romans
Anderton Canal Lift, 422
Anglesey, 197, 411
Anglo-Saxon England, 181
Animal power, 174, 223–6, 302, 323
Antiques, 208, 214
Aqueducts, 292, 293, 296, 297, 328, 412, 415, Plate 62
Archaeology
    classical, 28–9, 30
    culinary, 198–200
    ecclesiastical, 348
Archimedes, 221
Argentina, 186
Aristotle, 221

Arkwright, Richard, 119, 126, 133, 417, 418
Armstrong, Neil, 324
Artificial fibres, 138, 159, 160, 161, 406
Ashburnham, 427
Ashton, T. S., 36
Ashton Mill, 234
Ashton-under-Lyne, 303
Asia, South-East, 47
Aspdin, Joseph, 178
Association for Industrial Archaeology, 355–7, 369
Atomic power, 49, 223, 343, 399
Australia, 186, 370
Automobiles: *see* Motor cars
Avebury, 205
Avon and Gloucestershire Railway, 304, 305, 306, 436
Avon Navigation, 288
Avon, River (Bristol Avon), 78, 82, 268, 272, 288, 302
Avoncliffe, 297
Avoncroft Museum of Buildings, 422
Avonmouth, 83, 272, 432
Axmouth, 277
Ayr, 309
Ayrshire, 61, 397

Bacon, Roger, 154
Bage, Charles, 133, 134, 422, Plate 34
Baird, John L., 351
Bakewell, 133
Banking, 214
Barges, 288
Barlborough, 69
Barlow, W. H., 315
Barnsley, 61, 405
Barrels: *see* Cooperage
Barrow, 111, 405
Barrow Gurney, 330

Barry, 70, 273, 412, 415
Barton, 292–3
Bass Brewery Museum, 366
Bath, 69, 143, 212, 239, 288, 297
    buildings, 432
    glass, 180
    stone, 168, 169, 432, Plate 39
    waterways, 239, 288, 293, 297, 436
Bath Turnpike Trust, 280, 283–4
Bath, University of, 263, 355, 359, 361, 387
Bath and West of England Society, 185
Bathgate, 61, 160
Batley, 127
Battersea, 343
Baxter, Bertram, 302
Bazalgette, Sir Joseph, 335
Beachy Head, 425
Beale, 338
Beamish, 68, 70, 71, 364, 385, 405, 410, Plate 2
Bean Ing Mill, 127
Beaulieu, 108, 427
Bedford, 425
Bedfordshire, 173, 325
Beeching Report, 318, 320
Belfast, 111, 364
Belgium, 51, 105, 370
Bell, Alexander, 351
Bell, Thomas, 120
Bellis and Morcom, 256
Belper, 133, 137, 418, 422
Benz, Karl, 265
Berkeley Power Station, 343
Berthollet, C. L., 50, 159
Bessemer, Henry, 49, 91
Bethnal Green, 129
Bettws-y-coed, 279
Beverley, 124
Bibury, 168

Bicycles, 101, 108, 285
Biggleswade, 427
Bingley, 294, 410
Birkenhead, 111
Birmingham, 207, 249, 299, 309, 310, 329, 415, 417, 418
  buildings, 346
  canals, 293, 298
  City Museum, 309
  Soho Foundry, 249
Black, Joseph, 159
'Black Country', 92, 293, 417, 418
Black Country Society, 417
Blackpool, 323
Blacksmiths, 93, 95, 189
Blaenau Ffestiniog: see Ffestiniog
Blaenavon, 88, 412, 415
Blagdon, 254, 256, 330, 432
Bleaching, 50, 143, 157, 159
Blists Hill, 364, 416
Blisworth Tunnel, 294
Blorenge, 92, 412
Blucher, 307
Bluebell Railway, 427
Bodmin Moor, 146
Bognor Regis, 425
Bonawe, 399, 401, 405, Plate 11
Boots and shoes, 207
Botallack Mine, 436
Bottles, bottling, 201–2
Boulton, Matthew, 77, 95, 98, 101, 196, 249, 250, 336
Bourn Windmill, 228, 427
Boyle, Robert, 245
Bradford, 136, 410
Bradford-on-Avon, 126
Bramah, Joseph, 95, 112
Brass, 78, 82–3, 411, 415, 431
Brayton, 330
Brecon, 294, 415
Brendon Hills Railway, 436

Bressingham Steam Museum, 309, 427
Brewing, 200–206, 424
Bricks, 163, 172–7
Bridges, 279, 286–7, 379, 410, 413, 415, 427
Bridgewater, 3rd Duke of (Francis Egerton), 95, 273, 291–3
Bridgewater Canal, 293, 295, 406, 410
Bridgwater, 273
Bridgwater and Taunton Canal, 295
Brighton, 212–13, 341, 425
Brimscombe, 299
Brindley, James, 95, 113, 194, 292–3, 296, 299, 417, 422, Plate 63
Bristol, 60, 69, 82, 110, 123, 132, 145, 151, 152, 162, 168, 176, 199, 206–7, 210, 330, 436
  boots and shoes, 207
  brass, 78, 82, 431
  brick-making, 176
  buildings, 121, 142, 209, 313, 314–15, 320, 366, 436, Plates 66 and 67
  chemicals, 162
  City Museum, 81, 234–5
  coal, 60, 69
  cotton, 138
  glass, 150, 431
  lead, 82
  port, 110, 132, 268, 270–72, 273, 436
  railways, 310, 311, 313–14, 436, Plates 66 and 67
  sherry, 206
  soap, 142, 431
  study courses in, 386
  sugar, 199
  University, 27
  woollen cloth, 121–3, 431

Bristol Aircraft Company, 325
Bristol and Exeter Railway, 311
Bristol and Gloucestershire Railway, 304
Bristol Dock Company, 273
Bristol Tramways Company, 325
Bristol Waterworks Company, 330
Britannia Bridge: *see* Menai bridges
British Rail, 107, 300–301, 309, 310, 318, 320
British Waterways Board, 299
Brittany, 140
Britton, G. B., 207
Brixton Windmill, 427
Broad Plain factory, 142
Bromsgrove, 422
Bronze, 74, 84
Bronze Age, 73, 375
Brora, 57, 62, 401
Broseley, 210, 348
Brunel, I. K., 100, 102–3, 110, 111, 272, 273, 287, 311–15, 361, 436
Brunel, Marc, 100, 102
Bugsworth, 303
Building industry, 163–8, 213, 348, 425, 432
Burford, 168
Burnley, 406
Burns, Robert, 131
Burrow Bridge, 436
Burton Beer Museum, 422
Burton-on-Trent, 201
Bury St Edmunds, 227
Buses, 319, 323
Buttons, 207

Caen Hill, 299
Caister Motor Museum, 427
Caithness, 399
Calamine, 78, 82, 432
Calder, River, 294

Caldon, 303
Caledonian Canal, 279, 295, 399
Calver, 133
Camborne, 76, 77, 253, 365, 436
Cambridge, 173, 425, 427
Cambridge Economic History of Europe, 26
Cambridgeshire, 228, 333
Camden, William, 382
Canada, 153, 369
Canals: *see* Waterways
Candle making, 189
Canterbury and Whitstable Railway, 309
Carbon, 86, 88, 89, 91, 154, 155, 158
Cardiff, 70, 364, 412
Carding, 119, 156
Cardington, 325, 427, Plate 86
Carew Castle, 240
Carew Tide Mill, 415
Carmarthenshire, 411
Carpenters: *see* Wood (woodwork)
Carriages/coaches, 106–8, 252, 282, 283, 322
Carron, 92, 401
Cartwright, Edmund, 118, 119
Carus-Wilson, E. M., 37
Castles, 412
Catcliffe, 151, 410
Cattybrook, 176
Causey Arch, 302, 410, Plate 64
CBA, 31, 357, 358–9
Celestine, 83
Cement, 177–8
Cemeteries, 348
Chain making, 189
Chalk Farm 'Round House', 427
Chamberlain, Joseph, 347
Chapel Allerton, 234
Chapel-en-le-Frith, 303
Chapels: *see* Churches

Chappe, Claude and Ignace, 349
Charcoal, 86, 89, 155, 401, 425
Chard Canal, 295, 432, 436
Charles I, 142
Charnwood Forest, 170
Charterhouse, 436
Chatham, 274
Chatsworth, 211
Cheddars Lane Pumping Station, 427
Cheddleton, 147, 365, 422, Plates 26 and 53
Chelsea, 145
Cheltenham, 179, 212
Chemical industries, 41, 48, 50, 138-62, 405, 406, Plate 24
See also individual industries
Chepstow, 412
Cheshire, 141, 151, 164, 417
Chester, 210, 268
Chesterton Mill, 235
Chiltern Hills, 424
Chimneys, 134, 158, 177, 332-3
China, 40, 127, 144
China clay, 145, 146, 147, 431, Plate 25
Chirk Aqueduct, 297
Churches, 72, 121, 171, 348
Churchward, G. J., 107
Cider, 205
Cinemas, 351
Civic buildings, 346-7
Claverton, 239, 241, 436
Clay pipes, 209-10
Cleethorpes, 335
Clerkenwell, 328
Clerk Maxwell, James, 105
Clermont, 110
Clevedon, 213, Plate 85
Cleveland (Yorks.), 84
Clifton Bridge, 287, 315, 430, 436

Clocks, 93
Clothing industry, 206-7
Clyde, Firth of, 110, 111, 273, 274, 397
Clydeside, 111, 157, 158, 273, 274
Coaches, 106-8, 252, 282, 283, 322
Coal, 27, 33, 42, 45, 51, 55, 89, 112, 138, 157, 158, 245, 246, 273, 292-3, 378, 404-5, 411-12, 425, 431, Plate 65
development of industry, 55-72, 112, 245
geology, 56-62
and Industrial Revolution, 55, 125, 406
and the landscape, 69-72, 347, 404-5
London market for, 61, 245, 405
and waterways, 294, 295, 417
Coalbrookdale, 87, 92, 248, 304, 364, 416, 417, 422, Plate 10
Coalport, 422
Cocoa, 199, 432
Coins, 214
Coke, 45, 87, 339, 377, 416
Colchester, 427
Coleford, 436
Collingwood, R., 376
Cologne, 197
Combe Hay, 436
Combing, 119-20
Comet, 110
Communications, 46, 105, 348-52
See also Mass media
Computers, 49, 105, 106, 161
Conservation areas, 358
Consumer industries, 197-215
See also individual industries
Conway, 25, 287, 415
Cooke, William Fothergill, 350
Cookworthy, William, 145

Cooperage, 202, 214
Copper, 74, 75, 78, 82, 84, 178–9, 411, 430
Copper Age, 73, 375
Corby, 92, 418
Corn Laws (1846), 185
Cornish Engines Preservation Society, 77, 253, 263, 365
Cornwall, 166, 336, 431
  china clay, 145–6, 431
  engineering, 51, 77–8, 253–4, 333, 431
  granite, 170, 431
  metalliferous mines, 45, 63, 75–80, 430
  mining equipment, 51, 60, 147, 253–4, 313, 333, 365, Plates 1 and 4
  ports and harbours, 270
  salt, 140
  slate, 170, 171
  water wheels, 241
  windmills, 234
Cort, Henry, 88–9, 427
Cossons, Neil, 366, 368
Cotswold Hills, 123, 166, 168–9, 293
Cotton Famine (1862–5), 137, 346
Cotton textiles, 40–41, 44, 45–6, 48, 131–8, 156, 272, 346, 406
Cottrell, Fred, 244
Council for British Archaeology: *see* CBA
County Councils Act (1888), 285
Coventry, 129, 418
Coventry Canal, 248
Cowley, 109
Crafts, 139, 152, 413
  rural (agricultural), 124, 126, 187–91, 415, 425
  urban, 121–4, 192–215
  See also Domestic industries

Cranbrook, 234, 427
Cranes, 273, 427
Crapper, Thomas, 212
Crematoria, 348
Cressbrook, 133
Crewe, 107
Crich Tram Museum, 324, 422
Crimson Hill Tunnel, 436
Crinan, 401
Crofting, 399
Crofton, 436, Plate 57
Cromford, 133, 303, 345, 417, 418, 422, Plates 33 and 37
Crompton, Samuel, 118
Crossley, 335
Crossness, 335
Croydon, 303
Cruquius Engine, 254, 333
Crystal Palace, 211, 315
Cubitt, Lewis, 315
Cumberland, 61, 84, 272, 405
Curzon Street, 313, 418, 422
Cutlery, 189, 406
Cutty Sark, 227, 274, 360, 427

Dagenham, 109
Daimler, Gottlieb, 265
Dale, David, 136
Dalmellington, 401
Dams, 329
Darby, Abraham, 45, 87, 416, 422, Plate 10
'Dark Ages', 38, 141, 222, 235
Dark Mill Steel Works, 436
Darlington, 107, 307, 410
Dart Valley Railway, 320
Dartmoor, 170, 286, 306
Dartmouth, 436
Darwen, 134
Davy, Sir Humphry, 66, 68
Dawlish, 312

Dean, Forest of, 60, 87
Dee, River, 279, 297, 412
Dee Mill Engine, 410, Plate 59
Defoe, Daniel, 125
Delabole, 171
Delft ware, 145
Denbighshire, 411
Deptford, 341, 343, 427
Derby, 117, 129, 134, 145, 417
Derbyshire, 324
    coal, 60, 405
    cotton, 133
    glass, 179
    iron, 88, 418
    lead, 418
    millstones, 197
Derwent, River, 129, 133, 329, 417
Deutsches Bergbau-Museum, 369
Devizes, 297, 299, 437
Devon, 60, 91, 431
    china clay, 145-6
    mines, 45, 76
Dewsbury, 127
Dickinson, John, 152
Didcot, 342
Diesel, Rudolf, 265
Dinorwic Slate Museum, 415
Distilling, 203-5
Ditches/dykes, 331
Docks, 70, 268-76
Dogs, Isle of, 111, 270, 271
Dolaucothi, 83, 415
Domesday Survey (1086), 121, 140,
    235
Domestic industries, 124, 139, 192,
    199, 211-12, 212-13
    See also Crafts
Don, River, 406
Doncaster, 405
Donkin, Bryan, 338
Dorset, 160, 171, 318, 432

Douglas, 323
Dounreay, 399
Dovecotes, 199-200
Doveholes, 303
Dover, 62, 427
Drainage, 177, 331-3
Drinks, 200-206, 399, 424
Droitwich, 141
du Pont family, 155
Dublin, 201, 279, 412
Duchess of Sutherland, 309
Duddon Bridge, 88, 410
Dudley Castle, 247
Dumbarton, 401
Dundas, 303, 436
Dundee, 130, 398
Dunfermline, 398
Durham, 61, 171, 402
Durham, County, 61-2, 239, 302,
    330, 364, 378, 402
    coal, 56, 61, 69, 72
Dunkirk Mill, 436, Plate 32
Dursley, 125
Dyes, dyeing, 139, 143-4, 159, 161,
    213

East Anglia, 121, 125, 234, 310, 424
East Lothian, 401
East Pool Engine, 253, 342
Ecomusée de la Communauté, 370
Edale, 133
Eddystone, 275-6, 436
Edge tools, 189, 406
Edinburgh, 168, 204, 279, 364, 398
Edison, Thomas, 104
Education Act (1870), 159
Education and Science, Department
    of, 363, 388
Edward I, 412
Egerton, Francis: *see* Bridgewater,
    Duke of

Egypt, 131, 149, 220, 226
Eire, 130, 279, 394
Elan valley, 329, 415
Electricity, 83, 104, 223, 262, 266, 341–4
  and aluminium industry, 83, 342
  domestic, 211–12, 266
  electrical engineering, 48, 103–6
  generation, 103–4, 223, 341, Plate 84
  urban supply, 266, 341–4, 424
  and urban transport, 105, 223, 266, 322–4, 341
  See also Hydro-electric power
Electronics, 49, 105, 324
Elizabeth I, 76
Ellesmere Canal, 297, 412
Elsecar, 248, 410, Plate 56
Elterwater, 155, 405, 410
Enclosure Acts, 182–3, 184
Engels, Friedrich, 35
Engineering, 41, 93–115, 255, 405, 418, 424
  electrical: *see* Electricity
  engineers, 93–5, 112–15
England: South-East, 154, 202, 205, 234, 295, 423–27
  South-West, 121–4, 205, 234, 295, 311, 430–36
English Channel, 295, 350
English Sewing Cotton Company, 133
Environment, Department of the, 357, 359, 369
Essex, 123, 124, 164, 315
Eton, 173
Euston, 25, 301, 315
Evans, Oliver, 50
Evercreech, 318
Exeter, 273, 436
Exmoor, 286

Explosives, 159, 161
  See also Gunpowder; Fireworks

Fairbairn, William, 237, 261
Fairs, 346
Fakenham, 340, 427, Plate 82
Falkirk, 92, 398
Far East, 131, 137
Faraday, Michael, 103–4
Fareham, 89, 427
Farnham, 202, 427
Faversham, 156, 427
Fenlands, 185, 234, 315, 331, 418, 424
Fermenting, 201–2
Ferranti, Sebastian de, 341
Ffestiniog, 171, 310, 320, 411, 415
Fife, 61, 397
File grinding, 189
Filton, 325
Finch Foundry, 436
Fire service, 347–8
Fireworks, 83
  See also Explosives; Gunpowder
Fishing, 140, 200, 413
Flanders, 62, 124
Flax, 130–1, 422
Fleet River, 334
Flint, 422
Flint (Wales), 411
Flying Scotsman, 309
Food processing, 198–200, 424
Ford, Henry, 108
Forge Mill, 189, 190, 422
Forges, 91, 377, 410, 427, 436, Plate 16
Forncett St Mary Steam Museum, 427
Fort William, 153, 342, 399
Forth, Firth of, 287, 313, 397, 398, 401

Forth and Clyde Canal, 295, 401
Fosse Way, 277
Foster Beck Mill, 239, 410
Fourdrinier, Henry and Sealy, 152
Fowey, 147
Frampton Cotterell, 207
Framsden Mill, Plate 47
France, 51, 155, 157, 206, 264, 349,
    370
    aqueducts, 328
    eighteenth-century, 43
    imports from, 140–41, 206
    science, 50, 157, 245
    silk, 127
    telegraph system, 349, 350
    water wheels, 237, 242
Franklin, Benjamin, 50
Fruit preserving, 199
Fulham Gas Works, 427
Fuller's earth, 123, 143
Fulling, 26, 120, 121–4, 127, 143
Fulton, Robert, 50, 110
Furnace (Scotland), 399, 401
Furnaces, 78, 85–9, 377, 383, 410,
    415, 416, 422, 436, Plate 17
Furness, 84, 405
Furniture, 192, 207–8, 424
Fussell family, 189

Gainsborough, 108, 418
Gamble, Josiah, 157
Gardening, 211
Gas, 336–40, Plates 82 and 83
    engines, 264–5, 335
    urban, 160, 212, 337, 339–40
General Enclosure Act (1801), 183
Gentleman's Magazine, 185
George III, 184
Georgian architecture, 347
Germany, 51, 105, 370
    chemistry, 159

millstones, 197
mining, 76
    transport, 285, 298
Gilbert, John, 292
Gilchrist, P. C., 91
Gladstone Pottery, 148, 365, 422
Glasgow, 111, 158, 196, 204, 209,
    210, 256, 309, 329, 401
    chemical industry, 158
    City Museum, 309
    port, 132, 134, 138, 272, 273, 401
    textiles, 132, 134–6, 138
    urban growth, 346
    trams, 323
Glasgow, University of, 249
Glass, 149–51, 157, 163, 178–80,
    206, 379, 406, 410, 431, Plates
    19 and 20
Glengoyne, 205, 401
Gloucestershire, 83, 123, 125, 206–7
Gold, 74, 83, 214, 411, 415
Goole, 70, 273, 405
Gott, Benjamin, 127
Gough, J. W., 27
Grain milling, 193–8, 209
Grand Trunk Canal, 293, 417
Grand Union Canal, 294, 418, 422
Grand Western Canal, 295, 436
Grange-over-Sands, 348
Granite, 170, 431, 436
Great Britain, 110, 366, 436
Great Central Railway, 311, 318
Great Eastern, 111
Great Eastern Railway, 315, 319
Great Exhibition, 211
Great Haywood, 293
Great Northern Railway, 315, 319
Great Western, 110
Great Western cotton factory, 138
Great Western Railway, 107, 306,
    310, 313, 314, 319, 321, 350, 431

Greater London Industrial Archaeological Society, 343
Greece, 226, 234
Greenwich, 227, 274, 360, 424
Grimsby, 422
Grinding, 211, 413, 422
Guericke, Otto von, 245
Guilds, craft, 192
Gunpowder, 154–6, 264, 383, 405, 427
Gypsy Moth, 427

Haarlemmermeer, 254
Hackney, 208, 424
Hackworth, Timothy, 308
Hagley Museum, 155
Hampshire, 141, 143
Hampton Court, 173, 211
Hamsterley, 410, Plate 15
Handicrafts, 211
Hanley, 145
Harbours, 267, 268–76
Hardwick, Philip, 315
Hardwick Hall, 179
Harecastle, 296, 417, 422
Hargreaves, James, 117
Harlow New Town, 208
Harrison, John, 93
Harveys of Hayle, 253, 254, 333
Harwich, 427
Hastings, 425
Hat-making, 206–7
Hatnersage, 197
Hawksbury, 248
Haytor, 170, 306, 436
Heathrow airport, 271, 325
Heaton, Herbert, 126, 127
Hebrides, 156, 171, 399
Heckington, 422, Plate 48
Hedley, William, 307
Helmshore, 410

Hemp, 130–31
Hero of Alexandria, 221
Herstmonceux, 173
Hertfordshire, 202, 424
Hertz, H. R., 105
Hewes, T. C., 237
High Ham, 436
High Peak Railway, 418
High Wycombe, 208
Highbridge, 401
Higher Mill, 410
Hill, Rowland, 349
Hofmann, A. W. von, 159
Hogarth, William, 201
Holborn Viaduct, 341
Holidays: *see* Tourism
Holland, 230, 234, 370
   windmills, 331
Holmans of Camborne, 253
Holyhead, 279, 412, 413
Hops, 202
Horses, 202, 205, 223–6
Hosiery, 134, 422
Housing, 344–8, 379, 383
Huddersfield, 127
Huddersfield Canal, 294, 410
Hudson, George, 310
Huguenots, 127, 130
Hull, 272, 405, 406, Plate 79
Humber, River, 274
Humberside, 331
Hungerford Bridge, 287, 315
Hunslet, 107
Huntsman, Benjamin, 91
Hydro-electric power, 83, 103, 223, 342

India, 40, 130, 131
Industrial Archaeology
   definition, 22
   study of, 367–8, 372–89

societies abroad, 370
subject organization, 21–34, 355–71
teaching/study courses, 385–9
Industrial Archaeology (Raistrick), 368
Industrial Archaeology Review, 356
Industrial monuments, 21, 23, 81, 84, 116, 162, 192, 206
  archive, 27–8
  definition, 23
  description, 31
  preservation, 22–4, 25, 26, 68, 82, 91, 110, 121, 124–6, 129, 131, 133, 134, 151, 155–6, 162, 172, 186–7, 247–8, 250, 253–4, 279, 300, 310, 319, 328, 358, 360–61, 379, 412, 431
  protection, 357
  recording of, 22–4, 109, 186–7, 362–3
Industrial Monument Survey, 358–9
Industrial Revolution, 23, 35–52, 262, 275, 370, 404, 416
Industrial Revolution, 1760–1830 (Ashton), 36
Inglesham, 293
Institution of Civil Engineers, 94, 113, 279
Institution of Mechanical Engineers, 113
Internal combustion engine, 56, 105, 106, 110, 160, 223, 262, 264–5
International Commission for Conservation of the Industrial Heritage, 369, 370
International Conferences of the Conservation of Industrial Monuments, 369
Invention, 40–44, 221–2
Inverform machine, 152

Invicta, 309
Iona, 171, 401
Ireland, 279
Iron, 40, 41, 45, 74, 75, 83–92, 111, 179, 377, 383, 405, 412, 415, 416, 418, 427, Plates 10 and 11
  in buildings, 179, 213, 348
Iron Age, 73, 84, 221, 375, 377
Iron Bridge, 286, 358, 369, 416, 422, Plate 12
Ironbridge Gorge Museum, 364
Ironstone, 418
Irvine, 131
Irwell, River, 292, 296
Italy, 127, 129, 328, 370

Jacobs of Bristol, 150
Jam, 199
James II, 128
Japan, 51, 111, 370
Jarrow, 111
Jessop, William, 113, 271–2, 296, 303
Johnson, Samuel, 209
Journeymen Steam-Engine and Machine Makers and Millwrights, 114
Jute, 130–31

Kaolin: *see* China clay
Katrine, Loch, 329, 401
Keighley and Worth Valley Railway, 320, 410
Kelp burning, 156, 189
Kendal, 209, 410
Kennet and Avon Canal, 239, 293, 294, 297, 299, 303, 306, 436
Kent, 62, 87, 156, 202, 424, 425
Kew Bridge Pumping Station, 427
Keyhaven, 141
Keynsham, 82, 143, 436, Plates 27 and 28

Kildonan, Valley of, 83
Killhope, 79, 239, 240, 410, Plate 50
Kilsby, 418, 422
Kimmeridge, 160
King's Cross Station, 315, 427
Kingswood, 27, 207
Kingussie, 401
Kinlochleven, 83
Kinneil House, 250, 401
Kirkcaldy, 398
Knitting, 119

Labour-saving devices, 211–12, 220
Lady Isabella water wheel, 239, 406, 410, Plate 54
Lady Victoria colliery, 71, 401
Lake District, 60, 76, 156, 170, 171, 329, 405
Lanarkshire, 61, 397
Lancashire, 132, 263, 292
    canals, 294, 299, 406
    chemical industries, 151, 157, 405, 406
    textiles, 134, 137, 299, 405
Lancashire Cotton Corporation, 137
Lanchester, F. W., 108
Land's End, 77, 170, 253
Lavenham, 121, 164
Lavoisier, Antoine Laurent, 159
Law courts, 346
Lawrence, D. H., 72
Laxey, 239, 240, 406, 410, Plate 54
Laxton, 182, 422
Lea, River, 328
Lead, 27, 74, 75, 78–82, 83, 178, 432, 436
Leadhills, 401, Plate 7
Leather, 189, 214–15
Leblanc, Nicolas, 157, 158, 159
Lechlade, 293
Lee, William, 119

Leeds, 107, 127, 131, 206, 405, 410, Plates 30 and 52
Leeds and Liverpool Canal, 410
Leek, 194
Leicester, 60, 134, 294
    University, 387
Leicestershire, 170, 184
Leisure amenities, 192, 210–11, 345
Lenoir, Étienne, 264
Leonardo da Vinci, 42
Letter boxes, 349–50
Levant Mine, 253, 436, Plate 4
Liebig, Justus von, 159
Liège, 62
Lighthouses, 104, 274, 275–6, 341, 427
Lightships, 275–6
Lime, 177
Limehouse, 294
Limestone, 60, 157, 166, 168, 169, 177
Lincoln, 277, 418
Lincolnshire, 140, 234, 335, 418
Linen, 130–31
Liverpool, 309, 348
    buildings, 344, 346, 348
    City Museum, 309
    Polytechnic, 387
    port, 132, 134, 138, 270, 272, 273, 406, 410
Liverpool and Manchester Railway, 48, 301, 308, 310, 313, 319, 406
Llanfoist, 415
Llangollen, 297, 412
Lleyn peninsula, 171, 411
Lochgilphead, 401
Locks, 289–91, 294, 296–7
Locomotion, 307, 309
Lofthouse Colliery, 27
Lombe family, 50, 117, 129, 133, 422

London, 61, 112, 127-9, 201, 349
    Bridge, 170, 270, 328, 423, 427
    buildings, 168, 170, 176, 196, 270,
        314-18, 427
    docks, 270, 271, 272, 423, 427
    industries, 112, 128-9, 142, 145,
        201, 206, 208, 423-5, 427
    Pool of, 423
    port, 62, 206, 270-72, 294, 423,
        424
    public services, 328, 334-6, 349,
        424, 425
    transport, 105, 266, 279, 295, 303,
        310, 313, 322-3, 341-2, 412,
        418, 427
    *See also individual districts and
        institutions*
London and Birmingham Railway,
    315, 418
London and North-Western Rail-
    way, 319, 413
London Gas Light and Coke Com-
    pany, 337
London Passenger Transport Board,
    323
London to Brighton rally, 285
Long Melford, 121
Longbridge, 109
Longden-on-Tern, 297, 422
Longton, 422
Lundy Island, 170
Lune Aqueduct, 297
Luton, 109, 425
Lymington, 141

McAdam, John, 113, 281-2
Macclesfield, 129
Machine tools, 95-103, Plate 36
McNaught, William, 256, 259
Maerdy, 329
Major, J. Kenneth, 225

Malaya, 76
Malta, 302
Malthus, T. R., 47
Malting, 201-2, 203, 427
Man, Isle of, 239, 323, 406, Plate 54
Manchester, 98, 112, 132, 312, 329
    canals, 268, 298, 410
    industries, 98, 112, 132, 406
Manpower, 219-23
Marble, 170, 171-2, Plate 42
Marconi, Guglielmo, 105
Markets, 346
Marlow suspension bridge, 427
Marly, 245
Marple, 303
Marshall, John, 131
Marshall's Mill, Leeds, 410, Plate 30
Marshalls of Gainsborough, 108
Marx, Karl, 36
Marylebone, 318
Mass media, 105, 351
    See also Radio; Television
Masson Mill, 133, Plate 33
Matlock, 133, 417
Maudslay, Henry, 95, 98, 100, 101,
    112
Mayflower, 227
Mayhew, Henry, 334
Mediterranean, 220
Melingriffith water pump, 415
Mells, 189
Menai bridges, 279, 287, 313, 411,
    412, 413, 415
Mendip Hills, 27, 60, 75, 76, 78, 82,
    432, 436
Mersey, River, 111, 274, 293
Merseyside, 142, 157, 158, 272, 274
Merstham, 303
Merthyr Tydfil, 412
Metal industries, 33, 45, 73-92, 163,
    178-80, 189, 383, 406

Metcalfe, Jack, 280
Metropolitan Board of Works, 335
Metropolitan Water Board, 328
Mevagissey, 270
Mexico, 211
Middle Ages, 412
  agriculture, 181
  crafts and industries, 143, 214
  mining, 75, 78
  power, 236
  transport, 226, 278
  water, 328
Middle East, 40, 116, 131, 220
Middlesbrough, 60, 287, 410
Middleton, Sir Hugh, 328
Midland Railway, 310–11, 319
Midlands, 416–22
  agriculture, 182, 418
  canals, 293, 299, 417, 418
  coal, 55, 60, 417
  engineering, 112, 416–17
  metal industries, 88, 92, 416–18
  public services, 330, 335, 413
  salt, 141, 417
  textiles, 119, 134, 417
Midlothian, 61, 71, 397
Mileposts, 283–4
Milford Haven, 268, 413
Milk, 200
Millom, 84, 410
Millstones, 169, 197
Millwall, 111, 271
Millwrights, 93, 94, 95, 240
Mineral and Battery Company, 76
Mineral water, 206
Mines Act (1842), 67
Mines Royal, 76
Mints, 214
Monmouthshire, 92, 287, 294
Montagu, Lord, 108, 427
Moon landing, 324

Mordants, 143
Morden snuff mills, 427
Morley Park, 88, 422
Mortar, 177
Morwellham, 436
Mosse, Samuel, 350
Motor cars, 108–10, 160, 213, 265,
  285, 319, 324, 336
Motor vehicles, 101, 262, 324
Mumbles, 303
Murdock, William, 336
Museums, 70–71, 72, 81, 154, 198,
  205, 215, 248, 253, 265, 273,
  274, 294, 309, 320, 363–5, 385,
  415, 422, 427, 436
  folk museums, 124, 364, 401
  *See also names of individual
  museums*
Muspratt, James, 157
Mystic Port (Connecticut), 227

Nails, 189
Nailsworth, 436
Nantwich, 141
Napier engine, 401
Napoleonic Wars, 127, 131, 349
Nasmyth, James, 96, 97, 99
National Coal Board, 56, 57, 69, 71
National Maritime Museum, 71
National Monuments Record, 363
National Record of Industrial Monu-
  ments: *see* NRIM
National Survey of Industrial Monu-
  ments, 361
National Transport Museum, 309
National Trust, 253, 299, 365
Nationalization, 56, 319–20, 323,
  342, 344
Navy, 100, 274
Neath Abbey Iron Works, 415
Needles, 189, 190, 422

Nef, J. U., 37, 55, 62
Neptune's Staircase, 295, 401
Netham, 162
Nether Alderly Mill, 422
New England, 227
New Iron Age, 377, 382
New Lanark, 29, 134, 136, 345, 401,
    Plate 29
New River, 328
New Stone Age, 73, 180
New Towns, 208, 425
New World, 132, 186, 209, 222
Newark, 160
Newbury, 293
Newcastle, 151, 158
    See also Tyneside
Newcomen, Thomas, 51, 64-5, 77,
    246-9, 252, 257, 261, 328, 410,
    436
Newcomen Society for the Study of
    the History of Engineering and
    Technology, 24, 247, 333, 367
Newport (Mon.), 70, 287, 294, 412,
    415
Newry Canal, 291
Newtongrange: *see* Lady Victoria
    colliery
Noe, River, 133
Norfolk, 140
Norman Britain, 181, 214
Normandy, 227
Norse mills, 235, 241, 242
North Downs, 424
North-East coalfield, 62-3, 68, 69,
    72, 245, 302
North Leverton, 234, 422
North of England Open-Air
    Museum: *see* Beamish
North Shields, 158
North Star, 107, 321
Northampton, 207, 418

Northamptonshire, 84
Northern Mill Engines Preservation
    Society, 264, 410
Northumberland, 61, 402
Norwich, 123
Nottingham, 134, 302, Plate 80
Nottinghamshire, 60-61, 69, 160,
    168, 182, 234, 330, 405, 417
NRIM, 31, 361-2
Nuclear power, 342
Nylon: *see* Artificial fibres

Ogofau mine, 83
Oil, 61, 160-61, 336-7, 413
Old Stone Age, 180
Orkney Click Mill, 401
Oslo 227
Otto, N. A., 264
Ouse, River (Yorkshire), 273
Owen, Robert, 29, 134-5, 398, Plate
    29
Oxen, 223-4
Oxford, 288, 294, 425
Oxfordshire, 173
Oystermouth, 303

Paddington, 314-15, 322, 427
Palmer, John, 349
Pantiles, 176-7
Paper, 112, 152-4, Plates 21 and 22
Papin, Denis, 245
Papplewick, 330, 422
Par, 147
Parsons, Charles, 103, 262, 342
Parys Mountain, 411, 415
Pateley Bridge, 410
Paul, Lewis, 118
Pawtucket, 137
Paxton, Joseph, 211
Peak District, 75, 78, 133, 197, 329
Peak Forest Canal, 303

Peat, 57, 189
Pelton, Lesley, 242
Pembrokeshire, 240
Pendeen, 76
Penistone, 312
Pennines, 60, 78, 81, 126, 132, 294, 329, 405
Pennsylvania, 51, 70, 242
Penryn (Cornwall), 170
Penydarren tramway, 252, 255, 301, 302
Perkin, W. H., 159
Perth, 398, 401
Petro-chemical industry, 160, 161
Pewter, 74-5
Phoenicians, 226
Photography, 28, 31-2, 378, 379
  aerial, 378, 379
Piers, 213, 425
Pilgrim Fathers, 227
Pilkingtons, 151
Pillar boxes, 349-50
Pins, 207
Pittsburgh, 70
Plaster, 177-8
Plastics, 83, 112, 159, 160, 161, 379
Plato, 221
Plumbing, 212, 327-9
Plymouth, 145, 274, 276, 436
Police, 346
Pollution, 200, 335
Poncelet, Jean Victor, 237, 242
Pont Cysyllte Aqueduct, 297, 412, 415, Plate 62
Poole, 147
Population, 47-8, 222, 404
Port of Bristol Engineering Workshop, 272
Port Dundas, 401
Port Sunlight, 142, 157

Portland, 168, 169, 171, 178, 432, 436, Plate 41
Ports, 205-6, 215, 267, 268-76, 405
Portsmouth, 101, 111, 227, 274, 303, 349, 425, 427
Portugal, 234
Postal services, 349
Potteries, the, 145, 293, 417
Pottery, 144-9, 417
Power, 22, 33, 219-23, 244-66
Power stations, 341, 342-4, 427
Preservation: *see under* Industrial monuments; Railways
Preston, 406
Preston Mill, 401
Prestongrange, 401
Prestwick airport, 325
Priestley, Joseph, 159
Prince Regent (George IV), 212
Prior Park: *see* Allen, Ralph
Prisons, 346
Prussia, 51
Public houses, 72, 202, 211
Public services, 22, 33, 327-52
Puffing Billy, 307
Pumps, pumping, 44, 77, 160, 239, 241, 245, 248, 253-4, 266, 301, 313, 329, 330, 331, 333, 335, 415, 422, 427, 432, Plates 7, 57, 58 and 81
Purbeck, 171, 432
Pyramids, the, 226

Quarries, 168, 169, 170, Plate 42
Quarry Bank Mill, 422

Radio, 105, 212, 351
Radstock, 61
Railways, 46, 48, 171, 284, 318, 411, 418, 424
  buildings and stations, 106, 311,

313–15, 318, 320, 366–7, Plates
64, 66 and 67
*See also names of individual
stations*
development and decline, 298,
303–21
locomotives, 106–8, 252, 308, 309,
321, Plates 69 and 70
preservation, 25, 39, 107, 300–301,
309–10, 312, 313–18, 320, 411
Railways Acts, 302–4, 311, 319
Rainhill, 308
Raleigh, Sir Walter, 209
Ramsden, Jesse, 94, 97
Ravenglass and Eskdale Railway, 410
Reading, 425
Recreation, 192, 210–11, 345
'Red Flag Act' (1896), 285
Redditch, 189, 190, 422
Redhill, 143
Redruth, 77, 336
Refrigeration, 212
Regency England, 178, 179, 180,
213, 347
Regent's Canal, 271, 294, 427
Rennie, John, 113, 296, 297
Reservoirs, 328, 329
Resorts, 212–13, 425
Rheidol Valley Railway, 415
Richard of Devizes, 142
Richards, J. M., 202
Rivers: *see* Waterways
Road signs: *see* Roads (street furni-
ture)
Roads, 46, 69, 112, 267, 276–86, 399,
418
street furniture, 283–4, 286, 337,
349
Rochdale, 294
Rocket, 255, 308, 309
Roebuck, John, 157, 158–9, 161, 250

Rolt, L. T. C., 356, 368
Romans, 75, 78, 141, 221
buildings, 173, 176, 275, 286
metal working and mining, 78, 83,
178, 382, 411, 432
roads and transport, 277–8, 279,
282, 302
water supply, 327
water wheels, 221, 226, 235
Romney, 268
Rope-making, 215
Rostow, W. W., 49
Rotherham, 151, 406
Rotterdam, 274
Royal Albert Bridge, 287, 431, 436,
Plate 45
Royal College of Chemistry, 159
Royal Commission on Historical
Monuments, 363
Royal Navy, 100, 274
Royal Society, 336
Ruddington Hosiery Museum, 422
Rugby, 294, 418
Runcorn, 293
Russia, 51
Rye, 268
Ryhope, 330, 333, 410

St Austell, 146, 147, 431, 436
St Fagan's, 124, 215, 364, 413, 415
St Helens, 157, 158, 406, 410
St Katharine's Dock, 206, 270, 273,
423, 427
St Mary's (Scilly Isles), 234
St Pancras, 311, 315, 427
St Rollox factory, 158
Salt, 140–41, 157, 417
Salt, Sir Titus, 136, Plate 31
Saltaire, 136, 345–6, 410, Plate 31
Saltash: *see* Royal Albert Bridge
San Francisco, 71

Sankey Brook Canal, 291
Sapperton Tunnel, 293, Plate 61
Savery, Thomas, 64, 246, 260
Saxstead Green Windmill, 427
Scandinavia, 153, 235, 370
Science Museum (London), 101, 248, 250, 307-9, 325, 363, 364
Scilly, Isles of, 156, 234
Scotland, 151, 153, 166, 235, 268, 363, 397-401
  chemical industries, 151, 153, 397, 399
  coal, 60, 61, 378
  metal industries, 83, 92, 397
  oil, 160
  power, 83, 235, 342, 399
  rural crafts, 57, 156, 399
  textiles, 130, 398
  transport, 279, 397, 398
  whisky, 203, 204, 399
Scott, Sir Gilbert, 315
Scottish Survey of Industrial Monuments, 363
Scouring: see Fulling
Scunthorpe, 92, 418
Scutching, 120, 130-31
Seaham Harbour, 62, 70, 273, 410, Plate 75
Sedgemoor, 57, 188, 331
Selby, 330
Settle, 313
Severn, River, 234, 293
Severn Tunnel, 176, 254, 301, 312
Severnside, 111, 161, 274, 432
Sewage, 265, 334-5, 424
Shardlow, 422
Shaw, 410
Sheffield, 112, 151, 189, 197, 209, 248, 312, 323, 329, 406, Plate 51
Sherwood Forest, 69
Shetland, 235

Ships, shipbuilding, 110, 111, 227, 267, 269-70, 273-4, 405, Plates 76 and 78
Shoe making, 207
Shops, 72, 180, 215, 347
Shrewsbury, 133, 279, 422, Plate 34
Shropshire, 92, 210, 297
Shropshire Union Canal, 294, 297
Shuttleworth Collection, 325
Sicily, 127, 155, 302
Siemens, William, 91
Silk, 50, 117, 127-30, 422, 424
Silver, 74, 75, 78, 214
Skye, Isle of, 399, 401
Slate quarrying, 170, 171, 172, 411, 415
Slater, Samuel, 137
Slaughterford, 154
Slavery, 220, 222, 272
Slums, 345
Smeaton, John, 113, 237, 275, 295, 436
Smith, Adam, 39
Smith, William, 59
Smithies: see Forges
Snaefell, 406
Snowdonia, 171, 279
Snuff, 209, 427
Soap, 141-3, 157, 406, 431
Social regulation, 344-8
Society for Industrial Archaeology, 369
Society of Civil Engineers, 94
Soda, 156, 406
Soho Foundry, 249
Solent, 111
Somerset, 168, 431, 432
  coal, 60, 61, 69, 431, 432
  industries, 122-3, 154, 189, 207
  transport, 270, 273, 304, 318, 432
  water drainage, 331, 333, 432

windmills, 234
withies, 188
Somerset and Dorset Railway, 318
Somerset Levels, 432
Somerset River Board, 333, 436
Somersetshire Coal Canal, 303, 432, 436
Sorocold, George, 442
South Africa, 51
South Devon Railway, 312
South Foreland Lighthouse, 104, 276
South Uist, 156
Southampton, 60, 270, 425, 427
  University, 387
Southern Railway, 319
Southwark, 196, 335, 343
Sowerby Bridge, 294
Spain, 206
Spas, 212
Spinning, 94–5, 117–18, 120, 134, 156
Spitalfields, 128, 424
Sport, 211
Staffordshire, 145–8, 176, 247
Staffordshire and Worcestershire Canal, 293
Standedge Tunnel, 294, 410
Stanley Mill, 134, 401, Plate 35
State coaches/carriages, 252, 282, 283, 322
Staveley, 69
Steam power, Plates 3, 4 and 84
  development of, 45–6, 244–64, 331, 345
  electricity generation, 103, 341–2
  mines, 45, 65–6, 71, 77
  industries, 45–6, 132, 196
  steam engines, 45, 67–8, 71, 77–8, 94, 106, 223, 233, 244–64, 272, 436

transport and communications, 110, 111, 186, 202, 252, 301, 307, 308, 309, 322
turbines, 103, 262
Steel, 83–92, 377, 405, 415, 416, 436, Plate 15
  development of, 41, 89–91, 416
Stephenson, George, 66, 68, 113, 301, 304, 307, 308, 311
Stephenson, Robert, 113, 255, 308, 311, 313, 413
Sticklepath, 91, 436
Stirling, 61, 398
Stockport, 129
Stockton and Darlington Railway, 301, 304, 307
Stoke Bruerne, 294, 418, 422, Plate 60
Stoke-on-Trent, 145, 148, 293, 296, 303, 417
Stone, 163, 166–72, 432
Stone Age, 375, 377
Stonehouse, 134
Stourbridge, 151
Stourport, 299, 422
Stratford Canal, 299
Strath Kildonan, 401
Strathalan Aero Museum, 401
Strathclyde, University of, 351, 363, 387
Street, 207
Street furniture: *see* Roads
Stretham, 333, 427
Strontium, 83
Stroud, 125, 134, 431, 436, Plate 35
Strutt, Jedediah, 119, 133, 137, 418
Strutt, William, 133, 134, 418
Stuart England, 278, 328
Study techniques, 31–3
Styal Mill, 365, 422

Sudbrook, 254, 301, 313
Suffolk, 121, 123, 124, 164
Sugar, 112, 199, 432
Sumeria, 172
Sutherland, 83
Surrey, 271, 424
Surrey Iron Railway, 303, 304
Sussex, 87, 140
Swan, Joseph Wilson, 104
Swansea, 82, 303, 411, 412, 415
Sweden, 51, 177, 227
Swindon, 107, 309, 321, 436
Switzerland, 51, 105
Syracuse, 221, 302

Taff, River, 412
Talyllyn Railway, 310, 320, 415
Tamar, River, 287, 431, 436
Tanfield, 302, Plate 64
Tangye engine, 272
Taunton, 436
Tay, Firth of, 398, 401
Tea, 206, 271
Teddington, 328
Tees, River, 61
Tees-side, 92, 161, 405
Telegraph system, 46, 349, 350
Telephone, 46, 349, 350–51
Television, 105, 351
Telford, Thomas, 25, 51, 113, 271,
    279–80, 281, 287, 295–7, 361, 399,
    412, 413, 417, Plates 12 and 62
Telford New Town, 72, 358, 364,
    385, 416
Temple Meads, 313, 314–15, 320,
    366, 436
Tennant, Charles, 157, 158, 159
Terracotta, 177–8
Textile industries, 33, 112, 116–38,
    213–14, 156, 398, 405
  buildings, 121–2, 124–9, 131,

    133–7, 179, 347, 417–18, Plates
    29 and 30
  machines and processes, 37, 117–
    20, 124, 143, 211
  as urban crafts, 121–3, 213–14
    See also individual industries
Thames, River, 111, 170, 196, 271,
    274, 288, 303, 315, 322, 328,
    334, 335, 423
Thames and Severn Canal, 293, 298
Thirlmere, Lake, 329
Thomas, Christopher and Brothers,
    142
Thomas, S. G., 91
Tibet, 227
Tiles, 172–7
Timber: *see* Wood
Tin, 74–5, 78, 411, 430, 436
Tintern, 411, 415
Tiverton, 295, 436
Tobacco, 192, 209–10, 215, 432
Todmorden, 294
Tolgus Stream, 77, 436
Toll houses, 283, Plate 71
Tourism, 212–13, 323, 398, 411
Tower Bridge, 170, 423, 427
Tower of London, 271
Tower Subway, 322
Town and Country Planning Acts,
    357
Townshend, Charles, and Viscount,
    185
Toynbee, Arnold, 35
Trams/tramways, 105, 266, 301–7,
    412, 422, Plate 64
  colliery, 307
  electric trams, 323–4, 341–2
Transport, 22, 33, 46, 63, 105, 211,
    212, 341, 383, 398, 412
  urban, 321–4
    See also individual systems

Treadmill crane, 427
Trent, River, 234, 293
Trent, Vale of, 342, 417
Trent and Mersey Canal, 293, 296, 303, 417, 422
Trevithick, Richard, 77, 252, 255, 261, 301, 307
Trinity House, 276
Trossachs, 329
Trowbridge, 125
Truro, 368
Tudor England, 76, 130, 278, 328
Tull, Jethro, 185
Tunnels, 296, 379, 417, 418, 422
Turnpike trusts, 280, 282, 283 5
Tyler, Wat, 176
Tyneside, 61, 63, 64, 68, 69, 111, 112, 142, 157, 158, 302, 306, 307, 311

Ulster: see Ireland
Underground railways, 266, 322–4, 342
UNESCO, 369
United States of America, 29, 51, 101, 105, 131, 137, 320, 350
   Civil War, 137, 160, 346
   Declaration of Independence, 39
   See also America, North
Universities, courses at, 386–8

Vasa, 227
Vermuyden, Sir Cornelis, 288, 331
Versailles, 245
Viaducts, 312, 318
Victoria Embankment, 335
Victorian England, 37, 180, 212, 312, 337
Victorian Society, 356
Victory, 227, 274, 427
Vikings, 227

Vinci, Leonardo da, 42
Vitruvius, 221
Volta, Alessandro, 103

Wade, General George, 279, 281, 399, 401
Wagons, 187
Wailes, Rex, 234, 358–9
Wales, 125, 166, 411–15
   coal, 56, 57, 60, 69, 70, 72, 319, 411–12
   industries, 92, 125, 215, 411–13
   metalliferous mines, 76, 78, 83, 92, 411, 412
   slate, 170, 171, 411
   transport, 70, 252, 303–4, 319, 411–13
Waller, 338
Wandsworth, 303
Wanlockhead, 401
Wapping, 270
Ward, Joshua, 157
Ware, 328
Warrington, 142, 157, 158, 406
Warwickshire, 164, 235, 248
Wash, the, 288
Waste disposal, 334 5, 424
Watchet, 270
Water conservation, 330
Water drainage, 288, 331–3, 432
Water power, 86, 132, 209, 223, 234, 235–43, 345, 415, 417, Plates 28, 49, 50, 51 and 52
   industries, 45, 86–7, 123, 132, 143–4, 193–6, 209, 221, 243, 399, 413, 417
   mines, 64, 77, 239, 245, 406
   water wheels, 94, 143, 193, 196, 221, 239, 242, 245, 328, 406, 410, Plate 49
Water supply, 327–8, 424

Waterside, 196
Waterways (inland), 267, 288–99
    canals, 46, 95, 298–9, 397, 406,
    417, 418, 422, 432, Plate 62
    rivers, 286–7, 288
Watford Gap, 294
Watkins, George, 28, 259, 263
Watt, James, 26, 45, 77, 95, 101, 196,
    233, 248–50, 252, 257, 262, 336,
    349, 367, 401
Wealden Open-Air Museum, 427
Weapons, 74, 75, 93, 94, 221
Wear, River, 61
Weaving, 118, 134, 156, 413
Wedgwood, Josiah, 145, 293, 417
Welland Navigation, 291, 295
Wellington (Shropshire), 297
Welsh Folk Museum, 215
Welsh National Museum: *see* St
    Fagan's
Welsh Technological Museum, 415
Wendron Forge, 436
Wesley, John, 201
West Country: *see* England (South-
    West)
West Indies, 199
West Lothian, 61, 160, 250
Western civilization, 37, 38, 39, 47,
    52, 108, 144, 152, 193, 210, 220–
    23, 226
Wey and Arun Canal, 295
Whaley Bridge, 303
Wharves: *see* Docks
Wheal Martyn Museum, 147, 436
Wheatstone, 350
Wheelwrights, 93, 187
Whisky, 203–5, 399
Whitby, 57, 270
White, Sir George, 325
Whitechapel, 206
Whitehaven, 61

Whitworth, Joseph, 98, 406
Widcombe, 297, 436
Widnes, 158, 406
Wigan, 57, 135, 406
Wight, Isle of, 143
Willans, 259, 260
William III, 128
Wilkinson, John, 98, 249, 348
Wilmington, 155, 177
Wiltshire, 123, 154, 205, 432
Winchester, 215
Wind power, 209, 226–35, 244,
    Plates 46, 47 and 48
    windmills, 193, 227–35, 331–3,
    358, 422, 425, 427, 436, Plates
    46, 47 and 48
Windscale, 343
Windsor Great Park, 184–5
Wine, 206
Withies, 188
Wolverhampton, 60
Wolverton, 107
Wood: buildings and ships, 42, 44–5,
    153, 163, 164–6, 227
    fuel, 44–5, 55
    woodwork, 93, 95, 187, 188–9, 208
Woodbridge Tide Mill, 427
Woodhead Tunnel, 312
Wookey Hole, 154
Woollen cloth industry, 47, 121–7,
    142, 206, 378, 405, 431
    development of, 37, 47, 121–7,
    431
Woolley Park, 225
Woolwich, 424
Worcester, 145
Worksop, 61
World Wars: First, 55, 159, 186,
    319, 323; Second, 49, 56, 70,
    109, 147, 177, 186, 207, 265,
    283, 323, 325, 345, 351

Worsley, 292, 293, 406, 410
Wortley, 91, 410
Wrawby, 234, 422
Wren, Sir Christopher, 168
Wright, Orville, 324
Wyatt, John, 118
Wye, River, 133, 411
Wylam, 307

Yate, 83
York, 124, 309

Yorkshire, 72, 124, 281, 330
  coal, 27, 57, 60, 61, 70, 405
  industries, 92, 125, 206, 239, 299,
    378, 405
  transport, 70, 270, 273, 281, 294,
    299, 309, 312, 313, 324, 406
Young, Arthur, 185
Young, James, 160

Zinc, 82, 83, 411